WINDOWS NT TRAINING GUIDE

LIMITED WARRANTY AND DISCLAIMER OF LIABILITY

ACADEMIC PRESS, INC. ("AP") AND ANYONE ELSE WHO HAS BEEN INVOLVED IN THE CREATION OR PRODUCTION OF THE ACCOMPANYING CODE ("THE PRODUCT") CANNOT AND DO NOT WARRANT THE PERFORMANCE OR RESULTS THAT MAY BE OBTAINED BY USING THE PRODUCT. THE PRODUCT IS SOLD "AS IS" WITHOUT WARRANTY OF ANY KIND (EXCEPT AS HEREAFTER DESCRIBED), EITHER EXPRESSED OR IMPLIED, INCLUDING, BUT NOT LIMITED TO, ANY WARRANTY OF PERFORMANCE OR ANY IMPLIED WARRANTY OF MERCHANTABILITY OR FITNESS FOR ANY PARTICULAR PURPOSE. AP WARRANTS ONLY THAT THE MAGNETIC DISKETTE(S) ON WHICH THE CODE IS RECORDED IS FREE FROM DEFECTS IN MATERIAL AND FAULTY WORKMANSHIP UNDER THE NORMAL USE AND SERVICE FOR A PERIOD OF NINETY (90) DAYS FROM THE DATE THE PRODUCT IS DELIVERED. THE PURCHASER'S SOLE AND EXCLUSIVE REMEDY IN THE EVENT OF A DEFECT IS EXPRESSLY LIMITED TO EITHER REPLACEMENT OF THE DISKETTE(S) OR REFUND OF THE PURCHASE PRICE, AT AP'S SOLE DISCRETION.

IN NO EVENT, WHETHER AS A RESULT OF BREACH OF CONTRACT, WARRANTY OR TORT (INCLUDING NEGLIGENCE), WILL AP OR ANYONE WHO HAS BEEN INVOLVED IN THE CREATION OR PRODUCTION OF THE PRODUCT BE LIABLE TO PURCHASER FOR ANY DAMAGES, INCLUDING ANY LOST PROFITS, LOST SAVINGS OR OTHER INCIDENTAL OR CONSEQUENTIAL DAMAGES ARISING OUT OF THE USE OR INABILITY TO USE THE PRODUCT OR ANY MODIFICATIONS THEREOF, OR DUE TO THE CONTENTS OF THE CODE, EVEN IF AP HAS BEEN ADVISED OF THE POSSIBILITY OF SUCH DAMAGES, OR FOR ANY CLAIM BY ANY OTHER PARTY.

Any request for replacement of a defective diskette must be postage prepaid and must be accompanied by the original defective diskette, your mailing address and telephone number, and proof of date of purchase and purchase price. Send such requests, stating the nature of the problem, to Academic Press Customer Service, 6277 Sea Harbor Drive, Orlando, FL 32887, 1-800-321-5068. APP shall have no obligation to refund the purchase price or to replace a diskette based on claims of defects in the nature or operation of the Product.

Some states do not allow limitation on how long an implied warranty lasts, nor exclusions or limitations of incidental or consequential damage, so the above limitations and exclusions may not apply to you. This Warranty gives you specific legal rights, and you may also have other rights which vary from jurisdiction to jurisdiction.

THE RE-EXPORT OF UNITED STATES ORIGIN SOFTWARE IS SUBJECT TO THE UNITED STATES LAWS UNDER THE EXPORT ADMINISTRATION ACT OF 1969 AS AMENDED. ANY FURTHER SALE OF THE PRODUCT SHALL BE IN COMPLIANCE WITH THE UNITED STATES DEPARTMENT OF COMMERCE ADMINISTRATION REGULATIONS. COMPLIANCE WITH SUCH REGULATIONS IS YOUR RESPONSIBILITY AND NOT THE RESPONSIBILITY OF AP.

WINDOWS NT TRAINING GUIDE

James Turley

AP Professional

AP Professional is a Division of Academic Press

Boston San Diego New York
London Sydney Tokyo Toronto

AP PROFESSIONAL

An Imprint of ACADEMIC PRESS, INC.
A Division of HARCOURT BRACE & COMPANY

ORDERS (USA and Canada): 1-800-3131-APP or APP@ACAD.COM
AP Professional Orders: 6277 Sea Harbor Dr., Orlando, FL 32821-9816

Europe/Middle East/Africa: 0-11-44 (0) 181-300-3322
Orders: AP Professional 24-28 Oval Rd., London NW1 7DX

Japan/Korea: 03-3234-3911-5
Orders: Harcourt Brace Japan, Inc., Ichibancho Central Building 22-1, Ichibancho Chiyoda-Ku, Tokyo 102

Australia: 02-517-8999
Orders: Harcourt Brace & Co. Australia, Locked Bag 16, Marrickville, NSW 2204 Australia

Other International: (407) 345-3800
AP Professional Orders: 6277 Sea Harbor Dr., Orlando FL 32821-9816

Editorial: 1300 Boylston St., Chestnut Hill, MA 02167 (617)232-0500

Web: http://www.apnet.com/approfessional

This book is printed on acid-free paper. ♾

United Kingdom Edition published by
ACADEMIC PRESS LIMITED
24–28 Oval Road, London NW1 7DX

ISBN 0-12-703855-8

Printed in the United States of America
96 97 98 99 IP 9 8 7 6 5 4 3 2 1

To my parents, for a brain;
my wife, for courage;
and my children, for a heart.

Contents

ACKNOWLEDGMENTS

Whew! Finally finished.

Creating a new book is a group effort; the combined work of the publication staff far exceeds that of the simple author. It seems somewhat unfair to me that the majority of the people who bring a book together do not share in the recognition. So, to the folks at AP Professional, please accept my thanks for your very good work.

Jeff Pepper was the catalyst for this book; Gael Tannenbaum the conduit for information. Andrea Mulligan perfected the manuscript; Andrew Williams kept everything straight. Mihaela Miair and Darah Whelihan did their part as well. Michael Slater, Linley Gwennap, and Kimberly M. De Loney each helped in their own way, too. Thanks again, everybody.

And, as ever, thanks go to my young, attractive, and accomplished wife Kathy for her support, her understanding, and the terrific index at the back (enjoy it). And to Cari and David, who are now used to ignoring their Daddy for long periods. Cari created the picture in Chapter 4 and David helped with the typing. Thanks a bunch and I promise never to do this again—until the next time.

AN EASY FIRST TOUR OF WINDOWS NT

Welcome to Windows NT!

If you're new to Windows NT, this book is for you, and this chapter is the place to start. In the next few sections, you'll learn all the basic skills you need to start working with Windows NT. Working better, working faster, and working more easily.

What Is All This Stuff?

Let's start by just looking around on your screen. This is a time to get acquainted with your computer and with Windows NT. If your computer is already running, your screen should look something like the example in Figure 1.1. If you have more or fewer little pictures on your computer screen, don't worry about it. Everybody's computer is a little bit different and later on in this book you'll see how you can make yours special by changing the colors, sizes, and arrangement of everything to suit you.

Desktop Refer to Figure 1.1 as we orient ourselves with the new look of Windows NT. First of all, another name for your screen is the *desktop*. It's called a desktop because it's supposed to make you think of a real desk, and all the little pictures along the left side of

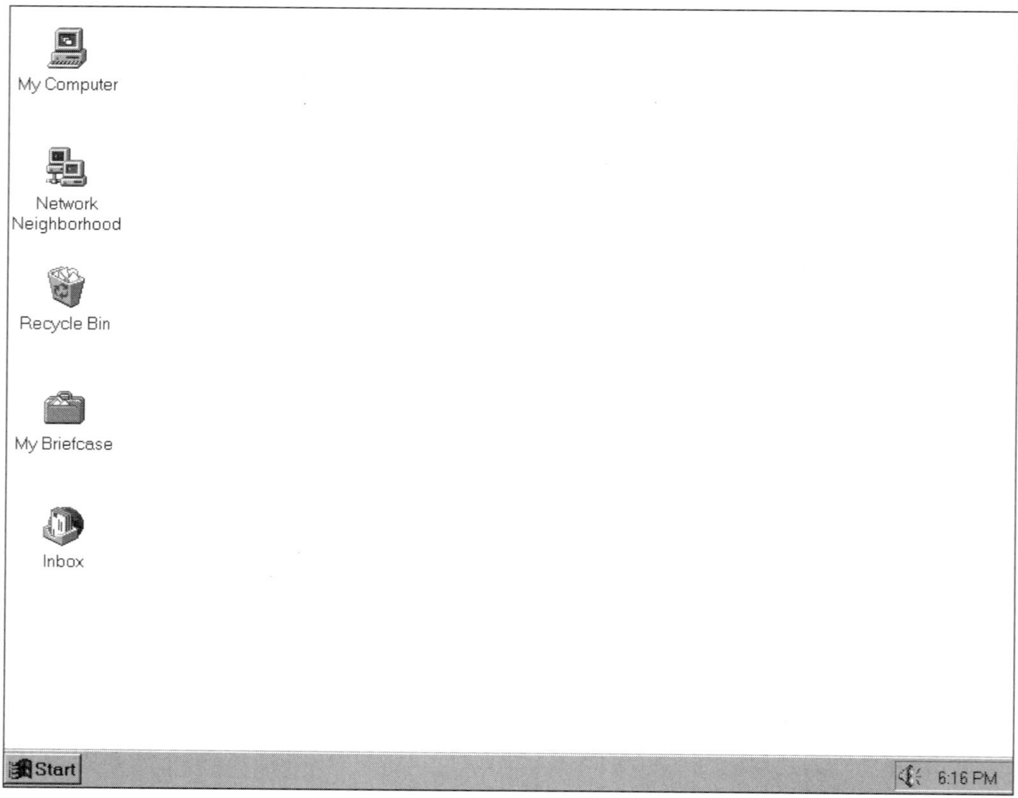

Figure 1.1: The Windows NT desktop, with five icons.

the desktop are like little objects you might have on a real desk. So when you read about your desktop, or finding something on your desktop, it's just another way of saying it's right there on your screen.

Icons There are lots of little pictures on your desktop, each one about the size of a postage stamp. In Figure 1.1 there are five of them, all in a row along the left side. In the computer world, the simple word picture is frowned upon—using the more exotic word *icon* is preferred. Now, icon is not a word most people use much. Icons have traditionally represented cultural or religious figures or paintings. But now, an icon can also mean a small picture on your computer screen. Each icon represents a physical thing. For example, the uppermost icon on your desktop represents your computer. As you can see, it's even called "My Computer."

Another icon represents a trash can or recycling bin. Can you find the Recycle Bin icon? Although there are only five icons in this figure, you will see many, many more icons as you start working with Windows NT. You'll even create some of your own. Each icon looks different, and the way it looks is supposed to remind you of what the icon really stands for. For example, the icon called My Computer probably looks a little bit like your computer does, and the Recycle Bin icon also bears a pretty good likeness to a real recycle bin or a trash can.

The arrangement of the icons on your desktop makes absolutely no difference. You are allowed to move these icons around on your desktop (that is, on your computer screen) any way you want to, just like you would move your stapler, telephone, and pens on a real desk.

The Taskbar Across the bottom of your desktop is a gray stripe. This is called the *Taskbar* and it will become very important to you later on. The appearance of the Taskbar will change as you use your computer, the way a speedometer moves as you drive a car. For now, the Taskbar has only two interesting items on it. These are on the far left and right ends, and they are the Start button and the clock.

The Start Button At the left end of the Taskbar is the *Start button*. It is one of the most constant and unchanging things you will ever see with Windows NT. The Start button never moves and it never changes. It's called the Start button because, obviously enough, it says Start on it in big letters, and because it's drawn to look a little like a push-button on your screen.

As you will soon find out, you really can push the Start button and something will happen. Let's save that for now and move on.

The Clock At the opposite end of the Taskbar is a digital clock. Don't be concerned if the time isn't right, you can fix that later. Your clock may also have a little picture (an icon) of a blaring speaker, or a fax machine, or some other little image next to it. These are not important for now.

Basic Mouse Skills

What is important is getting started with Windows NT! To really succeed with Windows NT you need to be able to use a computer mouse. Your mouse should be connected to your computer by a thin cord and look a little like a well-worn bar of soap.

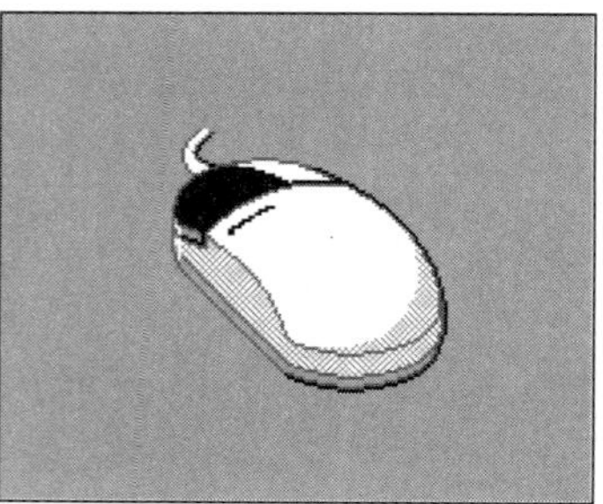

Your mouse should also have two or three buttons on it. If it has three, you should know right now that you will never use the middle button. You only use the left button and the right button when using Windows NT. Pressing the middle button won't hurt anything—it just doesn't do anything.

Using the mouse requires a little hand-eye coordination, the kind that seven-year-olds seem to be best at. It doesn't matter if you're not handy with a mouse yet. You will be soon enough. Besides, there's absolutely no penalty for being slow or awkward. Your computer is extremely patient and tolerant of mistakes. You can not harm anything while you're practicing so practice as much as you like.

Mouse Lesson 1 The idea behind a mouse is to be able to point to things on your screen without actually getting fingerprints on the glass. That's it. If you can point, you can use a mouse. And if you can click the two buttons, you can use Windows NT.

Rest your right hand on your mouse and roll it around a little bit on your desk (your real desk, not the computer-screen desktop). If you have the great good fortune to be left-handed, then by all means, use your left hand instead. As you move your mouse around, you should see a little white arrow like the one shown below moving around with you. When you roll your mouse to the right, the little arrow moves to the right. Moving left goes left. Moving the mouse toward you moves the arrow down. Try moving your mouse around in circles and curlicues until you feel comfortable with it.

Here's a couple of hints if you're having a tough time. First, if the little white arrow goes off the edge of the screen, it stops there. This is a mouse, not a lemming, and it won't run away. There's no way you can lose it off the edge of your screen.

Second, there's no penalty for picking up your mouse and setting it down again. Many first-timers run out of room on their desks and don't know how to get the arrow to move any farther. Pick it up. Move your mouse to a clear space and keep on rollin'.

Third, you should always point your mouse directly at your computer screen as you roll it. Don't tilt it to one side or hold it cocked like a pencil like the example in Figure 1.2. This is a subtle thing, but many people get tripped up by this. If you hold your mouse sideways, then the arrow on your screen won't move like you expect. That will look very confusing and it makes a big difference when you're just learning. Remember: point your mouse at your screen and hold it straight.

As a test, do a little slalom between the icons on the desktop of your own computer. Practice moving your mouse until you can make the little white arrow pass between each icon on the left and then on the right.

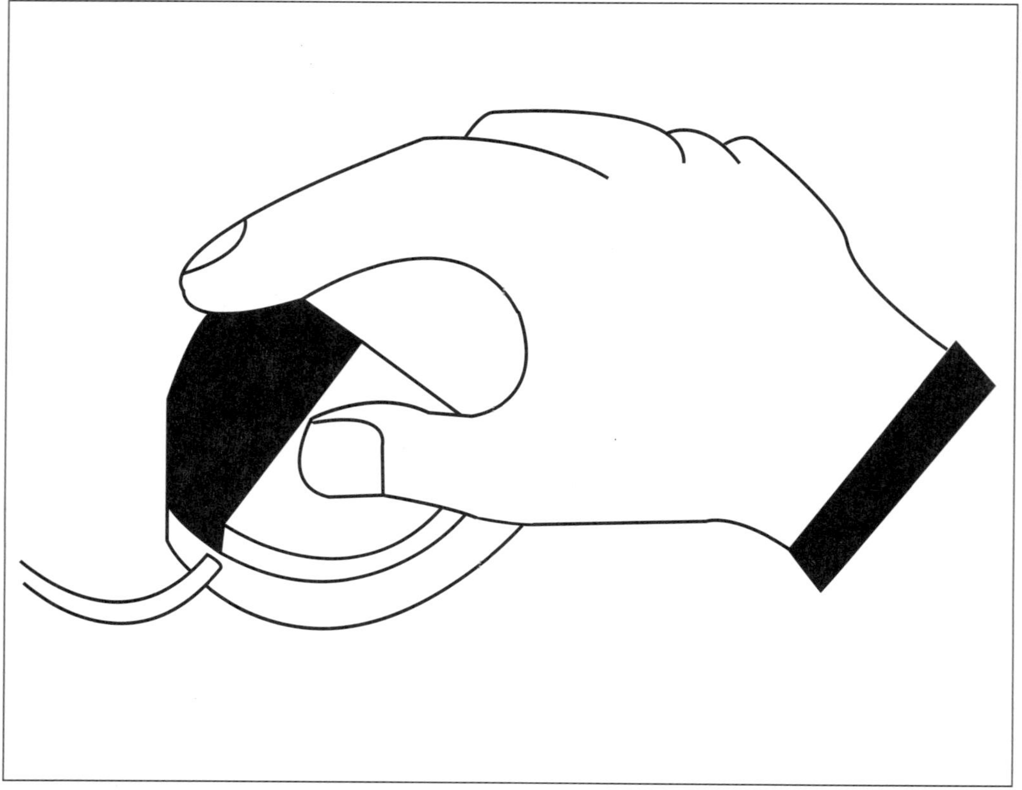

Figure 1.2: Don't hold your mouse at an angle or you'll have a hard time controlling it.

Mouse Lesson II That takes care of the hardest part of learning to use a mouse. You've mastered the steering, now how about the pedals? The two buttons on your mouse are there to let you carry out commands. Like the captain of a ship with a well-trained crew, all you have to do is point and gesture, and your commands will be carried out without hesitation. To carry out Windows NT commands, you first need to learn a very simple kind of gesture.

Start by moving your mouse so that the little white arrow (called the mouse pointer, or sometimes, the *cursor*) is in the middle of your screen. Make sure you're not pointing to one of the icons, or they will think you're "talking" to one of them. Press the left mouse button down briefly and then let go of it so the button comes back up. Repeat this procedure again, pressing and then releasing the left button. Done properly, it's a simple, brief, tapping motion, like dialing numbers on a touch-tone telephone or pressing keys on a calculator. Don't hold the mouse button down as if you were ringing a doorbell.

You've just mastered the next important step, called *clicking*. Get used to clicking your left mouse button, because you'll do it frequently as you use Windows NT. Clicking your left mouse button is the most common gesture you'll use to get Windows NT to do what you want. From now on, when you read about clicking, you'll know what to do.

Note for Left-Handers In medieval times, left-handed swordsmen were prized for their ability to fight while climbing a spiral staircase. These days, the advantages of being left-handed are few. So far, we've assumed that you're holding your mouse with your right hand. If you are among the left-handed elite, you may find it more comfortable to swap hands and keep your mouse on the left side. But that raises another question: do you also swap the mouse buttons? This choice is entirely up to you. Windows NT has the ability to swap the meaning of the left and right buttons on your mouse for you, if you choose to do so. (You'll learn how to do this in Chapter 5; it doesn't involve any surgery to your mouse.) Bear in mind that you'll be clicking the left mouse button (for right-handers) much more frequently than the right button. If this is uncomfortable, by all means swap the buttons. On the other hand, many portsiders prefer to stick with the right-handers' arrangement of buttons. One final note: Throughout this book, references to the left button and right button assume the right-handers' position. Your buttons will be reversed if you choose to swap them.

Mouse Lesson III Now that you've learned how to click, you need to know how to double-click. A *double-click* is nothing more than two clicks, one right after the other. The only trick to it—and it's an easy one to master—is to keep the two clicks close together. Don't let too much moss grow under your mouse between the first click and the second click or it won't be a real double-click.

Practice doing this faster and faster until you can hear your mouse go "click-click." If you can make you mouse button go "click-click" about as fast as you can say "click-click," you're doing fine. Don't strain yourself by trying to go any faster than that.

Mouse Lesson IV Almost done. This lesson's easy, really. So far, you have always clicked the left mouse button; you haven't clicked with your right mouse button (lefties, that's the left button for you). You won't need to click with your right button much, and you will never need to double-click it, but this skill will come in handy from time to time. Again, pointing to a blank area of your screen away from any icons, click the right mouse button once.

What happened? Did you see a gray box pop up? You should have, because clicking the right mouse button on a blank desktop is a command that Windows NT understands (even if you don't, yet). You should see a gray box with a list of words written on it, like the one in Figure 1.3.

This is your first real command, and also your first introduction to a pop-up menu. It's clear why this is called a pop-up, but why a menu? It's called a menu because each of the words on the gray box is a Windows NT command. Using your mouse, you can select one of

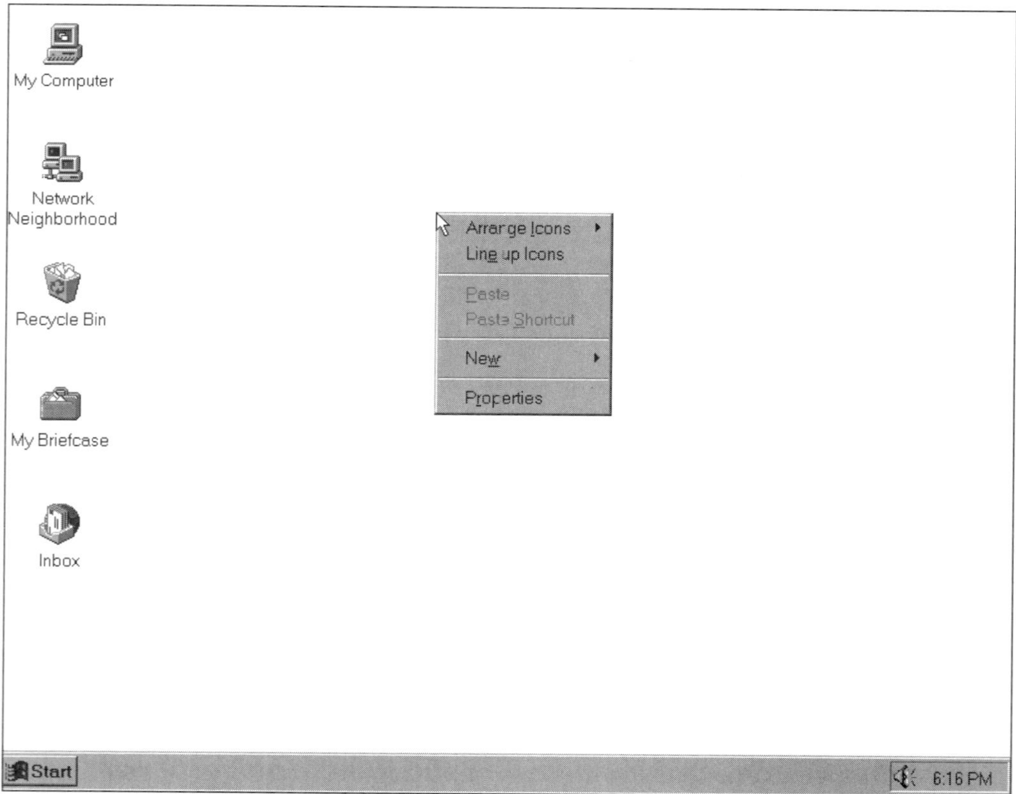

Figure 1.3: Right-clicking on an open area of the desktop causes a shortcut menu to pop up.

these commands, like selecting a side order off a menu. We'll practice that action later on.

Mouse Lesson V In this last lesson, you'll learn about a different kind of mouse-button click called the drag. Dragging is like a very long, drawn-out click. Less of a click really, and more of a thud.

To *drag* your mouse, you need to hold the left mouse button down. Don't just click it and then let go, press the mouse button and hold it down for a few seconds before you let it back up. You use this dragging technique to move icons (the little pictures) around on your desktop. Let's try it now.

Place your mouse pointer right over the icon near the corner of your screen called My Computer. Point right at the middle of it. Now press and hold your left mouse button down and—still holding the button down—move your mouse. After you've moved a few inches, let go of the mouse button.

Did My Computer move? You should have dragged My Computer across your desktop and placed it a few inches away, like Figure 1-4 shows. This is how you move items around on your desktop. Later on, you'll use this technique to move items around inside windows, too. After all, windows are what Windows NT is all about.

Before moving on, practice dragging. Drag all the items on your desktop to different places. Rearrange the icons so they're in opposite corners, or diagonal lines, or anything else you can think of. Be careful that you don't overlap any of them. When they're all skewed and rearranged, you can try issuing another Windows NT command.

Right-click your desktop (that is, click the right mouse button on a blank area of your screen) to get the pop-up menu. The second line on the menu should say Line Up Icons. Move your mouse just a little bit so that the arrow points right to the words Line Up Icons. The words should turn bright blue. When they do, click your left mouse button once. Voila! On your command, Windows NT straightens up your icons for you. See Figure 1.5 if you're having trouble finding the right command.

To review, you've learned four techniques, or gestures, with your mouse. You can:

- Click the left mouse button once (left-click)
- Click the right mouse button once (right-click)

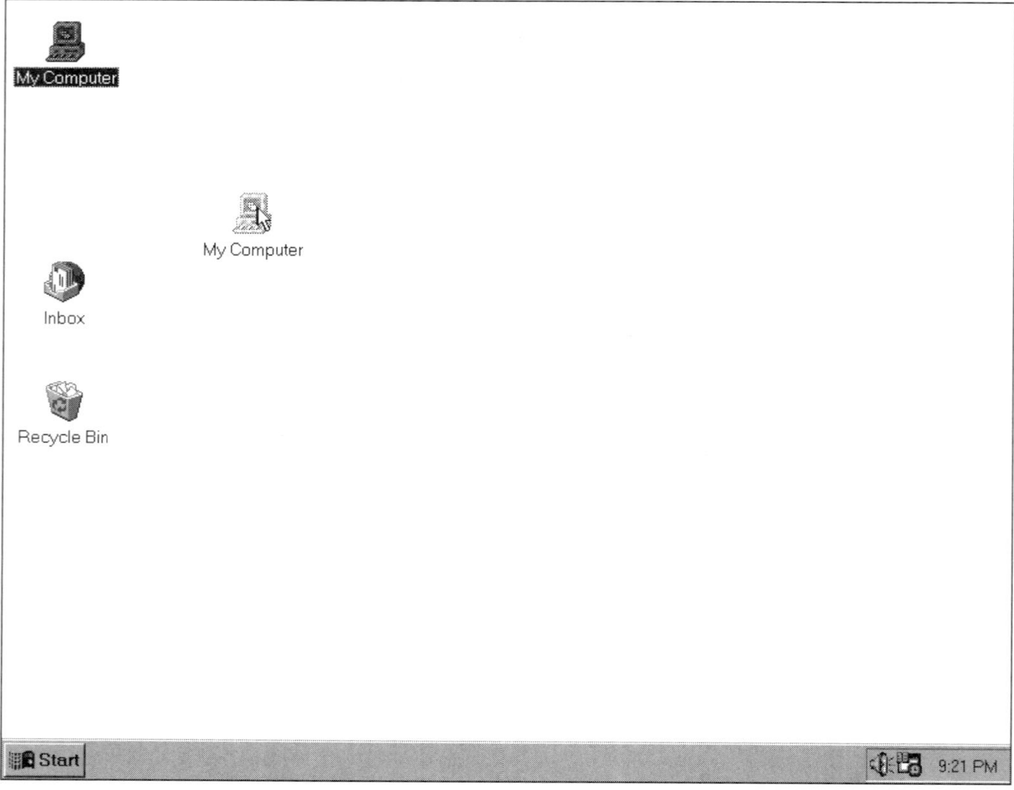

Figure 1.4: You can use the mouse to move, or drag, icons around on your desktop.

- Click the left mouse button twice in quick succession (double-click)
- Click and move using the left mouse button (dragging)

These four techniques, plus dragging with the right mouse button, are all you need to use Windows NT effectively. Now you can get on your way and start exploring some more!

Starting with the Start Button

Most everything you do with Windows NT will start by clicking on the Start button. The Start button is down at the bottom of your screen, in the lower left-hand corner. It has a Windows logo and the word Start on it in large, friendly letters and it looks like this:

The Start button is your entryway into the most important things you'll want to do with your computer. You can start using your applications to do work with Start; you can change the way your computer looks and behaves with Start; you can search for misplaced files with Start, and lots of other things, too. So let's get started!

The Start button always works the same way. To get started, move your mouse so the arrow is right over the Start button. When you're pointing right into the middle of it, click your left mouse button one

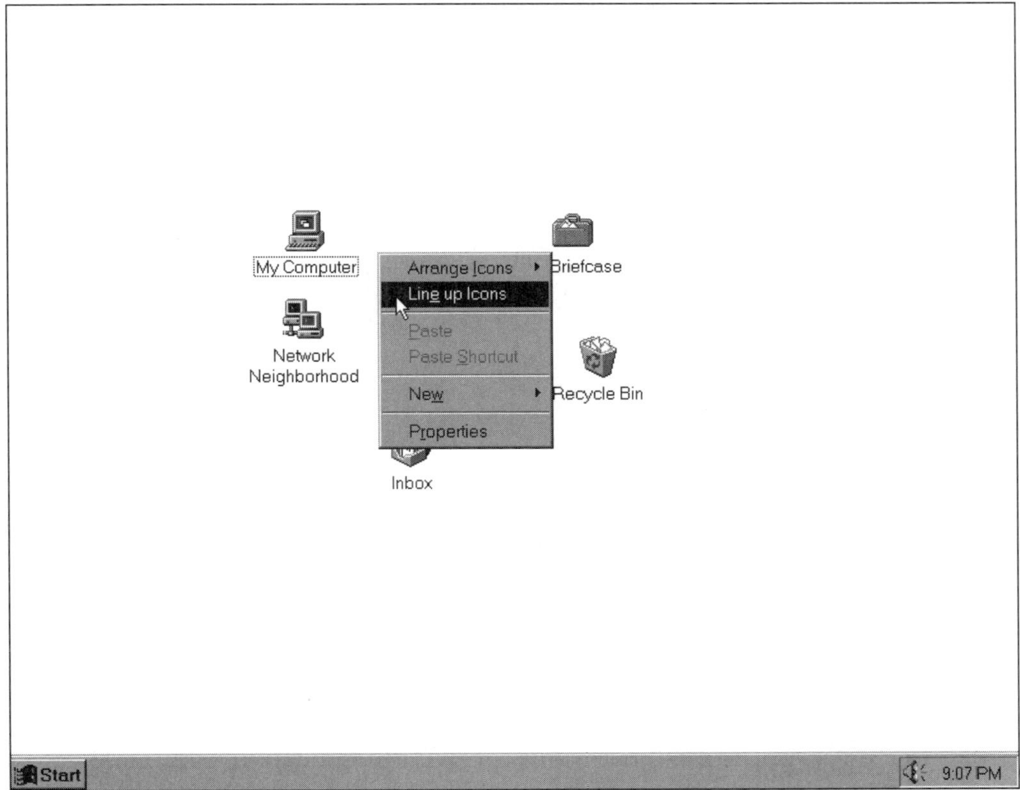

Figure 1.5: The second command on the short cut menu, Line up Icons, will straighten up all the icons on your desktop.

time. The Start menu will pop right up. Now your screen should look like the one in Figure 1.6.

You've already done the hardest part! As you can see, there are seven items on the Start menu. These represent seven different commands that you can carry out just by clicking your mouse. Each command has a little icon, or picture, next to it to give you a visual cue or reminder what the command is used for. If you look, you'll notice that the top four choices (Programs, Documents, Settings, and Find) have little arrows next to them. You'll find out in a minute what this means. For now, let's practice using the Start menu.

Without clicking or holding any mouse buttons, move your mouse pointer straight up the screen. Try to make the arrow on your screen go right up the middle of the Start menu. Notice how each of the commands is highlighted in blue as you pass over it? That's showing you what command would be carried out *if* you clicked your left mouse button. But don't click anything yet.

What happens if you move your mouse away from the Start menu? Try it! Nothing bad happens. You can move the little arrow all over the

Figure 1.6: Clicking on the Start button makes the Start menu pop up.

screen and the Start menu stays right where it is. When you move the arrow back over the Start menu it highlights commands exactly the same as before.

Again, without clicking or holding any mouse buttons, try placing your mouse's arrow pointer right over the word Programs at the top of the Start menu. What happens? Does your screen look like the one in Figure 1.7? When you place your mouse pointer over a command (like Programs) that has a little arrow on it, Windows NT is telling you the arrow is pointing to another menu off to the right.

This is called a cascading menu or a submenu—a menu that's part of another menu. The choices on this submenu are part of the Programs command. You can move your mouse pointer all around and over this menu, too, and watch how each of the commands is highlighted as you pass over it.

Some of the commands on this submenu have arrows next to them, too. Can you guess what would happen if you placed your mouse pointer over one of them? Try it! Move your mouse's arrow pointer

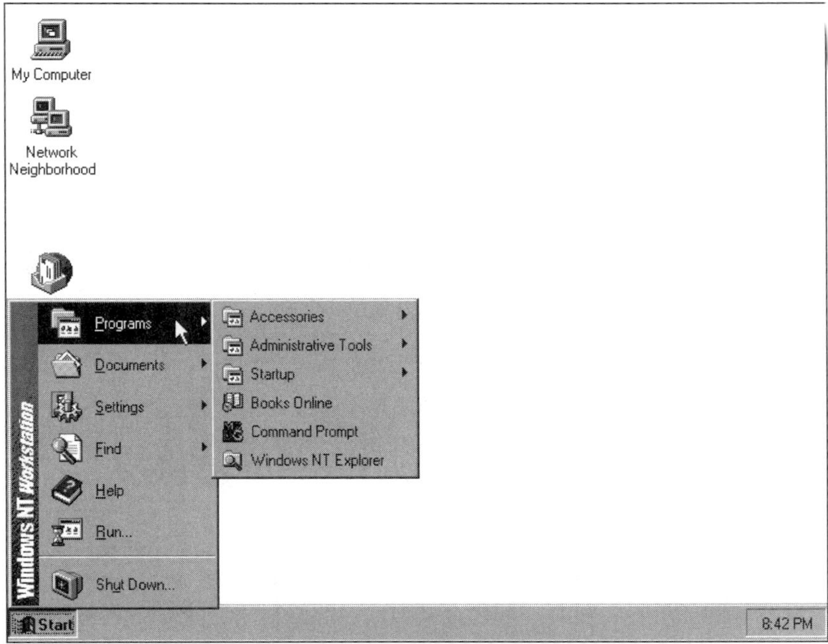

Figure 1.7: Highlighting one of the menu choices with an arrow on it causes a cascading menu to pop up.

over the word Accessories at the top of the submenu, and yet another submenu will pop up.

What do you do if you don't want all these menus and submenus? That's easy—just move your mouse pointer away from the menus, and click the left button once. If you're not pointing at a command (for example, at a blank area on your screen) then no command will be carried out. Try this now—point to a blank area of the screen and click the left mouse button once. All the menus disappear and you're back where you started, no harm done.

Choosing a Command Now that you know how *not* to select a command, it's time to stop avoiding work and learn how to select a command. As always, start by pointing to the Start button and clicking your left mouse button one time. Now move your mouse pointer over the word Help so that it's highlighted in blue. Now click your left mouse button one time again. That's it! You've just started the Help command and you should see a big new window like the one in Figure 1.8 that just about fills your screen.

We're not going to do anything with the Help command now. Instead, we're going to end it. When you're using Windows NT, stopping or ending a command is called "closing" it, like closing a window (get it?). Closing the Help command, or any other window, is just as easy as opening it was. Look in the upper right corner of the Help window, along the blue bar. You should see two little bitty boxes like these:

The gray box on the right with the X in it is called the Close Box. If you click on it, the entire window will close, and the Help command will go away, just as if it had never been here. Let's try that now. Move you mouse pointer so that the arrow points right into the middle of that X in the close box. When you've got it centered, click the left mouse button one time. The Help command disappeared!

Just as an exercise, repeat the entire procedure. First, click on the Start button to make the Start menu pop up. Second, click on the Help

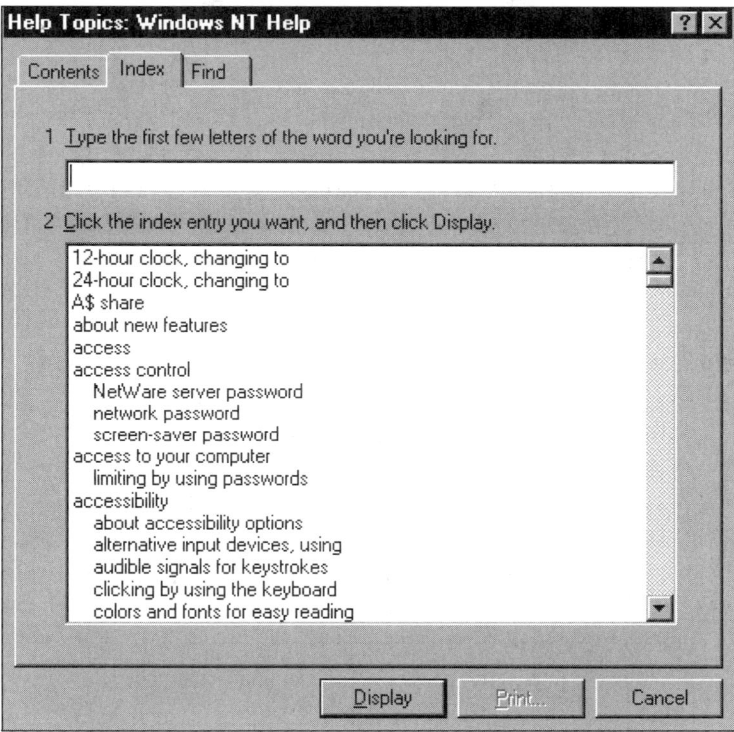

Figure 1.8: The Help function is always available from the Start menu.

command to open the Help window. Third, click on the close box to close the Help window. That's all there is to it! Every Windows NT command, application, and file window works just this way. When you learn those three simple steps, you've got 90% of Windows NT mastered!

Choosing a Different Command Now that you know where to find Help when you need it (and before long, you probably will), it's time to try out some of the other commands on the Start menu. As always, start by clicking on the Start button. This time highlight the Run command and click on it. The Run window should open, just like the one in Figure 1.9. We don't need to explore the Run command now, so just close it by clicking on its close box. Although the Run window is a different size and shape than the Help window, they both have the same kind of close box in the upper right corner.

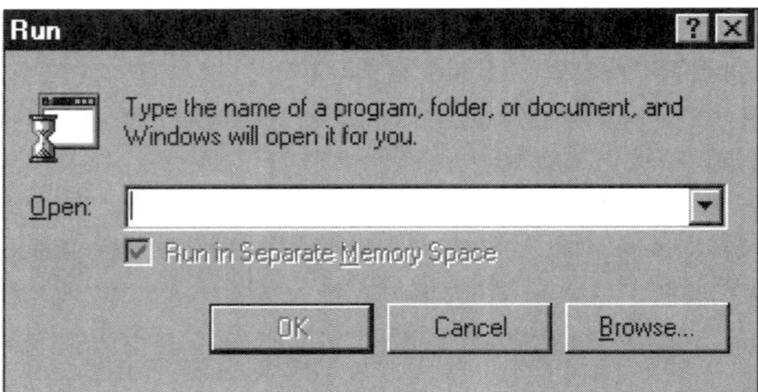

Figure 1.9: The Run command is always available from the Start menu.

As a third example, let's try out one of those strange submenus we saw earlier. Click on the Start button and highlight the Find command but don't click anything yet. As you move your mouse pointer over the Find command (called "hovering," like a hummingbird) the submenu for the Find command will pop up. Now move your mouse so that the arrow pointer moves to the right, highlighting the words "Files or Folders..."

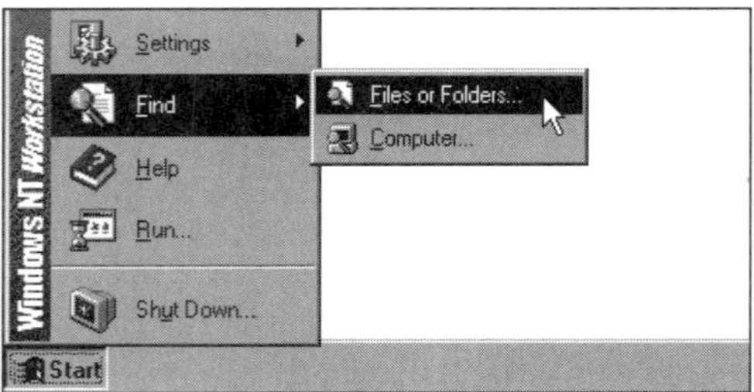

Now click once on the command. You should see the Find window, which looks pretty much like the Run window and the Help window. Just like the others, click on the close box to close the Find window and return to where you started. Now you know how to open and close windows, how to select commands from the Start menu, and how to make submenus pop up. With these basic skills you can do anything you want to with Windows NT.

How to Select Menus without a Mouse If your mouse ever breaks or gets disconnected from your computer, you need to have an "emergency plan" for selecting menus and commands. Although it's not convenient, you can always operate Windows NT without a mouse at all, using just your keyboard. Like most emergency procedures, you should practice this now so you're prepared.

If you look closely at any menu, you'll notice that most commands have one letter underlined. This is the emergency, or shortcut, key for that command. To select a command with the keyboard, first press the <ALT> key. Then press the underlined letter for the command you want. In the example in Figure 1.10, you would press <ALT> followed by F and then C to select the File menu and then the Close command.

Note that you should not hold the <ALT> key down while you're pressing the other keys. Just tap it once to turn the emergency menus on. Tapping <ALT> a second time turns the emergency menus back off.

You can also use your arrow keys instead of, or in addition to, the underlined letters. Pressing <DOWN ARROW> moves the highlight down any menu one command at a time, for example. When you've highlighted the command you want, press <ENTER> to select it.

Moving a Window around on Your Screen

When you open a window it doesn't always open up onto a convenient place on your screen. Maybe it's covering up something that

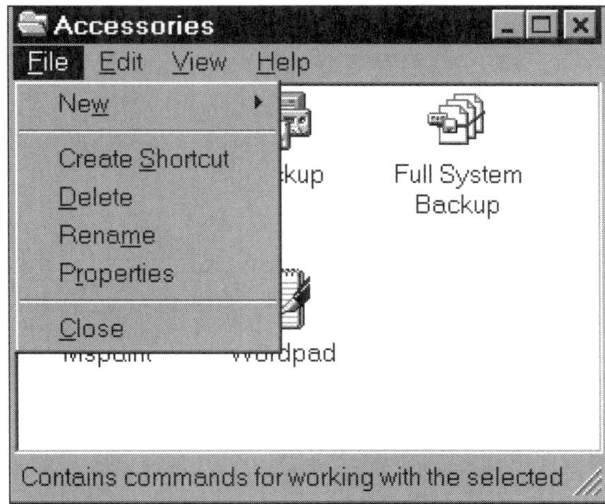

Figure 1.10: To select commands without the mouse, first press the <ALT> key on your keyboard, then press the underlined letter for the command you want.

you'd like to see, or maybe you just wish the window was someplace else. Well, that's any easy thing to fix.

To practice this little skill, we'll need a window. The best place to open a new window is from the Start button, of course, so click once on the Start button to pop up the Start menu. From the menu, select the Run command. When the Run window is open on your screen we're ready to begin.

Across the top of the Run window is a dark blue stripe. On the left of this stripe is the word Run (so you know what this window is for) and on the far right is the close box. To move a window to a different place on your screen, you have to "drag" it there. To drag something with your mouse, you have to be able to press a mouse button down and hold it while you move your mouse. This isn't like clicking the mouse button as you normally do. Dragging is different because you press the mouse button down the whole time and don't let up on it until later. Let's try dragging the Run window as an example.

Move your mouse so that the arrow is pointing somewhere along the blue stripe at the top of the window. It doesn't matter where on the stripe you point, as long as it isn't over one of the buttons. Point to the middle of the blue stripe just to be safe. Now press down on the left mouse button and keep pressing down while you move your mouse up a few inches. Now let go of the left mouse button.

Did the window move? It should have moved up your screen. Keep trying this, and move the window up, down, left, and right. You can move the window anywhere you want; just "drag" the colored bar with your mouse. When you're done, leave the Run window somewhere in the middle of your screen.

Opening Several Windows at Once One of the best features of Windows NT is also one of the ones that few people use. With Windows NT, you don't have to close each window when you're done with it before opening another one. Instead, you can just leave a window open on your screen while you open another one. There is no limit to how many windows you can have open at one time. This is a very useful and powerful feature, and one you should be comfortable with.

In this example, we're going to open a few different windows from the Start menu. Click on Start and select the Help command. Now go directly to the Start button again. This time highlight the Find command, then from the pop-up submenu select the Files and Folders command and click on it. If you had the Run window already opened from the previous example, your screen should look a little bit like the one in Figure 1.11.

As you can see, there are three windows open all at once: the Run window, the Find window, and the Help window. They all overlap, one on top of the other, just like real pieces of paper on a desk. And that is precisely the point: Windows NT is meant to work as much like a real desk, with papers and files and folders, as possible.

Now, since you already know how to drag a window, practice dragging these three windows around on your screen. Notice that as you click a window that is "behind" another window, that window comes to the front. You'll also find that it's easy to "lose" a small window

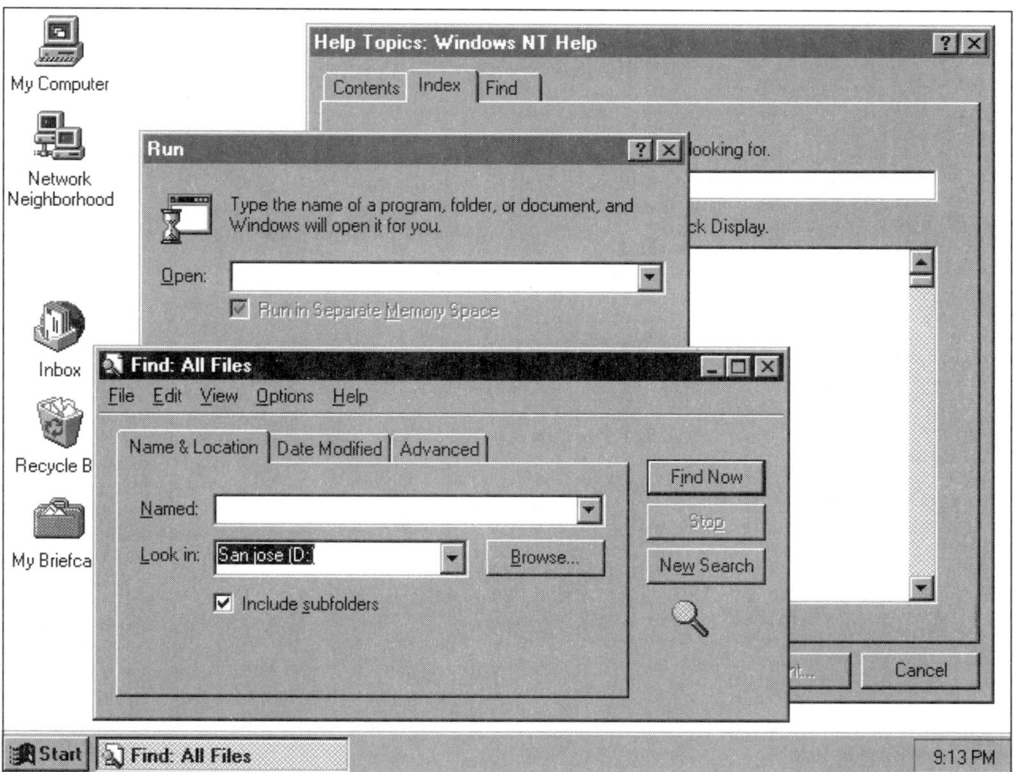

Figure 1.11: You can keep multiple windows open at the same time.

behind a bigger one so that you can't see it. You'll have to drag the bigger one to the edge or bottom of your screen to make the smaller window visible again.

Changing the Size of a Window There's more to windows than opening, closing, and dragging. Although that's all the skills you really need, you'll be happier if you know how to make windows bigger and smaller to suit your needs and your style. Here's how.

To explore this technique, we'll need a different window. Close any other windows you might have open on your screen (you do remember how to do that, right?). Now click the Start button and highlight Settings. When the pop-up submenu appears, highlight Control Panel and click on it. Your screen should look something like Figure 1.12. There's lots of interesting little icons in this window, but we're not con-

Figure 1.12: You can change the size of any window by dragging its lower-right corner or move the entire window by dragging it by the colored bar at the top.

cerned with those yet. Instead, take a look at the lower right corner of the window.

The lower right portion of the window has some diagonal "ridges" across the corner. If you happen to pass your mouse pointer over these ridges, the shape of the arrow pointer changes. To see what this means, press and hold the left mouse button down and drag the mouse down and to the right a little bit. Now let go of the left mouse button. Did your window get bigger? You can drag this corner of the window inwards, too, to make the window smaller. Try that now.

Although the lower-right corner of a window is a convenient place to drag around to change its size, it's not the only place this little technique works. Try placing your mouse pointer exactly along the right edge of the window. You'll know you've got it right when the normal arrow changes to a two-headed arrow. Now drag the edge of the window left and right. You'll discover that you can change the width of the window this way (left to right) but not its height (top to bottom). To make a window taller or shorter, place your mouse along the bottom edge and look for the two-headed arrow. When you see it, drag the bottom edge of the window up and down.

You can change the size of a window any time. It will not effect what's inside the window, only the way it looks. If a window is too big for your taste and covers up too much of your screen, feel free to drag it by the edge or the corner and resize it to suit you.

Making a Window Disappear If changing the size of a window doesn't do what you want, you can make the window disappear instead. Take another look at the open window on your screen. As always, there's a blue stripe across the top of the window, and the close box is at the very end. But what are the other two boxes? These are called the minimize button (on the left) and the maximize button (in the middle).

These both do really interesting things to your window. Let's say that a window is covering something behind it on your screen and you

can't seem to drag the window to a convenient location. If you want the window to temporarily disappear, all you have to do is click on the minimize box (the one with the flat line on it) one time, and presto! the window is gone.

Or is it? Look at the bottom of your screen, at the Taskbar. Right next to the ever-present Start button you should have a new button called Control Panel. Your window isn't really gone. It's been "stuffed into" the Control Panel button at the bottom of your screen, on the Taskbar. (The name Control Panel comes from the name that was written across the top of the window when it was open.)

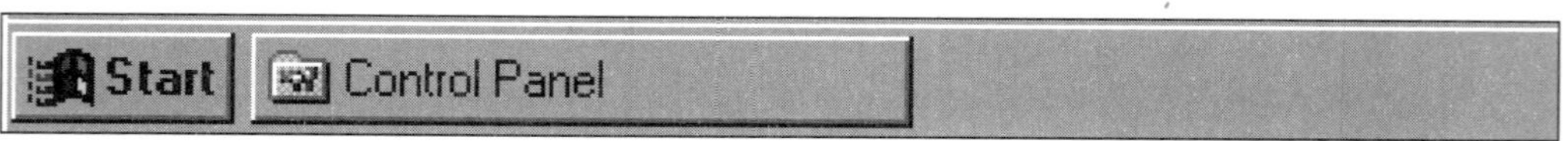

How do you bring the window back? You simply click once on its button on the Taskbar. Try it now. After you click on the button, the window reappears exactly as it was. The button on the Taskbar is still there too, but it looks pushed-in now. There's always one button pushed in on the Taskbar, and it's always the one belonging to the window that's in the front of your screen.

It's important to understand that clicking on the minimize button to shrink a window isn't the same thing as clicking on the close box to close a window. Shrinking (or minimizing) a window only makes it disappear from view—everything that the window was showing or doing is unharmed. On the other hand, closing a window ends its life, so to speak. Closing puts the contents of the window away, and if the window was running a command or an application for you, that work will stop. The work doesn't stop if you minimize a window. It does stop if you close a window.

This is an important distinction, particularly once you start opening multiple windows simultaneously and your screen starts to get cluttered. You might want to *minimize* windows from time to time to reduce the clutter and see what you're doing, but you'll only want to *close* the window when you're really done with the work you're doing in that window.

Making a Window Grow The opposite of the minimize box is, of course, the maximize box. When you click on this box (the one with the square drawn on it) your window will grow to fill your entire screen. This is as big as a window can possibly get. It blankets the entire desktop, covering everything except the Taskbar at the very bottom. You might want to do this from time to time to see more of what you're working on. (It's also a quick way to hide other windows on your screen from prying eyes.)

After a window grows to maximum size, the appearance of the maximize box changes. It becomes the return-to-normal-size box, and it looks like this:

Clicking on this box returns the window back to the way it was before you maximized it.

Using Scroll Bars in a Window When a small window holds a lot of items, you won't be able to see everything that's inside the window all at once. You see, Windows NT won't squeeze the items closer together to make them all fit. Instead, it keeps things spaced apart normally but gives you a way to see everything else. When a window is too small to show everything, it gets *scroll bars.*

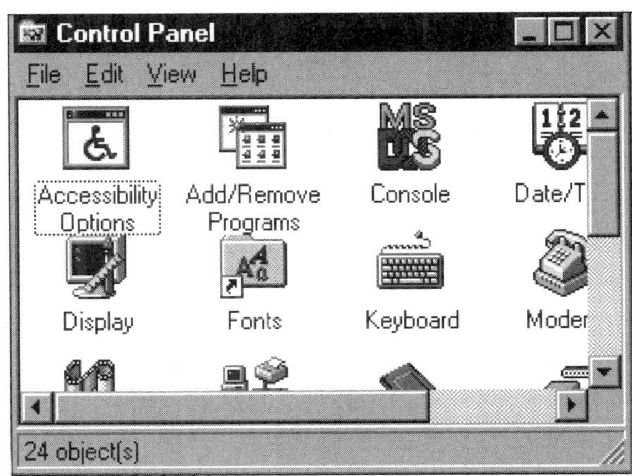

Scroll bars are different-looking borders along either the right edge or the bottom of a window, or both. You can use your mouse to click on the scroll bars to make the contents of the window move around, or "scroll," inside the window. This is hard to visualize if you've never seen it, so let's try it now.

If you don't already have it open, open the Control Panel window. (Click the Start button, hover over the Settings command, and click on Control Panel.) Now use your mouse to grab the lower right corner of the window, where the diagonal ridges are, and drag the corner up and to the left so that the window is much smaller. Did your window sprout scroll bars? Keep adjusting the size of the window until you have scroll bars across the bottom and along the right side.

Look carefully at the scroll bars and you'll see two arrows at each end of each scroll bar. You can click on these arrow buttons to make the insides of the window move over, or scroll, in that direction. Click on the arrow at the right end of the bottom scroll bar (it has an arrow pointing to the right). Did everything in the window move to the left? Now click on the opposite arrow button a few times—the one at the left end of the bottom scroll bar that points left. Did the contents of the window move back? Now try clicking on the up and down arrows.

Clicking on the scroll bars doesn't move the window (you already know how to do that), it moves what's inside the window. Clicking on the scroll bars will always let you see everything that's inside a window no matter how small the window gets or how much is inside it.

Now make the window bigger again by dragging the lower-right-corner of the window out. If you make the window big enough, the scroll bars will disappear. Scroll bars only appear on a window when they're needed. That's how you can tell whether or not you're seeing everything that's inside the window.

Scroll Bars, Part II There's another way to use the scroll bars (isn't there always?) to see what's inside a window. And although it might not be obvious the first time, the size of the scroll bars themselves is telling you something. Open and/or adjust a window on your screen so that it shows a scroll bar, like the one in Figure 1.13.

Between the arrow buttons at the ends of the scroll bar there is a big gray rectangle. The rectangle is like a thermometer: it moves up and down and changes size to show you how much of the window you are looking at. In other words, the rectangle represents the proportion of the window that's visible compared to the part that's not visible. If you can only see a small portion of the window (because it holds a lot of

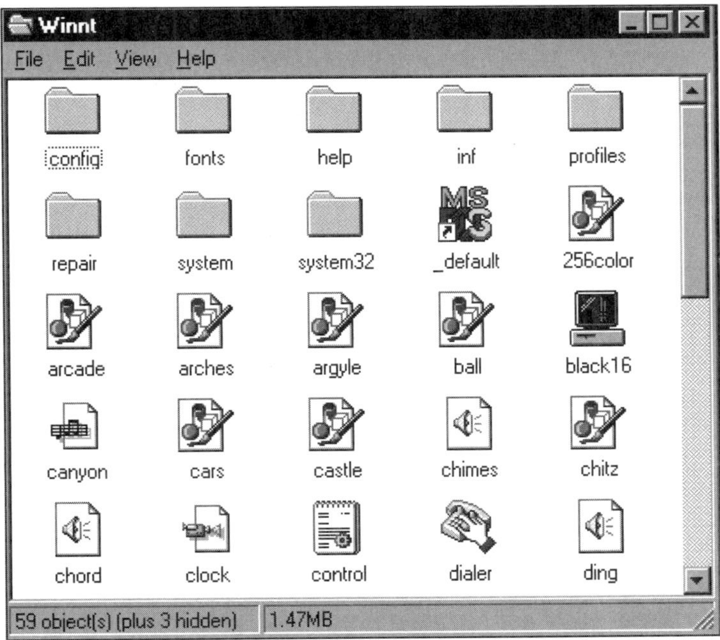

Figure 1.13: Scroll bars, like the one on the right side of this window, indicate that the window is too small to show everything it contains. The size of the scroll bar indicates what proportion of the contents is not visible.

things and you have shrunk it very small), the scroll bar rectangle will be very small. If you can already see most of the window, the size of the scroll bar will be larger. If the rectangle is half as long as the scroll bar, you can see half of the window.

The gray rectangle (called a slider) looks like another button, and it is. If you put your mouse pointer on that gray rectangle and hold your left mouse button down, you can drag the scroll bar up and down. As you drag the scroll bar, the contents of your window scroll along with you. The more you drag, the more your window scrolls. The faster you drag, the faster the window scrolls. When you finally let go of your left mouse button, the window stops scrolling and stays where you left it. This can be a handy way to quickly see everything that's inside a window.

One last trick: you can also click on the light gray area in the scroll bars to make the window "jump" in that direction. With a scroll bar visible on your window, click once on the light-colored area between the arrow at the end of the scroll bar and the darker rectangular slider. The slider will jump in the direction of your mouse. Move your mouse and click on the opposite end of the slider and it will jump back.

Working with Windows

Now that you've mastered all the basic skills, it's time to get some real work done. Whether or not you write much at your computer, this little exercise will walk you through all the basic steps of creating a memo or a letter and saving in on your disk. You'll see how to use drop-down menus and how to save your work in progress.

Writing a Brief Letter To start with, we're going to use one of the free applications that comes with Windows NT. Windows NT comes with not one, but two, word processing (writing) programs, called Notepad and WordPad. Notepad is the easier of the two to learn, and that's the one we're going to use now.

Opening a Notepad window is no different than opening any other window. Start by clicking on the Start button. When the Start menu pops up, highlight Programs. When the pop-up submenu appears, highlight Accessories. When the next pop-up submenu appears, click on Notepad. Figure 1.14 shows you where the Notepad command is.

The normal Notepad window should appear, like the one in Figure 1.15. Most of it is empty. Now, like any writer, you're staring at a blank sheet of paper. Across the top of the Notepad window is the ever-present blue stripe with the minimize, maximize, and close boxes all in a row at the right end. Near the left the window is labeled "Untitled - Notepad." That's there to remind you that your letter (or memo, or novel) is as yet untitled, and that you're working with Notepad.

The first thing to do is start writing! Start typing away, writing anything you'd like. It doesn't need to be spelled correctly or even be coherent. This is only practice. Be sure to type at least 10–20 words, so don't give up too easily. Also, *do not* press the <ENTER> key at the end of each line. This is not a typewriter, and you don't need to hit the carriage return every time you get near the edge of the page.

When you've successfully put in a dozen or more words, take a break and look at your Notepad window. If you've typed in enough words, there should be a scroll bar at the bottom of the window showing you that the window is not big enough to show all your writing at once. Experiment with the scroll bar and scrolling the window back and forth until you've seen the whole thing.

Now it's time to take a look at the special commands that come with Notepad. Just underneath the blue stripe at the top of the

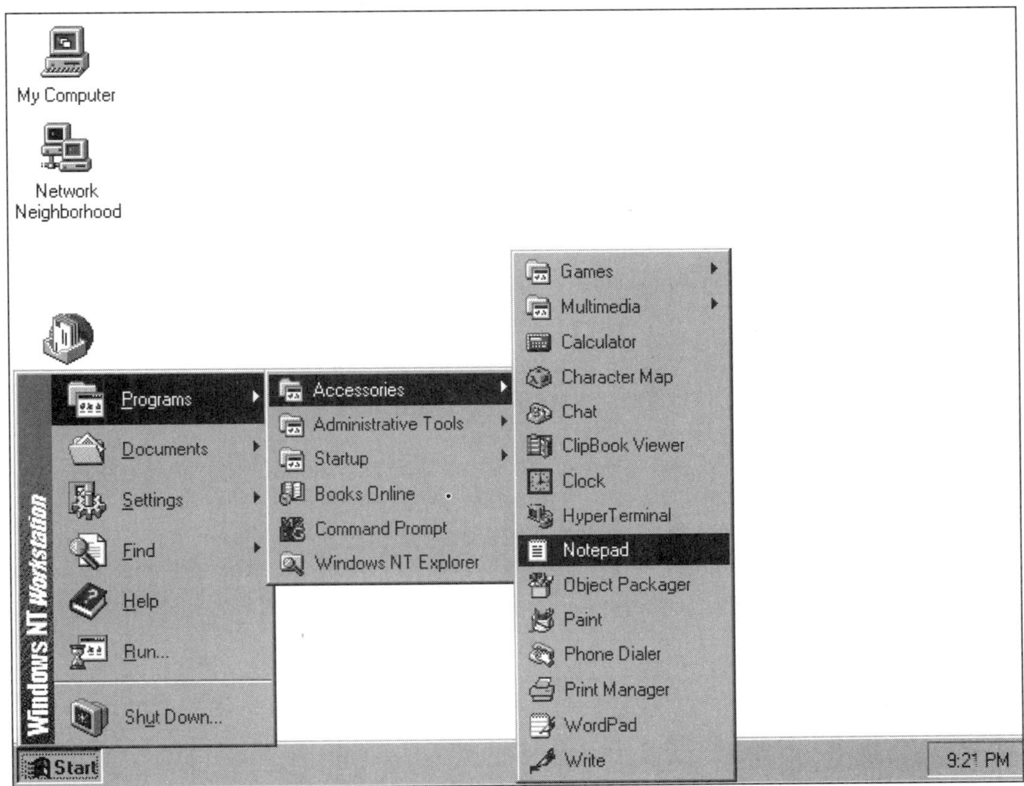

Figure 1.14: Notepad is a simple word-processing (writing) program that can be found through the Start menu.

window are four words on a gray stripe. This stripe is called the *menu bar* because each of those words is a Notepad command and each command has its own pop-up menu. To see how these work, click once on the word File. The Notepad File-command menu should pop up, as shown in Figure 1.16. If you move your mouse pointer up and down the File menu, each command will be highlighted in turn, just like they are on the Start menu.

If you move your mouse pointer over the other three menu commands (Edit, Search, and Help) you will see their menus pop up, too. Remember to do all this without clicking or holding your mouse button. Just hovering over the menus and the commands in the menus is enough.

Let's make it a little easier to read what you've written. Highlight the Edit menu, then select the next to last command, Word Wrap, and click on it once. The Word Wrap command makes all your words fit

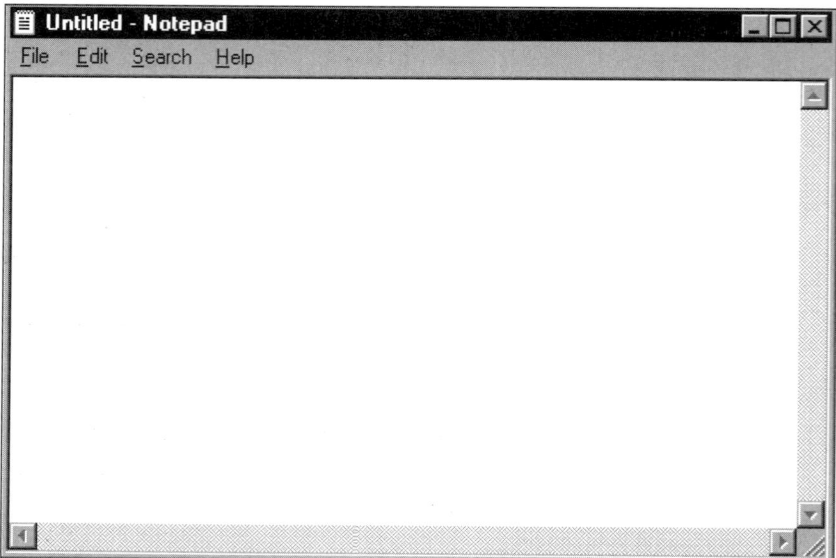

Figure 1.15: When Notepad starts, you are faced with a blank window.

inside the window by "wrapping" the words around the end of each line. Now your fabulous writing should be easier to read. Pop up the Edit menu again and look at the Word Wrap command near the bottom. There's a little check mark next to it to tell you this option is now in effect. If you click the Word Wrap command a second time, the check mark will go away and the word wrap feature will be turned off like before. You can switch this option on and off as often as you like, like flipping a light switch.

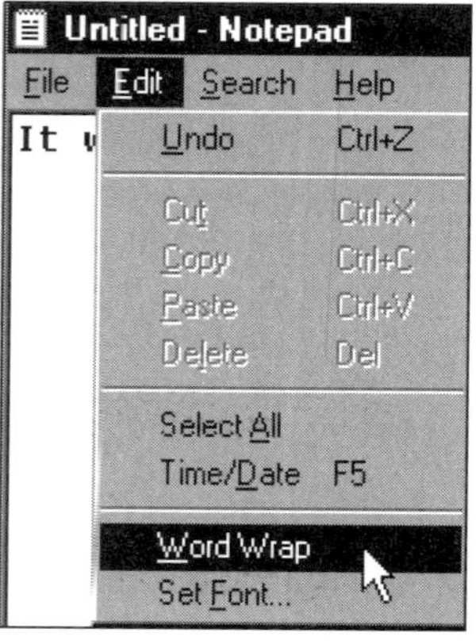

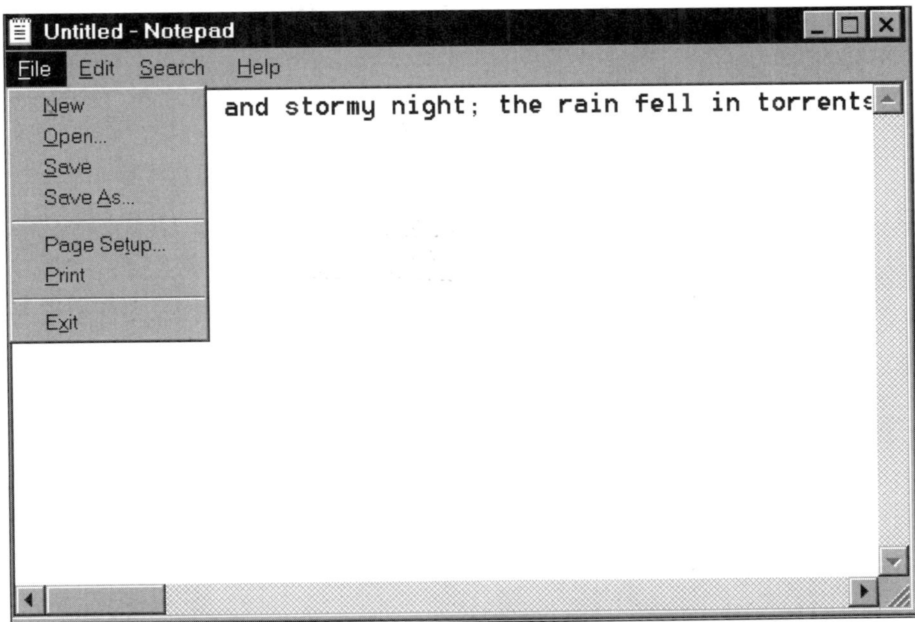

Figure 1.16: Notepad has four pop-up menus of its own, such as the File menu shown here.

Remember how you could grow and shrink a window by clicking on the maximize and minimize buttons? Try those again now. Click the maximize button (the one in the middle, with the square on it) and watch your Notepad window expand to fill the screen. You'll notice, too, that each line of your typing wraps in a different place now because the window is bigger. Click the back-to-normal box to return your window to its previous size. Now click the minimize box (with the underline on it) to shrink your window to a small button on the Taskbar. Even though your window has disappeared temporarily, Windows NT remembers all the typing you did. You haven't lost any work. Click the button on the Taskbar to restore your window (the button should say "Untitled - Notepad").

Finally, click on the close box (with the X on it) in the corner of your window. What happens? Windows NT is warning you that if you close the Notepad window, you will be throwing away all of your typing work (see Figure 1.17). Remember, closing a window is not the same as minimizing it. Closing a window ends your work session once and for all and you won't be able to come back to it later. Sure, you'll be able to use Notepad again to write something else, but the writing you did now will be tossed out, impossible to retrieve.

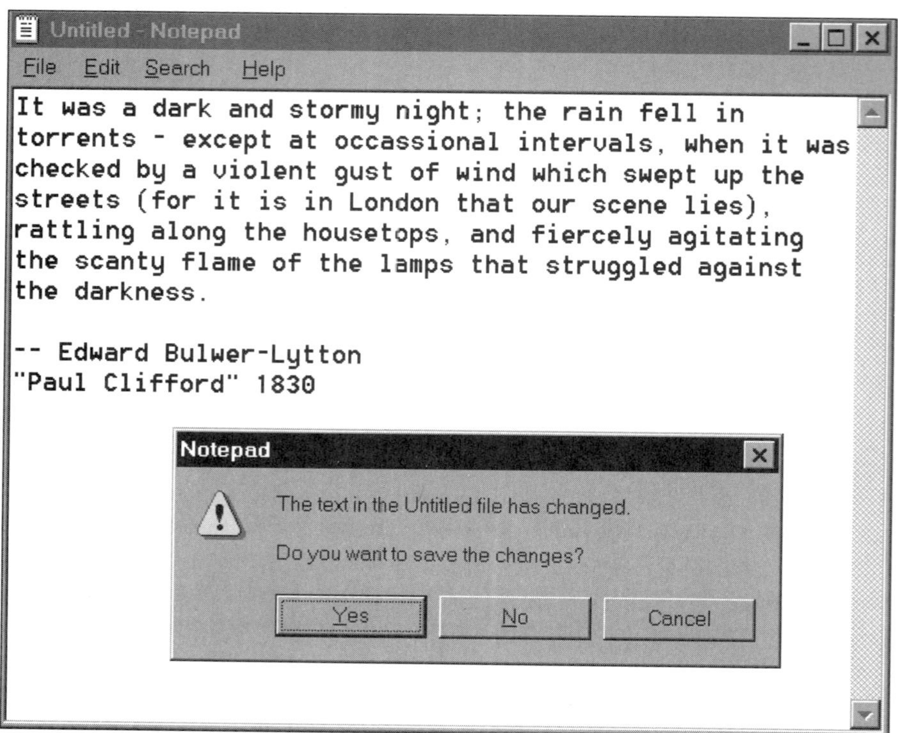

Figure 1.17: A warning box appears if you're about to lose some valuable work.

This was just a test. The correct answer here is to click in the Cancel button. That will cancel your request to close the window and everything is back to normal, no harm done. So if closing the window is not the right way to finish your work, what is the right way?

Saving a Work File Every application, including Notepad, has a command to save your work before you quit. It's usually on the File menu because saving your work is like filing it in a file drawer. Click on the File menu and then select Save. What you will see is a new and complicated window like the one in Figure 1.18. This is called a Save As window (check the name in the corner) because it lets you save your work as a new file on the computer.

Despite all the windows and icons and stuff in the Save As window, you really only need to decide on two things: what you want to name your work file and where on your computer you want to store it. You get to make up a name for each and every work file you create from

Figure 1.18: When saving your work to permanent storage, Windows NT allows you to choose the place and the name under which the file is stored.

now on. The name can be very long—up to 255 letters long—and it can be called anything you like. You should pick a name that you're going to remember later on. This name will be attached to your work file for the rest of its life, kind of like writing the title on the cover of a book.

The place to type the name of your new file is already highlighted near the bottom of the window. The working title so far has been "Untitled" but that's not very descriptive. Without clicking any mouse buttons or selecting anything, simply start typing a new name for your file. For this practice session, let's make up a name like "This is my First Notepad File." Type that name in now but don't press <ENTER> when you're done.

That takes care of the first part, naming your file. Now you have to decide on the second part: where on your computer you want to store this file. Windows NT is recommending that you store it on your desktop (see the top of the window), but that's not always the best place. If you always stored your work on your Windows NT desktop it would get pretty cluttered after a few days. Just like with a real office desk and real paper files, you should probably store your files in their appropriate file folders and not just strew them on your desktop.

Here's how to do it. The top line of the Save As window shows you where Windows NT is planning to store your file. The big center portion of the window shows you the alternatives. If you double-click on one of these other choices, Windows NT will change its recommendation and suggest that you save your file there. Try that now. Place your mouse pointer over the words My Computer and double-click it. The choice My Computer is now "promoted" into the area at the top of the Save As window as the suggested saving place. You also get a new list of alternatives in the big window. These each represent the disks inside your computer.

Let's repeat the process to choose one of them. Find your main disk (usually called disk C) and double-click on it. That disk is now promoted to the top of the window, and folders that are stored inside that disk are now presented as alternatives. You are, in a sense, tunneling deeper into your file cabinet, or your computer's disks. One more time, select a folder that seems appropriate (your choice) and double-click on it. When you're satisfied that this is a logical place to store your work file you can click one time on the big Save button near the lower right corner of the window.

Now your work is saved as a permanent file on your computer. If you shut your computer off and come back tomorrow your work file will still be there. You can work on it again another time and polish it up, making it just the way you want. In fact, let's try that now.

Loading a Work File Click the close box in the corner of the Notepad window. The window should close without any complaints this time because Windows NT knows that you've saved your work. Closing the window now won't harm anything, so Windows NT complies with your request. Now pretend that you're coming back to your computer another day to make changes to the document you just wrote. First, you need to open a Notepad window again.

As always, you can begin by clicking on the Start button and selecting Notepad from the series of cascading menus. Just like before, you'll get a big blank page on which you can type. But instead of creating something new, you want to edit (change) something older. How do you get your old work back into the new Notepad window?

Very simply. Click on the File command near the top of the Notepad window. Highlight the Open command and click on it. You should see a window that looks just like the Save As window you saw before. In fact, the only difference between the Open window and the Save As window is the word Open at the top. You use the window the same way except this time you're telling Windows NT where to get your file from, not where to store it to.

Using the same technique as before, double click on My Computer, then your disk, then your folder, and so on. When you reach the right folder you should see your work file listed in the big window, just like in Figure 1.19. Highlight its name and then click once on the big Open button near the bottom of the Open window.

Shortcut Hint: You can open a file by double-clicking on the file's name in the Open window.

Sure enough, your work appears in the Notepad window just like before. Now it's time to make some changes. This will help you practice basic Windows NT techniques for selecting and editing any kind of work, even if you don't do much writing.

Help! I'm Lost What if you can't find your file again? What if you took a wrong turn as you were clicking and double-clicking folders and wound up at a dead end? First of all, don't feel too bad, because nobody can memorize where each file and folder is, and everybody clicks the wrong one from time to time. Besides, it's not difficult to get back to where you want to be.

When you select a wrong folder, there are two ways you can retrace your steps. You can either click the "back up" button or you can press the <BACKSPACE> key on your keyboard. Either method works the same way. The "back up" button is part of the Open window and it looks like a yellow manila folder with an arrow on it.

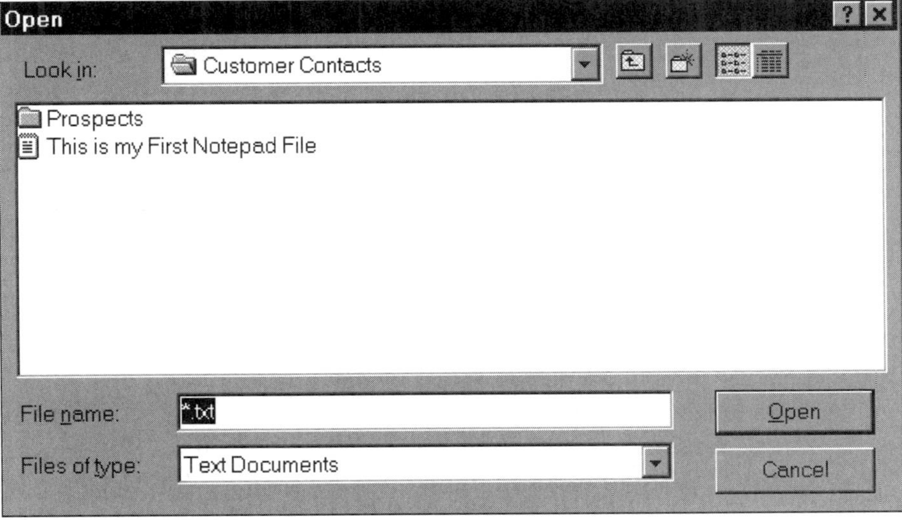

Figure 1.19: The Open box, like the Save box, lets you pick a file and its location.

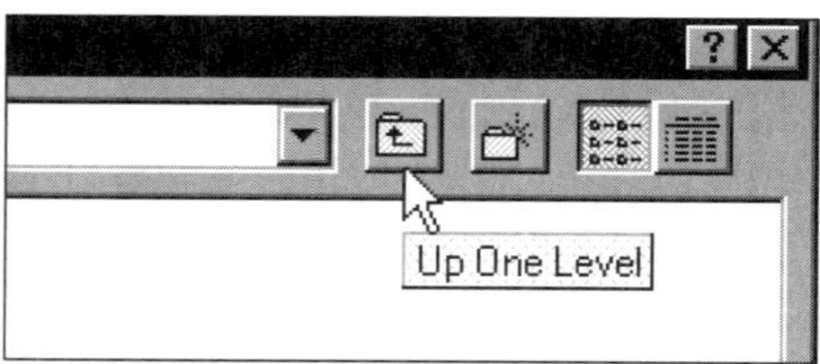

Clicking this button once takes you back one step. Clicking it again takes you back one more step, and so on. Pressing <BACKSPACE> does exactly the same thing. After one or two steps back, you should be able to head down the right path again and load your Notepad file.

Making Changes to a Work File The first thing you might want to do is turn the word-wrap option back on. Click Edit, then Word Wrap. To erase a word from your document that you don't want, place your mouse pointer over a word (the pointer looks like a skinny vertical line now) and double-click on that word. The entire word, plus the space and any punctuation marks around it, are highlighted. Now that you've identified the word you want to erase, click on the Edit menu and select the Delete command. Poof! The word is gone.

Shortcut Hint: You can erase a word by highlighting it and pressing the <DEL> key on your keyboard.

If you want to erase two adjoining words, you could repeat this process, once for each word, but there's a better way. Double-click a word but make sure you hold your left mouse button down after the second click. Now drag your mouse over the second word and it will be highlighted too. Practice dragging the mouse back and forth across your text, selecting more or fewer words as you go. When you've highlighted just the words you want to erase, let go of the left mouse button.

There's a third way to select multiple words, too. Instead of double-clicking, just click once and drag your mouse and you can highlight as much or as little as you want. This technique lets you highlight individual letters and punctuation marks, too, not just whole words. As you become more comfortable with Windows NT, you may settle on one or two of these techniques and they'll become your favorites.

Adding to a Work File So much for erasing. How do you add more words? That's no harder than typing is. The only thing you have to do before you add any more words is show Windows NT where you want to add. To do that, place your mouse pointer somewhere in the middle of a sentence and click the left button once. That places a marker (the flashing vertical line) in your document where the new words will go. After you've clicked, you can move the mouse away if you want to, and the marker will stay. Now just start typing and all your new words will be inserted in between the old words.

Cut & Paste in a Work File This is a really fun and useful technique that you could never do before with a typewriter or even pencil and paper. It's called cut & paste, and it gives you the freedom to make lots of changes to your work files without lots of erasing and re-typing.

Let's start by assuming that you have a long document, say, a contract. You decide, after reading it for the fourth time, that the opening paragraph would really look better at the end of the document. You could either erase the paragraph from the beginning of the document and then type it again at the end of the document or you cut use cut & paste.

Here's how to do it. Start by highlighting the words you want to erase. Then, from the Edit menu, select the Cut command. The highlighted words are gone, just as if you had erased them. But wait, there's more. Now point to the end of your document where you want to add the text back in. Click your left mouse button once to place the marker exactly where you want the new text to go. Then, from the Edit menu, select the Paste command. Voila! Your words have been moved from the beginning to the end and you didn't have to type anything over again.

Shortcut Hint: You can cut text by highlighting it and pressing <CTRL+X> on your keyboard and paste it by pressing <CTRL+V>.

Cutting text is kind of like erasing except that the text you cut is "remembered" instead of thrown away. When you cut words or letters, they go into a special storage area Windows NT calls the Clipboard. Although you normally don't see it, the Clipboard always holds the last thing you cut, no matter what it is or what application you were using when you cut it out.

Copy & Paste in a Work File Sometimes you don't want to erase something and move it elsewhere. Sometimes you might find yourself with a sentence so wonderful that you want to duplicate it several times in the same document. For example, you might want to repeat a quotation or somebody's name in different locations. Of course, you could type the words in every time, but there's a better way.

To make copies of the same words in different places in the same document, first highlight the words you want to repeat. From the Edit menu, select the Copy command. Nothing much appears to happen, but the text has been copied to the Windows NT Clipboard nonetheless. Now use your mouse to point to the first place you want those words repeated and click the left button to place the marker. Now select the File menu and click Paste.

Shortcut Hint: You can copy text by highlighting it and pressing <CTRL+C> on your keyboard.

If you want to duplicate the text a second time, just select the Paste command again; there's no need to copy the original a second time. The Clipboard can produce endless copies of anything it holds. It acts like a rubber stamp: after one Copy command you can repeat a hundred Paste commands. This is true of text you cut, too. You can cut the words once, and paste them back in a hundred times. The contents of the Clipboard are remembered until you shut down your computer; they don't survive overnight.

More about Saving Your Work Files When you save a work file to disk by clicking on the Save command (on the File menu) you are making a copy of the contents of that window. If you make more changes afterwards, they are *not* automatically saved for you. If you want to save the latest, updated version on disk, you have to click in the Save command again. The second time you click on Save, you won't see the Save As window like you did the first time. That's because Windows NT already knows what your file is called and where it is supposed to be saved. It's like having a perfectly efficient office assistant: the very first time you want to file something you have to explain where you want it, but after that, the file always goes back into its proper folder with no questions asked.

Every time you click Save, Windows NT saves the current version of your work as it appears in the window. It also erases the previous version of that file. That means that there is always only one revision of your work saved on disk. This is normally what you want, but what if you prefer to keep multiple different revisions on disk all at the same time? Is there a way to save newer versions of a file without erasing the older versions? You betcha.

On the Edit menu is a command similar to Save called Save As. When you click Save As, Windows NT gives you a chance to save your work under a different name, or in a different place. You can save a copy of this work file in a different folder, on a different disk, even (if you have a network) on a different computer. You can also change the name of the file. You could, for example, use the Save As command to save different revisions of a contract in the same file with names like "Bichlmaier contract, first draft" and "Bichlmaier contract, revised September 17th" and so on. Use your imagination.

Be careful with this technique. Once you save a file with a different name or in a different folder, that name becomes the standard name for this file. If you click on the Save command again, the file will be saved again under the new name, not the older name. This may or may not be what you wanted. The title at the top of the window will remind you what name you are working under.

More about Cut & Paste You already know how to cut text from one part of a file and paste it into another part, but did you know that you can cut from one file and paste into a completely different file? It's just as easy as before, and you can try it with two different Notepad windows.

With your original Notepad window open on your screen, open a second Notepad window by selecting it from the Start menu. You should see a second Notepad window that overlaps the first one. Click on the original window and highlight some text. Choose the Copy command (or press <CTRL+C>) to copy the highlighted text to the Clipboard. Now click on the new Notepad window and select the Paste command (or press <CTRL+V>). You should see your text duplicated in both windows, like the example in Figure 1.20.

Even though these are different Notepad work files, you can cut (or copy) and paste information between them. But wait, it gets better. You can also paste information between two different windows in two different applications. For example, you can paste words from a word processing window into a financial plan in a spreadsheet window, or vice versa. You can paste information from any window into any other window, within reason. This is a very powerful and useful technique to master because it means you can create much more interesting (not to mention more reliable) documents when you don't have to re-type anything. The rule of thumb is, you should never have to

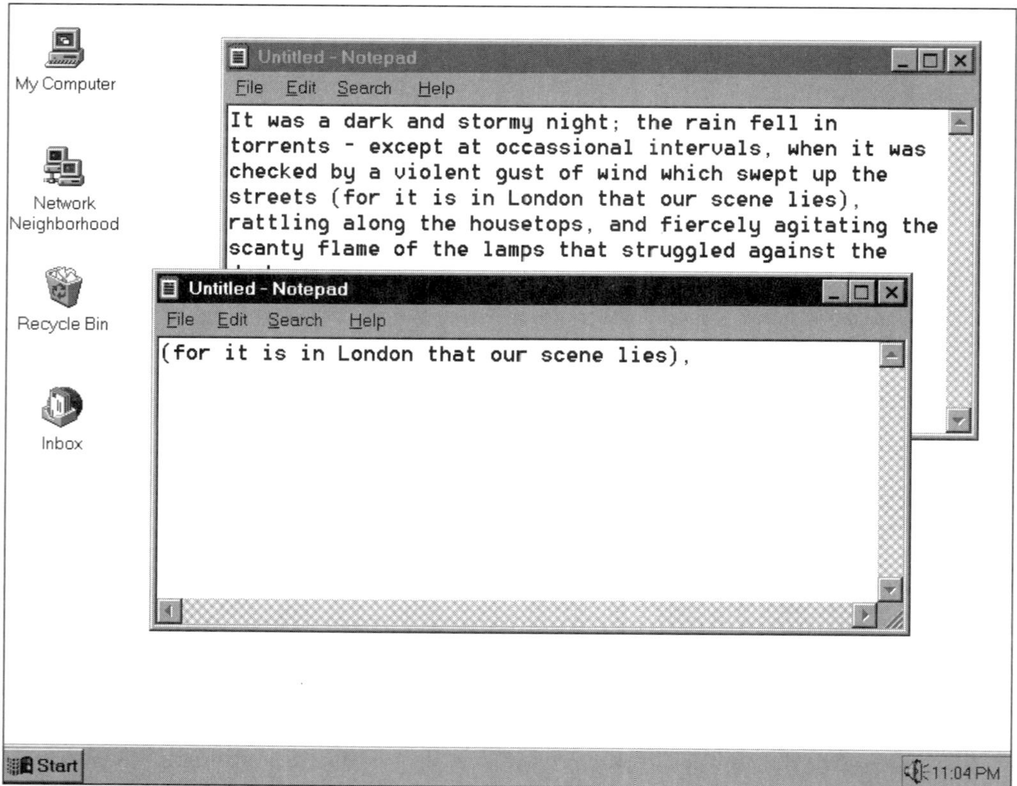

Figure 1.20: You can copy writing from one window to another or within the same window.

type anything more than once. After that, you should paste copies wherever you need to.

More about Loading a Work File You already know how to load a work file by using the Open command from an application's File menu. But there's a shortcut you may prefer that's right on the Start button. Click the Start button now and follow along.

If you highlight the Documents command on the Start menu and hover over it a bit, you'll be rewarded with a list of all the work files that you have opened. The list shows your work files in alphabetical order. If you've been busy, the Documents list can be up to 15 items long (after that, older items get dropped from the list to make room for new items). See Figure 1.21 for a sample of what the Documents list looks like.

If you click on an item from this list Windows NT opens it for you directly. Windows NT even remembers what application (Notepad,

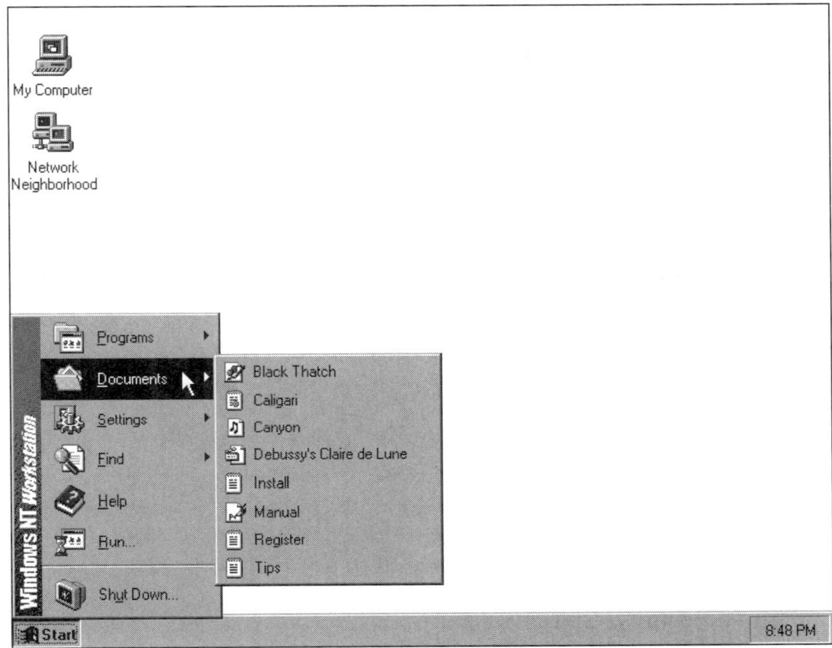

Figure 1.21: The Documents menu automatically lists the last 15 files you opened, read, edited, or worked on.

Paint, Media Player, etc.) you used to open it with and starts the appropriate application.

Exploring Your Computer

You can start using all your favorite applications by clicking on the Start menu. When an application's window opens (like Notepad, for example) you can do your work, whether it be writing, calculating, creating graphics, or whatever. Before you close the window, you save your work onto disk so that you have a permanent copy filed away for later.

But where exactly do those work files go? Sure, they're stored on your computer's disk, but how can you find them again? You also need a way to organize your disk into folders so that you can arrange your work files and find them again. Just like a real filing cabinet, your computer works better if you sort or group your files instead of just throwing them all in and slamming the door.

With Windows NT, you organize, sort, and browse through your computer by clicking on the icon labeled My Computer. That's the first step to making your work more organized and more easily accessible. As you work along with the following examples remember that there's no right or wrong way to organize your computer. At first, you'll just be looking at where some files are already stored on your disk. Later on, you'll be able to impose your own order and organization (or lack of it) any way you want to.

To begin looking inside your computer, locate the icon in the upper left corner of your screen labeled My Computer. Put your mouse pointer over it and double-click the left mouse button.

That should open up the first window onto your computer (or is it My Computer?). The window should look something like the one in Figure 1.22, although you might have more or fewer disk icons. This window is an overall "bird's eye" view of the storage places on your computer. Each icon represents a different storage medium. Let's take a look at the different kinds now.

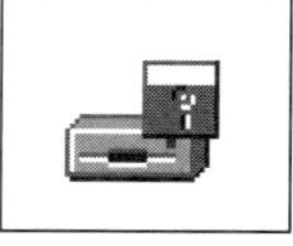

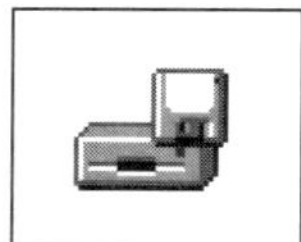

These two icons represent floppy disk drives. Your computer probably has one of these, or maybe both. Windows NT likes to give each disk drive in your computer a letter, and the floppy disk drive is almost always called A. If you have two floppy disk drives, they will be called A and B.

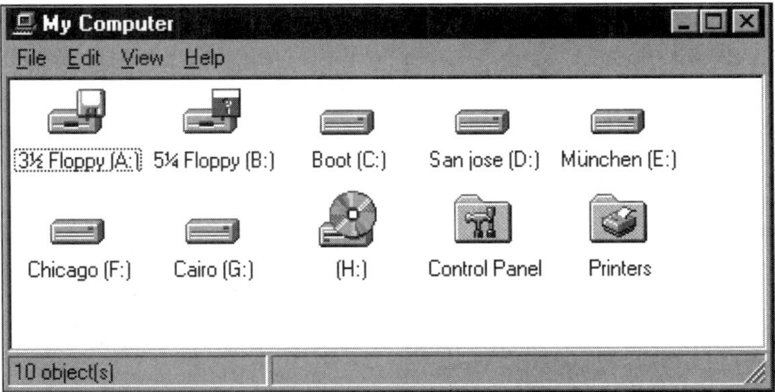

Figure 1.22: Double-clicking on My Computer opens a window showing all the storage options on your computer.

This icon represents a hard disk drive (sometimes called a fixed disk or a Winchester disk). Your computer definitely has one of these, and maybe more. These are the high-speed, permanent storage areas inside your computer where most of your work is stored. Windows NT itself is also stored on a hard disk. Hard disks also get assigned letters, usually starting with the letter C.

If your computer is equipped with a CD-ROM drive, you'll see one of these icons in the My Computer window. A CD-ROM (which stands for the technical term *compact disk, read-only memory*) holds a lot of information, but you can't store your own work on one, you can only load information off of it.

This icon represents a hard disk that isn't really part of your computer. It's part of somebody else's computer and the two of you are attached by a network. You can use the disk just like it was your own, but the little wire underneath the hard disk in the picture reminds you that the disk isn't really in your own computer.

Browsing through Your Computer Opening the My Computer window is a little like looking at the outside of a filing cabinet: you can tell files are stored in there but you can't tell how much, what they are, or where. Now it's time to look further inside your system. Highlight the first hard disk on your computer, usually called C, by clicking on it once. Next, click on the File menu and select the Open command by clicking on it.

Shortcut Tip: You can also open a drive window by double-clicking on the drive icon.

Now you should see a window like the one in Figure 1.23. This window shows you what's stored on this disk. It's like opening a file drawer but without looking into each of the folders yet. As you can see, there is a collection of different items: folders, work files, and other assorted icons. The folder icons look like manila folders. These hold more things inside them, but you can't see their contents yet. The other icons are "loose" files, like pieces of papers that aren't inside any file folder. As you become more accustomed to using Windows NT, you'll see that it's common to mix files with folders.

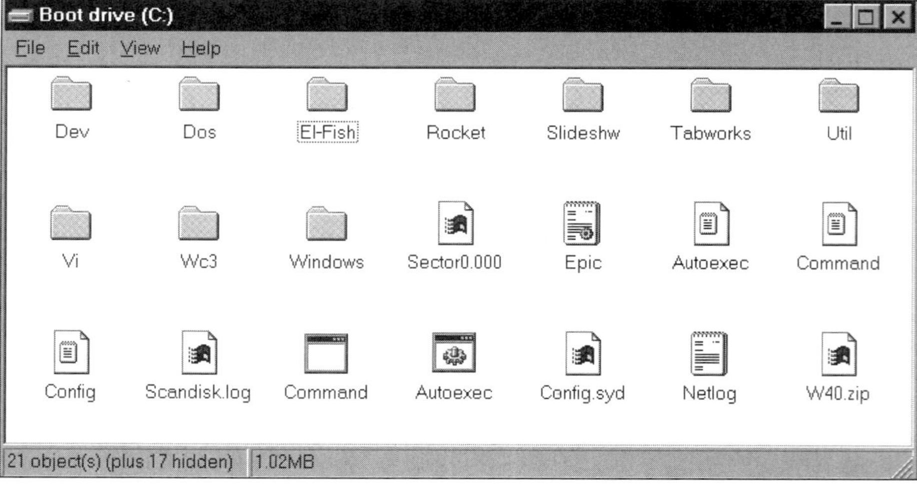

Figure 1.23: Double-clicking on a disk icon opens a window showing all the folders and files stored on that disk.

You could open one of the files in this window now, but let's explore some of the folders instead. Pick a folder (any folder) and highlight it by clicking on it once. Then click on the Edit menu and select the Open command. This will open the folder so you can see inside.

Shortcut Tip: You can open a folder by double-clicking on its icon.

What you see inside the folder depends on what folder you picked. If the folder has just a few files in it, it might look like Figure 1.24. If it has a lot of files and/or other folders inside, it might look more like Figure 1.25.

The icons in each window mean something. In the early versions of Windows NT the original purpose of these icons was to identify a document (a work file that you created) versus an application (a program file that a professional software developer created). Over time, the icons got fancier, so that you could tell a word processing file (like a memo) from a spreadsheet file (like a financial plan) from a dozen different other types of files. Now, as you can see, there are hundreds or thousands of different icons, and each one seems different.

Some of the files you see are work files that you could edit, and others are applications that you could use. Still other icons represent system files—special files that are needed to make your computer run. Most applications (in fact, probably all of them) will be on your Start menu or one of its pop-up submenus so you should never need to search for an application by browsing through your computer like this. But you should become familiar with browsing through your system to find your work files. Just as with a real filing cabinet, you will be more efficient and better organized if you know where everything is and how to look for it.

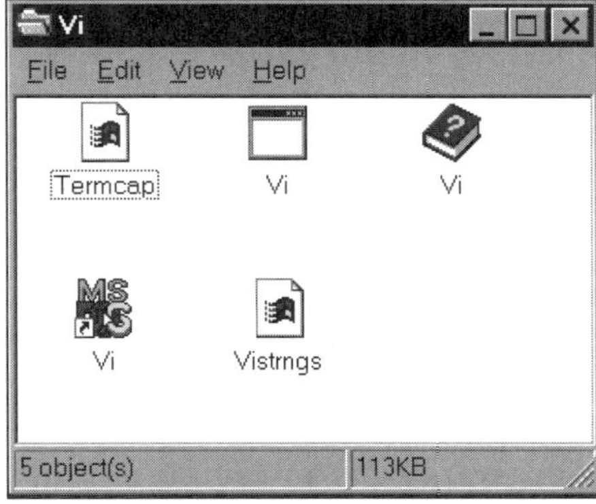

Figure 1.24: Double-clicking on a folder icon opens a window showing all the files (and additional folders) stored in that folder.

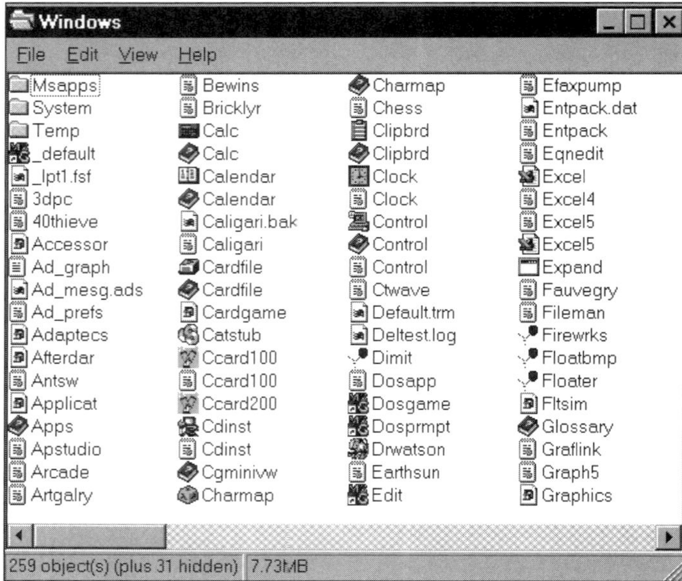

Figure 1.25: If a folder contains a lot of files, they will be displayed with smaller icons, and the window may have scroll bars.

Organizing Your Files

As you saw from the previous examples, your disk contains folders, and those folders can contain more folders, and so on. Those folders can also contain files. Files and folders can be mixed with other folders in any order. The purpose of folders is to let you organize your work, nothing more. They're only there as a convenience. Consider the alternative: you probably have more than two hundred files on your disk, and if they were all jumbled together it would be very hard to pick out the ones you wanted when you needed them. Your work files would be mixed in with the Windows NT system files and applications. Nothing would be organized, and as time went on, it would get worse.

By creating folders you can sort and collect similar files together in an imaginary manila folder. But these folders are better because they never get overstuffed, ripped, or lost. A folder can contain one file or one thousand files. A folder can also contain other folders inside it. For example, if you are a salesperson, you might create a folder to hold all your customer contacts, and another folder to hold product information. A third folder might contain personal correspondence and games. Within the folder for customer contacts, you might have another folder just for prospects who are not yet your customers. You might even have another set of folders inside that one for each geographical region.

How to Create a New Folder Let's try creating exactly that kind of organization now. Starting from the beginning, open My Computer by double-clicking on it. Now choose a hard disk icon and open it by double-clicking on it. You should be looking at the contents of your hard disk, which already has various files and folders in it. To create a new folder, click the File command and hover for a moment over the New command. When the pop-up menu appears, choose Folder (the topmost choice) and click on it. A new folder is created inside the window with the unexciting name of New Folder.

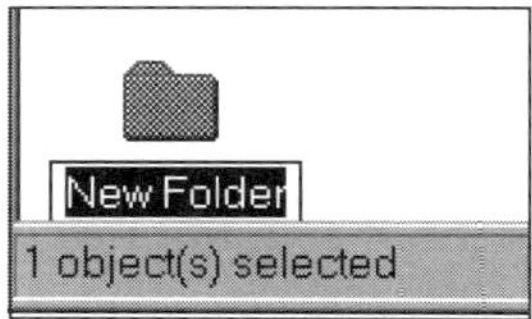

First things first. Let's change the name of the folder to something more descriptive. If you need to highlight the new folder, click on it once. Then, from the Edit menu again, click on the command Rename. The name under your folder will be highlighted, ready for you to type in a new name. Type Customer Contacts and press <ENTER>. Now your folder should look like this:

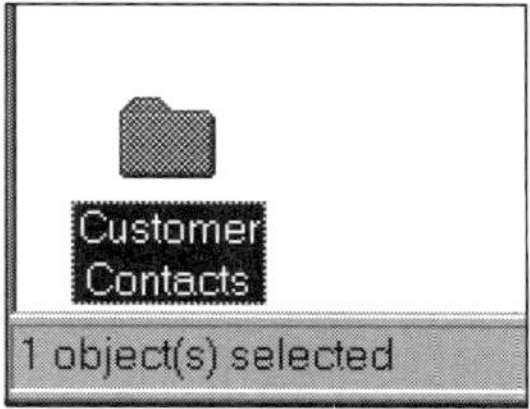

So far, so good. From now on, you can save your customer contact information in this folder. Repeat the same process to create the Product Information folder and the Personal folder. You should now have three new folders on your disk.

Continuing with your file-organization blitz, you decide to open your Customer Contacts folder and create some new folders inside it. Double-click Customer Contacts to open it. Then repeat the process you used before to create one new folder. This time you'll take a short-cut to renaming your new folder. Notice that when a new folder is first created, its name is already highlighted. As long as you don't carry out any other commands first, you can start typing a name for this new folder right away. Type Prospects and press <ENTER>. You should now have a Prospects folder inside your Customer Contacts folder, as shown in Figure 1.26. Finally, inside the Prospects folder, create three new folders called West, Central, and East.

Now you're organized! The next time you open a Notepad window to create a memo, you'll know where to save it. And, the next time you need to refer back to an old customer letter, you'll know where to look for it. In fact, let's create a few new documents now.

Creating New Files from Scratch You already know how to open Notepad and other applications to start using them. First you start typing, and then you save your work as a new file. But you can also do it the other way around: create a new file first and then open it with the proper application.

If you want to compose, say, a new letter to a west-coast prospect, open the West folder (inside the Prospect folder, inside the Customer Contacts folder). From the File menu, hover over the New command for a moment, just as if you were about to create another new folder. But this time, click on the line that says Text Document. A brand-new document is created called (unsurprisingly) New Text Document. Take advantage of the fact that its name is still highlighted and type "Letter to Acme in San Francisco" and press <ENTER>.

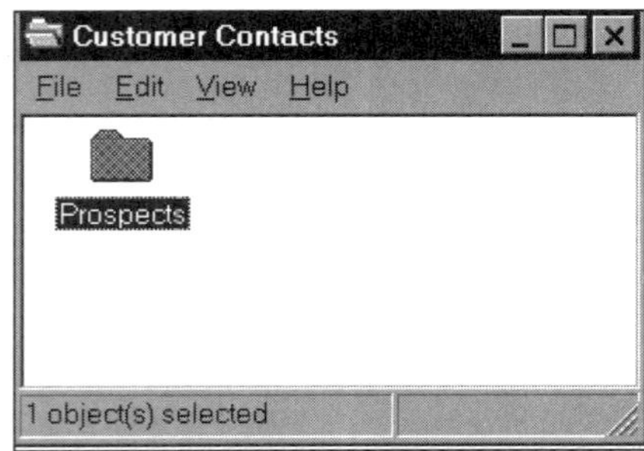

Figure 1.26: You can create new folders within other folders using the File menu.

Now that you've created a new file, what does it say? Nothing at all—it's like a blank sheet of paper. To start filling that blank sheet, double-click on it and watch what happens.

Notepad opens and automatically loads your file for you (notice the name at the top of the Notepad window). Does it look like Figure 1.27? Type a few lines as though you were writing a letter. Best of all, when you're done typing, save the file (click File, then Save) and Windows NT won't ask you where to save the file or what to name it—it already knows. Creating a file first and then editing it is often much more convenient than opening an application and then creating a file. You can use whichever method appeals to you more.

Moving a File from One Folder to Another There may often be times you wish you'd saved a file in a different folder. You might save the San Francisco letter in the East Coast folder by mistake, or you might reorganize your territory some day into North and South and have to rearrange all your files. Moving files from one folder to another is easy and straightforward. All you have to do is drag the file from one place to another.

As an example, let's move the San Francisco letter to the East folder and then back again. Open the West folder so you can see the letter you just created. The West folder should look like Figure 1.28. Arrange the windows on your screen so that you can see the East folder and the West folder at the same time. The East folder does not have to be open, just visible. Now drag Letter to Acme in San Francisco until it is over the East folder. Let go of the mouse button. Refer to Figure 1.29 to see what this looks like.

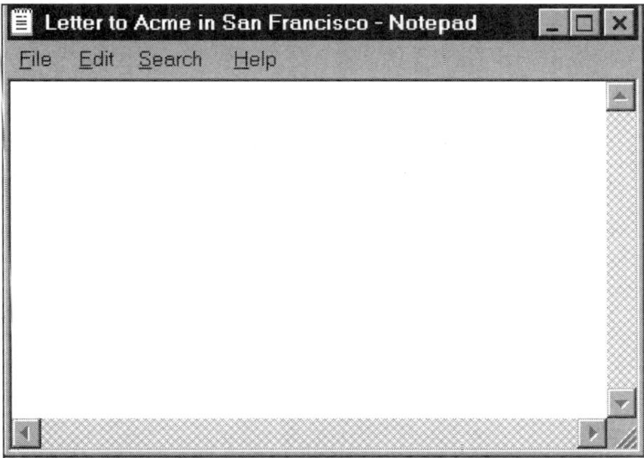

Figure 1.27: You can create a new, blank document using the shortcut menu and open it later by double-clicking on it.

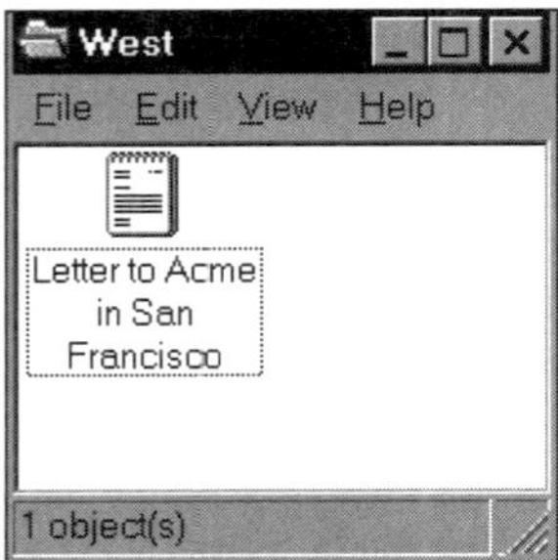

Figure 1.28: So far, this folder contains just a single file.

This is called a "drag and drop" file transfer because you drag the file from one folder and drop in into another folder. This works for any kind of file and any kind of folder. You can move files from disk to disk this way, too. Now repeat the same technique to move the file back where it belongs.

Another Way to Move a File In addition to the drag-and-drop method, there's also the cut-and-paste method. Open the East folder and highlight your file by clicking it once. From the Edit menu, choose Cut. Now open the West folder (if it isn't already open) and from its File menu, choose Paste. Your file has been moved. You can cut and paste entire files just as easily as you can cut and paste a few words in a document. Neat, huh?

Shortcut Hint: You can cut by pressing <CTRL+X> and paste by pressing <CTRL+V>.

Making Duplicate Copies of a File Perhaps there's a particular document that you're especially fond of. Or you've written some

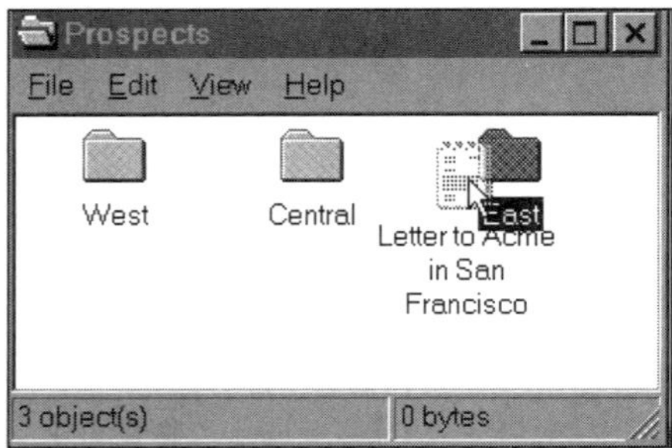

Figure 1.29: To move a file from one folder to another, simply drag it to where you want it to go.

"boilerplate" text that you want to use as the basis for a number of different documents. Whatever the reason, you may find yourself wishing you could photocopy your electronic files and have duplicates of them.

Well, you can, and it is very easy. First, highlight the file you want to copy by clicking on it once. From the Edit menu, choose Copy. To make a duplicate, open the folder where you want the duplicate to go, and select the Paste command. The second file will be exactly like the first one; they'll even have the same name.

Shortcut Hint: You can copy by pressing <CTRL+C> and paste by pressing <CTRL+V>.

You can also place copies in the same folder as the original file. In that case, the copy will be called "Copy of…" followed by the name of your original file.

As you can see, the only difference between moving a file and duplicating a file is the difference between using the Cut command (CTRL+X) or the Copy command (CTRL+C) on the original file.

How to Get Rid of a File Eventually you'll want to throw some computer files away. Just like paper files, the files on your computer may become out-of-date and unnecessary. Files also take up space on your computer and although your disk can hold lots of information, its capacity is not infinite. The day may come when you find yourself running low on disk space and need to do some housecleaning to free up more room. You can do all these things simply by dragging some files into the Recycle Bin.

The Recycle Bin sits on the left side of your screen, on the desktop. It's like another folder, but a special one. When you drag files to the Recycle Bin they are removed from your computer.

To test this theory, let's throw away a file. Find your earlier letter in your West folder. Open the West folder if necessary so that you can see the file. Also make sure that you can see the Recycle Bin at the same time. Now drag the file icon over to the Recycle Bin and release the left mouse button. Your file's gone!

Shortcut Hint: You can throw a file into the Recycle Bin by highlighting the file and pressing the <DEL> key.

Actually, like most real recycle bins, you can often rescue your file if you threw it away by accident. There are a number of ways you can do this.

How to Rescue a File from the Recycle Bin Find the West folder from which the file originally came. Click on the Edit menu and then select Undo Delete. Your file will pop back to its original location, none the worse for wear. (Actually, you can use the Undo Delete command from any window at all; it doesn't need to be the window that the file came from.)

Another Way to Rescue a File from the Recycle Bin You can double-click the Recycle Bin itself to open it, just like a folder. The Recycle Bin window will open to show you everything that's inside the Recycle Bin. Your file should be at the very top of the list.

To retrieve your file, highlight it by clicking once, select the File menu, then click on Restore. Your file will be restored to its original location.

Yet Another Way to Rescue a File from the Recycle Bin With the Recycle Bin window open, drag the file you want to rescue out of the Recycle Bin window into another window. This will remove the file from the Recycle Bin and put it wherever you drop it. This technique has the added advantage that you don't have to put the file back where it came from; you can drag and drop the file anyplace.

How to Really, Really Delete a File As you can tell, throwing a file into the Recycle Bin doesn't really remove it from your computer after all. It just puts the file into a kind of limbo, from which it might be rescued if you try. The Recycle Bin is nearly bottomless; you can throw files into it for years and still have a chance of pulling them back out years later. That's both a blessing and a curse. It's good because it means you don't have to worry about deleting a file by accident. It's bad because if you throw out a lot of files with the intention of making room on your disk, you won't be making any room at all. It's also bad because another person could retrieve files from your Recycle Bin that you don't want them to see.

If you really and truly want to throw something away, you have to empty the Recycle Bin. To do that, open the Recycle Bin window by double-clicking on the Recycle Bin icon. Then, from the File menu, choose Empty Recycle Bin. Windows NT will ask you one last time if you really want to do this.

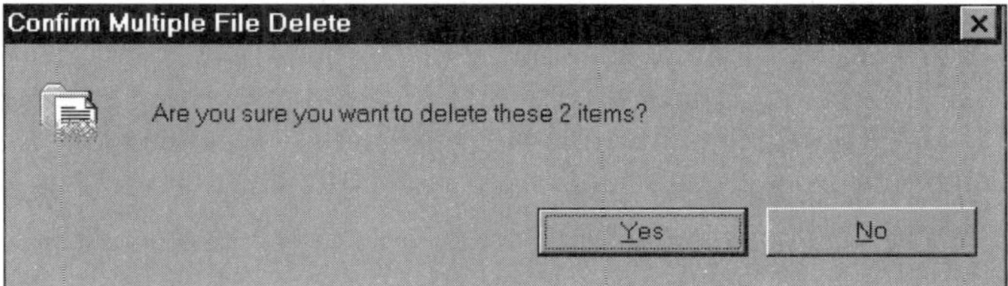

If you answer Yes, all the files in the Recycle Bin are really gone. The Recycle Bin will be empty again and the disk storage those files used will be free. There is no way to get these files back. When the Recycle Bin is empty, it even looks empty.

Recycle Bin Gotchas! You may have gotten the impression from the previous few sections that you might not always be able to rescue a file from the Recycle Bin. That's correct. You can *usually* pull a file back out after you've thrown it in, but not always. Sometimes the Recycle Bin empties itself, and you might not be able to predict when.

There are two times when this might happen. First, the Recycle Bin can be set up to empty itself every time you use it (you can learn how to do this in Chapter 10). In that case, it works more like a fireplace than a recycling bin. Files thrown into it are instantly gone. On the plus side, Windows NT does warn you every time you throw something into it.

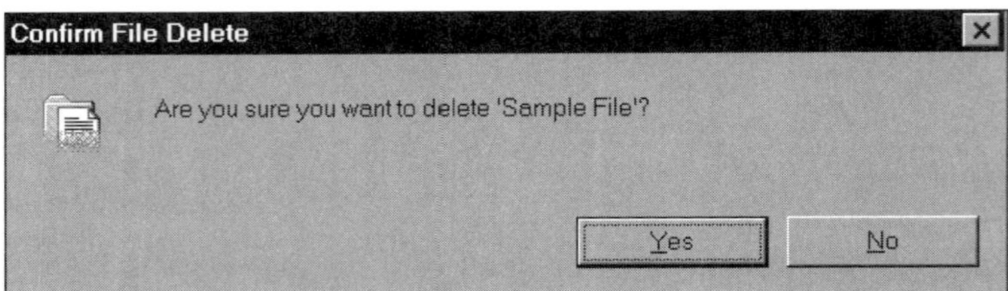

The other time your files might be irretrievable is after the Recycle Bin periodically empties itself. When it gets too full, the Recycle Bin quietly removes some of its contents without telling you. Generally, it removes the oldest files first when this happens, but not necessarily; big files are particularly vulnerable to being emptied.

People have snickered at the use of a recycling bin as a metaphor for deleting files from a computer. Why not a garbage can, they ask, or a paper shredder, or even an incinerator? Actually, the image of a recycling bin is particularly apt. When you throw a file into it you are recycling the disk space the file used to take up. And the system is 100% efficient—all the space that went to the old file can now be used for a new file, with no waste.

How to Reorganize Folders You can drag and drop entire folders exactly the same way that you can drag and drop files. If you want to move an entire folder (and everything inside it) to another disk or another folder, just select the folder icon (you may have to close the folder window first) and drag it to its new destination.

If you prefer, you can use the cut and paste method instead. After selecting the folder you want to move, choose Cut (or Copy, if you want to make a duplicate folder) from the Edit menu. After selecting the destination disk or folder, choose Paste from its Edit menu. That's all there is to it.

How to Change the Name of a File, Folder, or Disk When you create a new work file and save it, you get an opportunity to give that file a name. The same is true when you create a new folder. If, after you've created a file or folder, you want to change its name, how do you do that? It's really quite easy, and there are at least two different ways you can do it.

The first way is to click on the icon once to highlight it, then click on the File menu and select the Rename command. The name of the file will be highlighted, with a flashing editing bar at the very end. Because the entire name is already highlighted, if you press any key now, the entire name will be erased. In the example in Figure 1.30, pressing A will replace the entire name with the letter A. If you prefer to leave the name intact and add something to the end of it, press the <RIGHT ARROW> key first, then type in your additions.

Another Way to Change the Name of a File, Folder, or Disk

The other way to change the name of a file or folder involves clicking on it twice. Click on the icon once to highlight it, and then click directly on its name a second time to select it. This is not the same as double-clicking on the icon—you must be careful not to click too rapidly, or Windows NT will open the file. After the second click, the file's name should be highlighted and you can enter a new name, just as described above.

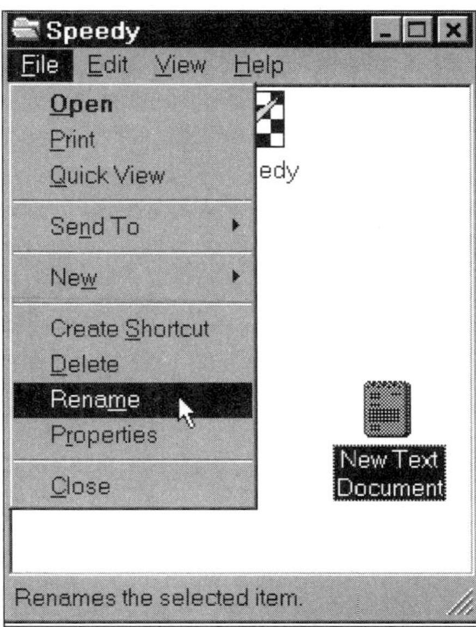

Figure 1.30: To change the name of any file or folder, hightlight its icon and select Rename from the File menu.

Chapter 2

USING WINDOWS NT EVERY DAY

In the previous chapter you saw how to do all the things you really need to know to make Windows NT work for you. In this section, you'll also pick up a lot of handy new tricks that can make your work easier. These are shortcuts and new techniques that are quicker than the usual commands. You'll also see how to keep your work from getting lost, and what to do if it does anyway, learn a new way to explore the contents of your computer, find out how to keep your work files consistent between your work computer and your home computer, and discover how you can train Windows NT to start your work for you when you turn your computer on.

Using Your Right Mouse Button

Using just your right mouse button, you can bypass a lot of menus and carry out some of the most commonly used Windows NT commands. These right-mouse "shortcuts" can save you time. There are even some commands you can only carry out with your right mouse button.

Discovering Shortcut Menus If you click on an icon with your left mouse button, you just highlight it. But if you right-click on an icon, you will get a special pop-up menu called a shortcut menu. The shortcut menu for each icon is different, but will usually include commands to open the file, print it, move or copy it, change its name, and to modify its properties. For example, right-clicking on a Text Document icon gives you a shortcut menu to open the file, print it, send it to someplace else, copy it, cut (delete) it, and many other options. Right-clicking on a disk will give you a completely different set of options. Right-clicking on the Recycle Bin gives you a chance to empty it, and right-clicking on nearly any item allows you to rename it.

You can also right-click on window borders, the Taskbar, and the desktop. In many dialog boxes, such as Open, Save, and Save As, right-clicking on buttons and drop-down lists will explain what those features do. As you become more familiar with Windows NT, you should experiment often with using your right mouse button to discover the shortcut menus that are attached to every icon.

Right-Dragging vs. Left-Dragging You saw earlier how to move a file from one folder to another by using your left mouse button to drag the icon. This is the most common way to copy or move files, but it's not the only way. If you learn to use your right mouse button, you'll find that there are many more options available.

To review, left-dragging a file will either copy the file or move it, based on a simple rule. If you drag a file to another folder on the same disk, Windows NT will move the file. However, if you drag the file to a folder on a different disk, Windows NT will make a copy of the file instead. Even though you are doing exactly the same thing, the outcome is different. The only hint you get that something different is happening is a small indicator next to your file just before you drop it. Look closely at the example in Figure 2.1. If you drag a file from the left window to the right window, which is on a different disk, Windows NT displays a small plus-sign indicator to show you that it is about to make a copy of the file, not move it. If you were dragging the file to a folder on the same disk, Windows NT would not display this little indicator.

If you use your right mouse button to drag files instead, you have the choice between copying and moving. Repeating the example above, if you right-drag the file from the left window to the right window and drop it there, Windows NT displays a shortcut menu allowing you to choose whether to copy the file, move the file, make a shortcut to the file (described later), or cancel the whole operation. Notice the difference in Figure 2.2.

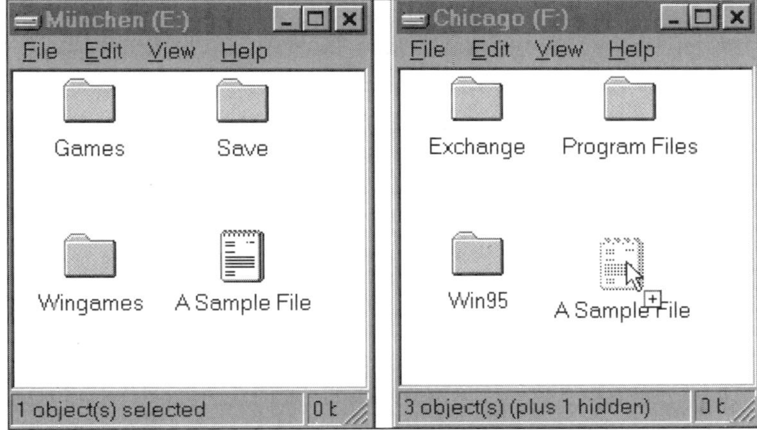

Figure 2.1: When dragging files to a different window, the small plus sign tells you Windows NT is making a copy of the file.

Searching for Files on Your Computer

Can't find a file? Afraid you deleted important financial records? Can't remember which folder you put that memo in? The Windows NT Find command can fix all these problems for you. Find searches your entire computer looking for anything you ask it to. It can tell you where files are stored, or whether they're on your computer at all, or even on somebody else's computer across a network. Find is your own

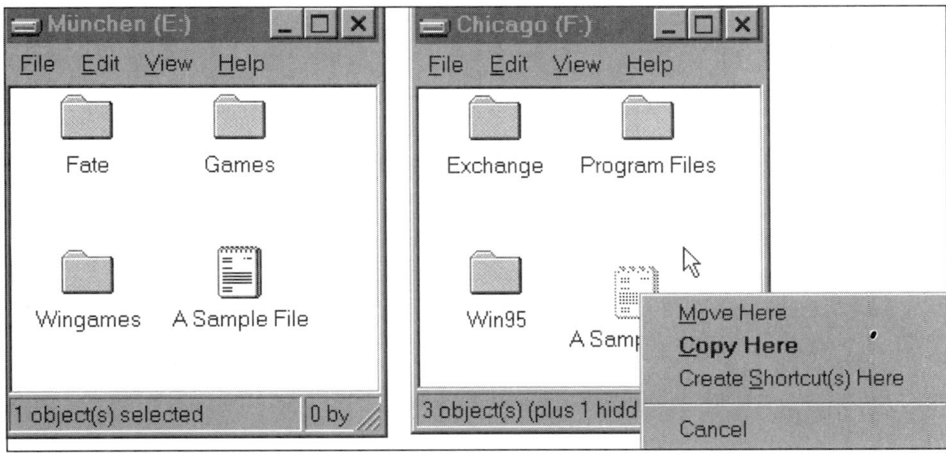

Figure 2.2: When you right-drag a file, Windows NT displays a short menu of options.

digital bloodhound. It can be a lifesaver when you can't find something but you just *know* it's in there somewhere.

If you go halfway up the Start menu you'll find Find. As Figure 2.3 shows, Find has two basic options: finding your own files and folders; finding other peoples' computers, files, and folders through your office network. Your own computer may not offer both of these choices, and that's okay. At any rate, you'll generally want to use the first option shown in the figure, "Files or Folders."

Selecting Find Files or Folders pops up a normal Windows fill-in-the-blanks window, shown in Figure 2.4. The window has three tabs, but we'll ignore those for now. For starters, there's only two basic things Find needs to know before it starts: what is the name of the thing you are looking for, and where you want to look. You answer the first question by typing something into the first fill-in line, which is labeled Named. As for where to look, Find gives you a drop-down list of choices, labeled Look In.

The idea behind Find is that you type in the name of a file, or just part of a name, and Find will locate the file for you. It may find the one exact file you're looking for, or Find may locate lots of files that all match the name you typed. For example, if you use Find to find a memo by typing "Memo to Jon Doyle regarding January Contract" then Find will probably find exactly that file. On the other hand, if you type something like "memo" then Find will probably find lots of files that have the word memo in their name.

You can decide for yourself how detailed you want to be with Find. If you don't remember the exact name of a file, just type in the part you

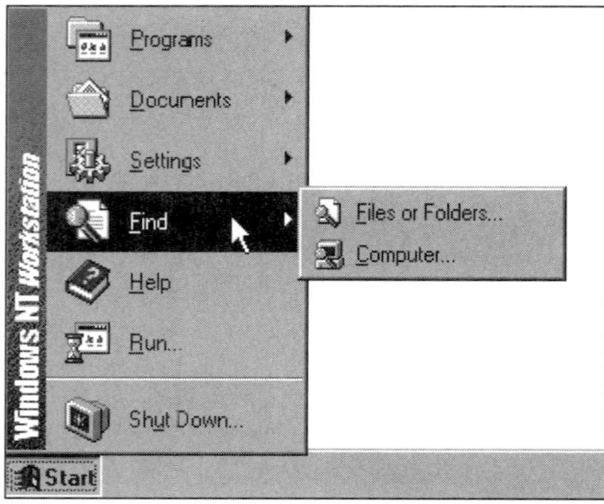

Figure 2.3: The Find command is vital on large systems with lots of files.

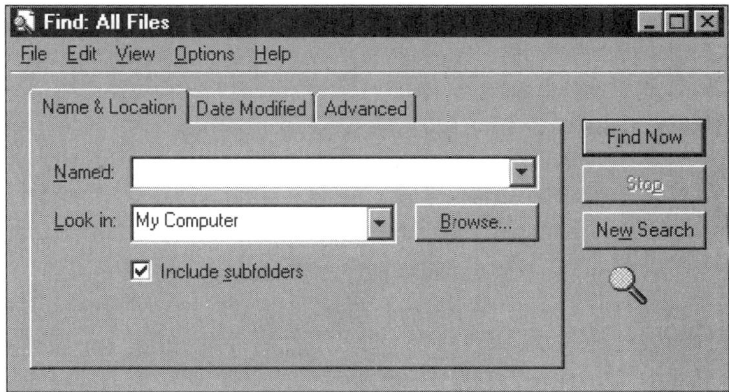

Figure 2.4: To find a file or folder, simply fill in the blanks.

know. There's no harm in being a little vague—it just means that Find will probably locate a lot of extraneous things that you weren't interested in. Don't go too far overboard, though. Typing just the letter E will probably find hundreds of files you don't want.

Entering a longer name will give Find more to work with and you'll probably be happier with the result. Be careful of your spelling—Find is very picky about matching what you type exactly. In the example above, if you had typed John Doile's name wrong, Find would not locate your memo. Lastly, if you're an old MS-DOS user, you don't need to use the MS-DOS wildcard characters (* and ?) with Find. Just type your search key and leave the rest blank.

As for *where* to search, Find offers you a drop-down list of the disks in your computer. By clicking on the drop-down list, you can pick one of those disks for Find to search. If you don't know which disk you should search, or if you just want Find to search your entire computer, chose My Computer at the top of the list. This will even search floppy disks and CD-ROMs, if you have any in your computer.

Directly underneath the drop-down list for disks to search is a check box labeled Include Subfolders. If you check this box, Find will *start* searching in the disk or folder you name, but it will also continue searching inside any folders within that disk or folder. This is usually the right thing to do. If the box is not checked, Find will not peek inside any folders. In other words, the file you're searching for must be stored "outside" of any folders except for the exact one that you've picked.

After you enter a file name (or part of a name) and choose a disk or folder, click on the big Find Now button or press <ENTER>. Find will start its work, and within a few seconds the Find window will open up at the bottom to show you what it's found.

If Find found a lot of things that match your description (say, a dozen or so), then they will probably overflow the space provided in the bottom half of the Find window. In that case, you can use the little vertical scroll bar on the right side of the window to scroll the list up and down. Or, you can stretch the entire Find window to make it longer. Just grab one corner of the window and drag it.

Advanced Finding Normally, Find searches for your files based on the name (or part of a name) that you type. If you wish, you can be much more specific about what you want Find to locate. The two extra tabs in the Find window, labeled Date Modified and Advanced, will help you. You don't need to use these options if you don't want to, but they do come in handy from time to time.

Searching by Date or Age Normally, Find pays no attention to how old a file is. The Date Modified tab lets you change that and narrow your search to only those files that were changed between two dates (which you get to specify). It can also find files that are newer than a certain number of days or months (which you also get to specify).

This is a wonderful tool for locating all the files you've edited in the past week so that you can give copies of them to a colleague or assistant. It's also handy for copying recently altered files into your Windows NT Briefcase. (If you're not familiar with the Briefcase, you can read about it later in this chapter.)

To select the Date Modified tab, just click on it to see your options, which are shown in Figure 2.5. As you can see, the top radio button is normally selected, meaning that Find pays no attention to dates at all. If you click the second option, you will "switch on" the special date-searching features of Find.

You have three options, and there's a place to click for each one. You can only choose one of these options, so think about what you want to find.

The first choice lets you specify two dates, and Find will only locate files that were either created between those two dates or that were modified (edited and changed) between those two dates. Click the "Between" option and type in two dates.

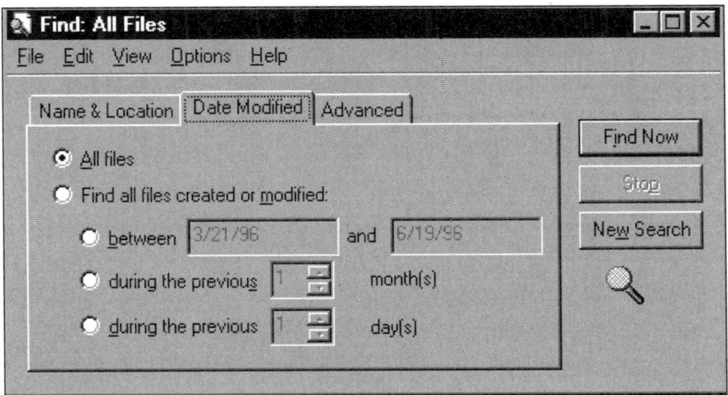

Figure 2.5: You can restrict your search to files created or modified between two dates.

The second choice tells Find to ignore any files that are older than a certain number of months. Click this option and type in your time limit. Or, you can use the tiny up and down arrows to increase and decrease the number of months without typing.

The third option is just like the second, but the time is measured in days. Again, click the option and fill in a number. Or, you can use the tiny up and down arrows to increase and decrease the number of days without typing.

Remember that if you use either the second or third options, the time limit will change each day. In other words, if you search for files that are 10 days old on Monday, and search for them again on Friday, Find will locate a different set of files because they've all aged by four more days. This is particularly important if you're going to save your search criteria (explained later) because the time limit you save will not change from day to day.

Searching by Type of File The Advanced tab is useful because it lets you start three completely new and different kinds of searches. You can search for different kinds of files, or files that contain something specific, or files that are bigger or smaller than a given size.

Look at the Advanced tab, pictured in Figure 2.6, and you'll see the three different fill-in areas. The first is the most ambitious, and it lets you search for specific kinds of files. Windows NT knows about lots of different kinds of files, and it has names (or classifications) for all of them. Rather than try to type in the exact wording that Windows NT

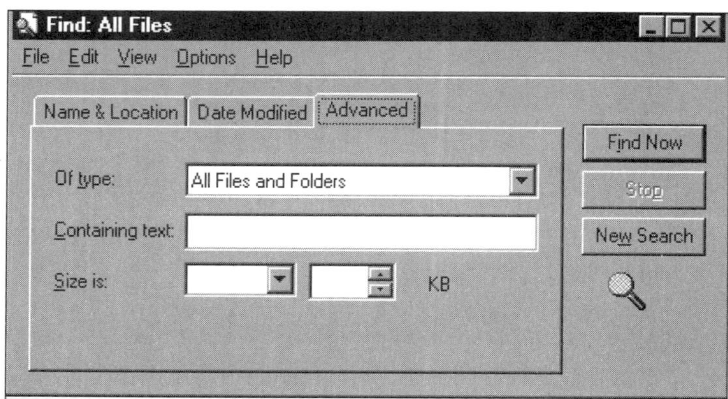

Figure 2.6: You can also restrict your search to only certain types of files.

uses for different classes of files, you should use the drop-down list. Click on the down-arrow to activate the drop-down list.

As you can see, there are many kinds of files that Find can search for. You can search for applications, bitmaps, control panels, font files—you name it. Pick one item from the list by clicking on it and that file type will be filled in for you.

Searching for a Key Word or Phrase Instead of searching for a file by what it's called, you can search for a file by what's inside it. In other words, Find can locate files based on their contents instead of (or in addition to) their names. This is like using the index in a book as opposed to the table of contents.

The next fill-in box lets you type in some words that you think your file contains. If you can't remember a file's name but you do remember what it says, type in a few words exactly the way you think they appear in the file. Find will search for the word or phrase that you type. You can use this option to locate all documents that have your name in them, or that contain the name of a certain company. This feature alone can save you enormous amounts of time and effort. In time, you may wonder how you ever got along without it.

Searching by File Size Finally, the third fill-in area allows you to narrow down the search to files that are bigger than, or smaller than, a certain size. This is handy if you want to locate all the files that are larger than 1.44 megabytes (the capacity of one floppy disk) before you try to copy them to a floppy disk. Or, you could locate all the biggest files on your hard disk and see which ones you could delete to free up some disk storage.

Complex Searches Remember that all three tabs work together. The name that you type in the Name & Location tab, plus the dates you enter in the Date Modified tab, plus the file type, file size, and key words you enter in the Advanced tab are all checked simultaneously when searching for your file. If you select options from all three tabs, that's going to be a very narrow search, indeed. Especially if Find is only searching one or two folders. On the other hand, you can leave the space for a file name blank (on the first tab) and just select date options or file-type options. Nobody said you have to search for a file by name. It's just the most common method, not the only one.

Clicking on the big New Search button clears out all your options at once and sets them back to their normal settings. It's like pressing a big red reset button. Windows NT will warn you and give you a chance to change your mind before doing this.

One last note: Normally, Find doesn't care about capitalization. But if you click the Options menu and select Case Sensitive, Find will be picky about matching uppercase and lowercase letters exactly the way you've typed them.

I Found It! Now that you know where to find the file or files you were looking for, what do you do? Well, you could simply close the Find window and put it away, content in the knowledge that your files were safe and sound right where you left them. More likely, though, you'll want to edit or print or copy one of the files that Find found. There's at least three ways you can do that.

The first way is to simply put away Find and go edit or print or copy (or whatever) your file some other way, such as by opening WordPad and making changes. The other way would be to open a My Computer or Explorer window and zero in on your file that way.

But the best and quickest way is to let Find help you. Once the file you want is listed in the bottom half of the Find window, you can double-click it and launch it right away. For example, double-clicking on a text document file in the Find window launches Notepad with the file already loaded for you.

You can also right-click on the files in the Find window, and do all the things you could normally do by right-clicking. You can delete the file, rename it, create a new shortcut to the file, alter its properties, or just about anything else. The point is, once you've found something with Find, don't just put it away. Take the easy road and use Find to get you started.

If you're going to do something with a whole bunch of files at once (like copy them to a floppy disk) you can select multiple files in the normal way, by holding down the <CTRL> key and clicking each one. Under the Edit menu, there's a little-used option called Invert Selection that can come in handy from time to time. If you have a long list of files, and it's easier to highlight the ones you don't want instead of the ones you do, this command can help. Highlight the file or files you don't want and click the Edit menu, then Invert Selection. All the files you didn't highlight will be highlighted and vice versa. Strange, but useful.

Here's another neat feature: although you can't tell just by looking, you can adjust the width of each of the columns with your mouse. For example, the second column, labeled "In Folder" is usually too narrow to show you what folder the files you found are in. To be able to read that folder's complete name, you have to make the column wider. Simply place your cursor over the dividing line between the "In Folder" column heading and the next column over, which is called "Size." Look at Figure 2.7 to see where this is. Then, just drag the dividing line a little bit to the right and you're all done.

You can also make these columns narrower by dragging the column headings the other way. Notice that once you widen a column, there's less room for the other columns. Unless you've got a really big screen, you'll probably lose something off the right-hand side. To remedy this, you could squeeze the size of, say, the "Type" column because maybe you don't really care about what's there. Simply drag the dividing line on the right edge of the "Type" column heading and make it as narrow as you want.

If you still can't see all the stuff in the Find window, remember that you can always use the horizontal scroll bar laying across the bottom of the window to pan right and left inside the window.

Find Gotchas! Something that's very easy to forget is the fact that Find can only find files that aren't invisible. That means that if Windows NT is hiding some files from you, Find won't be able to locate them, either. When would you ever hide files? You might already be hiding hundreds of files on your computer and not even know it.

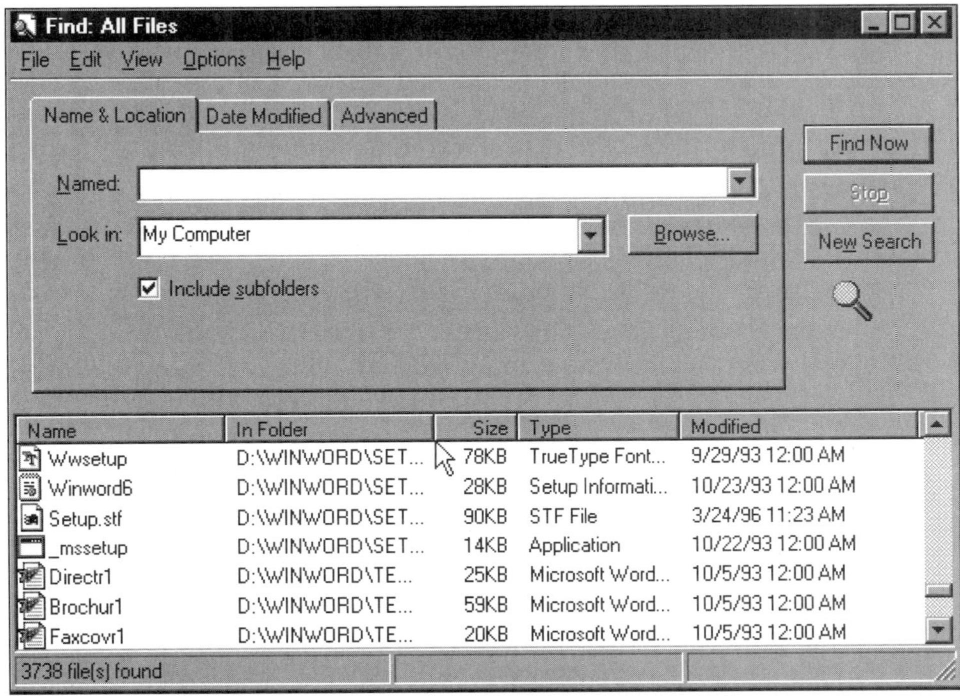

Figure 2.7: Once Find has found your files, you can alter the display by dragging the column heading left and right.

Windows NT normally hides many of its own system files from view so that they don't clutter up your windows. You can turn this feature on and off. Briefly, you need to open a file window, select the View menu, then Options, then select the View tab, then click the option that says Show all Files. You can read more about this by turning to Chapter 5, which describes file views and options for displaying files.

You can also hide your own files by turning on their "hidden attribute." You might hide files to prevent unauthorized eyes from finding them. To hide (or unhide) a file, simply right-click on it, select the Properties command, and check (or uncheck) the box that says Hidden. If a file is hidden in this way, Find will not be able to find it.

If a file is hidden and you want Find to be able to locate it, you can either unhide the file by turning off its hidden attribute, or you can leave its hidden attribute on but tell Windows NT to display all hidden files as described above. If you don't know how to do this yet, see the explanation of hidden files in Chapter 5.

Another Way to Find Find Now you've seen how to use Find and how to pop it up from the Start menu anytime you want it. That's good to know, because the Start menu is always available when you need it. But there is another way to access the Find command that you may find even more useful. If you right-click on the icon for any folder, you will see a shortcut menu and you can select Find easily from the shortcut menu. Figure 2.8 shows what this looks like.

The advantage to starting Find through the shortcut menu is that Find will automatically search the folder you clicked on—you don't have to type in its name. This is very handy if you want to search a particular folder and not your entire computer. Just right-click on the folder in question, select Find, and off you go!

That works if the folder is closed. Another place to find Find is in the corner of every file window. If you have a window open, there will be an icon of either a disk or a folder in its upper left corner. Normally, that icon isn't used for anything, but if you right-click it, you'll get a shortcut menu and you can select the Find command from there. Just like before, the Find window will already be filled in the name of the folder you clicked.

If You Use Find Frequently Find seems like such a mundane command, but it's really very useful and you may find yourself using it

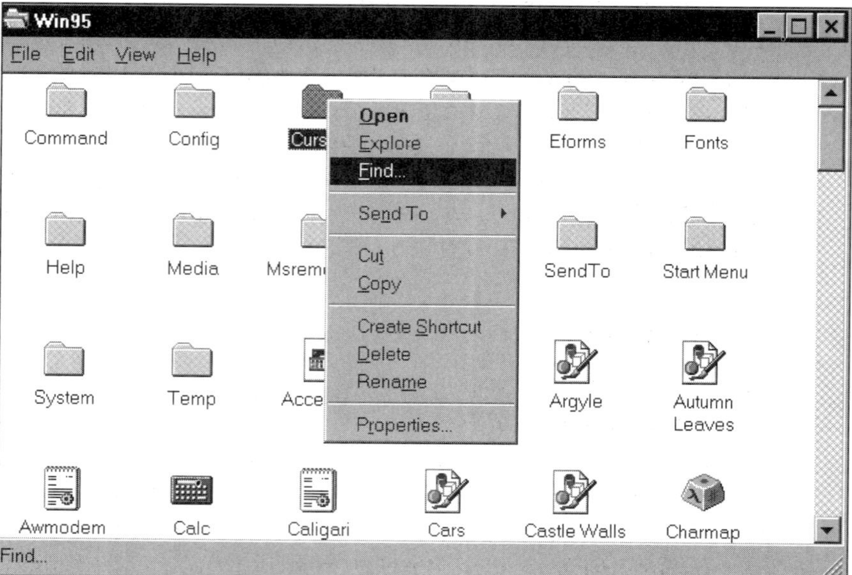

Figure 2.8: The Find command is also available by right-clicking for a shortcut menu.

quite frequently. Some of the Advanced options are particularly useful for rounding up all your received fax files, or for corralling all the documents that mention a certain client so that you can put them all in a special folder.

If you seem to be using the same Find options over and over, there's a shortcut just for you. It's called the Save Search command, and it's located on Find's File menu. First, set up Find the way you want it: enter all the names, dates, and options that you want. Then click the File menu and select the Save Search command. Windows NT will create a special shortcut on your desktop that freezes all of your search criteria.

You can double-click on this icon any time and Windows NT will automatically launch Find with all of your options and entries just the way you want them. The only thing left for you to do is click the big Find Now button and Find will be on its way. If there are several different special searches you do often, save a different setup for each one.

In addition to saving the set-up information for a search you can save the results of a search, too. Before you click the Save Search command, click on the Options menu and select the Save Results command. Find will now save names of all the files it found along with the criteria you used to find them.

All about Shortcuts

Windows NT has a nifty little feature that works like a Star Trek transporter. It's called a shortcut, and you can use shortcuts to make your files appear anywhere you want them to. You can make shortcuts to your favorite applications appear on your desktop. Or you can make July's sales figures appear in the July folder and also in your year-to-date folder, with a third copy appearing on a colleague's computer across a network. You can use shortcuts to make any file appear in any number of places, without ever making a copy of the file. And no matter where the shortcut appears, Windows NT always knows where the "real" file is at all times.

Before shortcuts, if you wanted to keep multiple copies of a file in different places, you had to copy the file. That wasted disk space because each copy took up as much space as the original. Worse than that, it meant that you had two or more copies of the same information on your computer, and updating one did not update the other. If you wanted the copies to all be identical, you had to be very careful about making new copies and deleting the old copies every time any little thing changed.

With shortcuts, all those problems are solved. Shortcuts appear to be copies of a file but are really just additional icons for the same file. You can place these duplicate icons anywhere you want to—in different folders, on different disks, on another person's computer—and not waste disk space by duplicating information. Clicking on a shortcut icon is exactly the same as clicking on the icon for the real thing. Better yet, because shortcuts don't really copy the information in your file, you don't have to worry about multiple copies getting out-of-date or unsynchronized. No matter how many shortcuts you make, there is always only one original file.

Making a Shortcut You can make a shortcut to anything: a file, a folder, an application program, a disk, a file you saw on a network once, or even the Recycle Bin. Some shortcuts make more sense than others, but you always have the ability to make a shortcut if you want to.

To make a shortcut, simply right-click on the object (file, folder, etc.) you want to make a shortcut for, and select Create Shortcut from the (yes!) shortcut menu.

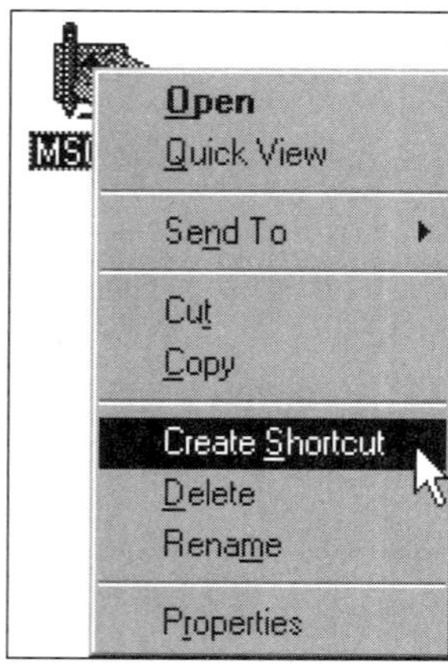

When you click this command, Windows NT makes a shortcut for you. The shortcut icon looks just the same as the icon you selected, but with a little shortcut telltale in the lower left corner. The shortcut is named, appropriately enough, "Shortcut to ..." your file.

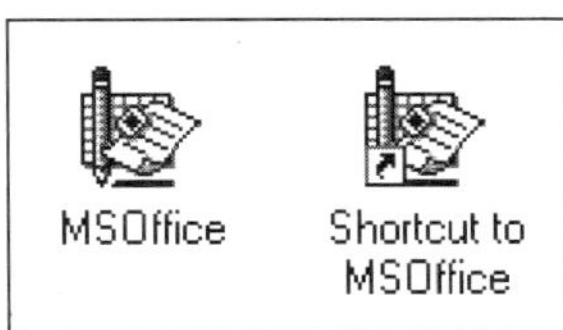

Now you can move this shortcut anywhere you'd like. If it's a shortcut to an application you use a lot, you might want to put it right on your desktop so that it's always available. Or you might like to put the shortcut inside a folder that holds a lot of the data files you work on with that application. You could make more shortcuts and place one on each disk. Do whatever suits your style.

Making shortcuts to documents and work files is more common than making shortcuts to applications. After all, you should be able to reach all your favorite applications from the Start menu. But keeping several shortcuts to a document means never having to search for the document or trying to remember where it's stored. Just keep a few shortcuts in handy places, and your document will always be there when you want it!

More about Shortcuts Shortcuts take up almost no space on your computer. They use just a few hundred bytes of storage—far less than a duplicate copy of most files would. Don't be shy about making lots of shortcuts to the same file; Windows NT will manage to keep them all straight. Also, you should feel free to change the names of the shortcuts after you move them. You don't have to stick with the generic name "Shortcut to ..." if you don't want to. Each shortcut can have a completely different name. Although you might have a hard time remembering what the shortcuts are for, Windows NT always remembers.

Treat a shortcut exactly as you would treat the original file. You can double-click it, you can choose it from an Open or Save dialog box, you can rename it or change its icon, and you can copy or move it. You can even move the shortcut off of your computer to another person's computer. If your computers are connected over a network, you can move the shortcut by dragging it to the icon that represents the other person's computer or disk.

About the only thing you can't do with a shortcut is give it to somebody else on a floppy disk. Although Windows NT will let you move or copy a shortcut onto a floppy disk, when the other person receives it, their computer will not be able to locate the original file the shortcut points to. That's only natural; because a shortcut is not a duplicate of a file; giving someone just a shortcut is not the same as giving them a copy of the file.

Shortcuts have properties, too, just like real files. Right-clicking on a shortcut and selecting the Properties command reveals a property sheet. This property sheet looks pretty normal, except that there is an extra tab labeled "Shortcut," as you can see in Figure 2.9. This tab tells you a little about the file the shortcut points to. The name of the

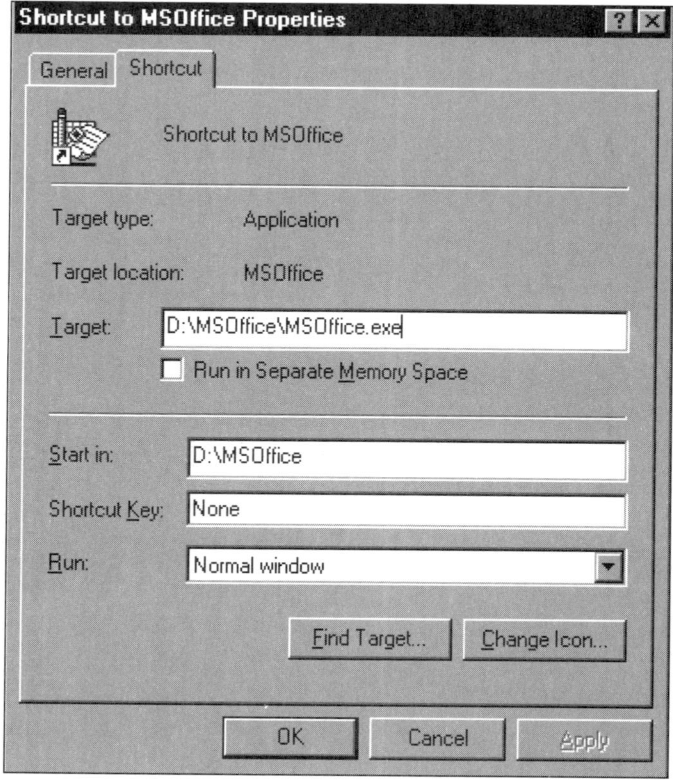

Figure 2.9: Examining the properties of a shortcut shows you what folder and file the shortcut points to.

original file (called the Target on the property sheet) is listed here, along with some basic information about how the file will be opened.

The property tab also gives you an opportunity to change the shortcut's icon so that it no longer matches that of the original file. No matter what icon you pick, a shortcut will always have a little telltale arrow in one corner. If you click the button marked Find Target, Windows NT will take you to the place where the original file is stored.

You can create a shortcut to a shortcut, and Windows NT is smart enough to make the second shortcut refer to the original file, not to the first shortcut. That way, if you delete the first shortcut, the second shortcut will still be able to "find" the original file it points to.

Moving Shortcuts You can move a shortcut to anyplace on your computer. That's partially the point, in fact. But what happens if the original file gets moved? Can the shortcut still find it?

That depends. Windows NT is pretty smart about keeping shortcuts linked up with their original files, but it's not foolproof. The rules are simple: If you move the original file to another folder on the *same* disk, the shortcut will still work. If, however, you move the file to a *different* disk on your computer, the shortcut will get lost and not work.

In that case, the next time you try to use the shortcut, Windows NT will launch a search expedition to locate the original file. If it doesn't locate the file (and it usually won't) Windows NT will pick a file that it thinks might be the original and ask you if this is the right one (it usually isn't).

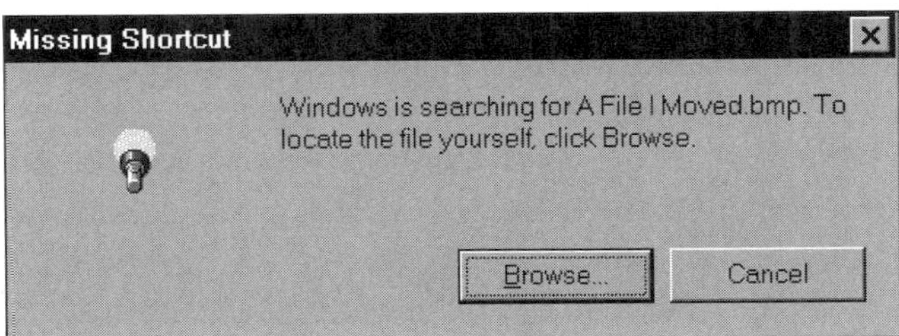

You can call off the search prematurely by clicking on the Browse button. This opens a normal browse window so that you can navigate through your files and folders looking for the original file. Once you've located it, Windows NT will link the file up with its shortcut again.

The same problem occurs if you rename the original file. If the file stays on the *same* disk, the shortcut will still work even though the original file has a different name. If the file moves to a *different* disk, the shortcut won't work. Note that if you change the name of the original file, the name of the shortcut will not automatically change to match it.

If you delete a file, its shortcuts are not automatically deleted with it. Deleting a file is no different than moving it to another disk.

Special Shortcuts to MS-DOS Programs

If you make a shortcut to an MS-DOS program (as opposed to a Windows application program), Windows NT will create a special kind of shortcut called a PIF file. A PIF (for program information file) shortcut looks different from other shortcuts, but you treat it exactly the same way. These special shortcuts also have more property tabs on their property sheets. All of these issues are covered in more detail in Chapter 8.

You can make a shortcut to any object you see on your computer, including My Computer and the Recycle Bin. Creating a shortcut to the Recycle Bin is a little unusual, but not as strange as it might sound. You might want shortcuts to the Recycle Bin in some of your work folders, for instance, so that you can delete old work files without looking for the Recycle Bin on your desktop.

Be cautious with a Recycle Bin shortcut. It works just like the real thing. Dragging files onto the shortcut will delete them just as surely as deleting them by any other method. It is also dangerous to change the shortcut's icon because you might forget (or another user might misunderstand) what the icon is for.

To delete a shortcut to the Recycle Bin, you would, of course, drag it to the Recycle Bin.

Windows NT Explorer

Windows NT comes with something akin to the File Manager that came with Windows 3.x. It's called Explorer, and it's an advanced tool for people who want to really look inside their computers and find out where everything's stored. Explorer's not for everybody, and not everybody needs to learn how to use it. But if you consider yourself a "power user"—or if you're just the curious type—give Explorer a try. You never know what you might find.

Explorer is also a lot like opening the My Computer window. Opening Explorer and opening My computer both show you what's stored inside your computer: files, folders, applications, and so on. For most people, the My Computer window is a friendlier, less complicated way to look at these things. Explorer, on the other hand, gets a little deeper into the guts of your computer and knows how and where your files are stored. It lays out your subdirectory structure and lets you navigate up and down directory trees. Explorer also gives you more information about file sizes and types and what the files do. It's like taking a magnifying glass to your disks.

How to Start Windows NT Explorer The easiest way to start using Explorer is to open it from the Start button. Explorer is part of the Programs group on your Start menu, so if you click on the Start button and hover over Programs for a moment and you should see the Windows NT Explorer.

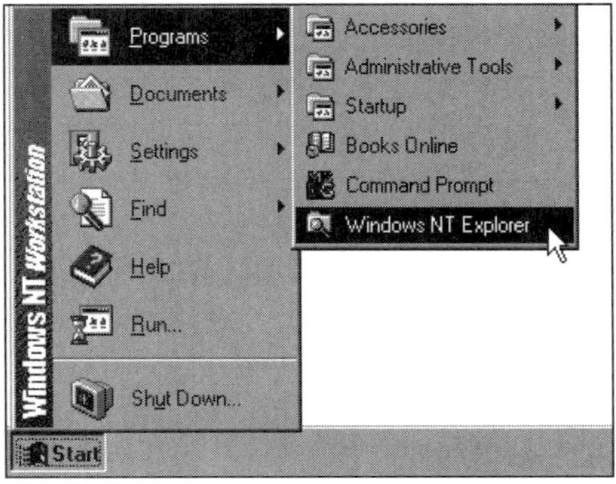

Another Way to Start Windows NT Explorer You can also start Explorer from a shortcut menu. If you right-click on the My

Computer icon on your desktop, the shortcut menu that pops up will have the Explore command listed on it. Naturally, clicking on Explore will open Explorer.

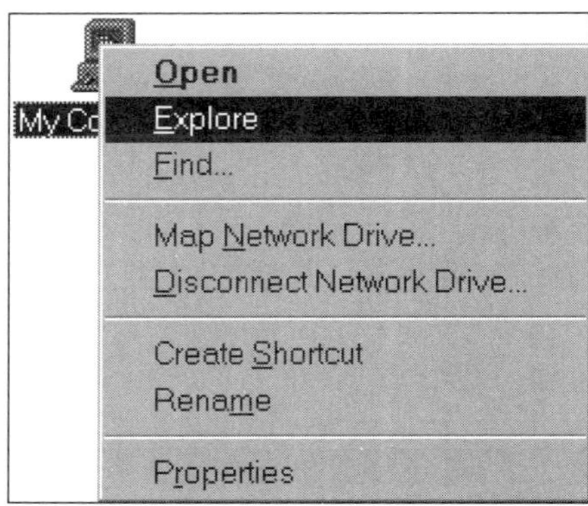

This technique also works on all your other disks and folders. Any time you see a folder icon or a disk icon, you can right-click on it and choose Explore from the pop-up shortcut menu. This technique also has the advantage of starting Explorer with the folder or disk you selected already opened up for you to examine.

Understanding the Explorer Window Either way you start Explorer, when it opens, you will see Explorer window like the one in Figure 2.10. It looks a lot different than opening My Computer! The Explorer window is divided into lots of sections with lots of information everywhere. To avoid information overload, let's take a look at each area one by one.

Across the top of the Explorer window, you have all the usual items: a blue stripe and below it, the menus. Below the menus is a drop-down list and a row of buttons on a toolbar. (If the toolbar isn't showing on your computer, click View and then Toolbar to turn it on.) Below the toolbar are two simple descriptions of what you see. We'll get back to that later.

The major portion of the Explorer window is divided down the middle into left and right panes. The left-hand pane is a bit smaller because it doesn't have to display as much information as the right-hand pane. Both of these panes probably have scroll bars in them across the bottom and their right sides. Finally, across the bottom of

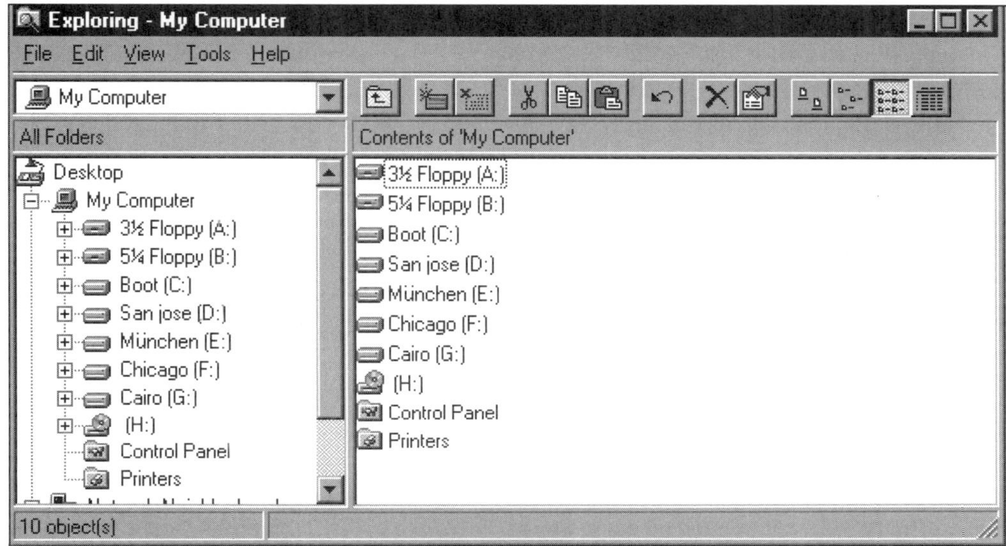

Figure 2.10: The Windows NT Explorer is an alternative to My Computer, with much more detail.

the window is a line with some status information, like how many objects (files and folders) are on your disk.

Objects on the Left Side of the Window The Explorer is just another way of looking at the files on your disk. What the Explorer emphasizes (and My Computer windows tend to gloss over) is how your files are arranged on the disk. That is, Explorer shows you your directory structure all at once. This is what the left-hand pane is showing. Starting with your Desktop at the top of the left-hand pane, Explorer draws My Computer under it, and your computer's disks under that. Furthermore, under your first hard disk (which was labeled Boot drive (C:) in Figure 2.10) Explorer indicates what folders are stored on that disk.

Explorer draws dotted vertical lines in the left-hand pane to help you to visualize what folders are inside of other folders. As an additional visual aid, all the icons in this pane are indented to show which folders are subordinate to which other folders or disks. This whole diagram is called your directory tree. It looks a bit like an upside-down tree, too, with the "root" at the top and the "branches" forking out as your go downward. It could also be compared to an organization chart, with subordinates shown underneath their superiors. If the

Explorer window is too small to show the entire tree, you can either enlarge the window or use the scroll bars to examine it from end to end.

If you study the top portion of the left-hand pane in the Explorer window you will see that it exactly matches the way objects are located on your desktop. If you follow the line straight down from Desktop, it touches everything that is stored on your desktop. For example, it shows that My Computer is indented one level directly "below" the desktop, meaning that it is subordinate to, or stored on, your desktop. Sure enough, the My Computer icon is on your desktop, isn't it? The line in Figure 2.11 also touches Network Neighborhood, the Recycle Bin, and My Briefcase. As the figure shows, all of these items are located on the desktop, too.

If you have individual files stored on your desktop, they won't appear in the directory tree in the left-hand pane. That's because the left-hand pane is reserved for disks and folders—things you can open or things that can hold other things. The left-hand pane shows your bird's eye view of how your files are organized, not the files themselves.

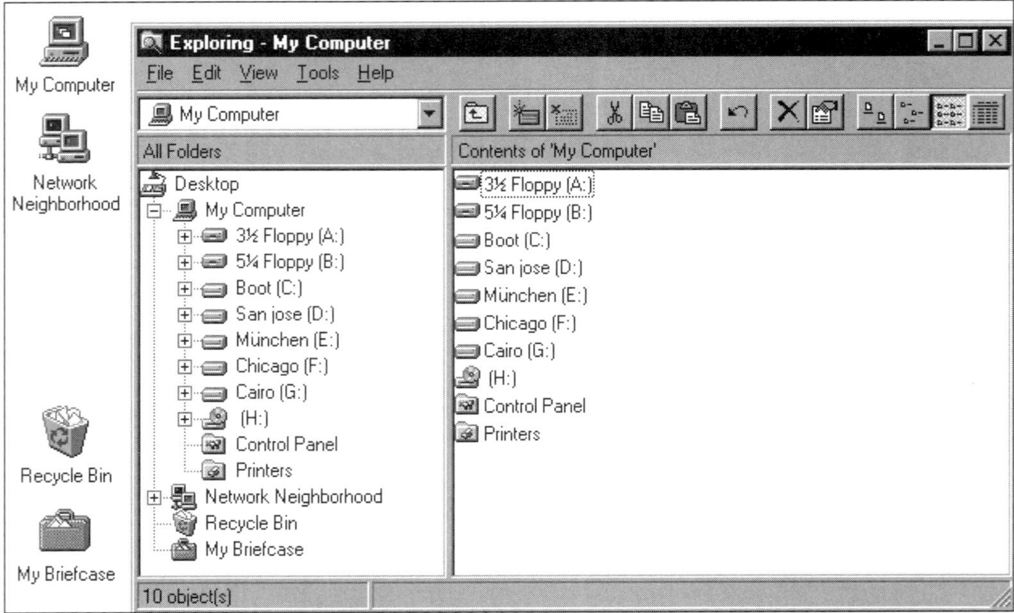

Figure 2.11: The left-hand side of the Explorer window displays a map of how your disks, folders, and files are organized.

Sometimes the dotted line drawn down from the Desktop has little boxes in it, and sometimes not. Sometimes those boxes have plus signs in them and sometimes they have minus signs. What's the difference? These are Explorer's way of telling you that there are more things inside this item than what you can see. The plus sign inside the box means that this item (whether it be a disk or a folder) has other branches (other folders) inside it that Explorer is not showing you. A minus sign inside a box means that there are more items inside this one than Explorer is showing you. No box at all means that there is nothing more inside this item. In the figure, the icon for My Computer has a box with a minus sign meaning that My Computer does contain more branches to the tree (in this case, seven disks and three folders) and that Explorer is already showing you what they are. Farther down, the Network Neighborhood icon has a plus sign in a box. That means that there is more to be seen inside this icon but that Explorer has not "unrolled" the entire tree yet. Finally, the Recycle Bin and My Briefcase have no boxes, signifying that there are no additional branches (folders) inside these items.

If you click on a box with a plus, it becomes a box with a minus and Explorer unrolls the directory structure inside that item so you can see it. Clicking the box again rolls the structure back up and changes the minus back to a plus. You can roll and unroll any item in the left-hand pane of the Explorer window this way. If unrolling an item (like a disk) discloses other items inside it (like folders), they may have plus signs next to them, too. You can click all of these to open them, and so on, and so on.

Objects on the Right Side of the Window So if the left-hand pane illustrates how your disks and folders are organized, what does the right-hand pane do? It shows you the actual files that are in the item you're examining in the left-hand pane. If the picture on the left is your bird's eye view of your disk, the right-hand pane is your magnifying glass. This is as close as you can get to where and what your files are. If you're an MS-DOS user, this is Windows NT's nearest equivalent to the DIR command.

When you click an item in the left-hand pane, its contents are instantly displayed in the right-hand pane. For example, in Figure 2.12, the folder called Adaptec is highlighted and the contents of that folder appear in the right-hand pane. This is the way you examine the contents of a folder or find a file. Use the directory tree illustration in the

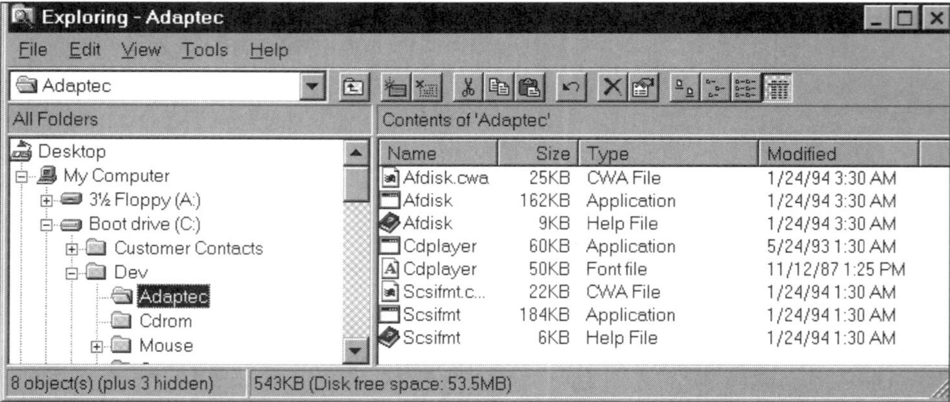

Figure 2.12: When you highlight a disk or folder on the left side of an Explorer window, its contents are displayed on the right side of the window.

left-hand pane to navigate your way to the proper disk and/or folder, and then highlight that folder. Its contents (including other folders) will appear on the right side of the Explorer window.

You can click anywhere on the directory tree in the left-hand pane and Explorer will instantly open that folder for you. This is one of the advantages Explorer has over My Computer windows. With My Computer windows, you must sequentially open folder after folder to "drill down" to the last folder you want to open. With Explorer, you can take a shortcut and open the folder you want directly. When you click on a folder in the left-hand pane, remember that you must click on the folder icon or its name; clicking on the little square next to it will either roll up or unroll that item's directory structure. When a folder is selected, its icon changes to one of an open folder and its name is highlighted.

Shortcut Hint: You can unroll a folder and display its underlying structure by double-clicking it on the left side of the Explorer window. Double-clicking again will roll the folder's directory structure back up.

More Explorer Navigation The right-hand pane of the Explorer window isn't much different than a normal My Computer window. It simply displays your files and allows you to examine them or sort them. Although Explorer usually displays files using the so-called Details view, you can switch to a more icon-oriented view by clicking on the View menu and selecting one of the other choices.

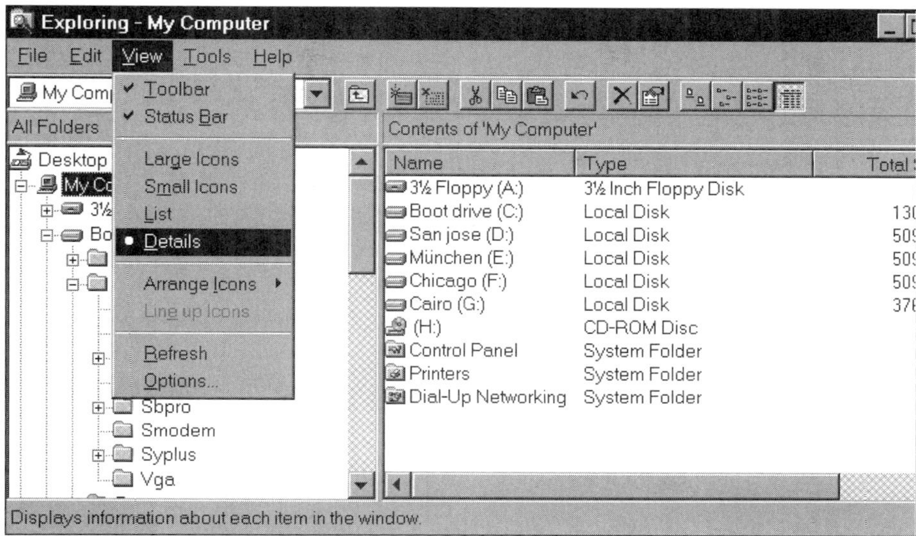

The Details view includes column headings over the right-hand pane to explain what you're looking at. Just like any file-display window, you can click these column headings to sort the files and folders by that column. Clicking on the Size heading, for instance, sorts the files in the window by their size. Clicking Size a second time sorts them by size, but in reverse order (biggest to smallest). You can also change the width of each column by dragging the column headings with your left mouse button. You can move the dividing line between the left- and right-hand panes by dragging it, too.

Highlighting a file by clicking on it once will highlight it and display some basic information about it on the status line at the bottom of the Explorer window. Right-clicking on the file produces a pop-up shortcut menu with the normal assortment of choices. The exact options presented depend on what kind of file you right-clicked. Double-clicking on a file will open it using whatever application is appropriate for that file. Double-clicking on a folder will open that folder and show its contents, just as if you had selected it in the left-hand pane.

Pressing the <BACKSPACE> key at any time takes you one level "up" the directory structure. Whatever folder you are looking into, you will move directly to its "parent" or enclosing folder. This takes you one step nearer the root of your directory tree. You can get the same result by clicking on the first button in the toolbar. It has a upward-pointing arrow on a folder to indicate its function.

Finally, you can move up and down the directory tree by using the drop-down list near the top of the Explorer window. Clicking on this window drops down a simplified diagram of your computers' directory tree. Only the first-level items are shown, plus the folders leading to the folder you are exploring. If you have a large and disorganized computer, the simplified display on this drop-down list can be easier to navigate than the more-detailed one in the left-hand pane of the Explorer.

Keep in mind that Explorer won't display files that are hidden. In this respect, it is exactly like a My Computer window. If you have configured Windows NT to hide certain type of files from view, or if you have hidden individual files yourself, Explorer will not display them. To make Explorer (and My Computer) display hidden files, you must configure Windows NT to un-hide them. You can do this with the View menu.

To un-hide files, click the View menu and then select Options. The first tab includes two radio buttons. If the second option is checked Windows NT hides all files of the types listed in the central window. Clicking the first option will make Windows NT un-hide all the files on your computer.

If you have hidden an individual file and want to un-hide it, you must first un-hide all the files on your computer, then select the file you want to un-hide and remove the "hidden" attribute from the file's property sheet. Then use the View menu again to re-hide all the remaining files on your computer.

Special Explorer Features The Explorer is smart about what folder it is showing you. Rather than always listing files by their name, rank, and serial number, Explorer alters its appearance on the fly. It will quickly and silently customize itself depending on what you're exploring. If you're new to Explorer, you might not even notice what's happening. Explorer is aware of the Recycle Bin, Briefcases, and special Windows NT folders, just to name a few.

As an example, locate the folder where Windows NT itself is stored. This is probably called Windows, or WinNT, or something similar. Locate that folder in the left-hand pane of an Explorer window and click on the little plus sign next to it to unroll its subordinate folders. Click on the View menu and make sure you've selected the Details view.

Now highlight a few folders in the left-hand pane and see how they are all displayed the same way. The folders named Command, Config, and Help, for instance, are all typical folders with normal files. Now highlight the folder called Fonts. The column headings in the right-hand pane have changed. A new heading called Font Name is now visible. The tools on the toolbar have changed, too. And, if you click on the View menu, you'll see that some completely new views have been added. Click on the new choice, List Fonts By Similarity (you could have also done this by clicking one of the new toolbar buttons).

Now all your font files are sorted by their appearance, not by such technical criteria as file names or sizes. With fonts, this is a really useful feature that you can't get any other way. It allows you to critically view your font collection and determine if there are any you don't need or others you need to fill in. Notice that you even get a new drop-down list near the upper right of the Explorer window that lets you select a font with which the others will be compared.

As another example, locate the Printers folder. It will most likely be near the bottom of the list of items stored under My Computer in the left-hand pane. Highlighting this folder turns the right-hand pane into a print-management window. Explorer lists your printers and the print jobs queued up at each one.

Finally, locate the Control Panel folder and highlight it. In the right-hand pane, Explorer displays a description of each control panel along with its usual name.

Using Explorer Instead of My Computer As you have seen, the Explorer window is just like a My Computer window, only more detailed. They both show you what files you have stored in a folder. The difference is the Explorer uses one window all the time, while My Computer opens a new window for every folder you open. (At least, this is normally how it works; you can change My Computer to use one window, too.) Another difference is that Explorer splits the window in two so that you can see both the contents of a folder and its position relative to other folders all at once. Like the My Computer window, the Explorer window can display your files in icon form, by name, or with all the details.

You can copy and move files from an Explorer window. In fact, you may find it more convenient to use an Explorer window than a My Computer window when you're copying or moving. Explorer lets you see all your folders at once and dragging a file from one folder to another can be easier when you can see both folders at the same time. As usual, use your left or right mouse button to drag a file from the right-hand pane onto a folder in the left-hand pane. Explorer will either move or copy your file according to the usual rules. If you're moving a file to another folder on the *same* disk, Explorer will move the file. If you're moving it to a folder on a *different* disk, Explorer will make a copy of the file instead. If you're eagle-eyed, you can see the little plus sign Explorer shows next to your mouse pointer when it's about to make a copy.

To really move (and not copy) a file to a different disk, use the right mouse button and select Move Here from the pop-up menu.

If the left-hand pane is too small to show your entire directory structure, and you can't see the folder you want to drag to, you can take advantage of Explorer's automatic scrolling feature. If you drag a file from the right-hand pane into the left-hand pane and hold it very near the top or bottom edge of the pane, Explorer will scroll the window for you until you reach the folder you want.

You can also right-click any blank space in an Explorer window and get a shortcut menu. From the shortcut menu you can create a new, blank work file, change your view, change properties, and so on.

Using the Windows NT Briefcase

It wasn't so long ago that having access to a personal computer was a rare and extravagant thing. "Just think," the early PC ads used to read, "my own IBM computer." Now having a PC is no big deal and having two is commonplace. Many "power users," people who use their computers regularly and often, think nothing of having one computer at the office, another at home, and a notebook computer for traveling.

One problem few people foresaw in those earlier days was the need to keep duplicate work files in two or more locations. Before computers, you could take your work home with you by stuffing papers into a briefcase or valise. The next morning, you returned your papers to their rightful place in your office. Nowadays, with electronic files, that becomes a little bit trickier, but the same basic problem applies. If you copy files onto a floppy disk to take home, you have to be sure that you copy the files back onto your office computer when you get back. Otherwise, the files on your PC at work will get out of date.

The problem gets more complicated if you have two computers that you use regularly and you keep copies of your work on both PCs. If you work a little bit here and a little bit there, how do you make sure that both computers always have the most up-to-date files?

Windows NT can handle all those problems for you. Harking back to simpler days when files were real papers and you always knew where they were, Windows NT has created a briefcase for you to transport your files. Briefcase is a special folder you can use to keep files up-to-date between two or more computers.

Where's My Briefcase? You may already have a Briefcase icon on your desktop. It looks pretty much like you would expect it to, and it's called simply My Briefcase. (You can change its name later if you want to, but we'll assume the standard name for now.)

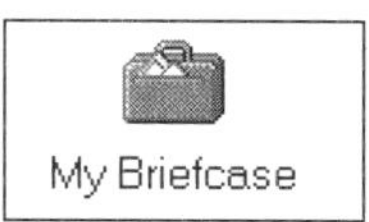

If you don't have a Briefcase already and you want one, just right-click on any blank area of your desktop and select the New command. When the pop-up menu appears, select Briefcase and a new Briefcase will be created for you on the desktop.

Like any other file or folder, you may move the Briefcase icon to another place on your disk if you prefer not to have it on your desktop.

Many people like to keep it on the desktop, out in the open, so that it's always easy to find.

Assuming that you have two computers that you use frequently, you need only one Briefcase between the two computers. In fact, it's important that you *not* have more than one Briefcase. The Briefcase is the central repository for all the files that are going back and forth between your computers and if there's more than one Briefcase, things get very confused, indeed.

How Does the Briefcase Work? Briefly (how else?), this is how the Briefcase works. Just like a real briefcase, you move all the files you want to transport to another computer into the Briefcase. Then you move the Briefcase itself to the other computer and open it. After you finish your work on the other computer, you put all the files back into the Briefcase and return it to the first computer. Simplicity itself.

So far, you could substitute the words "floppy disk" for "Briefcase" in the description above and it would be nothing special; people swap files between computers all the time. But this is where the magic of the Windows NT Briefcase comes in. When you take the Briefcase to your other computer, Windows NT checks the contents of the Briefcase against the contents of your other computer. If the files in the Briefcase are newer, they are copied over. If the files on your other computer are newer, they are copied into the Briefcase. The same is true when you return the Briefcase to your first computer. The newer files are copied from the Briefcase, and the older copies are left behind. Thus, with very little help from you, both computers always have the latest, most up-to-date files and you don't have to worry about editing a file that's already out of date or wasting effort repeating the same work you did last night.

The Briefcase does its magic by comparing the date, time, size, and contents of every file inside the Briefcase against the original files on both of your computers. It is an intelligent intermediary between your two computers. All you have to do is copy files into the Briefcase and back out—the rest is automatic.

As far as physically transferring the files in the Briefcase between computers, you can do that with a floppy disk, over a network, through a null-modem cable, or over the telephone lines with a pair of modems. The way you connect your computers is almost irrelevant; the techniques for moving files in and out of the Briefcase are the same no matter what. We'll cover connection-related issues later.

How Do I Use the Briefcase? Using the Briefcase couldn't be simpler. You just copy files into it. But don't copy files out of it—that would defeat the whole purpose of the Briefcase. You should always let the Briefcase copy its files onto your computer. That's the only opportunity it has to check dates, names, sizes, and contents to make sure it's giving you the latest version.

As an experiment, create a simple text file on your computer and save it with the name "Sample Briefcase File." Now drag the file onto your Briefcase and drop it there. Windows NT will make a copy of your file (files are generally copied into the Briefcase, not moved) and put it in your Briefcase.

Now double-click the My Briefcase icon to open it. The Briefcase window looks a little like most other file windows except that it displays your files in Details view. (You can use the View menu to change to the view you prefer, but don't do that yet.) Your Briefcase contains one file, as Figure 2.13 shows. In the second column, labeled Sync Copy In, Windows NT lists where the original file (technical term, the synchronized copy) is located. Under the heading of Status, Windows NT lists the file as "Up-to-date." The headings for file type, size, and last date modified are pretty self-explanatory.

From this window, you can click on your file and do most of the things you could normally do with a file. It is still completely accessible even while it is in the Briefcase. For example, if you double-click on it, it will open a window for editing. You can also print the file from here, and so forth. One minor difference is the file's property sheet. Right-click on the file and select Properties from the shortcut menu. As you can see from Figure 2.14, there are two property tabs instead of one; the second tab provides the file's update status. Selecting this tab forces Briefcase to perform a quick synchronization check and then it

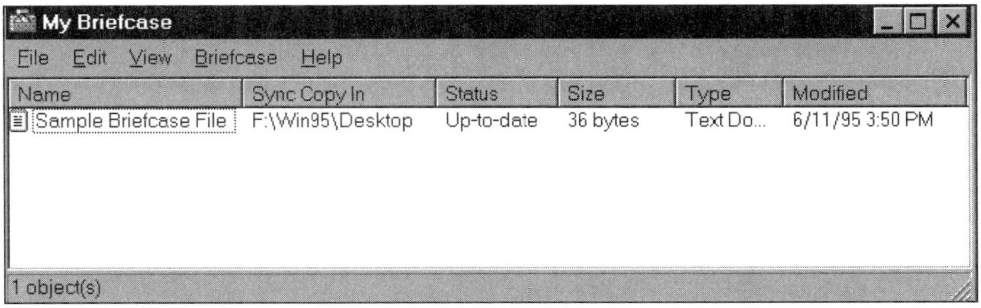

My Briefcase

File Edit View Briefcase Help

Name	Sync Copy In	Status	Size	Type	Modified
Sample Briefcase File	F:\Win95\Desktop	Up-to-date	36 bytes	Text Do...	6/11/95 3:50 PM

1 object(s)

Figure 2.13: The Briefcase is a bit like a magical folder.

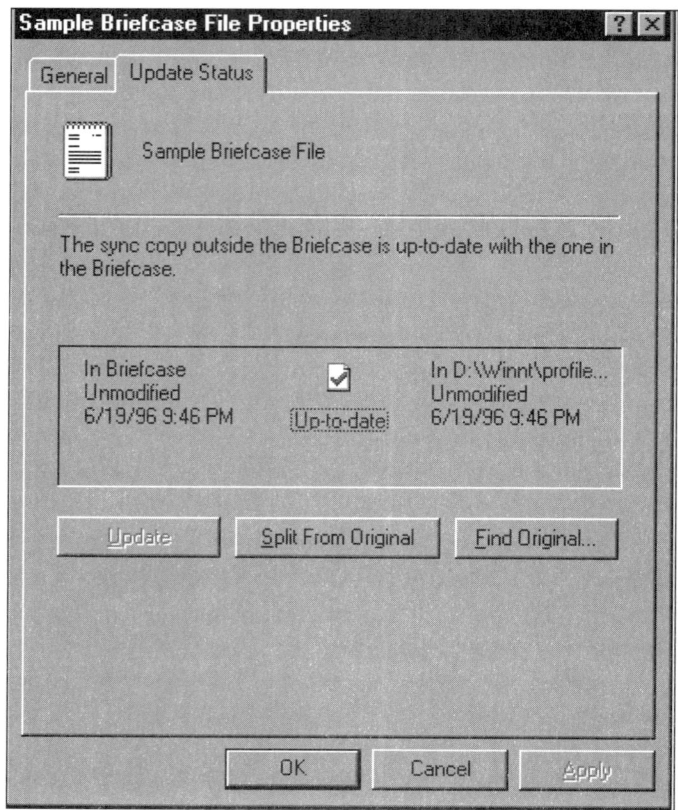

Figure 2.14: Files within the Briefcase gain an additional property: synchronization with their partner file on another disk or computer.

displays the happy news: your files are both up-to-date. There are also some buttons on this tab (Update, Split, and Find), but we'll come back to those later. For now, close the property sheet by clicking Cancel.

Now it's time to pretend you are taking this file away to your other computer (if you don't have to pretend, so much the better, but play along anyway). Put a floppy disk into your computer's floppy disk drive. The floppy disk doesn't have to be completely blank, but it does have to be formatted and it needs enough free space to hold your Briefcase. Close the Briefcase window (if it's still open). Now right-click on the My Briefcase icon and highlight the Send To command. From the pop-up menu, select your floppy disk. Windows NT will move (not copy) the entire Briefcase to your floppy disk. That's it for the first step. Notice that your original file is still on your computer but that the Briefcase is gone. Your files are now officially in transit.

Shortcut Hint: You can move your Briefcase onto a floppy disk by dragging the icon of the Briefcase onto the icon of the floppy disk and dropping it there.

If you have a second computer handy that is also running Windows NT, you can simply insert the diskette in that computer. If not, leave the diskette where it is in your original computer. Open the My Computer window (if it's not already open) and then open a window for your floppy disk drive by double-clicking on it. You should see a window that looks roughly like the one in Figure 2.15.

Now double-click the Briefcase to open it. There inside is the copy of your original file. To edit the file while it's still inside the Briefcase, double-click on it. When the editing window opens, make a few changes to the file and then save it. Close the editing window. Close the My Briefcase window. Drag the Briefcase icon from the floppy disk onto your desktop (notice that Windows NT moves the Briefcase instead of copying it). Now you've successfully imitated the motions of copying a file to your Briefcase, walking away with it, making changes, and returning with it. What happens now?

Double-click the My Briefcase icon to open it. Click on the Briefcase menu and select the Update All command. After a quick file-synchronization check, Briefcase will show you the Update window, like the one in Figure 2.16.

Briefcase has correctly determined that the version in your Briefcase is newer than the version on your computer. It recommends that you replace the out-of-date version on your computer with the newer one in the Briefcase. If you agree, you can click on the Update button and Briefcase will update the old file for you. If, for some reason, you don't want to do that, you have other options.

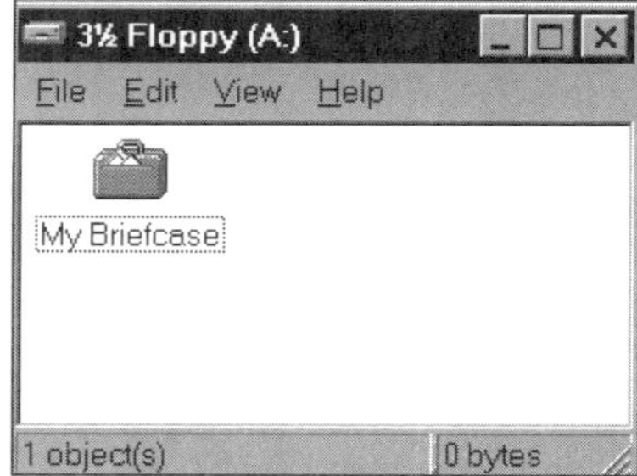

Figure 2.15: You can transfer synchronized files between computers by copying your Briefcase to a floppy disk.

How to Update Your Files When you move files between computers and work on them independently, the two copies of that file are bound to become out-of-date (in the technical vernacular, unsynchronized). When you try to bring the files back together, there are several possible outcomes:

- Neither file has been updated, in which case Briefcase has to do nothing

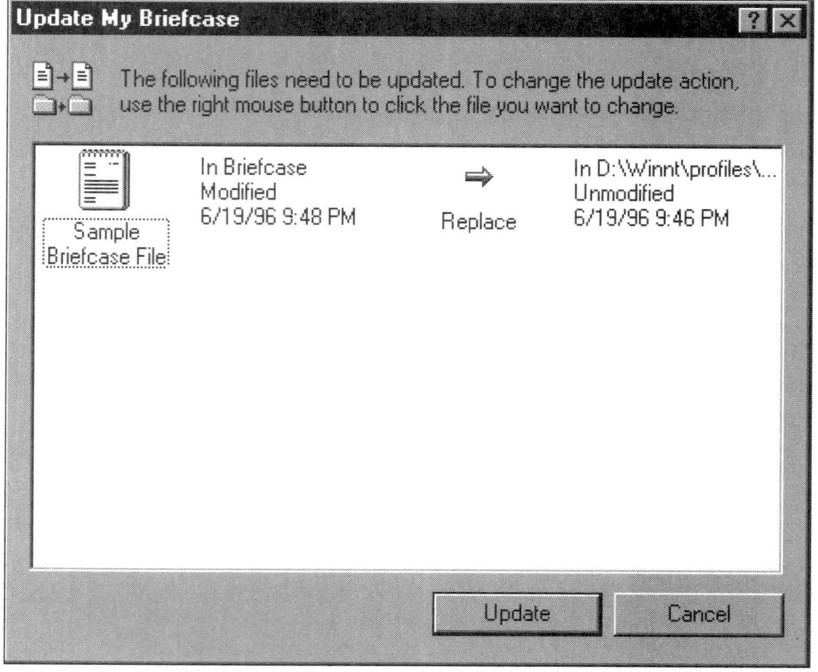

Figure 2.16: Updating the Briefcase sometimes shows that one copy of a file has been altered.

- The file was changed on the second computer
- The original file was changed on the first computer
- Both copies have been changed, one on each computer
- One of the files has been deleted
- One of the files has been renamed

Briefcase can determine all these things in a few moments when you click the Update All command. Then it will recommend a different course of action for each file, depending on its situation. Briefcase presents a window with all of its recommendations and gives you a chance to overrule its suggestions. To do this, simply right-click on the action you don't like and select an alternative. When you're happy with the proposed course of action, click on the big Update button.

In the first case, nothing needs to be done. Both versions of the file are identical and Briefcase will skip over the file.

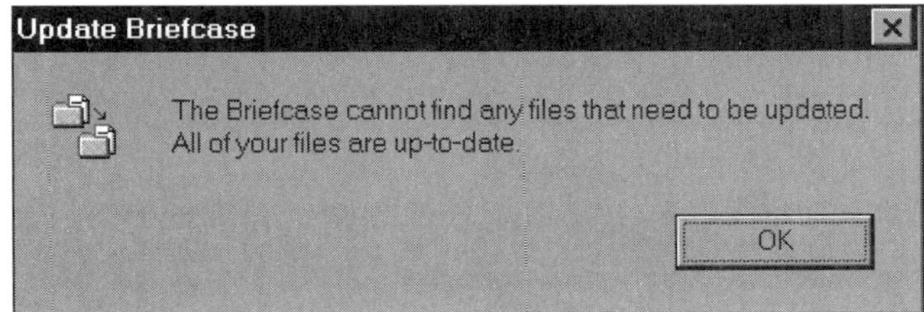

In the second case, as you saw earlier, Briefcase recommends replacing the out-of-date file with the newer version. This is true in the third situation as well, although Briefcase obviously recommends replacing the other file.

The fourth situation is harder to deal with. If both copies of the file have been modified since it was put in the Briefcase, there is no easy way to resolve the situation. This might happen when you copy a file into your Briefcase and take it home. Before you return with the updated version of the file, somebody else uses your computer and modifies the same file in your absence. When you return, Briefcase will correctly identify both versions as new. As Figure 2.17 shows, it cannot recommend replacing one file with the other, so it suggests leaving both files alone. If you have multiple files in your Briefcase, this one will be skipped over when the others are updated.

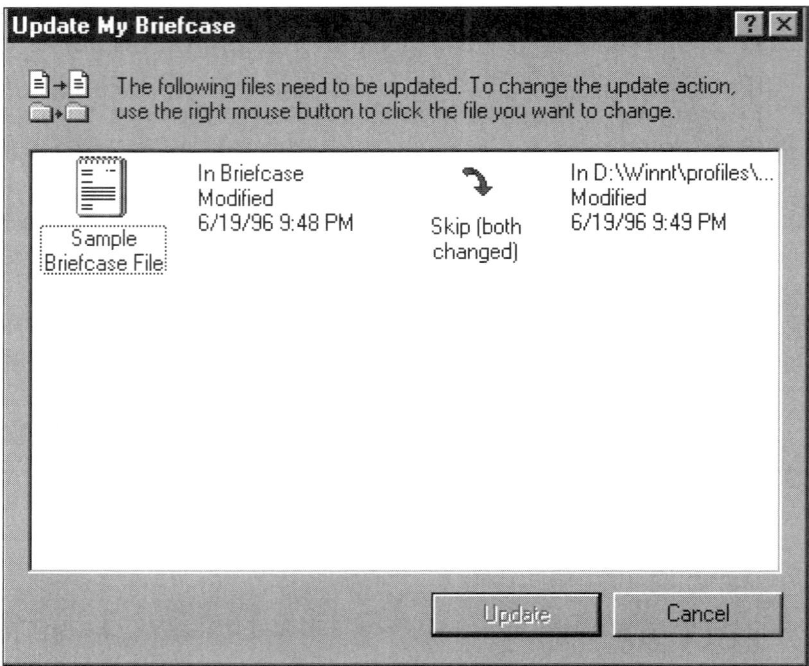

Figure 2.17: If both copies of a file have changed, Briefcase cannot synchronize them anymore.

When a file has been deleted from one computer but not the other, Briefcase obviously cannot synchronize them. With a big red X it suggests that you delete the "extra" copy so that both computers will match. If you disagree, you can right-click on the window and choose to either create a second copy, delete the extra copy, or leave the extra copy alone, as Figure 2.18 shows.

The last alternative is not much different than the previous one. If you rename one of the files, Briefcase cannot match it to its sibling, and recommends that you delete the "orphaned" one. As before, you can right-click on the window to choose a different course of action.

How to Orphan a File Briefcase will do its level best to keep track of every file you have in your Briefcase. You can move the original files into different folders, copy them to other disk drives, change their contents, and Briefcase will still keep it synchronized with its identical twin in the Briefcase. Usually, that's what you want, but what if you change your mind? What if you edit a file so much that you decide you don't want it synchronized with its twin? Once a file has been copied

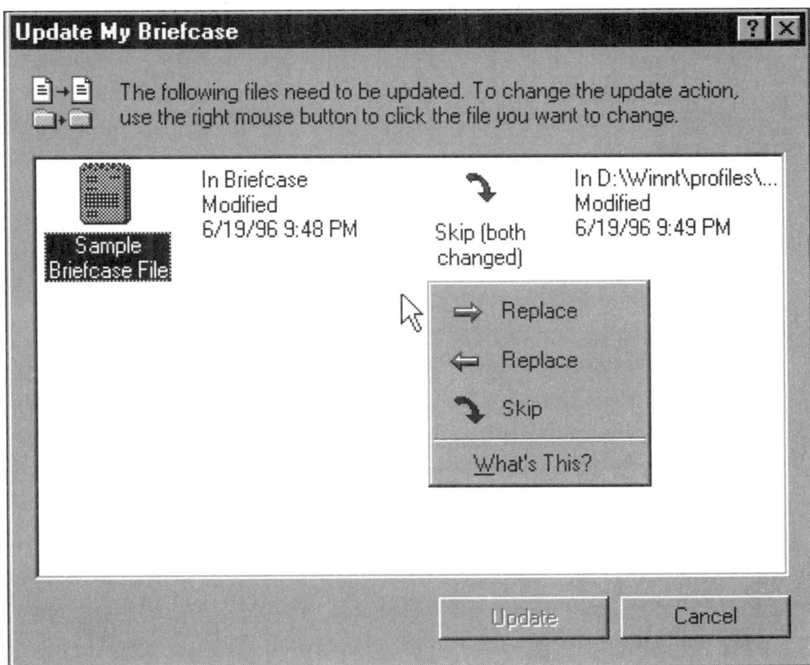

Figure 2.18: By right-clicking, you can choose to override Briefcase's recommended behavior.

to the Briefcase, how can you break the unbreakable bond between them?

The answer is: by orphaning the file. In the Briefcase window, you can select the file (or files) you want to orphan. Then click on the Briefcase menu and select the last command on the menu, Split from Original.

When you split, or orphan, a file, Briefcase will no longer track that file at all. It becomes just a superfluous bit of data in the Briefcase. You can still copy the file out of the Briefcase (and probably should) but it no longer has an invisible link to any other files in your computer.

Shortcut Hint: You can also orphan a file in the Briefcase through its property sheet. Right-click on the file, select Properties, select the Update Status tab, and click on Split From Original.

Helpful Briefcase Hints The Windows NT Briefcase is one of those things that you'll either use all the time or not at all. If you have only one computer, or if you don't share your files with a colleague very often, then you can probably ignore the Briefcase. On the other hand, if you're a power user and a road warrior, you'll learn to rely on the Briefcase and trust it with your most valuable work. In that event, here are some pointers to help you get the most out of your Briefcase.

Make sure you maintain only one Briefcase, and use it for all your file transfers. Even if you have three or more computers that you use frequently (and who doesn't?), you should still use a single Briefcase for all of them. Having more than one is asking for trouble.

If you share data with a computer running DOS (or an older version of Windows), the Briefcase will still work—sort of. When you transfer files from your Windows NT computer to the older computer, the Briefcase won't work. You will have to copy the files off the floppy disk yourself, so be careful about replacing newer files accidentally. Going back the other way, the Briefcase will work correctly and identify files the older computer has modified.

Feel free to move your files out of the Briefcase to work on them. There's no rule that says they must stay in there. If it's more convenient, copy them to a work folder and edit them from there. Just so long as you put the finished work files back into the Briefcase when you're done, Briefcase's file-synchronization feature will work fine.

You can also use the Briefcase to exchange files between two people who are working together on different computers. If you and a colleague are collaborating on a project and you want to share files with her, you can put your work files into a Briefcase and she can pull them back out. That way you're both sure that neither one of you is working with an outdated file.

If you use a network (as opposed to a floppy disk) to transfer files between computers, you should put the Briefcase on the computer you use less frequently. For example, if you have a big desktop computer that you use most of the time, and a little notebook computer you use once in awhile, keep the Briefcase on the notebook. That's because when you have the two machines joined together (via the network or cable), your Briefcase will already be on the computer you're going to take away; all you have to do is copy the files from one computer to the other over the network. If you are moving your Briefcase with a floppy disk, you can ignore this advice.

Briefcases and Networks So far, we've assumed that you are using a floppy disk to transfer the contents of your Briefcase between computers. That's a typical situation but it's not the only one. You might also have your two computers attached to each other via a network (also called a LAN).

If both computers are attached to a network, you should be able to see the disks of one computer on the desktop of the other computer. Likewise, you should be able to move and copy files from one computer to another just as you would on your own computer. That being the case, you can copy files from one computer into the Briefcase located on another computer.

More Briefcase Hints When you have a Briefcase on your computer, there are several ways you can copy files into it. The easiest method, by dragging the icon, you've already seen. There are two other ways as well. First, you can highlight a file by clicking on it once, then click on the File menu in the file's window, select the Send To command, and click on My Briefcase.

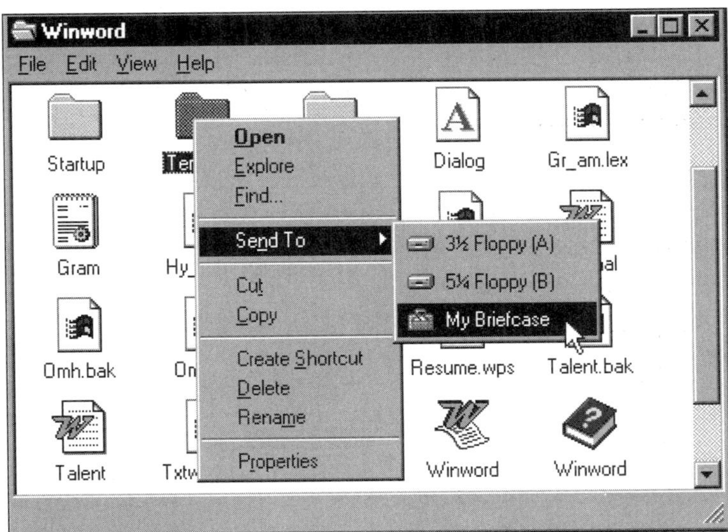

Another, quicker, way is to right-click on the file, select Send To, then click on My Briefcase.

When you open the Briefcase window, it shows you the files within it by name along with each file's type, size, last date of modification, and update status. Each of these headings is written on a kind of "button" over each column. You can click on these column headings to sort the files differently. For example, clicking the heading Size sorts the files by size. Clicking Size a second time sorts them by size in reverse order (largest to smallest). Clicking the Modified, Type, Status, Sync Copy, and Name headings all do the same thing.

If the columns are too narrow to read, you can make them wider or narrower by dragging the column heading "buttons" with your mouse. Dragging on the "groove" between two column headings lets you move the divider between those columns. Try it.

Like any other browser window, the Briefcase window has an optional toolbar. Clicking View, then Toolbar, lets you turn the Briefcase toolbar on and off. With it on, you get an assortment of icons across the top of the Briefcase window (see Figure 2.19) that let you carry out the most-used Briefcase commands with a single click.

In fact, the Briefcase window really is just another browser window, like My Computer. Browser windows are sensitive to what folder you're browsing, and if you select My Briefcase, the tools on the toolbar change accordingly. Technically, you never really need to open your Briefcase to look inside or do your file synchronization. You could just as easily use any browser window to open your Briefcase with the same results.

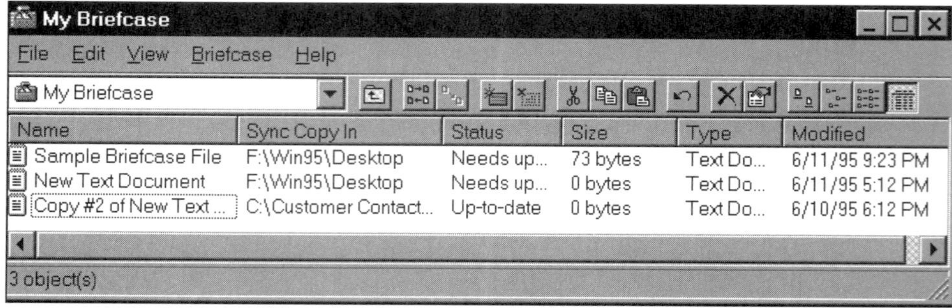

Figure 2.19: Briefcase has an optional toolbar for one-click access to the most commonly used functions.

Starting Applications Every Time You Start Windows NT

If you're like a lot of busy professionals, you may find yourself doing pretty much the same thing every morning after you turn your computer on. Maybe it's reviewing the latest financial figures, or updating last night's report. Wherever your work takes you, if you need to start the same tasks every time you turn your computer on, Windows NT has a way to make your work just a little bit easier.

Windows NT has a special feature that you can use to start the same applications or open the same documents automatically every time it starts. You can have Windows NT open one application, or a list of dozens. If you want to, you can also have windows open your work files for you. If your computer is shared among different people, each person can have their own work files opened when they start Windows NT, too.

To make an application or document open automatically whenever Windows NT starts, you simply need to put it (or a shortcut to it) in the special StartUp folder. The StartUp folder is a group of files on your Start menu. If you click the Start button now and look at your Start menu, you'll probably see an empty StartUp folder, like the one shown in Figure 2.20. An empty folder means that Windows NT won't start anything automatically. At least, not yet.

Adding something to your StartUp folder is easy. There are at least three ways you can do it. You can use the Taskbar Properties sheet, or My Computer, or Explorer. We'll look at each method now.

How to Add an Item to the StartUp Group The easiest way to add an item to the StartUp group is to use Windows NT's own Start menu manager. This is also called the taskbar Properties sheet, and you can access it by right-clicking on the taskbar at the bottom of your screen. When the pop-up menu appears, click on the Properties command. The Taskbar Properties sheet has two tabs; click on the second one, designated Start Menu Programs. Figure 2.21 shows what this tab looks like.

To begin, click on the Add button. The first thing you need to fill in is the name of the application or work file you want opened when Windows NT starts up. You can type in the name of any file here (full path name only, please, including the drive and the folders), or you can click the Browse button and point to the file you want. This is usually the easier method. After you've identified the file you want (either by browsing or by typing its name) click the button marked Next> at the bottom of the window.

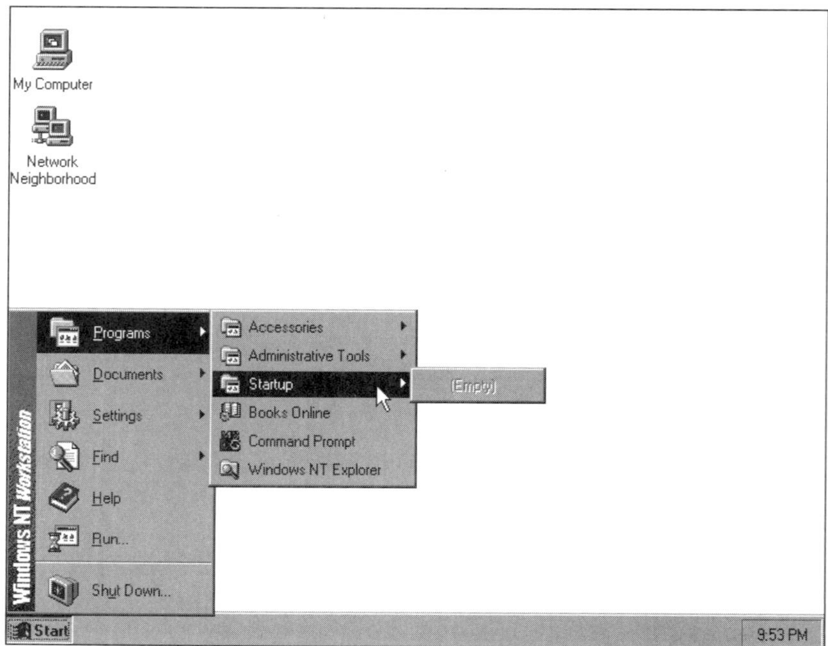

Figure 2.20: The Startup group, while initially empty, can hold applications or documents you want started automatically every time you start Windows NT.

The next step is to tell Windows NT where you want this item to be located on your Start menu. Since we're adding something to the StartUp group, you would obviously click on the StartUp folder. The StartUp folder is highlighted in Figure 2.22. After you've highlighted your StartUp folder, click the button marked Next> at the bottom of the window.

The final step is to give your item a name. This step is not vitally important, but it does allow you to create your own name that will appear on the Start menu. Type in anything you like, including spaces and punctuation, and then click the Finish button. That's it!

Another Way to Add an Item to Your StartUp Group There's another way to add an item to your StartUp group if you prefer dragging files around. The StartUp folder that appears on your Start menu is just like any other folder. That means that you can drag and drop files into it, or pull files out of it.

To modify your StartUp group this way, open My Computer by double-clicking on its icon. Now locate the disk that contains all the

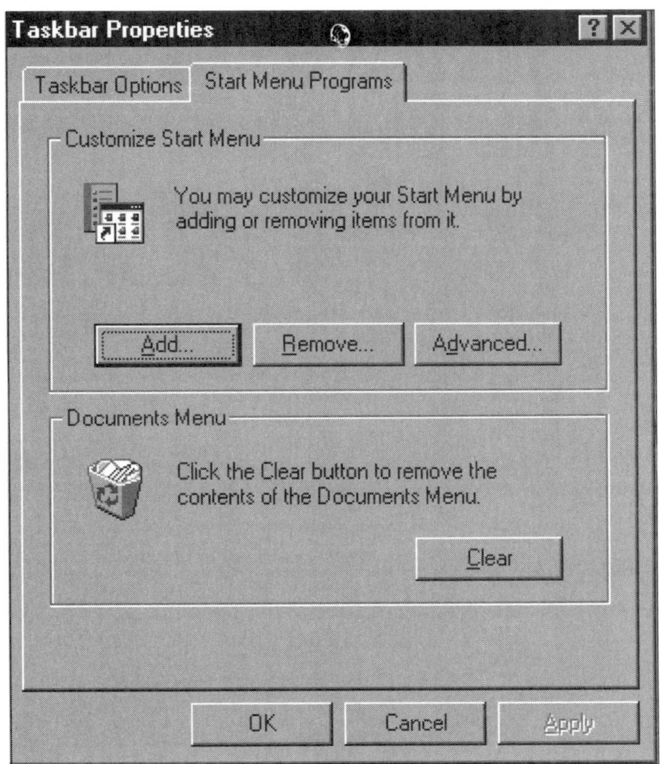

Figure 2.21: You can add items to the Startup group by right-clicking the Taskbar and following the directions.

Windows NT files and double-click on it to open it. Continue opening folders starting with the Windows NT folder itself, then Start Menu, then Programs, then StartUp. With the StartUp folder open, you can now drag files or applications into the StartUp group. You should always copy shortcuts into the StartUp group, not the original file or application. That way, if you delete the item from your StartUp group later on, you won't be deleting the actual file or application.

Yet Another Way to Add an Item to Your StartUp Group If you prefer using Explorer to My Computer, you can open the StartUp group by exploring the Windows NT directory, then "drilling down" through the Start Menu folder and the Programs folder into the StartUp folder. Now you can copy a shortcut to any file or application into the folder.

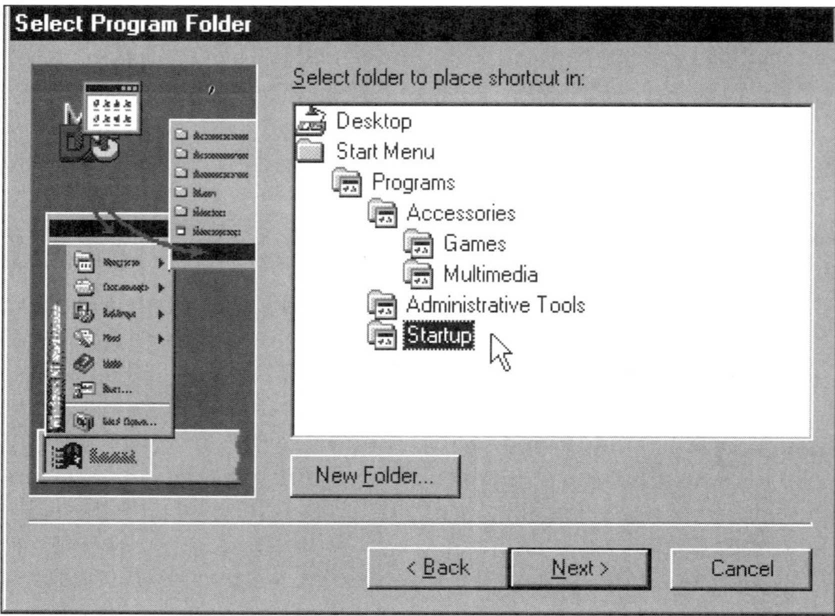

Figure 2.22: Be sure to select the Startup folder when adding items to the Startup group.

How to Remove an Item from Your StartUp Group

Removing an item is easier than adding one. If you're using My Computer or Explorer, just drag the offending item out of the StartUp folder and drop it in the Recycle Bin (make sure it's a shortcut first). If you clicked on the Taskbar Properties sheet, you can use the same method to remove an item. From the Start Menu Programs tab, click the big Remove button and highlight the item you want to remove. The next time you start Windows NT, that item will no longer be launched for you.

Shortcuts to Printing

You can print your work files in a number of different ways. Normally, to print something, you open the file with an application (say, a word processor like WordPad) and choose the Print command. Some applications also have print buttons in their toolbars. There are a few other ways you can print, too, that may be more convenient in some instances.

You can "drag and drop and print" with Windows NT. That is, you can drag the icon of a file and drop it on the icon of a printer, and it will print. The easiest way to do this is to keep a shortcut to your printer on your desktop, or another easily accessible place. You might want to make several shortcuts to your printer and keep them in convenient locations.

Another way to print is to the use Send To command on most items' shortcut menus. When you right-click on a file, the shortcut menu pops up. Hovering over the Send To command lists all the places you can send that file. Often your floppy disk drive, Briefcase, and e-mail manager are on the list of Send To items. If your printer is on this list, then printing a file is as easy as right-clicking it and sending it to your printer. (If you want to include your printer on the Send To list but you're not familiar with the procedure, see Chapter 5.)

You can send a second file to your printer before the first one has finished printing. In fact, you can send a whole batch of files to your printer at once, and Windows NT will make sure they're all printed in order. This is called a print queue. You can double-click your printer's icon (or a shortcut to it) to see what files have already been sent to the print queue. The print queue window lists all the files waiting in the queue in the order that they will print out. You can rearrange the order of the files simply by dragging them up and down the list.

You can also temporarily stop and restart printing either by using the Pause Printing command in the print queue window or by right-clicking the printer and choosing Pause Printing from the shortcut menu. The same shortcut menu also has a Properties command and you can control other aspects of your printer through its property sheet. One useful option is the Separator page. Choosing a separator page causes your printer to add an extra sheet of paper between consecutive print jobs. These make it easier to separate the files after they've been printed.

Using Long File Names

One of the most welcome features of Windows NT is its ability to use long file names. With MS-DOS, you could only give files and folders eight-letter names, and they had to be in all-capital letters. It was a real challenge for most people to create meaningful names for their work files with only eight letters. Now, with Windows NT's 255-letter limit, things are much easier.

In addition to just being longer, file names can now have spaces in them, meaning you can create names that are more than one word long. And, you can mix uppercase and lowercase letters. You can also use all kinds of punctuation marks in your file names. The only punctuation marks you absolutely cannot use are question marks (?), quotation marks ("), the greater-than and less-than signs (> and <), the backslash (\), the asterisk (*), the colon (:), and the vertical bar (|). Apart from those, you're on your own.

While these new features allow you a lot more freedom than before, there are some cautionary rules you should be aware of. First, although Windows NT permits mixed upper- and lowercase letters, they are treated as if they were all lowercase. For example, you cannot have one file called "XYZ" and another called "xyz" in the same folder. Don't try to create files that have different capitalization—it's a poor way to distinguish between your files and Windows NT won't allow it anyway.

Another drawback of long file names is that it becomes very easy to confuse two different files that have similar, but not identical, names. Take a look at the two files below. Can you tell the difference between them?

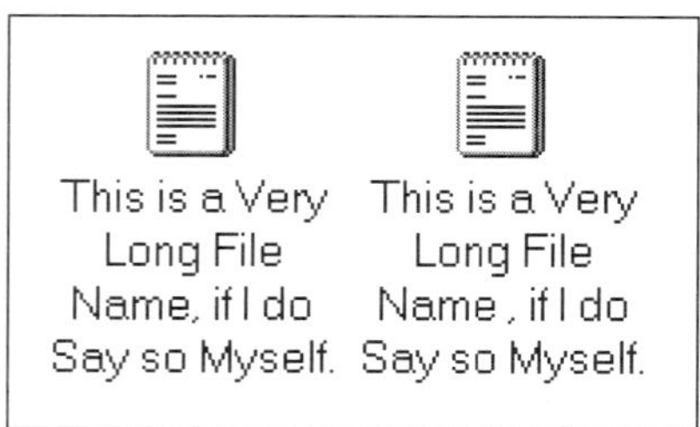

Keep in mind that even these file names are still less than one-third of the maximum length Windows NT allows.

A third problem with long file names is that not all programs recognize them. Even though Windows NT has no problem with 255-character names, most programs created before 1996 do not understand these long names at all. That means that your spreadsheet application, and your word processor, and all of your other applications will probably not allow you to use long file names if you purchased them before 1996. You will be forced to stick with eight-character names (all capitals) unless you buy new applications.

Although this limitation might be annoying, there's a bigger problem. If you change the names of any files or folders that these applications use, the application will likely start malfunctioning. For example, if you decide to name your customer contact folder "Customer Contacts," your pre-Windows NT application will not be able to access any of the files inside that folder. That's because the application cannot read the long name of the folder. You'll have to give the folder a name with only eight letters.

Every time you create a new file, Windows NT actually gives it two names: the normal, visible Windows NT name that you see all the time; and a second, invisible name for MS-DOS compatibility. Although you usually never see the second name, every file has one. You can see the MS-DOS name for any file by looking at its property sheet. The MS-DOS name is usually a conglomeration of the first few letters of the normal Windows NT name and some special symbols or numbers.

If you want to read a Windows NT file from an older application, and the file has a long Windows-type name, you will need to know its MS-DOS name. Right-click on the file and select the Properties command from the shortcut menu. Remember this name and use it when the application is ready to load your file.

Going the other direction, from an MS-DOS name to a Windows NT name, you can create a file with any legal MS-DOS name you want. The new file will have the same name when viewed from Windows NT. For example, a new file called XYZ.TXT will be called XYZ from Windows NT and have the icon for a Text Document (the .TXT extension). This is also true if you change a file's MS-DOS name; its Windows NT name will change to match the new MS-DOS name. You can change the new Windows NT name later, if you like.

Shutting Down

Windows NT makes it pretty difficult to lose your work by accident. If you write a letter with WordPad and then close the WordPad window, Windows NT warns you that you have not saved your work yet. You must either save your work or confirm that you really do want to throw it away before Windows NT will close the WordPad application. Other Windows NT applications work the same way.

You can use this to your advantage. When you're ready to shut down your computer at the end of the day, instead of saving all your open work files one by one and quitting each individual application, just go directly to the Shutdown command. As Windows NT shuts down your computer, it will close each open window and ask you to save any unsaved work. When the last file is saved, Windows NT shuts down.

CHAPTER 3

HELP WITH HELP

Considering how complex and powerful Windows NT is, there's bound to come a time when you'll get stuck and need to remember how to do something. Your first move, naturally, will be to pick up your well-worn, dog-eared copy of this book. But what if your book isn't handy, and there's no place to turn? Relax. In your time of need, you can rely on Windows NT itself to tell you what you need to know.

More so than with any previous version of Windows NT, you now have literally hundreds of pages of helpful information stored right on your computer—as part of Windows NT itself. There's an entire index to all the Windows NT commands, and it's all on-line (meaning it's stored on your computer for instant access). Whenever you feel the need, just call for help and Windows NT Help will be there.

Using the Help Index

There are a number of ways you can ask for help, but the easiest way is also the quickest. Right on your Start menu is a permanent entry for Help. If you click your Start button, you'll find Help halfway up the Start menu. Clicking on the Help command opens a big Help window right in the middle of your screen.

The Help window, shown in Figure 3.1, is like the index to a book. You can either browse through all the help topics in alphabetical order, or you can "ask the Help librarian" by typing in a few words to

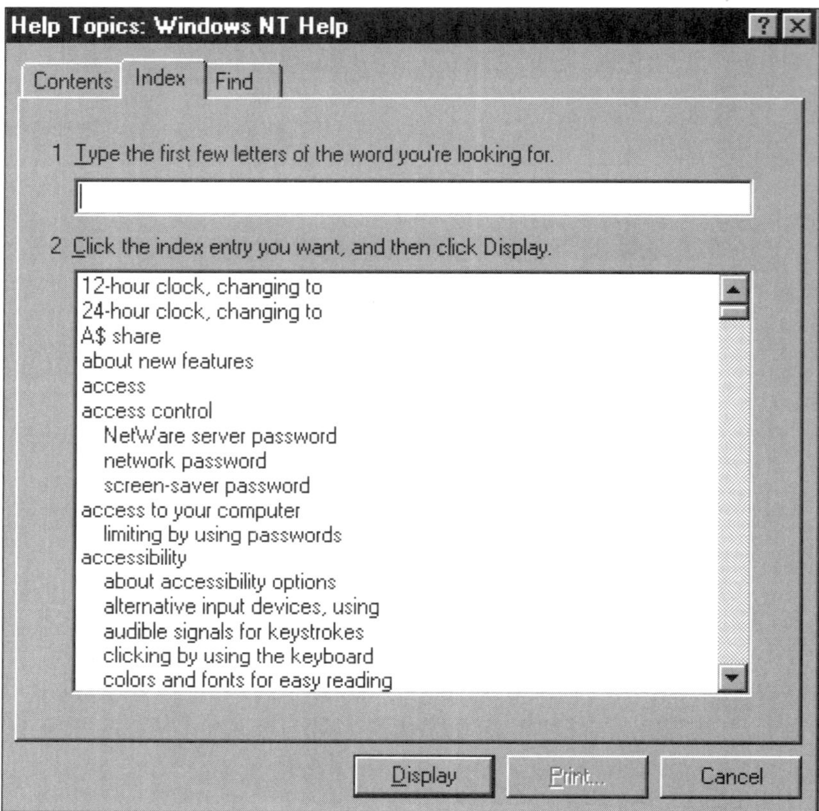

Figure 3.1: The Help command is conveniently located on your Start menu.

describe what you're looking for. Most everybody prefers the latter method, because it's a whole lot faster.

As soon as the Help window opens, it's all set to go. Follow along now and type in something that you might be curious about. Let's type the word Undo. If you type slowly, you'll notice that as you type each letter, Help begins to zero-in on the topic you want; first something beginning with U, then UN, then UND (perhaps "undeleting"), and finally Undo. The topic that Help found for you is now highlighted in the big index window. If you press <ENTER> now, Help will display that topic. If you prefer, you can click on the big Display button at the bottom of the window instead.

When you do, Help replaces the index (you don't need it anymore) with the nice, friendly, helpful description about Undoing shown in Figure 3.2. It briefly describes what you need to know about undoing your last command and even includes a few helpful tips.

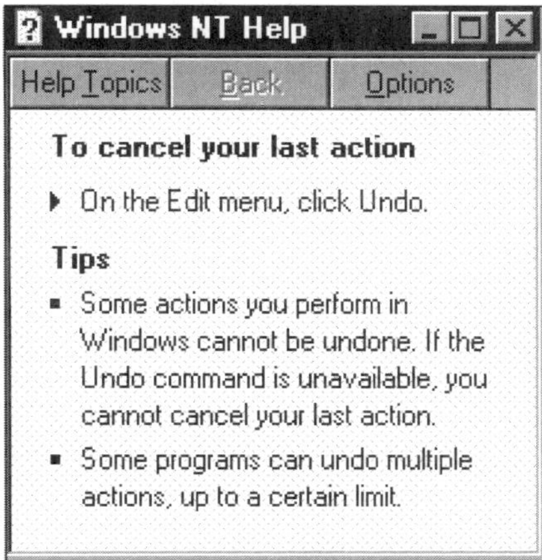

Figure 3.2: For each topic, there is a window that describes the concept or the steps to follow, like this one for "undo."

After you've read the Help message, you can either go back to the Help index to look up another topic, or you can dismiss the Help window. Clicking the little close box in the upper right corner of the window will close Help, just like closing any other window.

For now, let's return to the Help index. Click the big Help Topics button. When you find yourself back at the index, type in another topic. Let's say you're curious about how to change your computer's clock for Daylight Savings Time. Start typing the word Daylight until Help finds the right topic. Then click Display. Help displays another Help window much like the previous one, except this one has some sort of button in the middle of it (see Figure 3.3). If you read the description in the Help window carefully, you'll discover that this button actually works. Clicking it will take you directly to the window that controls Daylight Savings Time. Help is so helpful it even shows you the way.

If you read all the way to the bottom of this window, you'll discover another button. This button is marked Related Topics. Clicking it will display a list of topics that Help believes you might also be interested in.

The Back Button Before you go dodging off and changing your time zone, take a moment to experiment with some other features of the Help window. Next to the big Help Topics button, which you already know about, is a big button labeled Back. The Back button retraces your steps through the Book of Help. If you click Back now, Help will take you back to the description of Undo. From that win-

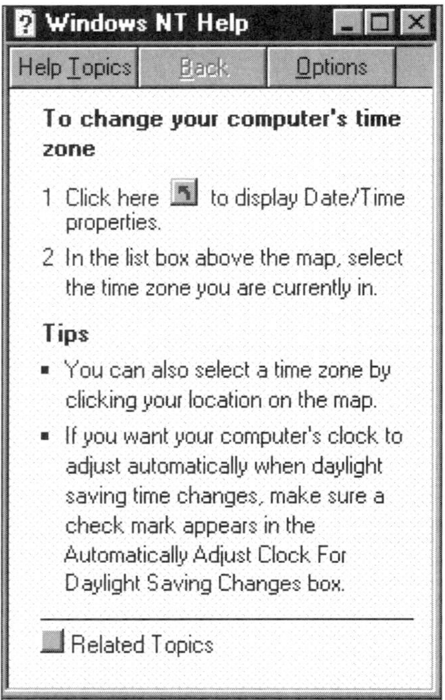

Figure 3.3: Some Help topics, such as this one on Daylight Savings Time, have a "hot button" that takes you directly to the appropriate command.

dow, clicking Back again will do nothing, for the simple reason that there's nothing to go back to—Undo was the first topic you looked up. You can use the Back button as often as you want. During a long Help session, it's a useful way to backtrack to a subject you just read about.

The Options Button The only other button on the Help window is labeled Options. Clicking Options allows you to print out a Help window so you can keep a permanent copy, or change the appearance of the Help window. There's also some other options we'll look at later on in this chapter.

Shortcut Hint: You can activate the Options menu by right-clicking anywhere inside the Help window.

One of the Options is called Keep on Top. If you let your mouse pointer hover over this option for a moment, you'll get three choices: Default, On Top, and Not On Top. Choosing one of these three options lets you control how the Help window operates. If you choose On Top, then the Help window will always be in front of all other windows, at the forefront of your screen. No other windows will cover it, even if you drag another window over it. The Help window is "magic" and can stay on top of any other window. This is very handy when you're trying to follow along with the instructions in the Help window and you don't want the instructions obscured by another window while you're trying to read.

Choosing Not On Top does just the opposite: Help will act like any other window, falling to the background when you move another window over it. Choosing the Default option allows Help to work in its normal, or default, manner. Sometimes Help will be on top of other windows, and sometimes it won't. Help is intelligent about what windows are what, and will try its best to be on top or underneath at the right time.

Multiple Choice Now you should return to the Help index and select a third topic. This time type Recycle Bin and press <ENTER> (or click Display). Help behaves differently this time. Instead of taking you directly to the Help window for the topic you entered, Help is displaying a list of related topics. As Figure 3.4 shows, there is a lot of information about the Recycle Bin and Help is asking you to pick one. Highlight the specific information you want, and then click Display.

Shortcut Hint: You can double-click a Help topic to display it.

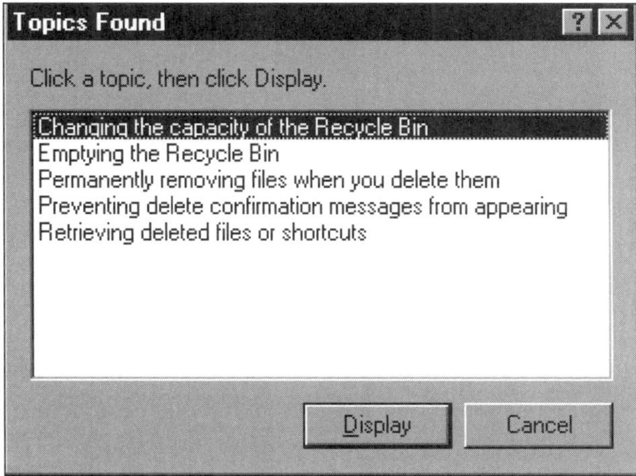

Figure 3.4: Some Help topics are ambiguous or have many parts, so Help lets you choose which subject you're interested in.

Word Definitions You should see a normal Help window like the ones you've seen before. If you've made a lucky choice, this window should have the words Recycle Bin underlined and written in green. If you place your mouse pointer over the green, underlined words, you'll see your mouse pointer turn into a hand. Clicking your left mouse button now will cause a special window to pop up, a window that explains what the underlined word or phrase means. In this case, the pop-up window explains what the Recycle Bin is.

Adding Your Own Notes to Help Sometimes the best helpful hints are the ones you discover yourself. Although Windows NT Help is lengthy and covers practically every topic, it would be nice to be able to add your own notes and observations. Well, with Help, you can. Anytime you're reading a Help window, you can add your own notes to, or annotate, the window.

To add your own personal annotations, click the Options button and select the Annotate command. (Remember, you can also right-click the window and select the Annotate command from the shortcut menu.) A small Annotate window, shown in Figure 3.5, pops up where you can type in your own notes. Your notes will be attached to the particular Help page you're reading at the time. You can type in anything you'd like, including cutting, copying, and pasting text from other documents. When you're finished making your annotation, click the Save button and your notes will be saved permanently.

When a Help page has an annotation attached to it, a little paper clip appears near the upper left corner of the window. When you see one of these paper clips, you know that somebody has annotated that page.

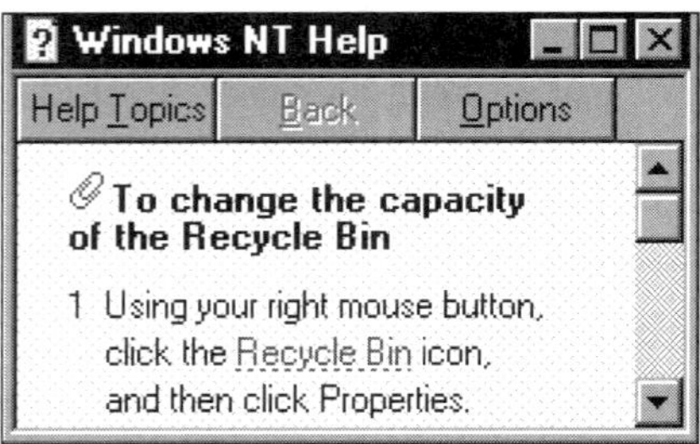

To read the annotations, click on the Options button and select the Annotate command. The existing annotation is displayed, and you

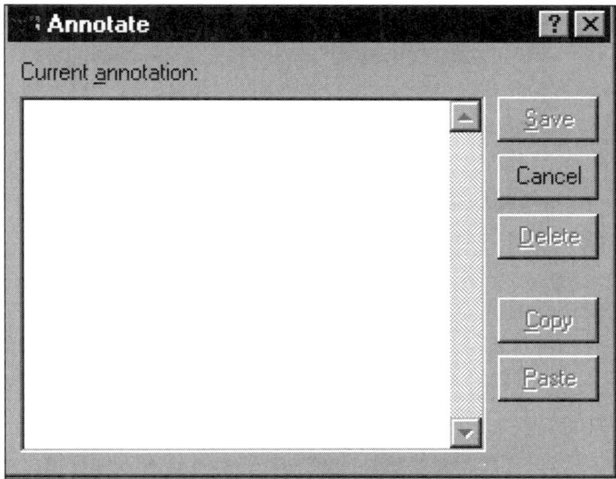

Figure 3.5: You can add your own personal notes and observations to Help using the Annotate function.

can add more notes to it if you want to. You can also select the Annotate command by right-clicking the Help window. If you want to permanently remove an annotation, you must first display it, and then click the Delete button in the Annotate window.

Shortcut Hint: You can read an annotation by clicking on the paper clip in the Help window.

Reading the Help Contents

The second way you can get help is by pressing the <F1> key on your keyboard. The <F1> key is almost always used as the Help key by most Windows NT Applications. Do you remember how selecting Help from the Start menu took you to the index of Help topics? Pressing <F1> works the same way, but it takes you to the Help Table of Contents. As you can see from Figure 3.6, the Contents tab is part of the main Help window just like the Index tab you saw earlier. The difference is that Contents has already zoomed into the application or window you are using.

If you press <F1> while you are using WordPad, Help will display the Contents tab for help with WordPad. If you're using Paint, Help will display the Contents for Paint, and so on. If you're not using any application, Help displays the Contents for Windows NT itself.

The Contents are arranged as a series of books. Each book holds a number of specific topics you can read. Rather than overwhelm you

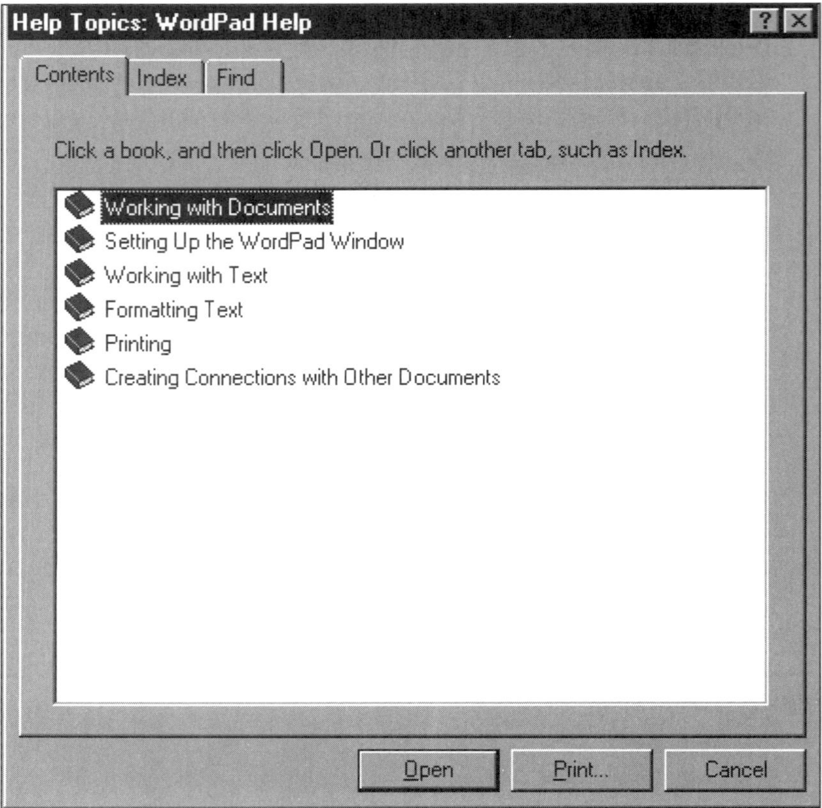

Figure 3.6: Help's table of contents sorts Help topics by subject, rather than alphabetically.

with choices, Help starts out with each of these books closed. When you've picked one that looks interesting, double-click the book, and it will open to reveal several "pages" of potential topics (see Figure 3.7). Double-clicking one of these pages displays it.

Searching for Help with Find

The third tab on the Help window is labeled Find. Using Help's Find tab is your last resort. If you can't find the subject you're looking for in either the Index or the Contents, then perhaps you will be able to locate it with Find. The Find tab hunts through every page of Help text on your entire computer searching for the words or phrase that you want.

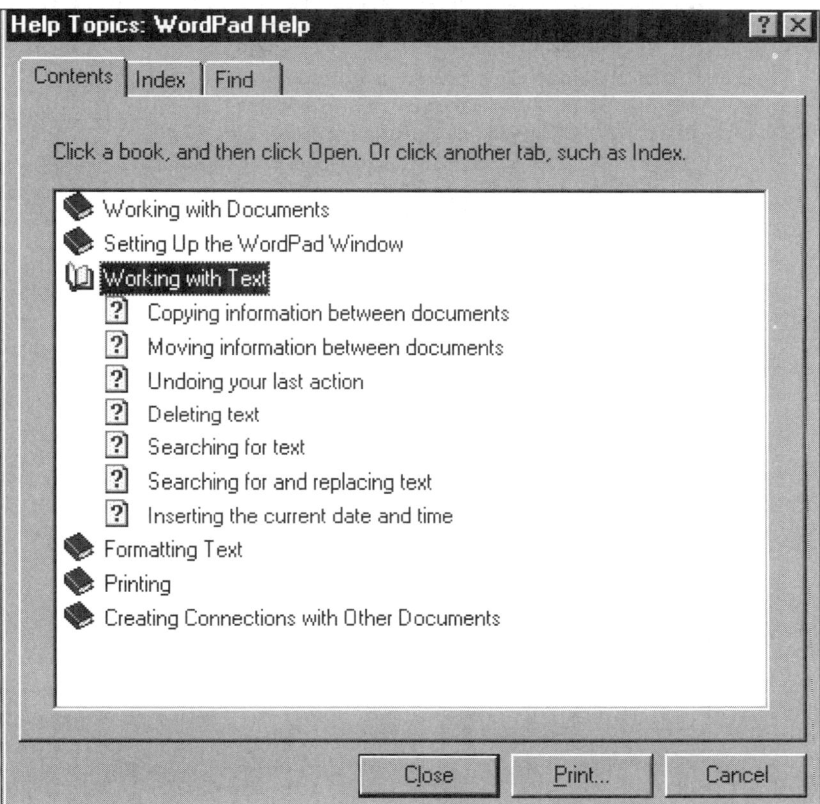

Figure 3.7: Double-clicking a Help "book" opens it to display more detailed topics.

The very first time you use the Find tab, Help will need some extra time to get started because it has never searched your Help pages before. You will see Help's Setup page, like the one in Figure 3.8, asking your permission to search and collate all the Help pages. You should carefully read the options here and make your choice. When you're ready, click the Next button.

Once the word list is created, the Find tab looks like the one in Figure 3.9. The Find tab is divided into three fields. On the top, you type what you're looking for. In the middle, Help displays the words that match what you have typed so far. On the bottom is a list of Help topics that contain those words and may be applicable to your search.

You should generally type slowly when you use Help this way. This is more to help you, not Help. As you type on the top line, Help will

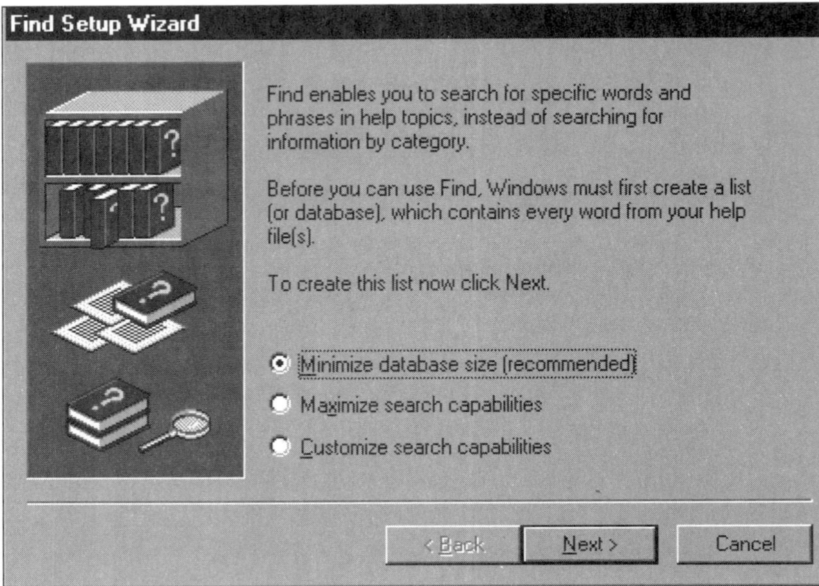

Figure 3.8: The first time you use Help's Find feature, Help will need to compile a list of words.

attempt to match each new letter with all of the words it knows. The more you type, the more it will narrow the search. For example, just typing the letter A doesn't narrow the search very much; there are hundreds of words on the Help pages that start with the letter A. Typing AR narrows the search to words like area, around, and arrow. Those words, in turn, let Help suggest some topics in the list on the bottom of the window. When a likely Help topic appears in this list, highlight it and click the Display button, or just double-click it.

The Helpful Question Mark

Sometimes you don't have to go looking for Help; sometimes Help comes to you. Many windows, applications, and property sheets have their own built-in Help function that works especially for that window. The built-in Help appears as a small question mark near the upper right corner of the window, next to the close box.

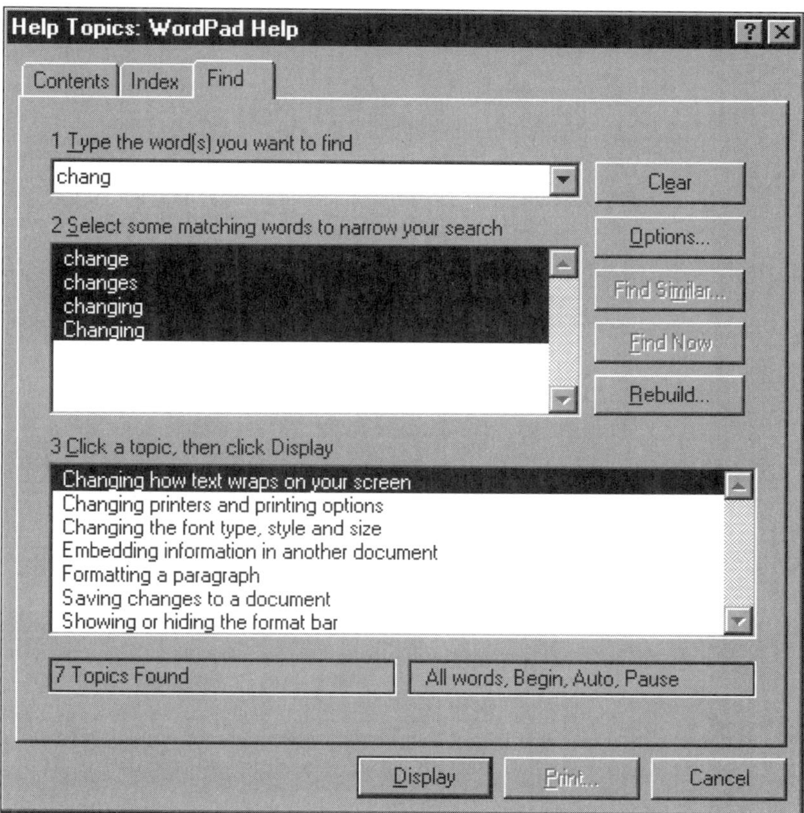

Figure 3.9: To find each occurrence of a word in the Help database, start typing the word in the topmost portion of the window.

Not all windows have this feature; you'll have to look and see which ones do and which don't. To use the built-in help, simply click once on the question mark. Your mouse pointer will change to a roving question mark; place it over the item in the window you're curious about, and click the left mouse button once again. A quick description of the item you pointed to pops up. In the example in Figure 3.10, the question mark on Display Properties sheet can explain what the preview screen is for. To make the pop-up help go away after you've read it, just click anywhere.

Keep in mid that the question mark cannot roam outside of its home window. In other words, you can't use the question mark from one window to ask about something in another window. In fact, the question mark disappears if you try to move your mouse outside the boundaries of the window.

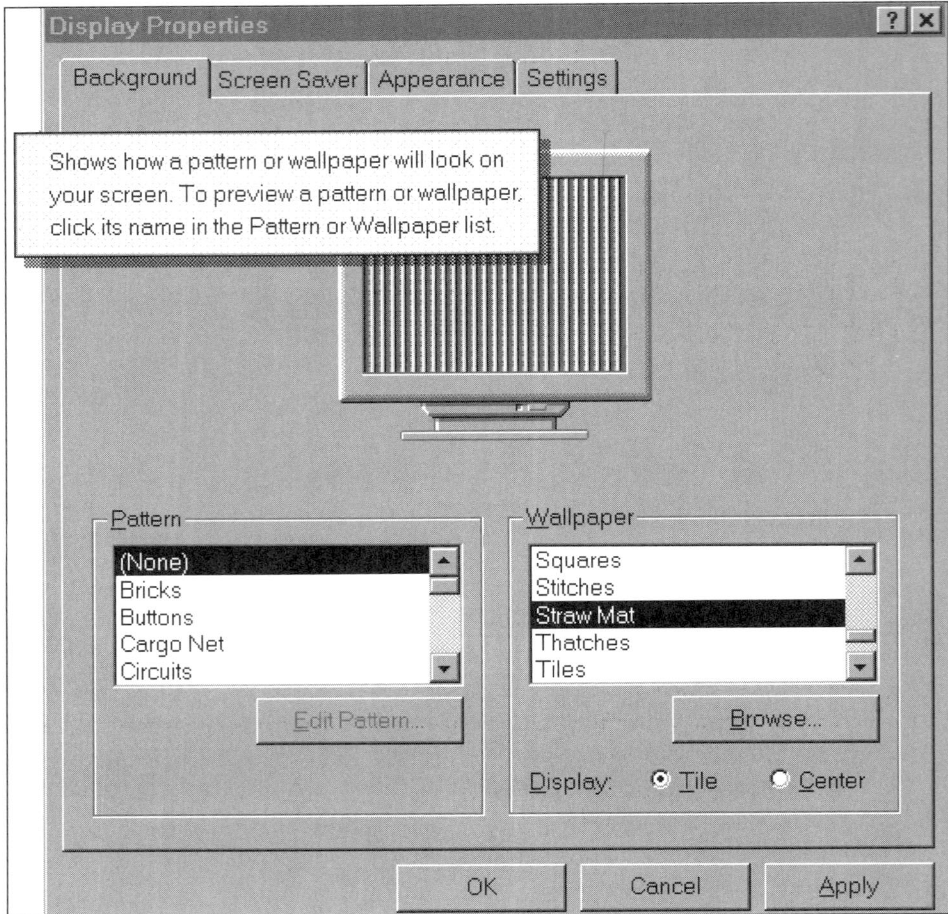

Figure 3.10: Many windows have their own built-in Help button. Click on the button and then at something in the window to see the descriptive text.

Shortcut Hint: You can access the built-in help by right-clicking the window and selecting What's This?

You can copy or print the contents of the pop-up help itself by right-clicking on it. This gives you an abbreviated pop-up shortcut menu. To cancel the shortcut menu, click anywhere except on the menu.

Chapter 4

USING WINDOWS NT'S FREE APPLICATIONS

Windows NT comes with a wealth of applications software—for free. You get a painting and drawing application, a telecommunication application, an application to dial phone numbers for you, and no fewer than two (count 'em) word processors. You also get a gaggle of games, for when you just don't feel like working. In fact, you could probably get most of your computing chores done with just the applications that come with Windows NT. In this chapter, you'll get a guided tour through each and every one of these applications so you can see how they work and how to put them to work for you.

WordPad

WordPad is the logical heir to Windows Write. They have similar features and look and operate about the same way. For those who are not familiar with Windows Write, WordPad is a word processor, and a pretty good one for the price. You can use it to write short or long documents like office memos, letters to friends and relatives, to-do lists, and schedules or programs. If you're a programmer, you can even use WordPad to enter source code. WordPad is also closely related to Word for Windows (which was also created by

Microsoft) allowing you to exchange Word for Windows documents with other people even if you or they don't own Word for Windows.

You can find WordPad by clicking Start, hovering over Programs, then over Accessories, and finally by clicking on WordPad. When WordPad starts, it gives you a blank page on which to begin typing, and you're ready to start. Figure 4.1 shows what a brand new WordPad window looks like.

The first thing to do is start typing! There are no preparations necessary. Even though WordPad is a much more capable (and complex) word processor than Notepad is, you don't need to concern yourself with features that you don't use. First things first: you should begin by typing at least some of your text before you begin the fancy formatting.

After you've entered your text, WordPad has an assortment of formatting and beautification options available to you. The great majority of these options are available both as buttons on WordPad's Toolbar and Format Bar as well as through the more-traditional menus. When you're formatting and beautifying text, the rule of

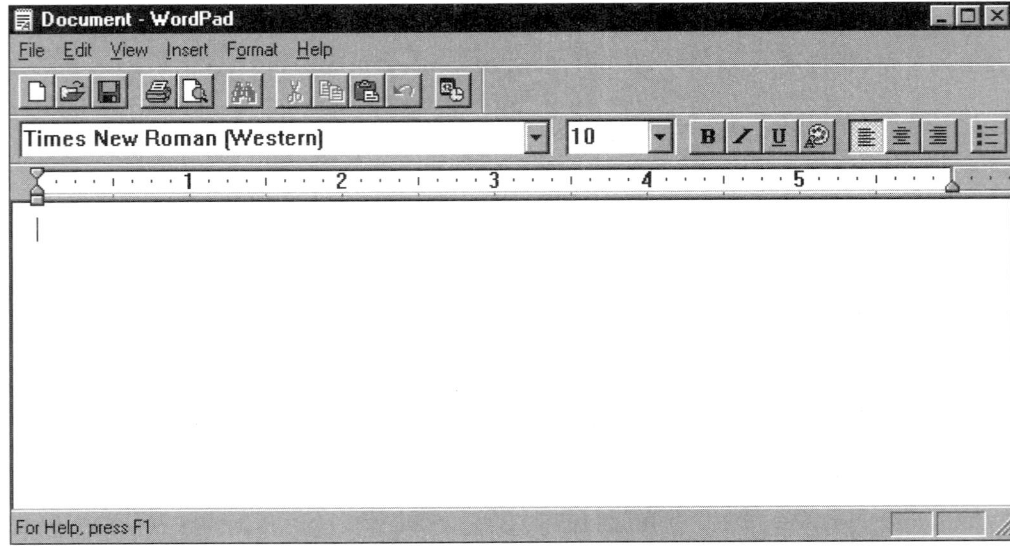

Figure 4.1: WordPad starts with a blank sheet of paper.

thumb is to always type the text first, then highlight it, then select the command you want to use on it.

Highlighting Text Since you should always start by highlighting your text, let's start by learning all the ways you can highlight. The first is to simply drag your mouse over the letters or words you want to highlight. Click and hold your left mouse button and drag across, up, or down until you've highlighted as much as you want to. Another way is to highlight individual words by double-clicking on them. By using a combination of double-clicking and dragging, you can highlight a series of consecutive words. Clicking three times in succession highlights an entire paragraph.

If you place your mouse pointer near the left edge of a paragraph, the arrow pointer flips over to the right. (There's only a very small space where this happens between your text and the left side of the WordPad window. It may take some practice to get this right.) If you click once there, you can select the entire line you are pointing to. Clicking twice selects the whole paragraph; clicking three times selects your entire document.

Bold, Italics, and Underlines After you've selected some words or characters, you can click on the Bold, Italics, or Underline buttons in the WordPad window. An alternate method is to click on the Format menu and select Font.

You can make your text bold, italic, and underlined all at once. Just click all three buttons and each style will be applied, one after the other.

Changing Type Size and Style Making your words bigger or smaller is very easy. After selecting the text you want to change, click once on the drop-down list for type size (this usually has a 10 or 12 in it when you start WordPad). The drop-down list shows you what sizes you can choose from. Not all characters can be printed in all sizes; the font you are using (see below) will affect your choices. Click once on the size you want, and the highlighted text will be converted to that size. These sizes are measured in points; a point, as any typographer can tell you, is 1/32 of an inch.

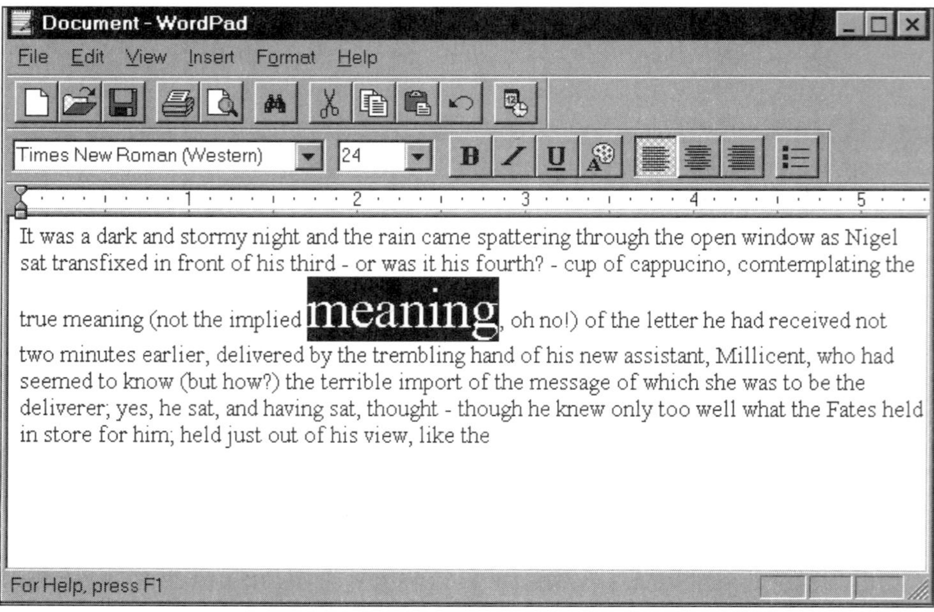

If you select a size *before* you start typing, everything you type will start out at that size.

You can also change the style of your text, called its font. Again, select your text by highlighting, then click once on the drop-down list for fonts. WordPad will list all the fonts that are loaded onto your computer. You may have quite a few of these if you're a font collector. The list doesn't show you a sample of what each of the fonts actually looks like; you'll either have to remember them or experiment with them. Click once on the font you want and your highlighted text will be changed.

You can even change the color of your words by clicking on the color palette button. WordPad give you a list of 16 different colors plus one called Automatic. These colors are fixed. You can't create custom colors like you can with Paint. The Automatic color assigns the color that gives the best contrast against the background—it "automatically" makes your text legible. This is usually black, but might change if you pasted your text onto a colored background.

Aligning and Indenting Normally, your text has a smooth left margin and a ragged right margin. This is also the way typewriters work.

If you choose, you can reverse this, making your text lay flush against the right margin with a ragged left margin. You can also center your text on the page. You cannot change the justification for just a single word or even a line; you must change the entire paragraph at once. Start by clicking anywhere in the paragraph (you don't need to highlight the whole paragraph) and then click one of the three alignment buttons: left, right, or center.

Tabs and Margins WordPad sets tab stops every half inch whether you want them or not. If you want different tab stops, you can set them with the Tabs command, or visually, by clicking on WordPad's Ruler.

To set tabs using the menu, click on the Format menu and select Tabs. The Tabs window will be empty, even though there are really tabs set at half-inch intervals. Here you can type exactly where you want the tabs to be. The units (inches, centimeters, etc.) are determined by the Options command in the View menu; go there if you want different units. After you type in a measurement for the new tab stop, click OK and the tab will be set. Note that tabs are only good for one paragraph. If you want the new tab stop to work throughout your entire document, you must highlight the entire document first.

A quicker way to set tabs is to simply click on the Ruler. Each time you click, a new tab stop is set. Again, these tab stops are only good for the currently selected paragraph; highlight the whole document if you want them to work everywhere.

You can indent a paragraph and change its margins by clicking on the Ruler, too. At the left end of the Ruler are three small controls. These control the left indent and first-line indent of the current paragraph. The third control moves the other two at once. There's a similar control at the right end of the Ruler. You might have to expand your WordPad window to see it.

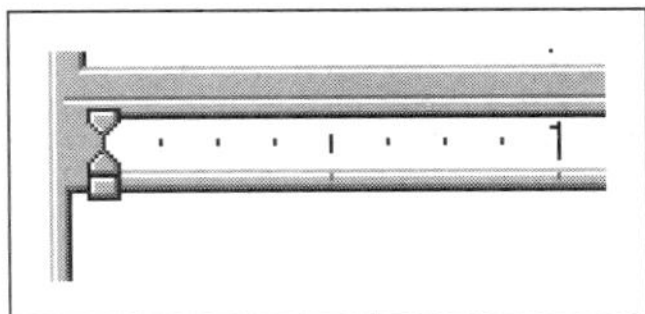

By dragging the uppermost control across the ruler you can set the first-line indent for the current paragraph. This offers a more convenient alternative to pressing <TAB> at the start of every new paragraph. To have a hanging indent, or an "outdent," drag the lower control instead. To indent the left margin of the entire paragraph, drag the boxy control that sits underneath the other two.

WordPad normally leaves margins of 1.25 inches on both the left and right sides of your paper. With 8.5 x 11-inch American paper, that leaves you 6" in which to type. If you want to change the page margins, click the File command and select Page Setup. Here you can change the top, bottom, left, and right margins as well as choose the size of your paper and whether its oriented right-side up or sideways (landscape mode).

Bullet Points If you're preparing a presentation or a memo with WordPad you might want to add some nice bullet points. Rather than typing asterisks for bullets and indenting your text, just type your list normally and then use the bullet-point tool. Clicking on the bullets button adds a bullet point in front of each paragraph you have selected and indents the text by a quarter inch.

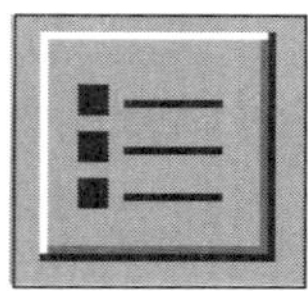

Opening and Saving Files WordPad can open four different kinds of text files and save your files in three different formats. This allows you to exchange documents with other people or other applications that do not have WordPad. Normally, WordPad saves files in a format that is compatible with Word for Windows and other commercial word processors. Your file will have a .DOC file name extension, which Windows NT recognizes as a Word for Windows file.

You can also choose to save your document as either a Rich Text Format (.RTF) file or as a basic Text Document (.TXT) file. These are most useful if you're planning to exchange files with another word processor. Both the .RTF and the .TXT formats take up less space on your disk than the .DOC format but they also lose some of the formatting features that you might have applied. The text-only format, in particular, throws away all of your formatting, making your document a generic ASCII file.

WordPad can also open other files in all three of these formats, plus the format used by Write, the word processor that came with Windows 3.x. WordPad can open these .WRI files but it cannot save them back again. You will have to convert them to one of the other two formats when you save your work.

WordPad's word-wrap setting is different for each type of file. See the Options command (on the View menu) to check this.

Fixing Spelling Errors WordPad does not have a spell checker, but it does have a search-and-replace feature. With it, you can tell WordPad to find all occurrences of a word or phrase and replace it with another word or phrase. This is handy if you discover you've been misspelling somebody's name all along. Rather than laboriously reading through your entire document hoping you catch all the errors, send WordPad on a "search and destroy" mission for you.

Under the Edit menu is the Replace command. Clicking on Replace pops up a simple Replace window where you get to type the word or phrase you're searching for and what you want to replace it with.

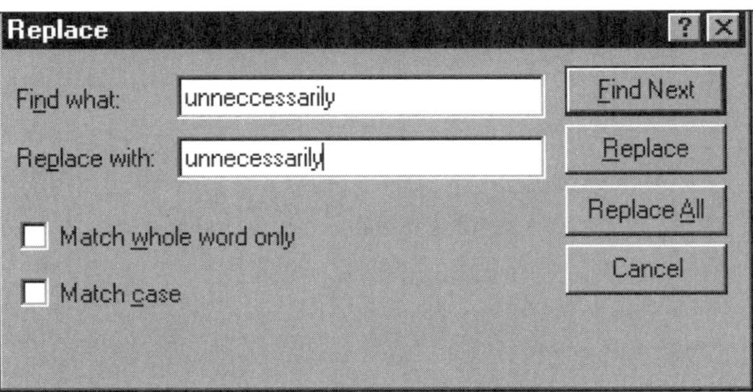

If you wish, you can restrict the search to complete words only. This is handy if you've typed something short like "the" as the search word. If you don't check the option for whole words, WordPad will find "the" in the middle of "together" and "rather." The other option, Match Case, tells WordPad to pay attention to capitalization and only find a match if it matches your typing exactly. Otherwise, WordPad ignores the difference between upper- and lower case letters.

Shortcut Hint: You can execute the Replace command by pressing CTRL+H.

You can either set WordPad on automatic pilot by clicking the Replace All button, or you can ride along by clicking the Find Next button. In the latter case, WordPad stops each time it locates your word or phrase and you can choose to either Replace that location or Find Next. This process repeats until WordPad has searched your entire document. Note that no matter where you start searching, WordPad will search your entire document, starting at the point where your mouse pointer is resting.

The Find command works just like the Replace command but without changing anything.

Shortcut Hint: You can execute the Find command by pressing CTRL+F.

Word Wrap and Tool Options You can choose whether the ruler across the top of the WordPad window uses inches, centimeters, points, or picas. To change this option, click on the View menu and select Options. Choose the first tab, labeled Options, and select the units of measure you prefer.

The check box for automatic word selection enables and disables WordPad's ability to automatically select whole words as you drag your mouse across your text. If you don't like that, and would prefer to select text a character at a time, uncheck this box.

The remaining five tabs set the same options for five different file types. For each type of file you can choose whether to display the WordPad Toolbar, Format Bar, Ruler, and Status Bar. You might choose to change these options for different file types so that you do not, for example, apply underlining to a file that is going to be saved in the Text Document format anyway (which does not save underlining). The Embedded tab controls "objects" that are linked or embedded in WordPad documents using a technique called object linking and embedding, or OLE.

Using Object Linking and Embedding (OLE) The technique of object linking and embedding (also called OLE) lets you mix different kinds of files into one file. For example, with OLE you can have a financial spreadsheet and a Paint picture in the middle of a WordPad document. Better than just copying and pasting, OLE creates "hot links" between these different file types so that you can change the picture in your WordPad document just by double-clicking on it. Paint will start up automatically, and your changes will be saved into your WordPad document.

The best way to get a feeling for OLE is to try it out. With your WordPad document open, click on a place where you'd like to insert a picture. Then click on the Insert menu and select New Object. WordPad will show you the New Object window, like the one in Figure 4.2. The list of objects in the Object Type list will grow and change over time depending on what applications you have loaded on your computer. All of your applications that can create OLE object (and not all of them do) will be listed here.

One application that uses OLE that you're sure to have is Paint. Paint creates pictures that are called Bitmap Images (.BMP files). To put a picture from Paint into your WordPad document, click on Bitmap Image and then click on the big OK button.

Now your WordPad window looks like a strange hybrid between WordPad and Paint. Your text is still visible in the window, but there's a big empty Paint canvas in the middle of it and all of the Paint tools have replaced the WordPad tools. You have successfully embedded a Paint object into a WordPad object.

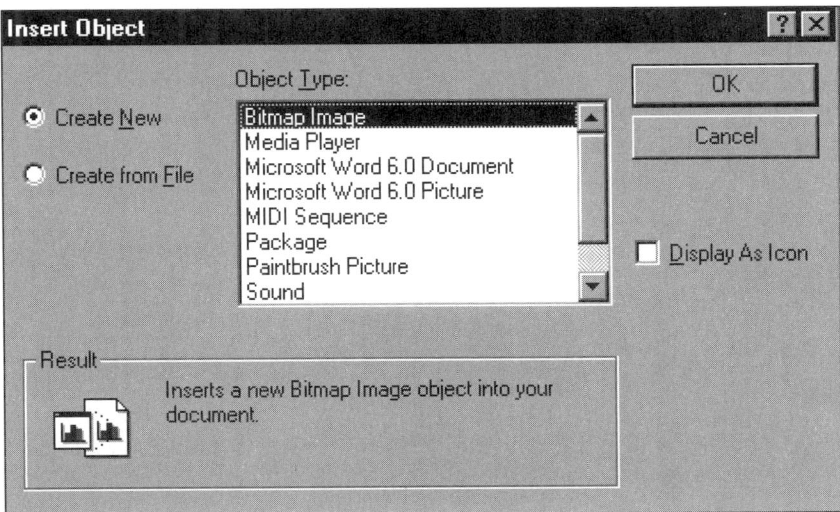

Figure 4.2: You can insert pictures and other "objects" into a WordPad document from the insert menu.

If you're not familiar with Paint, don't worry. If you are, feel free to create a little illustration like the one in Figure 4.3. When you're done with Paint, simply click your mouse somewhere outside of the picture and WordPad will return to looking like WordPad.

Although there's a big picture sitting in the middle of your document, WordPad still operates just the same way as you're used to. However, if you click on the picture, you will have access to a few new commands on the Edit menu. Selecting Object Properties lets you examine some specifics about this picture and even change it into an icon if you prefer. Double-clicking will actually open the application that created the picture (in this case, Paint) so that you can edit it just as before.

Note that even though you created the picture with Paint, you never saved it as a Paint file. The picture only exists inside this WordPad

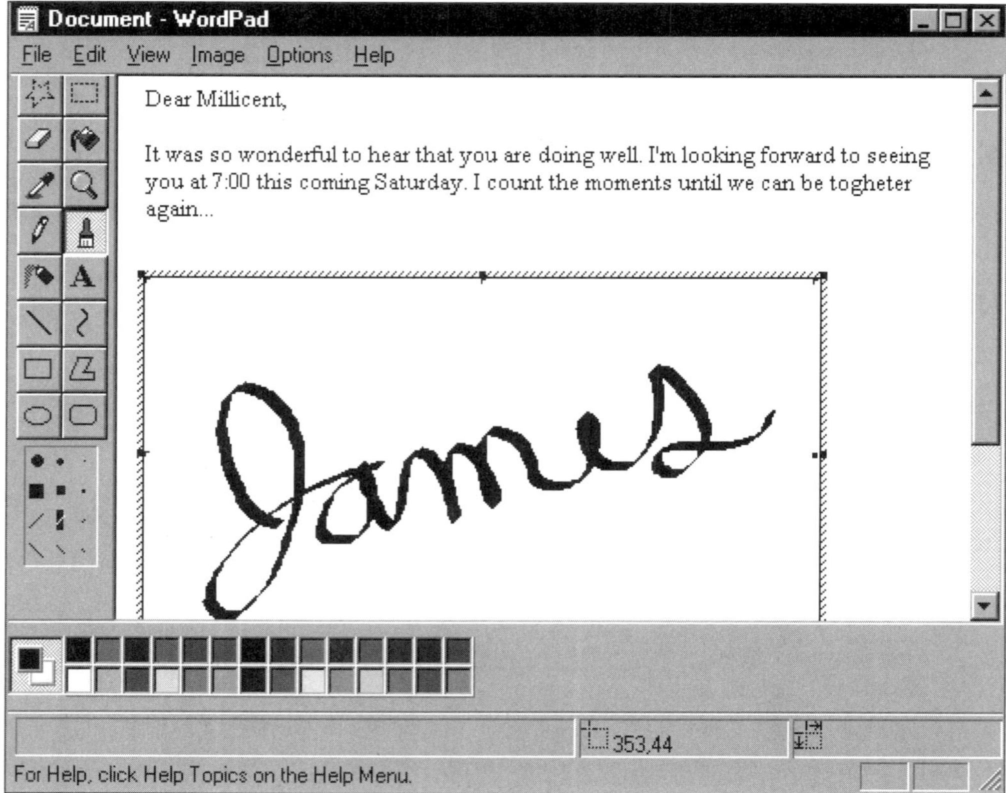

Figure 4.3: How a document looks after inserting a Paint object.

document and it is only saved as part of the WordPad file. This is called object embedding: the picture is "embedded" into your WordPad document like a marble embedded in a block of clay.

Object Linking Going back to the Insert menu and selecting New Object, you'll notice that there are two radio buttons near the left side of the Insert Object window. These make the difference between object linking and object embedding. If you select the Create New option (the normal choice), you will embed a new object. If you select Create from File, you will create a link instead.

What's the difference? There are a couple. When you embed an object (like the Paint picture you created earlier) you are storing the object as part of your main document. The object doesn't exist anywhere else and it has no file name of its own. You could not, for example, open Paint and load the embedded picture because it's embedded into your WordPad document.

When you link an object, on the other hand, you are creating a magic thread between two files. If you had linked your WordPad document to an existing Paint picture, the result would be the same but both files would be stored separately and independently. That means that your WordPad document will take up less space on your disk (because the whole picture isn't embedded inside of it) and it means that you could open the picture with Paint if you wanted to.

This brings us to the best part: when you link two objects together, changes in one will show up in the other one automatically. For instance, if you create a WordPad document and make a link to a Paint picture on Monday, and change the picture on Wednesday, when you print the WordPad document on Friday, it will have the new picture in it.

To create a link, click the radio button that says Create from File. Now you must select the file that holds the object you want to link with your WordPad document. You can use the Browse button to locate it on your computer. Just as before, you have the option of displaying this object as just an icon in your WordPad document rather than the full image. This is more useful for sound clips than it is for pictures. Finally, be sure you check the box marked Link, or else the file you select will be embedded in your WordPad document instead of linked to it.

Notepad

Notepad is the most basic of Windows NT word processors—a lowly text editor with absolutely no fancy features. With no bells or whistles to make it complicated, Notepad is the perfect application to whip out a quick note, edit Windows NT configuration files, or create easily readable files for nearly any purpose. In this section, we'll examine Notepad in all its minimalist glory.

Notepad was first introduced in Chapter 1 as a good way for first-timers to get started with Windows NT. That's still true, although now you're better-equipped to deal with the basics of handling and moving windows, and selecting commands from menus. When you first start Notepad, the first thing to do is start typing. No preliminaries here, Notepad is ready for you to type as soon as you see the Notepad window open up.

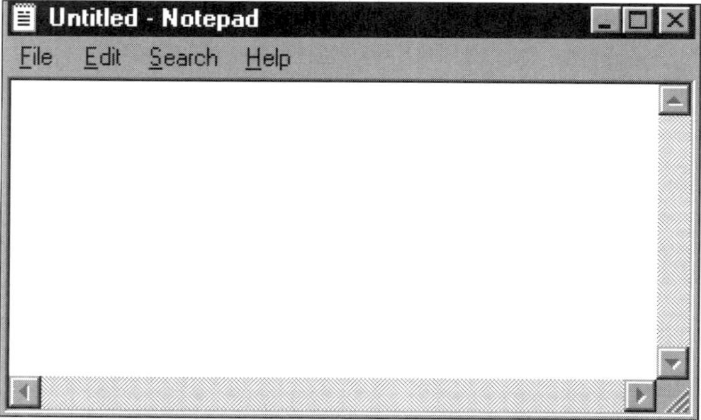

Notepad allows you to do the two most basic functions you would want to do with a file: save it and print it. Notepad also has a text search function you can use to find words inside your Notepad file. Notepad files are always saved as very basic, generic, text files. Windows NT classifies these files as Text Documents because they have the .TXT extension to their file names. Notepad does not allow you to save your files in any other format. These are "plain vanilla" ASCII files suitable for writing MS-DOS batch files, or feeding to a language compiler.

One annoying feature of Notepad is that it normally lets your words run off the edge of the window. As often as not, you'll want to click on the Word Wrap option in the Edit menu. This causes the text to "wrap around" at the edge of the window so you can read long lines. This option "sticks;" so once you select it, all Notepad files will have Word Wrap turned on.

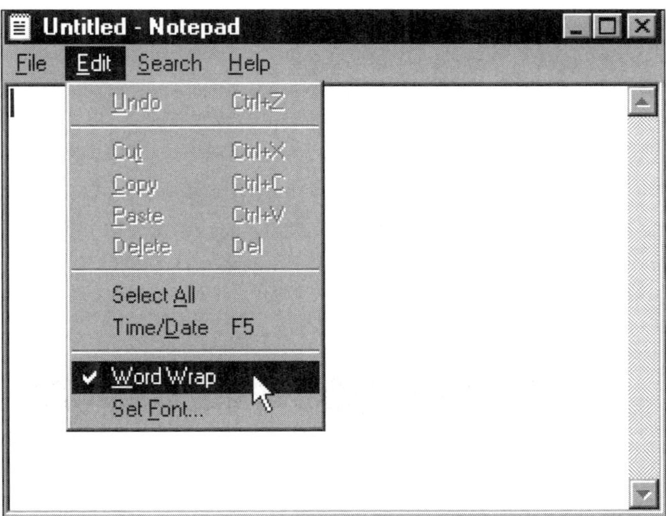

The only semi-fancy feature of Notepad is its ability to type the current time and date for you automatically. This is also under the Edit menu. Every time you select this command, Notepad types both the time and the date at the location of your cursor. There's even a shortcut—you can press <F5> and get the same result. You can't change the way that either the time or the date is displayed, although you could always edit them afterward if you need to.

There is a hidden, magic feature associated with this. If you type the magic word ".LOG" on the very first line of your Notepad file (note the period at the beginning), Notepad will add the current time and date at the *end* of the file at the moment you open it. Why? So that you can create yourself a log file that keeps its own record of every time it is opened. This has the odd side effect of modifying the file for you every time you open it, even if you never really change anything. To keep the log accurate, be sure to save the file every time you close it.

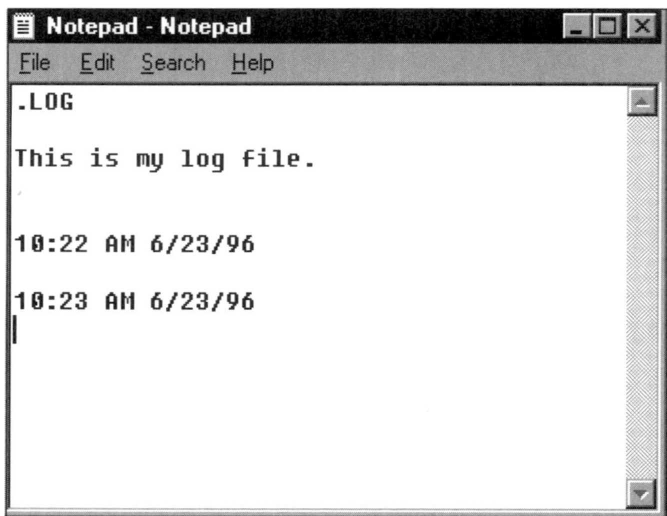

Notepad has only the most basic text-beautification commands for changing the font (type style) it uses. It also has only the most basic cut, copy, and paste commands for editing. Drag-and-drop editing is not supported. Selecting the Set Font command from the Edit menu allows you to change the text in a Notepad file but it has the strange side effect of changing all the text in all Notepad files anywhere on your computer. That is, its sets the standard font for Notepad itself. If you have two or more Notepad windows open, Windows NT will remember the font you selected on the last Notepad window you closed, and it will become the new standard Notepad font.

ClipBook Viewer

The ClipBook is your own personal electronic scrapbook. With the ClipBook, you can store little snippets of your work that you want to save, or share with others, or use again and again. Examples might be a company logo that you've drawn and want to reuse, or your signature in script, or a paragraph from a standardized form letter, or whatever. With ClipBook you can squirrel away just about anything you want—words, pictures, or both—and use them again later.

You can find the ClipBook with the other Accessories as part of the Program group on your Start menu. When you open the ClipBook window you'll see two smaller windows inside it, Figure 4.4 shows. One of these is called your *Local ClipBook* and one is called the

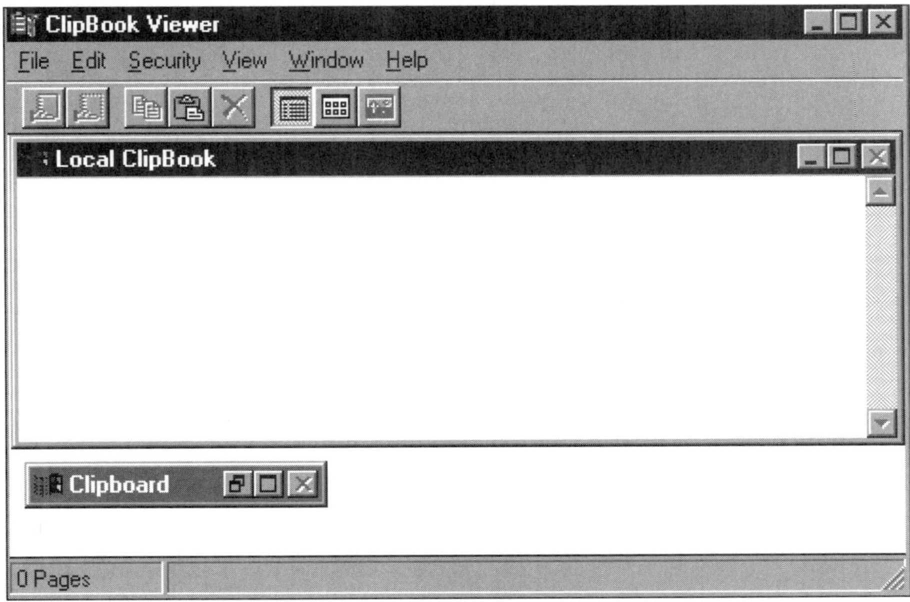

Figure 4.4: The ClipBook includes two smaller windows, the local ClipBook and the Clipboard.

Clipboard. It's important to keep these two different windows straight in your mind.

You use the Clipboard all the time without even knowing it. Every time you cut or copy something in an application, it magically appears in the Clipboard, automatically. That means every time you use Notepad, WordPad, or the other Windows NT applications, and use the copy or cut commands, the thing that you copy or cut winds up on the Clipboard. When (or if) you paste something back in, it gets pasted from the Clipboard. The Clipboard is your magical, invisible holding area where items—text, pictures, or anything—are held temporarily until they're pasted back in. It's not until you open the ClipBook and look at your Clipboard that this becomes apparent.

When you open the ClipBook and look at the Clipboard window, you'll see that the last thing you cut or copied has been placed there. The very next time you cut or copy something, the current contents of the Clipboard will be discarded and replaced with the new item. The Clipboard can only hold one item at a time. Again, this happens all the time without any special work on your part. If you leave the ClipBook window open while you work with Notepad (or any other Windows NT application), you'll be able to see the Clipboard at work.

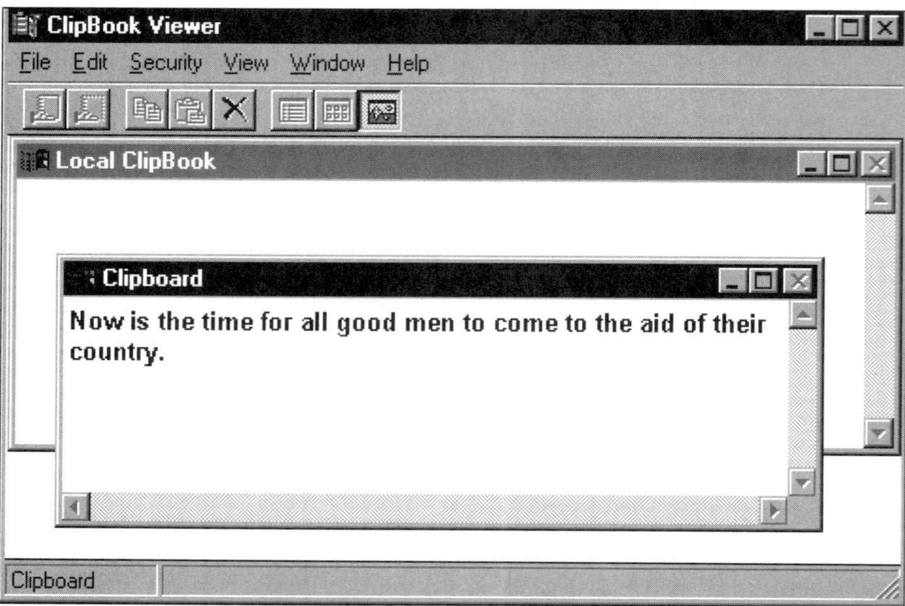

Where the ClipBook gets interesting is when you want to make a permanent copy of the item on the clipboard. At first, your ClipBook will be empty—you haven't stored anything in it yet. If you've cut or copied something you want to save, you need to paste it into your ClipBook. You can paste as many "keepsakes" into your ClipBook as you like, and you can even share them with your colleagues, if you want.

To paste a permanent copy of the Clipboard into your ClipBook, use the mouse to highlight the Local ClipBook window. From the Edit menu, choose the Paste command (you can also use the Paste button on the toolbar, if you prefer). When you do, the ClipBook will ask you to give this new "page" in your electronic scrapbook a name.

Type in any name you want for this item. The name will only be for your reference, so make up something that will help you remember what you're pasting. If you check the box labeled Share Item Now, you'll be presented with several options for controlling who you want to share this item with and what privileges you want to give them. You can share individual items or pages of your ClipBook, and not others.

When the Clipboard window is highlighted (as opposed to the Local ClipBook window), you have several options for viewing the contents of the Clipboard. As Figure 4.5 shows, the ClipBook can hold pictures as well as text. The View menu gives you several options for viewing the picture on the Clipboard. These options will change depending on what's on the Clipboard at the moment. You can never edit the contents of the Clipboard, only view it.

Character Map

The Character Map is a simple but useful tool for writers, whether full-time or part-time. It lets you see what all the characters (letters, numbers, and symbols) of your current font (printing style) look like.

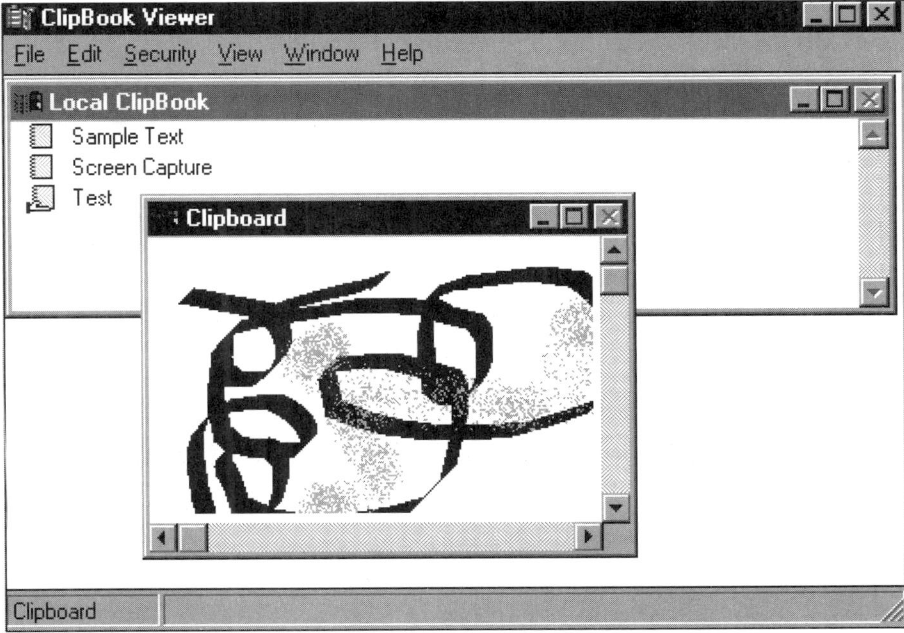

Figure 4.5: The Clipboard always holds a copy of the last thing you cut or copied from another window.

Without Character Map, it would be hard to know how to type a ® symbol or get a ß to print.

Granted, these are probably not tasks you need to do every day, but that's partly the point. Anybody can find A-Z and 1-9 on their keyboard; it's the "funny" characters that are hard to find. Opening the Character Map window displays a full set of characters, like the one in Figure 4.6.

A full assortment of 256 characters displayed, arranged in eight rows. These are all the characters that can be displayed or printed in the font you have selected. You can change the font by clicking on the drop-down menu near the upper left corner of the Character Map. All the fonts that are loaded on your computer will be listed here, and you can choose whichever one you want. Character Map displays a helpful "TT" reminder next to all the fonts that are stored in the TrueType format (the kind that Microsoft recommends).

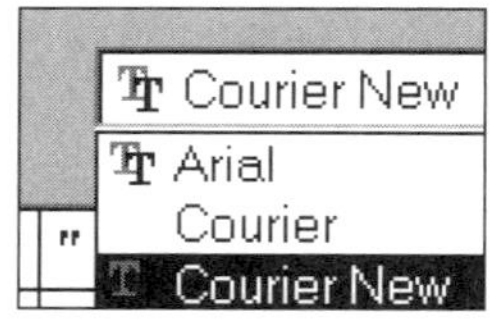

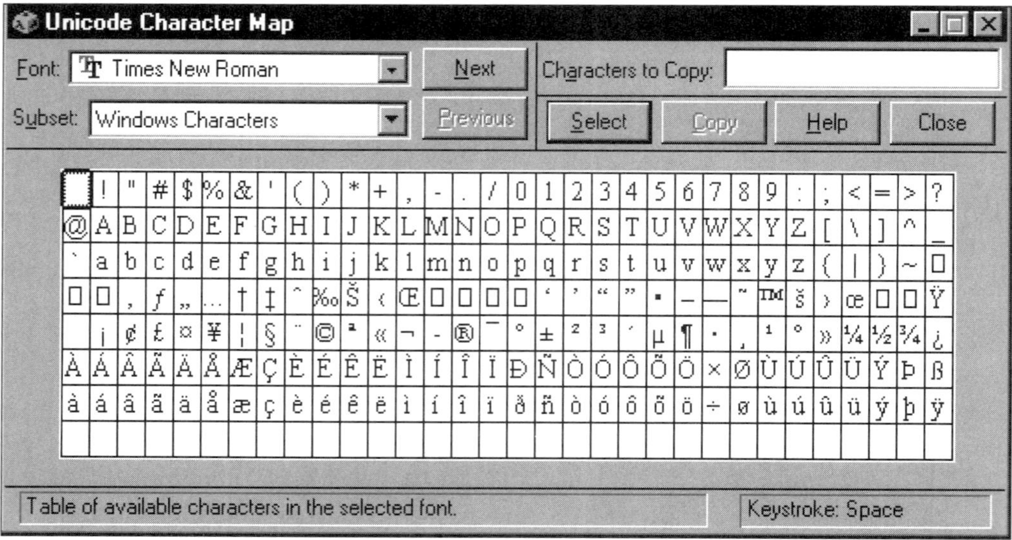

Figure 4.6: The Character Map accessory lets you see and select all of the unusual characters your PC can print.

The drop-down list below the Fonts list is labeled Subset. You can use this list to display even more characters within the selected font. If you click on the drop-down list you'll see that dozens of different subsets, or variations, are listed. Not all fonts use these subsets—in fact, most don't. But if you're curious, they're worth browsing through.

You can use Character Map just to browse and marvel at all the wonderful symbols you probably aren't using, or you can use it to actually enter those characters into a document. Character Map doesn't do any of the typing for you but it does act as kind of a special multilingual Clipboard.

When you click on a character in the Character Map, the character is highlighted and its special key code is displayed in the lower right corner of the Character Map window. For example, the ® symbol in the MS Sans Serif font uses the key code ALT+0174. That means that if you hold down the ALT key and type 0174 on your numeric keypad, you can type a ® symbol in your document.

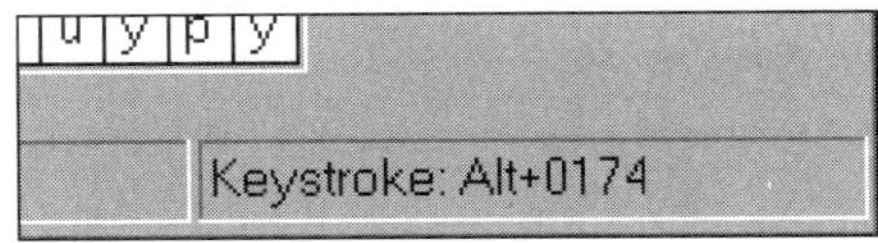

Shortcut Hint: Be sure to use the number keys on the far right side of your keyboard, called the numeric keypad, when you enter special key codes. The number keys across the top of your keyboard will not give the same results. You must type all four digits of the key code, even if the first digit is zero.

This is the technician's way to enter special characters. There's an easier way preferred by most people who don't care to memorize special key codes. If you highlight a character by clicking on it, you can then click the big Select button on the Character Map window and that character will be put into the Copy window near the upper right corner of the Character Map. This is a storage place for your special characters. Highlighting a second character and clicking Select again adds that character to the Copy window, and so on. You can "spell out" the sequence of special characters you want this way without typing a single key code.

Shortcut Hint: Double-clicking on a character places it in the Copy window.

When you've selected the special character or characters you want, be sure to click the big Copy button *before* you close Character Map or else your characters won't be copied to the Clipboard. Once your special characters are on the Clipboard you can paste them anywhere, just like always.

If the small characters in the Character Map are a little hard to see, you can point to one and hold down your left mouse button to see a magnified view of it.

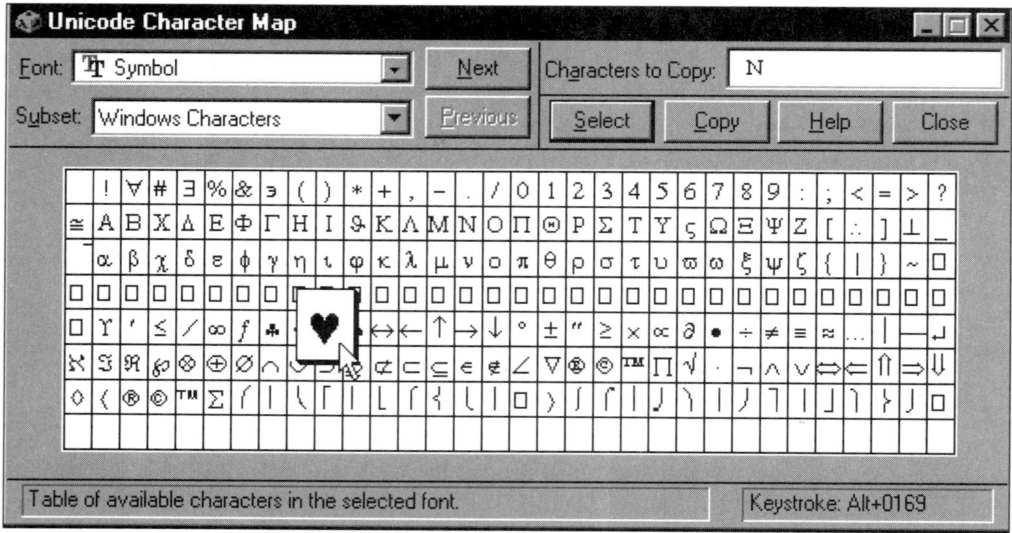

Calculator

The Windows NT Calculator is no better than one you'd get for free by opening a new bank account or digging in the bottom of a cereal box. Nowadays, calculators more powerful than this one fit into wristwatches and run off bright sunlight. Nobody expects you to have a fancy calculator on your computer, but on the other hand, you'd feel pretty silly sitting in front of a $2,500 computer and not be able to tally up a series of numbers without using your fingers.

The normal Calculator looks just like the one in Figure 4.7. It has big buttons, an easy-to-read display, and four red memory keys. The "advanced" functions are on the right: percent, square root, and reciprocal.

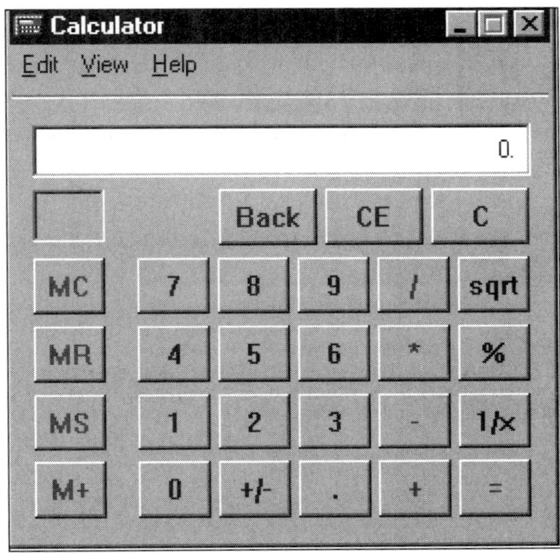

Figure 4.7: Using the Calculator is as easy as it looks.

Although you can click on the Calculator buttons to use it, most people find it more comfortable to use their keyboard to enter numbers. The number keys on the far right side of your keyboard (called the numeric keypad) are especially useful for this. Be sure you have pressed the <NUM LOCK> key first to make these keys work.

Calculator is a simple four-function calculator. It adds, subtracts, multiplies, and divides. To add two numbers, type 1 + 2 and press the <ENTER> key. The <ENTER> doubles as an "equals" key on the Calculator, and there's one conveniently located in your numeric keypad. The minus sign and the divide symbol are easy to find; the asterisk is your multiplication symbol. All these keys are located on your numeric keypad.

If you want to use the square root, percent, or reciprocal functions, you can either click their keys on the calculator or press the <@>, <%>, or <R> keys on your keyboard, respectively.

The red memory keys allow the Calculator to remember one number. Clicking the MS (memory store) key copies the number on the Calculator's display into a memory storage place. Later, clicking the MR (memory recall) key brings that number back. The M+ key adds the number on the display to the number stored in memory. Finally, the MC (memory clear) key erases the Calculator's memory. These keys also have shortcuts. They are CTRL+M, CTRL+R, CTRL+P, and CTRL+L, respectively.

So much for the basics. If your calculating needs are more advanced, you can turn the mild-mannered Calculator into a complex "scientific" calculator with lots of functions. From the View menu, select the Scientific command, and the Calculator will change into the one shown in Figure 4.8.

This Calculator has many more functions, as you can see. It also has the ability to calculate in different number bases, like base 2 (binary), base 8 (octal), and base 16 (hexadecimal). These are useful for computer scientists and engineers, and terrifying to the rest of the community. Rather than explain what each key and function does, you should explore the scientific Calculator for yourself if you are interested in it.

Each key on the Calculator—even the scientific functions—has a matching shortcut key on your keyboard. If you forget what the shortcut key is, just right-click on the Calculator key and select the What's This? command. Finally, if you want to copy the result of your calculations to another document or application, you can click on the Edit menu and select the Copy command.

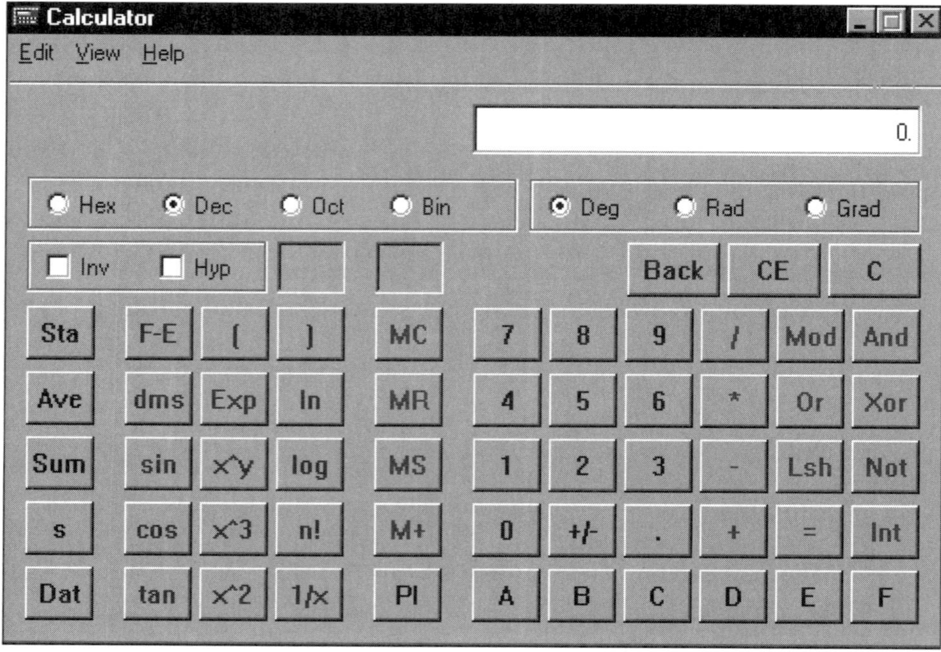

Figure 4.8: The Calculator has a second face, one with more scientific features.

Paint

Paint is a fun little application that's also very useful. What WordPad is to word processing, Paint is to graphic arts. You can create color pictures with Paint that you can paste into your documents, use to add a personal touch to letterhead, illustrate maps, decorate the refrigerator, or create your own screen background. Paint is easy to use and you can save your pictures, exchange them with friends and colleagues, and even edit existing pictures.

Paint has menus across the top of its window like most applications, but the real tools are along the left-hand side, as shown in Figure 4.9. These take the shape of 16 buttons you can click to get various painting tools. Each of these tools will be described shortly. Underneath the

Figure 4.9: The paint application gives you a whole box of paintbrushes, pencils, erasers, and colors to play with.

16 buttons is a small gray area called the option area. Different things will appear in this area from time to time so that you can select options. Across the bottom of the Paint window is your collection of colors, called the color palette. You can dip your electronic paintbrush into these colors any time you wish. In fact, your paintbrush can hold two colors at once, something real paintbrushes can't do very well. The two colors on your brush are shown in the two overlapping colored squares in the lower left corner of the Paint window. One of these is your primary, or foreground, color. The one behind it is your secondary, or background, color.

If you're doing precision drawing, the numbers along the bottom of the window will help you. These tell you the exact coordinates of the tip or your brush. The coordinates are measured in pixels starting from the upper left corner of the Paint window and working down and to the right. The second set of numbers tells you how far you are from the last point you made. These will make more sense when you start drawing squares and rectangles. For now, let's get started with Paint!

Pencil The Pencil is the most basic drawing tool and the one most people start with. It works very simply: you hold down a mouse button while moving your mouse around and it leaves a pencil trail on your picture. With a little practice you can sign your name or draw stick figures this way.

Pencil lines are always skinny; you can't change the thickness of the Pencil. You can change its color, however, by clicking on one of the colored squares in the color palette across the bottom of the Paint window. Left-clicking on a color sets the foreground, or primary, color. Right-clicking sets the background, or secondary, color. After you pick two colors, you can draw with either one by holding either the left or right mouse button while you "write" with the Pencil.

Paint Brush The Paint Brush is the companion to the Pencil. It works very much the same way, but the Paint Brush makes fatter, more interesting lines. The Paint Brush is your best freehand tool unless you want pencil-thin lines.

After clicking on the Paint Brush tool, you can select from an assortment of different "brush shapes" in the option area. There is a total of twelve brushes at your disposal (some are very small and hard to see). Three brushes are round, three are square, and the remaining six are angled like calligraphy pens (three to the left and three to the right). Each type of brush comes in small, medium, and large, for a total of twelve brushes. Click on a brush shape and you're ready to begin painting.

Your Paint Brush holds two colors of paint at once. Clicking and dragging with the left mouse button paints with the primary color. Dragging with the right mouse button paints with the secondary color. If you want to change the primary and secondary colors, use the left and right mouse buttons to choose new colors from the color palette near the bottom of the Paint window.

Spray Painting The Spray Can tool lets you put rough patches of color in your picture that look a little like poorly applied spray paint. Simply click on the Spray Paint tool and then use either your left or right mouse button to "spray" color wherever you want it. The standard rules apply: left button sprays foreground color, right button sprays background color. Moving your mouse slowly will give you better coverage; holding it still while you spray will saturate a spot with color (it won't drip).

The three options in the option area let you choose how wide your Spray Can sprays. Click on one of the blotches to select an option.

Eraser The Eraser is kind of an interesting tool and never seems to work quite the way people expect it to. Erasing seems simple enough: removing unwanted lines or colors. But when you're creating a color picture, what gets erased and what stays behind? A tough question. Maybe that's why there are no color erasers in real life.

Start by clicking the Eraser tool. The option area gives you four sizes of Eraser to choose from. Then you need to decide whether you want to use the dumb Eraser or the smart Eraser. The dumb Eraser acts more like a paintbrush than an eraser. It simply leaves a color trail behind it as you drag it around with your left mouse button. The color you have selected as your foreground color is the color it leaves behind, regardless of what color you're erasing.

To use the smart Eraser, drag it around using your right mouse button. The smart Eraser looks for a particular color and replaces it with another color. All the other colors are left alone. That's what makes it a smart Eraser. Pick the color you want to remove by left-clicking it on the color palette. Then pick the color you want to replace it with by right-clicking on it. In other words, the smart

Eraser replaces the foreground color with the background color. This is handy for removing unwanted spray paint or pencil lines from a multicolored background.

Paint Can The tool with the overflowing can of paint will quickly fill in an entire area with one color. The Paint Can fills in for you automatically, so you don't have to laboriously color something in with the Pencil or the Paint Brush. If you had a hard time staying inside the lines with your childhood crayons, the Paint Can is for you.

Like most tools, the Paint Can can paint in either the primary or secondary color depending on which mouse button you use. To "spill" your can of paint, position the paint can somewhere inside the area you want painted, and click once. The color you selected will instantly fill the entire boundary.

That boundary is important. You can only paint an enclosed area. Otherwise, your paint will "overflow" the area and get into others parts of your picture. Be sure that the area you are painting has a continuous, unbroken border around it. If you paint something and the paint overflows, you can use the Undo command (under the Edit menu) to fix your mistake.

Straight Lines The Line tool lets you draw lines that are much straighter than if you had drawn them with the Pencil. Your lines can be tilted at any angle, or you can make them horizontal. You can also make lines at perfect 45-degree angles.

Clicking the Line tool presents you with five options in the option area. You can pick five different line widths, from thin to thick. All the lines you draw will be of that thickness. The line thickness you choose here also affects any circles, ovals, or polygons you might draw later.

To draw a straight line, you must drag the mouse. Don't click one point and then click another because that won't draw anything. If you want your lines to be perfectly vertical, horizontal, or diagonal (45 degrees), hold down the <SHIFT> key while you draw and your line will "snap" into place. Drawing a line with your left mouse button draws in the primary color; drawing with the right mouse button uses the secondary color.

The Line tool is also the first one to use the second set of coordinates on the Paint window. Notice that as you draw a line, these numbers show you how far you are from the other endpoint of the line. If you want to make a precision drawing, like a floorplan, this is a useful feature.

Curves Next to the Line tool is the Curve tool. Curves start out as lines, but then you get to distort them. Curves are not like freehand curves you draw with the pencil; these have a bit more mathematical precision to them and, thus, less freedom.

There are two ways you can draw a curve. The first way is to click the Curve tool and drag out a straight line with your mouse, like you would with the Line tool. Then, click your left mouse button near the line and drag it out of shape until you're happy with it. You can click a second time in another place and distort the line again if you want. Two clicks is the limit, though.

The other way to draw a curve is to click once to place one point and click a second time to place the other point. Then click a third time to distort the closed loop you've created.

Rectangles and Squares You can draw either rectangles or squares by clicking on the Rectangle button. Clicking this tool gives you three options in the option area: rectangle with no fill (outline only); rectangle with a fill; and fill only (no outline). You can also pick two colors, the outline color and the fill color. Clicking your left mouse button on a color in the color palette sets the outline color. Right-clicking a different color sets the fill color. You can't pick the thickness of the outline directly. Instead, rectangles "inherit" the thickness of the last straight line or curve you drew. To change the line thickness, first click the Line tool (or the Curve tool) and choose a line thickness from there.

To draw your rectangle, just click and drag your mouse to the shape you want. When you release the left mouse button, your rectangle is drawn in the colors you choose. Holding down the <SHIFT> key with your other hand while you draw will make your rectangle into a perfect square. If you use your right mouse button to draw your rectangle/square, the outline and fill colors will be reversed.

Rounded Rectangles and Squares Diagonally across from the rectangle and square tool is the Rounded Rectangle tool. This works just like the rectangle tool does except that the corners of your rectangles and squares are rounded off instead of squared off.

Ovals and Circles Clicking the Oval tool lets you draw both ovals (ellipses) and perfect circles. As with the Line tool, the <SHIFT> key is your helper. In this case, holding it down makes your ovals into circles.

Like rectangles, you can draw ovals and circles in three styles: outline only, fill only, and filled outline. If you want to change the thickness of the outline, you must change it with the Line or Curve tool. Just like the other shapes, you can choose two colors for your oval/circle: the outline color and the fill color. Left-clicking on the color palette sets the outline and right-clicking sets the fill.

Polygons You can make irregularly shaped polygons with the Polygon tool. Like rectangles and ovals, polygons can be outlined and/or filled. Their outline width is also taken from the last straight or curved line you drew. And, the outline and fill colors can be selected with the left and right mouse button.

To start a polygon, drag your mouse to create a straight line. You can make this line vertical, horizontal, or diagonal by using the <SHIFT> key. After the first line is drawn, you can click once to add more lines to the first one. Add as many lines as you want this way. Right-clicking instead of left-clicking reverses the colors of your polygon-in-progress. To finish the polygon you can double-click the last point and Paint will close the endpoints of your polygon together for you.

Typing Words in Your Picture Paint has some nice features for adding words to your picture. While it's certainly no word processor, you can choose different fonts and sizes, make your text bold face, underlined, or italics, and even put colored backgrounds behind it.

To start, click on the Text tool with the big A on it. This gives you a cross-hair cursor which you then use to drag out an outline into which your text will fit. Pay attention to this step because it determines how high and how wide your text will be. You can change these aspects later, but it's better to get them right the first time. After you've created an outline, a Fonts window appears. (If the Font window does not appear, click on the View menu and select Text Toolbar.) You can either play with the Font window now, or ignore it and come back to it later. You can also move it if it's in your way.

You can start typing right away, and your text will fill the box as you type. If you get to the right edge of the box, Paint will wrap your words, just like a good word processor. You don't need to press <ENTER> at the end of each line or at the end of your typing. When you're done typing, simply click somewhere outside of the box to finish.

Before you finish typing, you should turn your attention to the small Fonts window that's hovering somewhere over your picture. This allows you to change the font, size, and style of your text before you finish typing it. Making changes here will cause instant changes to your text, so you can preview what the changes will look like. After you've finished typing and clicked outside of the text box (or clicked on another Paint tool button) it's too late to go back and change your text. You'll have to erase it and start over.

The two colorful options in the option area let you choose whether your text will have a colored background or not. If you select the upper option, the outline you created before you started typing will be filled in with the background color. In other words, the entire rectangle will be opaque. You won't be able to see "through" your letters. If you choose the lower options, on the other hand, the background will not be filled in and your letters will overlay whatever is behind them. Although text is normally black, you can change that by selecting a different foreground color by left-clicking on the color palette while you type.

Magnifying Glass The Magnifying Glass, as you might suspect, gives you a close-up look at your picture. You can zoom in twice as close, six times as close, or eight times as close as normal. Naturally, you can also zoom back out again.

Simply click on the Magnifying Glass tool and select one of the four magnifications offered in the options area (1x is normal size—you're already looking at that). Or, you can ignore the option area and just place your mouse pointer over the area of your picture you want magnified and click the left mouse button. This always selects the 8x zoom for you.

You can continue to work on your picture while it's magnified. This allows you to do some fine tuning to the details of your picture. When you are through examining your picture, click the Magnifying Glass tool again and click anywhere on your picture to bring it back to normal size.

Rectangular Cut and Copy You can cut, copy, and paste portions of your picture like words in a word processor. You can make "rubber stamps" by copying a portion of your picture and pasting it over and over in different areas. You can snip a section of your picture and save it as a separate file. Or, you can cut a section out of an existing picture and draw something new in its place.

The key to all these creative acts is selecting the area you want to copy or cut. If the area you want is rectangular, simply click on the Rectangular Select tool and then drag out the rectangular area you're interested in. (If it's not rectangular, see the next section.) After the area is selected, a four-headed arrow will appear. This is optional, but if you want to move the selected area, click and hold the left mouse button and drag the area to wherever you want it to be. The Draw Opaque option changes how this works. With Draw Opaque checked (see the Options menu), the entire rectangular area will move, background and all. With Draw Opaque unchecked, only the foreground colors will move, and you will be able to see through them to the background.

Shortcut Hint: You can choose between the two Draw Opaque options by clicking on the two icons in the option area.

There are several other things you might do with the selected area. Rather than move it around, you can right-click on the area and get a list of choices from the pop-up menu that appears. Most of the choices are self-explanatory, but the Copy To... and Stretch and Skew commands are kind of unusual. Copy To... allows you to save the selected portion of your picture as a different file. You could load this portion at a later time to paste into a different picture. Stretch and Skew, on the other hand, lets you distort the selected area of your picture in new and unusual ways including elongating it either vertically or horizontally, or tilting it to one side. Experiment with this one for some fun.

Star Select Tool The star-shaped tool works just like the Rectangular Select tool except that you can define odd and irregularly shaped areas in your picture, not just rectangles. To try this, click on the tool button and drag your mouse around the area you want to select. Paint will leave a pencil line behind as you draw so that you can see where your border will be.

Your border can be as irregular as you like, and you do not have to close the ends together. When you release the mouse button, Paint selects the area you have defined. If the endpoints of your border do not meet, Paint cuts in a straight line between them. Despite the rectangular box around your selected area, you really have selected an irregular portion of your picture. As before, you can copy, cut, or distort the area as you see fit.

If you use the four-headed arrow to move your selection around the screen, the movement may be a little jerky and uncoordinated. That's because it takes a lot of work for your computer to calculate and draw an irregular, colored shape on another irregular, colored background. The faster your computer is, the smoother this motion will be.

Color Picker The Color Picker tool, which looks a little bit like an eye dropper, lets you pick up a color from your picture and make it either your foreground or your background color. To use it, simply click on the Color Picker tool and place the eye dropper over a sample of the color you want to get. As you might have guessed, clicking the left mouse button makes that color the foreground color, while clicking the right mouse button makes it the background color. This tool is useful if you have loaded a picture that does not use the usual 28 colors that come with Paint.

More about Colors Paint normally gives you a palette of 28 colors, including black and white. These are basic colors like you'd get in a small box of crayons. If you want, you can replace these colors with different colors that you can mix yourself. Then you can save your newly mixed colors as a separate color palette so that you can use them again and again—your own private box of crayons.

To replace one or more of the standard colors with a custom color, click on the Options menu and choose Edit Colors. You will see the Edit Colors window, like the one in Figure 4.10. The 16 white boxes near the bottom of the window are where you can store up to 16 new colors that you create. The 48 colored squares above them are starting points for your custom colors.

To create a custom color, click on the big Define Custom Colors button. If you want, you can select one of the 48 colored squares first to use as a starting point. Otherwise, you'll create your color from scratch.

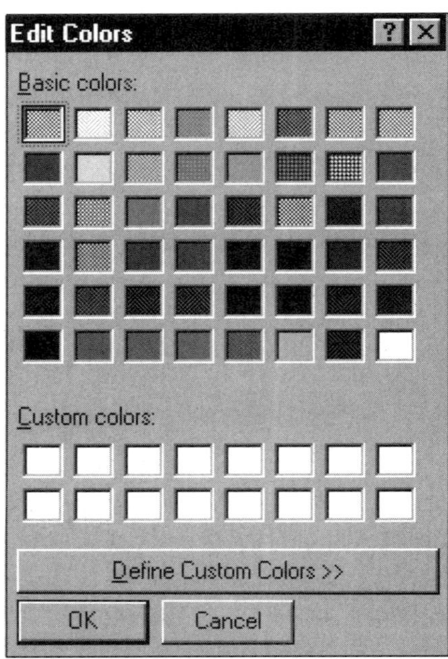

Figure 4.10: With Paint, you can use the colors provided or mix new colors of your own.

When you click the button, the Edit Colors window doubles in size to show you the full color spectrum, as Figure 4.11 shows. This is a kind of three-dimensional color selector. You can move the cross-hairs on the big color wheel (even though it's square) by clicking or dragging with your mouse. Moving left or right changes the color's hue while moving up and down changes its saturation. You can also change the luminance (darkness or lightness in your color) by dragging the little arrow up or down along the color "thermometer" on the right edge of the window. Most people just do this by eye. Between the two-dimensional movement of your mouse across the color wheel and the up-and-down movement of the luminance thermometer, you have three dimensions in which to dabble with custom colors.

Shortcut Hint: To choose 100% color saturation, press ALT+O.

For the numerically minded, you can also type hue, luminance, and saturation values directly into the three fill-in boxes provided. Or, you can type in the red, green, and blue components of your color. You cannot do both; entering one set of numbers changes the other set.

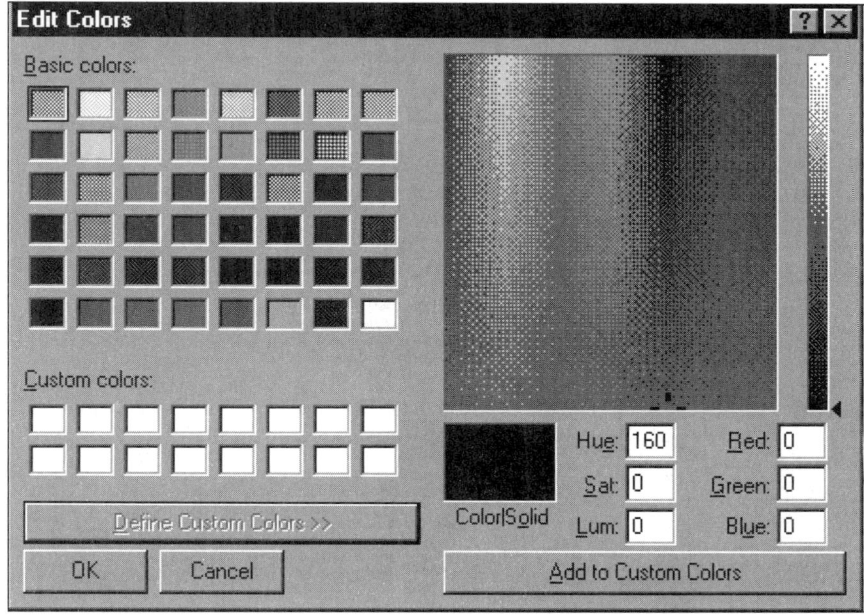

Figure 4.11: Paint allows you to mix your own custom colors.

Rather than entering these numbers, you might choose to write them down somewhere after you create a particularly pleasing color so that you can remember its "formula."

When your color is just the way you want it, click the big Add to Custom Colors button at the lower right and your color will be added to one of the 16 unused custom colors. If you want to replace a specific custom color, click on its box before you start mixing its replacement color. When you're satisfied with your colors, click OK.

If you want to save these colors permanently, click on the Options menu and select Save Colors. You will see the standard Windows NT Save box, which lets you choose the disk and the folder where you want to save your custom color palette. You should also give your palette a name; the extension .PAL will be attached to it automatically.

Conversely, if you want to use a different color palette that you saved before, click Options and then Get Colors. You can now browse through your computer until you select the color palette you want to load.

Opening and Saving Pictures Paint can open and edit pictures that you've created previously with Paint, obviously, as well as pictures that others have created. These pictures are all stored in the Windows Bitmap format, or .BMP files. Paint can also open pictures stored in the .RLE format, which is a compressed version of .BMP that takes up less disk space. Files with the .RLE extension are not very common, with the notable exception of the old Windows 3.x logo that was displayed every time you started Windows.

When you save your pictures, you can only save them in the Windows Bitmap, or .BMP, format. In the bottom of the Save As window, you can choose exactly what *kind* of Windows Bitmap file. That is, you can decide to save your file with all its colors intact, or as a black and white picture. You can also choose the 256-color or the 16-million-color (24-bit) format. These require a little explaining.

Normally, Paint allows you to paint with 24 different colors, as you have seen. Paint has its usual box of colors and you can mix in custom colors of your own. If you mix custom colors frequently as you paint, you might have dozens or even hundreds of colors in your picture when you're finished. The reason Paint gives you four different choices when saving a picture is so that you can conserve disk space if you have relatively few colors. The four choices (2-color, 16-color, 256-color, and 16-million-color) each require successively more disk space to store. A black and white picture takes the least amount of space, and so on. These four choices are based on the way your computer saves colors, so if they seem like big leaps (say, from 16 colors to 256 colors) that's because they're necessary. If your picture has the usual assortment of 24 colors, you should save it in the 256-color format because the 16-color format will lose some of your colors. Blue and brown, for instance, might be stored as the same color. For most pictures, 256 different colors is plenty. Probably the only time you'd ever need more colors than that is if you were retouching a color photograph that had been scanned in and you wanted to save the changes accurately.

Painting Your Own Wallpaper Paint has a fun option that allows you to paint your own background design on your screen (also known as desktop wallpaper). At any time you're working on a picture, you can click on the File menu and select either of the two wallpaper options provided. These will instantly change your screen's background pattern to match your picture.

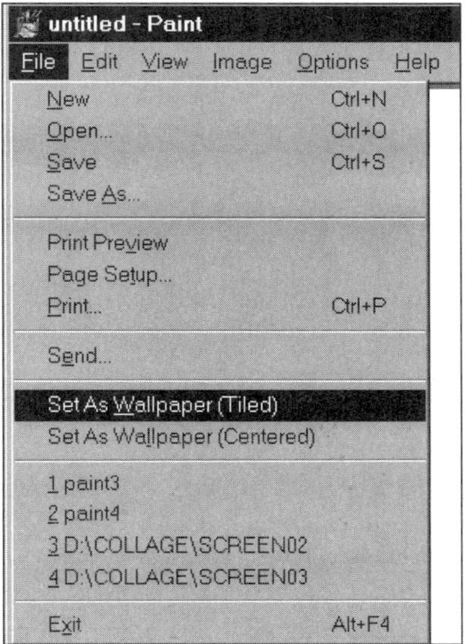

The two different wallpaper options are tiled and centered. These are purely aesthetic choices that are left up to you. If you choose centered, your picture will be placed in the center of your screen, actual size. If your picture is not big enough to fill the entire screen (it generally isn't), the rest of the screen will stay the same. This effectively leaves a frame around your picture. If you choose to tile your picture, the same picture will be repeated as many time as necessary to fill the entire screen, like painted tiles. This is particularly attractive if you can manage to paint a picture that has edges that match up when the picture is tiled.

The other way to create your own wallpaper is to save your picture in the normal way, and then use the display properties background tab to select your own wallpaper file from the list.

Changing the Size of Your Picture You can change the size of your "canvas" as you paint your picture. If you find yourself painting off the edge of your picture, you can increase the area you have to work in. To set the size of your painting area, click on the Image menu and select Attributes.

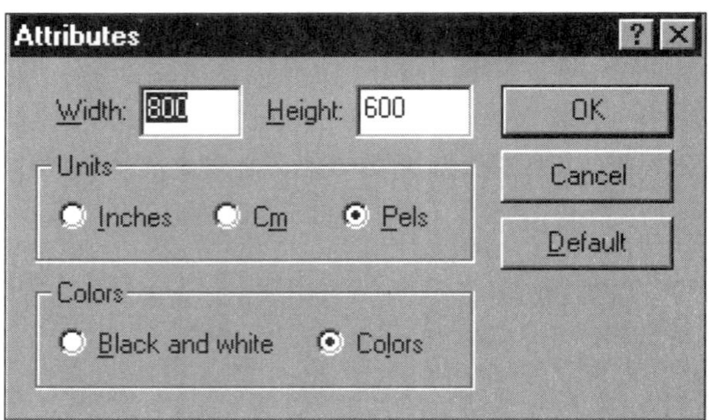

The Attributes window lets you set the size of Paint's canvas. You can measure it in inches, in centimeters, or in pixels (dots of light on your screen), inexplicably identified as "Pels" in the Attributes window. Click one of the three radio buttons and then type in the height and width you want to use.

Note than you cannot grow or shrink the picture itself, only the blank area you have to work in. If you've drawn something too big, you'll either have to erase it and start over, or buy a more sophisticated graphics program than Paint.

Phone Dialer

The telephone dialer is an odd little accessory application that might come in handy. As the name implies, the Phone Dialer dials telephone numbers for you. Why would you want to have thousands of dollars' worth of computer hardware dial your telephone? Because it can.

You must have two things before you can use the Phone Dialer: a modem and a willingness to let your computer dial your telephone. A modem is an additional product that you have to buy for your computer that allows it to use normal telephone lines to communicate with other computers, networks, and fax machines. Using the Phone Dialer instead of your index finger does have some advantages. Phone Dialer has eight "speed dial" buttons you can use to store frequently called numbers; it can automatically insert a special calling card access number if you use such a thing; and it keeps a log of the numbers you've dialed recently.

When you open the Phone Dialer from the Accessories menu, it looks something like the one shown in Figure 4.12. You've got your basic 12-key telephone pad complete with letters on the keys, eight speed dial buttons that you can customize, and a space to type in telephone numbers.

Dialing a Number The most basic way to dial a number is to press the telephone keys with your mouse. Unlike a real telephone, you have to click the big Dial button when you're finished dialing, or else Phone Dialer won't know you're finished. Phone Dialer uses your modem to place the call, which you should be able to overhear through your modem's own speaker. When the other party answers, you must pick up the receiver on your real telephone and click the big Talk button that appears on your screen. If you don't click Talk, the other party will not be able to hear you.

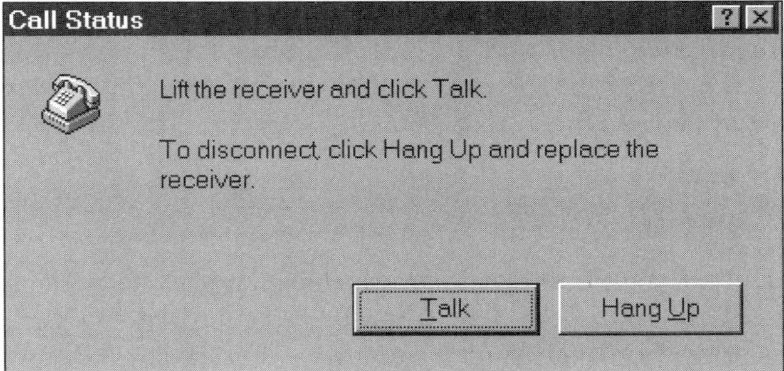

Instead of clicking numbers with your mouse, you can also just type the number in the space provided and press <ENTER>. If you type a telephone number, include parentheses around the area code, a plus sign before the country code (if you're calling internationally), and a space between the area code and the phone number. This will be important later on.

Another way to dial a number is to simply click one of the eight speed dial buttons, but this technique assumes that you've already programmed them. (You'll see how to do that in just a moment.) Finally, you can select a number by clicking on the drop-down list that

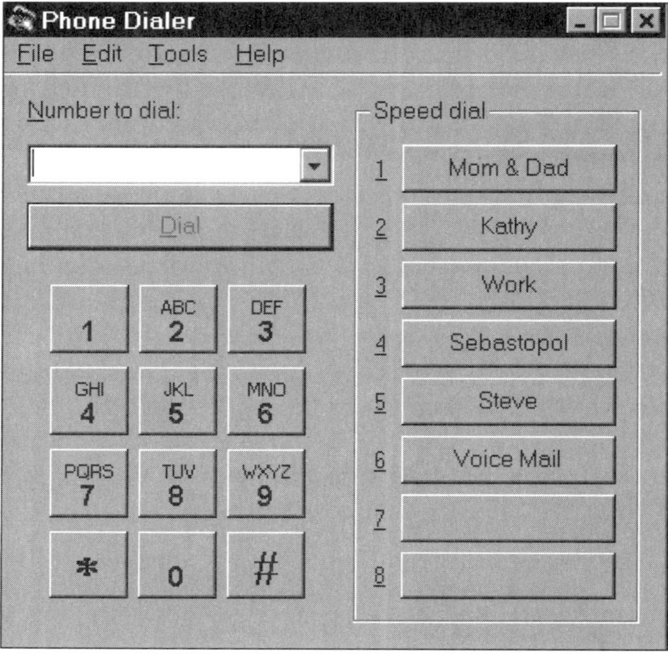

Figure 4.12: The Phone Dialer can store up to eight frequently used numbers.

you use to type in new telephone numbers. This stores recently dialed numbers even after you close the Phone Dialer window.

Programming Speed Dials To program the speed dial buttons, click on the Edit menu and select the Speed Dial command. The Edit Speed Dial window displays the eight buttons and two fill-in areas. In the space on the left, type in what you want the button to say. In the space on the right, type in the telephone number you want this button to dial. Include the area code, even if it's the same as the area code you're in now; Phone Dialer is smart enough to ignore the area code if it's the same as your own, but it will need the area code when you call from out of town. Phone Dialer automatically starts with the first speed dial button unless you click one of them first to select it (that's why the eight buttons are displayed for you).

Making Phone Dialer Smart If you use Phone Dialer on a portable computer with a modem, you can make it smart about traveling. Otherwise, using Phone Dialer on the road could be a trial. For example, when you're in the office, you might need to dial 9 before all outgoing calls. When you're in a hotel, you might need to dial a different number to get an outside line. And when you call from different area codes, you have to dial longer numbers to reach your office. Phone Dialer can handle all of these little complications for you.

Click on the Tools menu and select the Dialing Properties command. A big properties sheet, like the one in Figure 4.13, pops up. The idea here is to tell Phone Dialer everything about the place you are calling *from*. Based on that information, Phone Dialer will know how to get an outside line, what area code it needs to dial, and so on. You can assign a name to your current location, like Home or Office or Motel 6, and Phone Dialer will remember the particulars for each

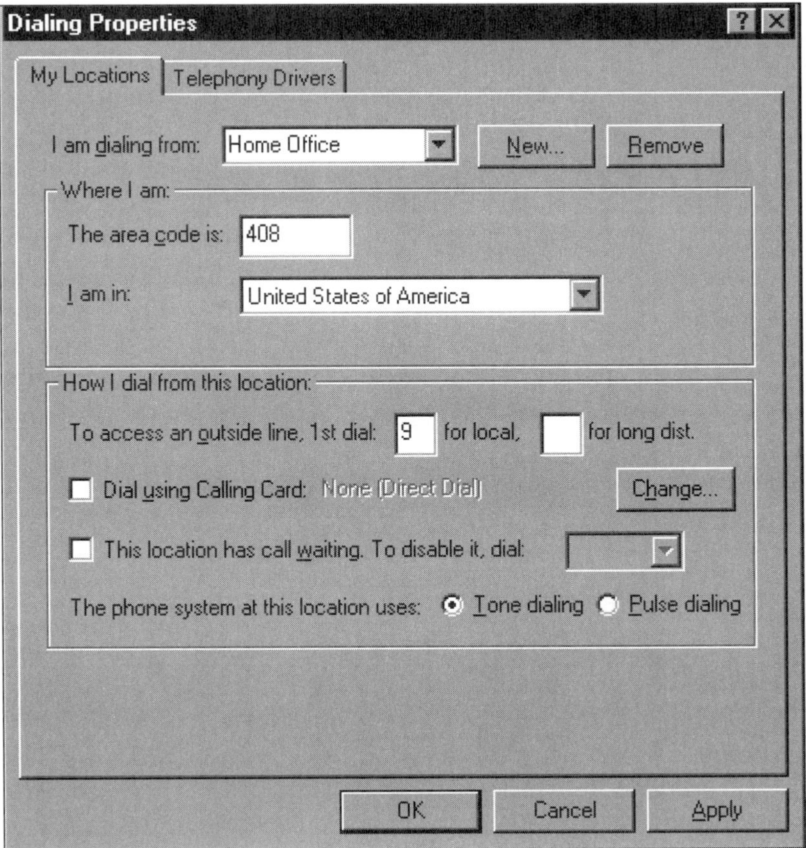

Figure 4.13: By informing Phone Dialer about the phone you're calling from, it can make the correct decisions about long distance numbers, access codes, and so on.

location. You would typically want to set up at least two or three different locations, one for each place you visit frequently.

Creating a New Location to Call From Starting at the top of the window, give the location a name and click the New button. The name can be anything that helps you remember where you are. Then fill in the area code for that location, the country it's in, the procedure for reaching an outside line, instructions for disabling call waiting, type of calling card, and so forth.

Selecting the Location You Are Calling From Before you make a call with the Phone Dialer, be sure you've selected the actual location you're calling from. Phone Dialer uses this information to place the call. When you take your computer to another location, like when you're traveling, be sure to select that location (or create a new one) before you place any calls from there.

Dialing Hints Although Phone Dialer's location names can be a real helper when you're on the road, they can sometimes get in the way. If you're using Phone Dialer to dial a colleague's four-digit extension from work, for example, Phone Dialer can get confused and try to add an area code to the number and botch the whole thing up. To bypass all of Phone Dialer's well-intentioned help, just enter the digits with no spaces, plus-signs, dashes, or anything. If you type "just plain numbers," Phone Dialer will dial just plain numbers. If you enter the phone number with parentheses, spaces, and whatnot like you normally should, Phone Dialer will evaluate the telephone number and step in as required.

HyperTerminal

HyperTerminal is a new twist on an age-old type of computer application, the modem communications program. HyperTerminal is used to call other computers or on-line services over the telephone using a modem. It's not very fancy—which is why it comes for free with Windows NT—but it is useful for communicating and exchanging information with other computers—which is why you should learn to use it.

If you subscribe to a commercial on-line service like America Online, CompuServe, or a similar service, you probably won't need

HyperTerminal. All these services come with their own special communications programs that are much more elaborate. But if you want to call a simple, basic service like the National Institute of Standards and Technology's on-line atomic clock, then HyperTerminal is just the ticket. In fact, we'll use NIST's on-line clock to walk you through your first HyperTerminal session.

HyperTerminal got its name because it allows your PC to act like a twenty-year-old computer terminal. Back before everybody had one, computers were big, ugly things that hid in a back room. To use one, you had to have a terminal on your desk. These so-called "dumb terminals" were just a screen and a keyboard plugged into a long wire that connected the terminal to the big, ugly computer in the back room. If you were far enough away, that wire might be a telephone cord and you would have to dial into the computer to get access. Well, those computers are still around, and sometimes you might need to call one of them.

Starting a HyperTerminal Session When you select HyperTerminal from the Accessories menu, you'll see a normal application window open up as shown in Figure 4.14. After a brief advertisement from its creators, you will see a window that asks you to enter a name and pick an icon.

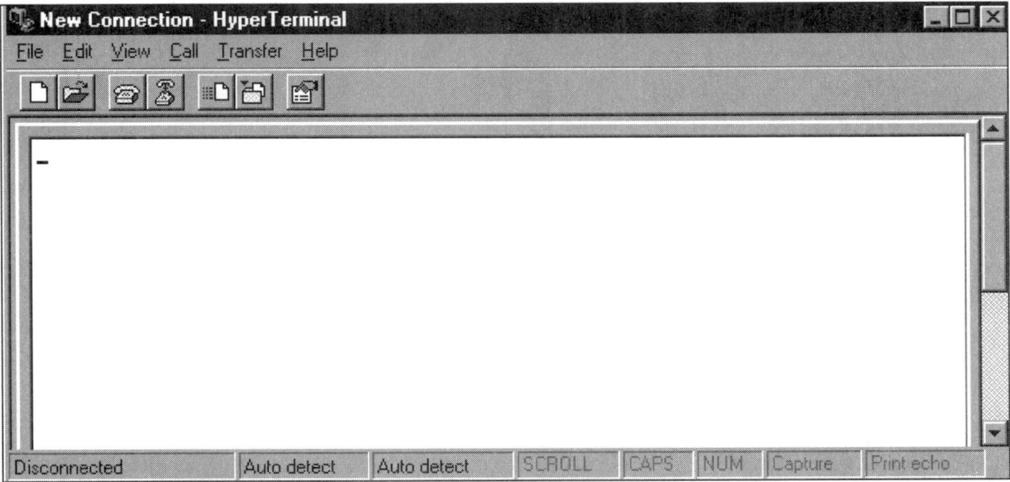

Figure 4.14: HyperTerminal acts as a remote terminal to another, remote computer.

What HyperTerminal is asking you to do is create a shortcut to the on-line service or computer you are about to call. After you do, HyperTerminal will create a new icon for you that you can double-click and be connected directly to that computer again. You won't have to go through this procedure every time, only the first time you connect to a new service. Since we're calling the atomic clock, scroll through the gallery of icons until you find one that looks appropriate and click it once. You should also type a descriptive name in the space provided, like NIST Atomic Clock in Colorado. See Figure 4.15 for examples.

After picking an icon, typing a name, and clicking OK, HyperTerminal shows you a second window asking for particulars about the location you want to call. Notice that if you've been through the setup procedure for Phone Dialer described above, HyperTerminal already knows what country you live in and what your area code is. In other words, HyperTerminal is assuming you want to call somebody or something in your local area. If you live near Boulder, fine. Otherwise, you'll have to change some of these settings. For the area code, enter 303. For the phone number, enter 494-4774. Check that the country and type of modem are correct, and click OK.

The third and final window is asking you where you are calling from. This information is also taken from the data you entered when

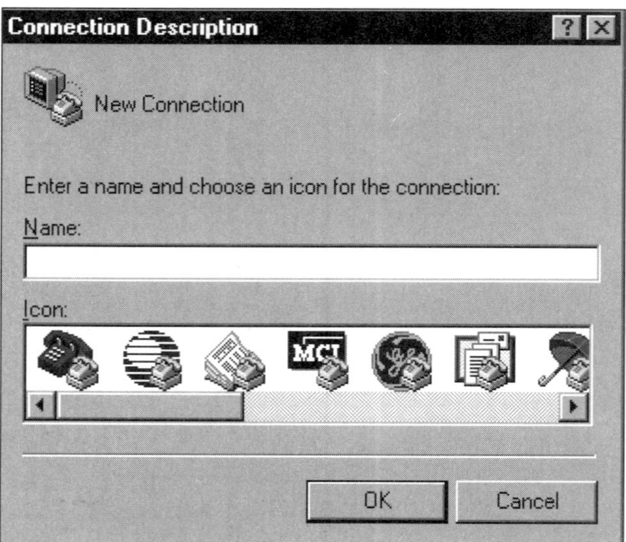

Figure 4.15: You should assign an icon to frequently dialled numbers to make them more convenient to reach.

you set up Phone Dialer. Select your current location from the drop-down list and HyperTerminal will make the remaining adjustments automatically. Clicking OK will make your connection.

If all goes well, the NIST computer should answer after one ring. It will then start reporting the exact time on your screen, repeating once every second, as Figure 4.16 shows. (You can use this information to set your watch or your computer's clock.) You can watch this for awhile if you like; the NIST computer will automatically hang up on you after 40 seconds. If you wish to hang up sooner, click the disconnect button on the toolbar or select the Disconnect command from the Call menu.

Before hanging up, you should try talking back to the other system. Although the atomic clock is not very interactive (after all, what could you ever tell it?), you can type a single question mark and it will display a screen full of helpful instructions. You might want to save these instructions and read them later using the technique for capturing input described below.

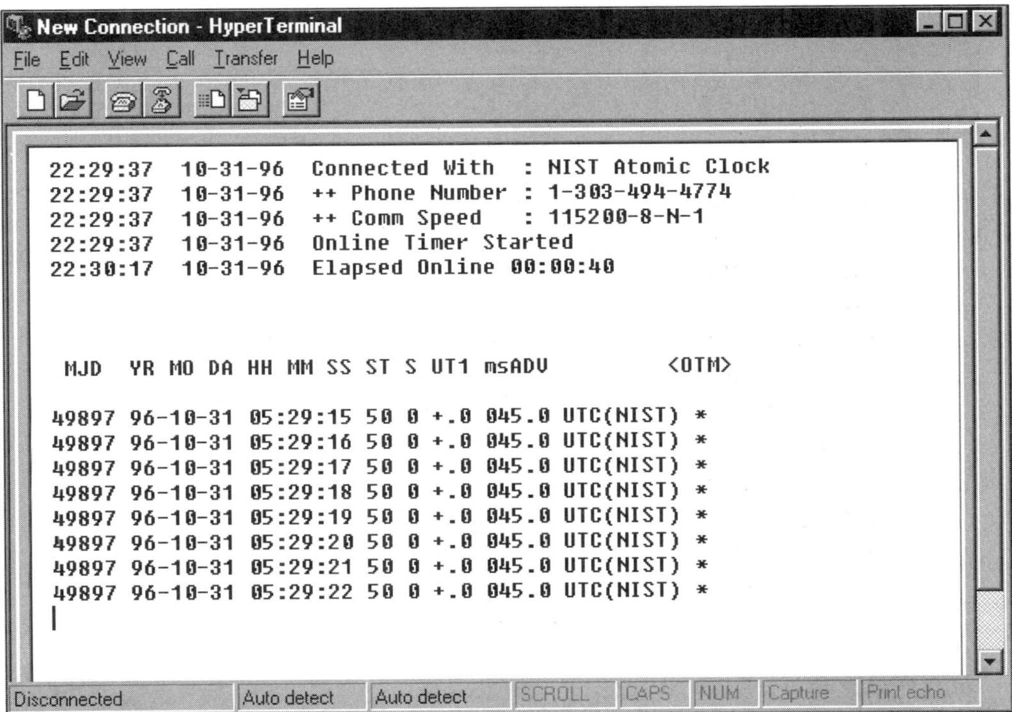

Figure 4.16: A test connection with the atomic clock assures that HyperTerminal is working correctly.

Communicating with Another Computer The basic use of HyperTerminal is to communicate with another computer. When you type on your keyboard, those keys are sent to the other computer, and when the other computer sends something back, that text is displayed on your HyperTerminal window. HyperTerminal will not display any fancy pictures or graphics—this is for pure text communication only. That's why the commercial on-line services have their own software.

You can also send files to the other computer and receive files from it. These files can be anything: pictures, spreadsheets, documents, system files, or whatever. HyperTerminal cannot display these kinds of files, but it can transmit and receive them. To send a file, click the Transfer menu, then Send File. (You can also click the Send icon on the toolbar.) HyperTerminal displays a window asking what file you want to send and how you want to send it. The latter question can be a little bewildering to the uninitiated. Over the years, many different methods have been developed for transmitting complex files over the telephone lines without scrambling the files. The Protocol drop-down list lets you choose one of these many methods. The method, or protocol, you use is irrelevant, as long as your computer and the other computer you are communicating with use the same one. If you have no idea what protocol the other computer uses, guess.

Receiving a file works the same way. Click the Transfer menu or the toolbar button and answer the questions about transfer protocol and the name to give the file you receive.

Keeping a Record of What You Do HyperTerminal can save, or capture, any incoming messages from your screen and save them in a file. Of course, you could highlight the text in the HyperTerminal window and use the normal cut, copy, and paste commands, but the Capture command is more automatic. Selecting Capture Text from the Transfer menu starts the process. All the data you receive on your screen from that point will be copied into a file that you name. The longer you stay connected to the other computer, the larger this file grows. You can stop capturing incoming text at any time by selecting the Capture Text command again, and then selecting Stop or Pause from the cascading menu.

Windows NT Games

Windows NT comes with an assortment of games that you can play (when you're not working, of course). These games may not have all been put on your computer when Windows NT was first loaded, so consider this section an invitation to add the rest of them to your PC.

Solitaire

The Windows NT Solitaire program has been around as long as Windows. Since every one of the millions of Windows users worldwide has a free copy of Solitaire, it's probably one of the most-played computer games of all time. If you're familiar with the actual card game, playing Solitaire will be no problem for you. If you're not, read on and learn how to have a little fun with your computer.

When you start a game of Solitaire, you should see a window more or less like the one in Figure 4.17. Your cards will be dealt differently, so don't be surprised if they're arranged differently than the example shows. You have seven cards arranged face up in columns, with the rest of the deck stacked up in the upper left corner of the window.

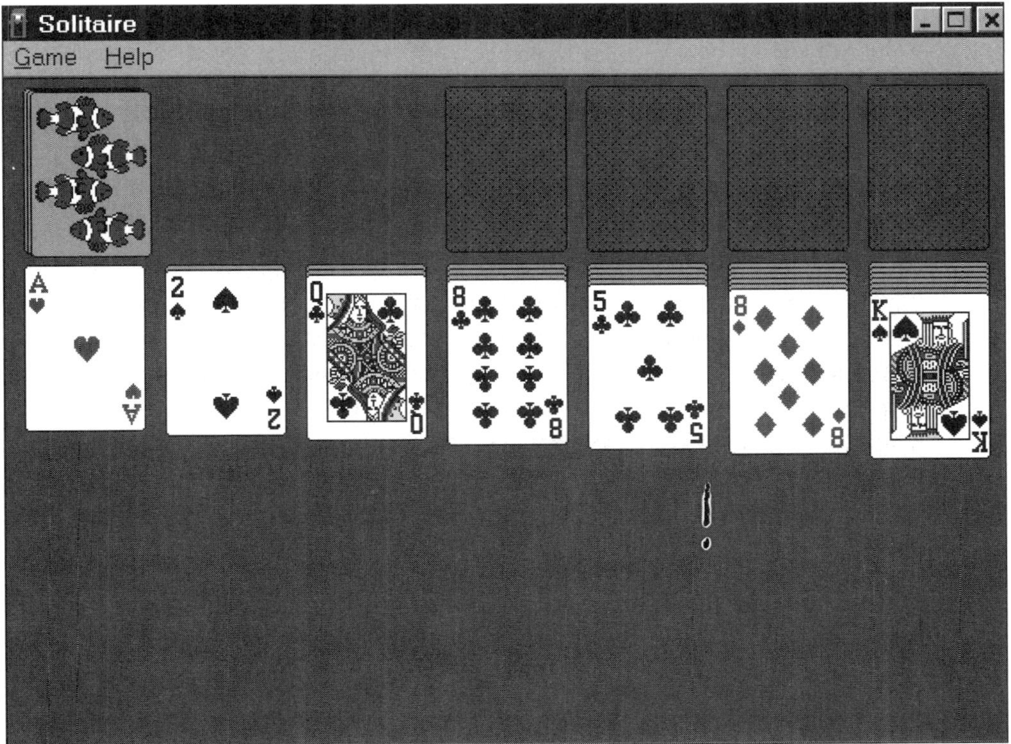

Figure 4.17: Everyone has time for a little Solitaire now and then.

There are also four shaded places near the top of the window for you to place your cards as you play.

Rules of the Game The game is very old, and is generally called Klondike by card-game aficionados. Although it is only one of a whole class of solitaire card games, most people are so familiar with it, they just call it solitaire. The object of the game is to get all 52 cards in the deck onto those four shaded squares near the top. All the hearts go in one pile, all the spades in another pile, and so on. The rules are easy, but winning the game is hard. Not all games can even be won, so don't feel bad if you have to play a dozen games or so before winning your first one.

You have to build the four piles in order: ace, two, three, and so on up to king. One pile is used for each suit, so after the ace of diamonds comes the two of diamonds, then the three of diamonds, and so on. When (or if) you build all four piles up to the king, you've won. Naturally, all the cards aren't dealt out in such a way that you can do this easily. That would be no fun. You have to move one card at a time, and only if the card is face up. In the example, the ace of hearts is already face-up, so you should move it directly onto one of the shared squares. Unfortunately, the two of hearts is not showing so you can't add it to the pile.

You can also move cards from one of the seven rows to another, but only if you follow the rules. First, the card has to be face up. Second, you can only place one card on another if they are different colors (hearts or diamonds on top of spades or clubs, and vice versa) *and* they are in descending order (seven on an eight, for example, or two on a three). Moving cards from row to row this way allows you to expose buried cards. When you move a card to another row and the card below it is face down, you can turn it face up. Eventually you'll have to turn all the cards face up to be able to put them in the stacks at the top, right? If you move the last card from a row, it leaves a gap in the rows. You can place a king there if you want to start a new row. Finally, as you work through the game you will build lots of cards arranged in black-red-black rows. You can move entire groups of these cards to another row the same way you can move one card.

Last rule: If you get stuck and can't make a move (this happens a lot) you can turn over new cards from the rest of the deck, which is stacked up near the upper left corner of the Solitaire window. This exposes new cards that you can play with.

Playing the Game Moving your cards is as easy as can be. Simply drag any face-up card to where you want it to be. When a card is face down, click it once to turn it face up. Same goes for the rest of the deck: click it once to turn over new cards. If a card can go to onto its pile at the top, double-clicking it will send it there. Solitaire won't let you cheat or break the rules: you can't drag a card to anyplace it isn't supposed to go.

Game Options Under the Game menu is an Options command. Selecting Options allows you to change one rule of the game and how the game is scored. Purists claim that you should always turn over three cards when clicking the deck, but it's easier to turn them over one at a time. You can also choose between Vegas scoring (in dollars, starting from -$52) and Standard scoring (in points, starting from zero), or no score. If you want a special challenge, you can also play a timed game.

Also under the Games menu is the Deck command. Clicking this command lets you pick the card backs for your game. Click on a design you like and then click OK. The same card design will be used forever until you change it again.

FreeCell

FreeCell is another type of solo card game, but it's much different than Solitaire. While it has not actually been proven, FreeCell is believed to be 100% winnable—if you're good enough.

Rules of the Game The object of the game is to take all the cards off the playing field and put them onto four stacks. Each stack is grouped by suit, with the cards stacked in ascending order from ace to king. So far, this sounds just like Solitaire. Like Solitaire, you move the cards around on the playing field and arrange them in descending order, alternating black and red cards as you go. To help you, there are four "free cells" in the upper left corner of the window where you can temporarily store four cards that are blocking your move—hence, the name of the game.

If a column becomes empty, you can also move cards into the empty column, but unlike Solitaire, you don't have to start a new column with a king. Thus, empty columns are kind of like additional free cells.

Playing the Game The FreeCell game is unique because it allows you to "stack the deck" before you play. This feature will let you play along with the example game in your book. When you start FreeCell, click on the Game menu and choose the Select Game command (or just press <F3>). FreeCell will ask you for a number. You can enter any number from 1 through 32,000. Each number deals the cards a different way. If you enter number 8046, your cards will be dealt exactly like they are in Figure 4.18.

There are two ways to move cards in FreeCell. The most common way is to click once on a card or stack of cards and then click again on

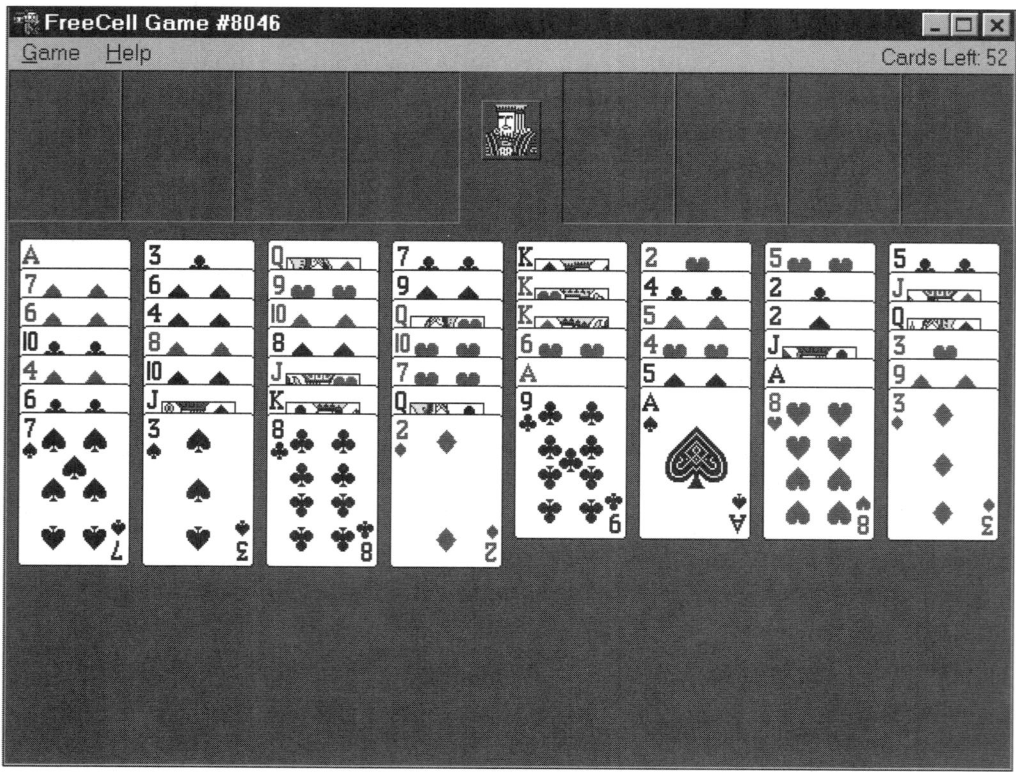

Figure 4.18: FreeCell is another solo card game that's much tougher than Solitaire.

the space where you want them to go. The second way is to double-click on a card to send it to a free cell.

Since the object is to move the cards, beginning with aces, up to the four cells near the upper right corner, and you have an ace of spades already showing, you can double click this card and it will automatically move to the correct space. Try it now. You'll notice that the card moves to a free cell first because you double-clicked it, but then it moves itself to the final stack.

Now click the two of diamonds and then click the three of spades. (The down-arrow marker indicates that you can make a legal move.) Double-click the queen of clubs to temporarily move it to a free cell. Move the seven of hearts over to the eight of clubs.

Watch as you move the nine of clubs onto the ten of hearts. This automatically releases an ace that was trapped under the nine. Move the eight of hearts onto the nine of clubs to release another ace.

Look at the fourth column of cards. See the 10-9-8 sequence? Those cards are in order, but they're in the wrong order. To reverse them quickly, let the computer do the chore for you. Click anywhere on that column, and then click on the jack of clubs. See how the computer uses the free cells to move all the cards in order for you?

Next click on the seventh column, where the eight of hearts is now, and move it back to the column that ends in the fourth column. The computer can only move the cards for you if there are enough empty spaces to accommodate the cards during the move. At the same time, you freed up a pair of twos. Nice work.

Move the seven of spades to the eight of hearts. Move the six of hearts to the seven of spades. Move the five of spades six of hearts and then move the four of hearts on top of it.

Bring the queen of clubs back down and put it on the king of diamonds. Move the five of diamonds to the six of clubs and then the four of clubs as well. Move all three (the four, five, and six) to the seven of hearts.

Double-click the four of diamonds to move it to a free cell. Move the ten of clubs to the empty column. Double-click the three of diamonds to move it to a free cell, then move the nine of diamonds to the ten of clubs. Notice that the three of hearts automatically moves to the home cells. Your deck should now look like Figure 4.19.

Double-click the six and seven of diamonds to send them to their home cells. Move the four of diamonds to the diamonds' home cell. You need to free up the five of diamonds. Do this by moving the four of clubs to the five of hearts, then move the five, six, and seven of dia-

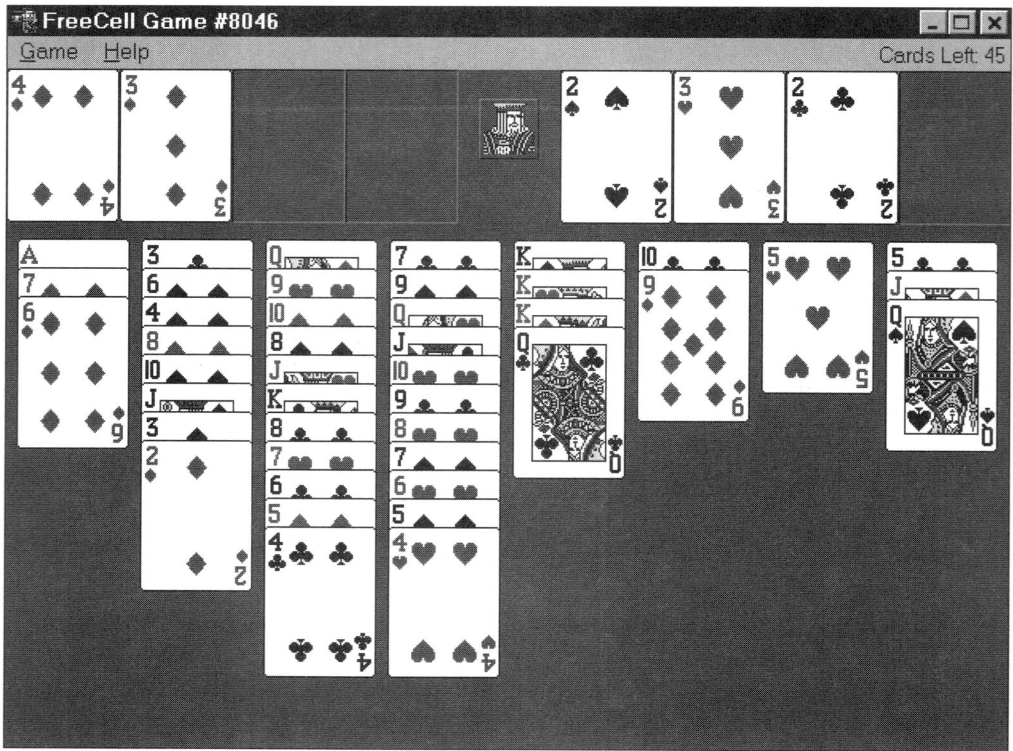

Figure 4.19: Almost ready to win at FreeCell.

monds to their home cell. Double-click on the jack of spades, ten of spades, and eight of diamonds to move them to free cells. The four of spades will automatically fly to the home cell. Next, double-click the six of spades and watch the cards fly.

Can you move the queen of spades and jack of diamonds to free up the five of clubs? From here on out, there's plenty of maneuvering room, so see if you can free up the rest of the cards and win the game. Good luck.

Game Options You can right-click a partially obscured card to see what it is. You can also disable the ability to double-click a card and send it to a free cell. And, you can undo your last move by clicking the Game menu and selecting the Undo command.

Minesweeper

Minesweeper is a fun game and the kind of game that you could only play on a computer. Your job is to clear an area of explosive mines. You have to do this through a combination of guessing, deduction, and plain luck. If you clear all the mines without setting one off, you win. There are many skill levels, so Minesweeper can be a challenge for years to come.

Rules of the Game When Minesweeper starts, you are looking at your "minefield," as Figure 4.20 shows. It's a field of 64 squares in an 8-by-8 grid. Under ten of those squares there are mines. Your job: find them.

The two sets of numbers are the quantity of undiscovered mines remaining (on the left), and the elapsed time, in seconds (on the right). Assuming you win, your score is determined by how quickly you cleared the minefield. The happy face in the middle is largely for show. To start, either click the happy face, or—the more conventional approach—click the Game menu and select New. You can also press <F2> to start a new game.

Every square in the game is either a mine or not a mine. If it's not a mine, the square will contain a number that tells you how many mines are next to it. Those numbers are your only tool to discover where the

Figure 4.20: Mine Sweeper is a simple game of chance and logic.

mines are. Through careful clicking and logical deduction, you can figure out where all the mines are, based on the numbers.

Playing the Game Your first step is to click a square at random. Hopefully, this won't uncover a mine or your game is already over. Otherwise, it will uncover either a number or a blank space. Each number is the number of adjacent squares that contain a mine. It won't tell you which square(s) contain the mine(s), only how many there are. Your job is to figure out which squares those must be. If a square has a 3 in it, like in Figure 4.21, then three of the eight adjoining squares contain a mine.

You can cautiously click around the immediate area of the first square, or click an entirely different square. Sometimes you get lucky and locate an area with no mines nearby. In that event, Minesweeper automatically uncovers all the adjacent squares that also have no mines nearby. That doesn't really give anything away, it just saves you a little tedious clicking.

You don't have to rely entirely on your memory when playing Minesweeper. You can use your right mouse button as a helper. If you believe a particular square contains a mine, right-clicking that square places a red flag on it. If you're not certain, right-clicking again will place a question mark on the square. Right-clicking a third time will remove the flag or the question mark.

Figure 4.21: There are three mines nearby. Can you find them?

Chapter 5

CHANGING APPEARANCES AND CUSTOMIZING WINDOWS NT

Windows NT is all about appearances. It's visual. You look at icons, you open and close windows, you drag scroll bars, you push buttons, and you pull down menus. Those windows, buttons, and menus are what make Windows NT Windows NT. And you know what? You can change the appearance of every one of those elements. Windows NT gives you an amazing amount of freedom to customize, tinker, and tweak until your computer is looking and acting just the way you want it to. In this chapter, you'll learn about dozens of useful and little-known ways you can put your own personal imprint on Windows NT.

Changing Your Start Button

Everyone likes to customize the Start button. It's one of the newest and coolest parts of Windows NT and the most obvious change from earlier versions of Windows NT. The Start button keeps your most commonly used programs and documents at your fingertips, just a mouse-click away.

When you start using Windows NT, you will see a handful of items on the Start button that its creators thought would be useful. The Run command, the Find command, Help, and others are all there. If you upgraded from an earlier version of Windows NT, most or all of your original Program Manager groups should be there, too. But there's no reason you have to stick with the programs and groups Windows NT gives you. You can customize your Start button to have all the things you want, and to remove the things you don't.

There are only a few things on the Start menu that you can't change. All seven items on the Start menu shown in Figure 5.1 (Shutdown, Run, Help, Find, Settings, Documents, and Programs) are permanent. You can't really change the list of recent documents in the Documents menu; Windows NT does that automatically as you open new documents. You can customize the Programs item, though. Although the Programs item itself is permanent, you can change the programs it points to. In addition to these seven fixed items, you can add as many more menu items as you like.

Like most things in Windows NT, there are many different ways you can add and remove items from the Start button. It doesn't really matter which of the following methods you choose; work along with the examples and try them all.

How to Add Something to the Start Button Perhaps the slickest and easiest way to add something to the Start button is to simply drag it there. If you see the icon of the item you want, drag it directly on top of the Start button, and you're done. It doesn't matter if you use the right or the left mouse button to drag the item.

The only drawback to this approach is that the new item always appears at the top of the Start menu, above the Programs item, as Figure 5.2 shows. You can't add items to the cascading menus for the Programs group this way. Also, there's no way to remove items this way—you can't drag things off the Start button.

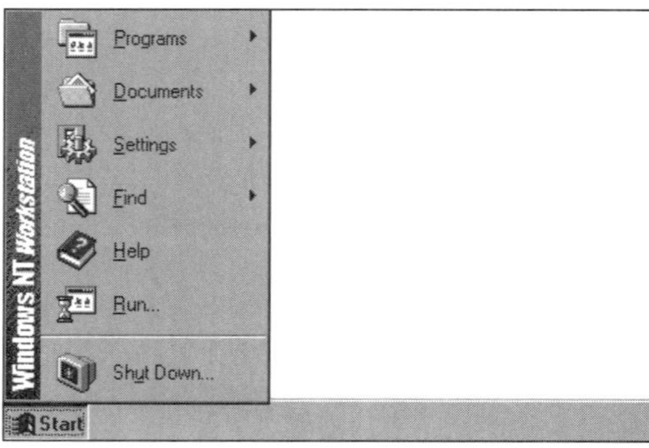

Figure 5.1: The first seven commands on the Start menu are permanent.

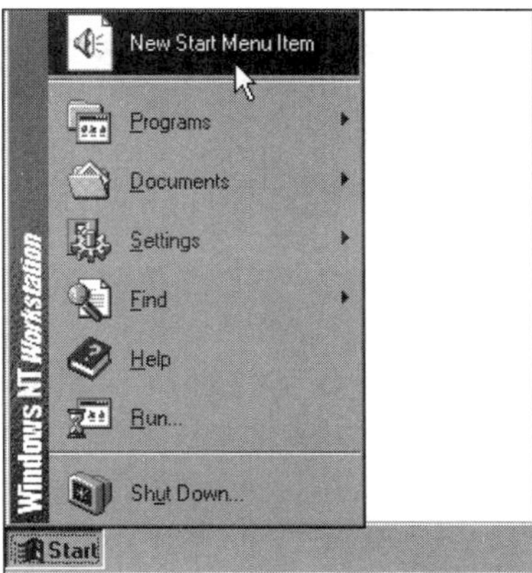

Figure 5.2: Dragging an icon to the Start menu adds it to the top of the list.

Another Way to Add Something to the Start Button If you right-click on the Start button, you'll see a short pop-up menu. Selecting Open displays the Start Menu folder with the Programs folder inside it. You can drag any icon into the Start Menu folder to add it to top of the start menu. If you prefer, you can double-click the Programs folder to open it and then drag items into one of its folders, like Accessories or StartUp. Opening the Accessories folder will let you add items to one of its groups, like Games or System Tools.

Yet Another Way to Add Something to the Start Button We'll start by clicking on Start. Then hover over the Settings command, move right, and click on Taskbar. You'll see a properties sheet with two tabs like the one in Figure 5.3. The first tab, Taskbar Options, doesn't help you, so click on the other tab, called Start Menu Programs.

The Start Menu Programs tab, shown in Figure 5.4, actually lets you do two things at once: change the programs on the start menu and clear out the recent documents listed in the Documents command. To add or remove programs on the Start button you should use, obviously enough, the Add and Remove buttons, respectively. We'll look at the Advanced button a little later on. For now, click the Add button.

1. Clicking the Add button starts you on a little three-step journey. The first thing Windows NT needs to know is the name and location of the item you want to add. This is not necessarily the title you want to appear on the Start menu, but the

Figure 5.3: The Taskbar's property sheet includes a tab for modifying the Start menu.

file's technical description: the name of the file, its path, and what disk it's stored on. Rather than type this in, it's almost always better to just click on the Browse button.

Clicking on Browse opens a file-browsing window similar to the one you get when you're using the Explorer or when you load or save a document. A disk is listed in the drop-down list at the top of the window, and the folders within that disk are arranged in the big area below. Your job is to point to the item you want to add to the Start menu. It means you'll have to know where that program is stored and click your way to it, but Windows NT is patient. Click on folders until you find the item you want. If you have to search a different disk, click on the drop-down list near the top of the window. When you find the exact program you want, double-click on it. Windows NT obediently fills in the onerous technical path and file name, and takes you back to the previous window.

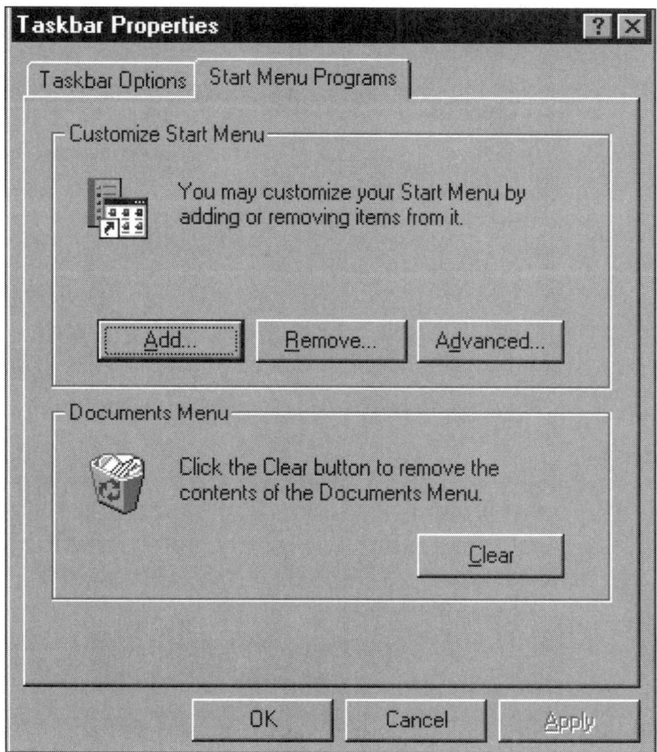

Figure 5.4: To add something to the Start menu, just click on Add.

Your first step is completed. Leave the path name alone and click the Next> button to proceed.

2. Now you need to show Windows NT where exactly on the Start menu you want this new item to go. Windows NT shows you a little diagram of how all the current items are arranged, and you get to point to the place you want your new item to go. Take a moment to study this little diagram. Some items are indented to the right, which shows you that they are actually cascading menus from other items on the Start menu. For example, in Figure 5.5, Games is indented under Accessories, which is itself indented under Programs. Sure enough, clicking the Start button shows Programs; hovering over Programs reveals Accessories (among other things); hovering over Accessories reveals Games. After you've figured out where you think this new program belongs, highlight that folder.

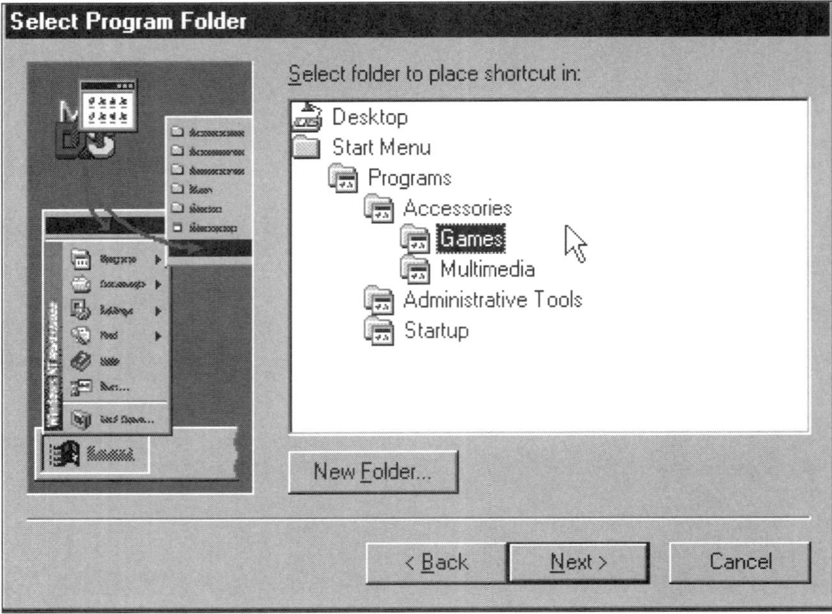

Figure 5.5: Windows NT walks you through the procedure for adding items to the Start menu.

By the way, there's no wrong answer to this question. This is purely aesthetics. You can arrange things on your Start button any way you'd like. If you don't like the indented structure already in place, you can add another cascading folder of your own by clicking on the New Folder button.

When you've highlighted a location for your new item, click on the Next> button.

3. Now to the fun part. You can type in anything you want to title your new item. Windows NT will suggest something mundane here, but feel free to give your new item a more descriptive title. You can tell by the size of the fill-in box that you've got a lot of space to enter a name. When you're done, click the Finish button. That's it!

   Windows NT takes you back to the first add/remove tab of the properties. If you want to add another item, repeat the last three steps. If you're done adding and removing items from the Start button for now, click on OK at the bottom of the window. Try out your new Start button!

Still Another Way to Add Something to the Start Button This way is not really very different from the previous method, so it only counts as a slight variation. To begin, right-click on the Taskbar at the bottom of your screen. Be sure to pick a blank space on the Taskbar, not on top of one of the application buttons (the far right end is a good place). When the mini-menu pops up, select Properties. You'll find yourself at the Taskbar Properties sheet just like in the previous exercise. Continue from Step 1 there.

One More Way to Add Something to the Start Button The Start button is really just another folder in the Windows NT main folder. If you're handy with the Explorer, you can see what's already in the Start menu and add or remove things from it. (If you're not familiar with Explorer and would like to learn, turn to Chapter 2.) Here's what to do:

1. To start Explorer, click on the Start button. Hover over Programs, then move right and click on Windows NT Explorer.
2. Find the main folder for Windows NT. You might have to navigate a bit to find the right disk, too. When you've found the Windows NT main folder, double-click it. Now look for the folder called Profiles and double-click it. Double-click one of the user's folders (Administrators, All Users, John, Mary, and the like). Finally, open the Start Menu folder. There are probably more folders inside the Start Menu folder, such as Programs, and even more folders inside Programs, like Accessories and Games. Keep clicking and opening up the folders until you've opened up the entire Start Menu directory structure, as shown in Figure 5.6.
3. If you highlight each of the folders in turn, you will see what programs and/or documents are stored in each one. Each file corresponds to an item on the Start menu and each folder corresponds to a category or a group of items. You can organize and rearrange these files and folders any way you like. Moving files from one folder to another will move its corresponding item on the Start menu. Try it!

   You can also place items in the Start Menu folder itself. When you click the Start button, you'll see your item at the

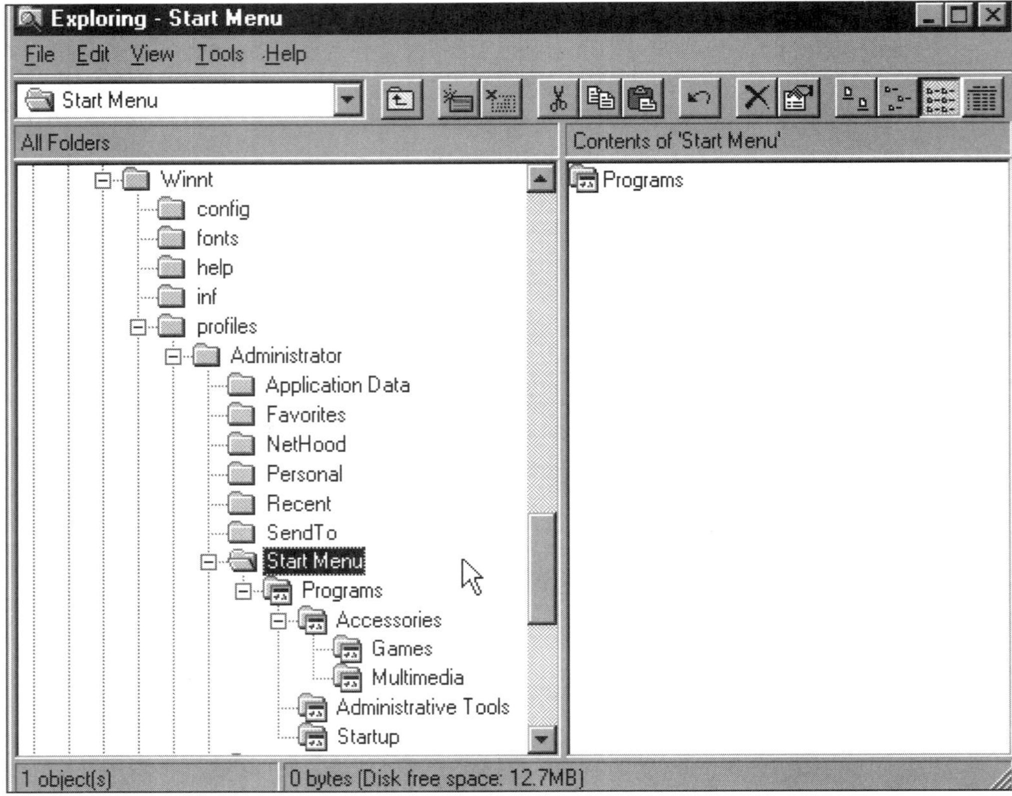

Figure 5.6: You can also add items to the Start menu by dragging them to the proper folder.

very top, just above the Programs item. Just like all the other menus, you can add as many items as you want this way.

Notice that all the folders contained within the Start Menu folder can have a mixture of files and other folders in them. An example is the Accessories folder, which has several programs in it as well as one or two additional folders, like Games. Some people like to organize their Start menu so that each level of the menu (or branch of the tree, if you like) contains only other folders (branches) with no items (or leaves) until the end.

If you enjoy tinkering with Explorer, try renaming the Programs folder inside the Start Menu folder and watch what happens to the Start menu. Nothing changes. You can even move the entire Programs folder someplace else (try it) and it won't effect the Start menu. The Programs folder is magic and its name and location are hard-coded into Windows NT.

The Final Way to Add Something to the Start Button If you're not comfortable using the Windows NT Explorer, you can accomplish the same result as in the previous example by double-clicking on My Computer. This opens up a somewhat more friendly window with a view into your disks. Just like in the previous example, you need to find the Windows NT home folder, then open the Start Menu folder. You can place new items in the Start Menu folder, or you can open up the folders inside it and place your new item in one of them.

Changing the Taskbar

The Taskbar across the bottom of your screen is one of your most useful tools. You rely on the Taskbar (or you should) to switch between running applications, to see what's already running, and to start and stop applications. But did you know that you can move the Taskbar? Or that you can make it thicker so that it holds more buttons? Well, you can.

Changing the Location of the Taskbar You can place the Taskbar on any one of the four sides of your screen. It's traditional to have it across the bottom, but if you prefer another side, move it! To move the Taskbar, simply click on an empty space (this may be difficult if you have many tasks running) and drag the Taskbar to any edge of your screen. If you place it on the right edge, your screen will look like Figure 5.7.

Changing the Thickness of the Taskbar You can also make the Taskbar thicker, so it can hold more buttons without crowding. Simply place your mouse pointer along the upper edge of the Taskbar (assuming it's still on the bottom of your screen) and drag it upwards slightly. The Taskbar will "click" into place. If you have a full bar, some of the buttons will move to the second row. You can make the Taskbar as thick as you want, creating room for dozens of buttons. You can make the Taskbar thinner again by dragging it back down.

If the Taskbar is placed on the right or left edge of your screen, you can still make it thicker or thinner, but it does not "click" into various thickness. Instead, you can control exactly how thick you want the Taskbar to be.

Making the Taskbar Disappear The Taskbar has a property sheet, just like most other items. To see it, right-click on a blank area of the

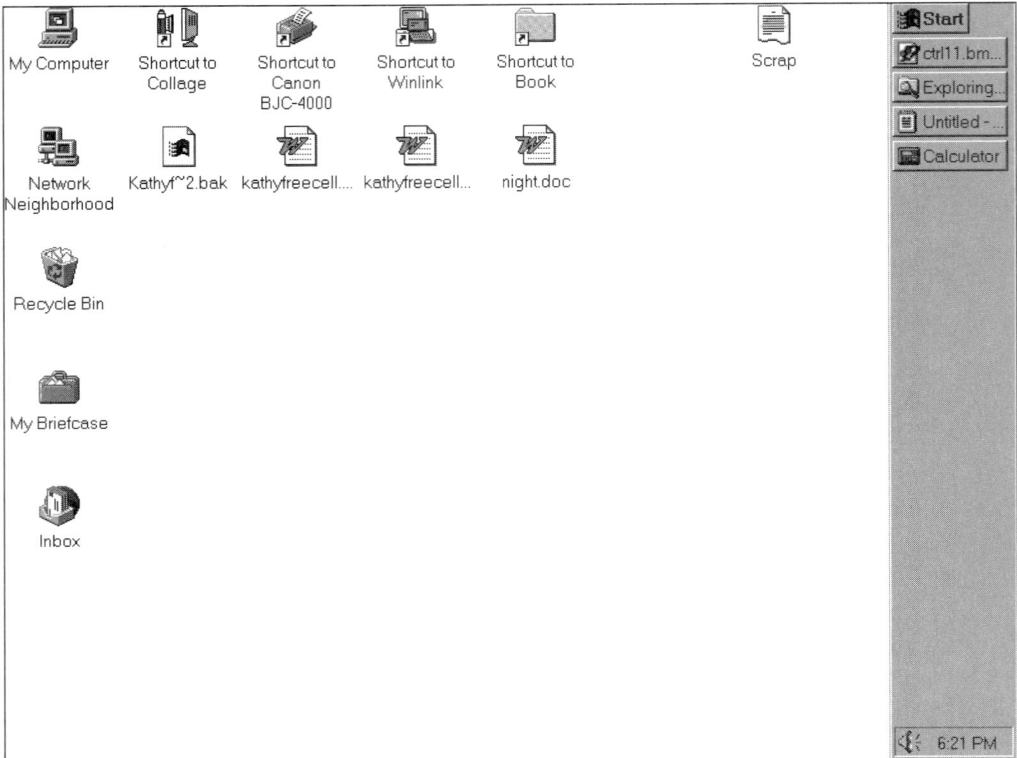

Figure 5.7: You can move the Taskbar to any side of your screen.

Taskbar and select Properties from the shortcut menu. The Taskbar Properties sheet, shown in Figure 5.8, has four options you can select.

The first option guarantees that the Taskbar is always visible, even if you try to cover it with another window. If this option is not checked, the Taskbar can be covered, which you may not want to happen.

The second option makes the Taskbar disappear right after you use it. It will hide until you click the Start button or one of the other Taskbar buttons again. If this option is checked, the Taskbar shrinks to a small gray line at the bottom of your screen. Placing your mouse pointer over it will make the Taskbar reappear.

The third option selects between big and small icons on the Start menu; choose whichever option you prefer. The fourth and final option allows you to either hide or show the Windows NT clock. If you prefer to see the clock, make sure this option is checked.

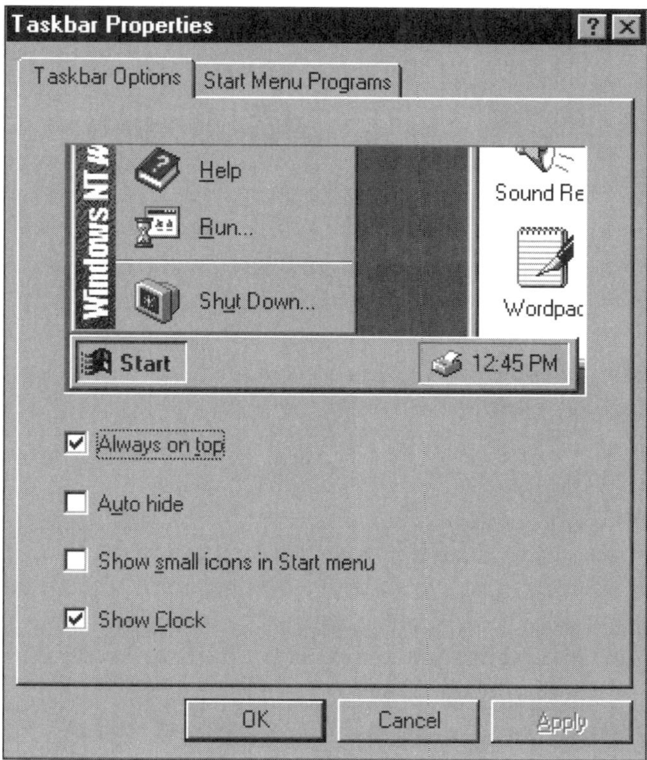

Figure 5.8: The Taskbar property sheet gives you four options for controlling the appearance of your Taskbar.

Changing What You See in a Window

When you double-click the icon called My Computer in the upper left corner of your screen, you'll see a window open up onto your entire computer. Through this window, and other ones like it, you can see everything that's stored on your PC. Every application you have installed, all your work files, the system files that make Windows NT work, and everything else that's stored on your computer will appear in these windows. All you have to do is open the window and look in.

Double-click in the My Computer icon now and you should see a window not too different from the one in Figure 5.9. This window is showing you an icon for every disk inside your computer, plus a couple of extra folders filled with goodies. The computer in the figure has seven disks: a floppy disk drive, five hard disks, and a CD-ROM. You might have a different number of disks on your computer.

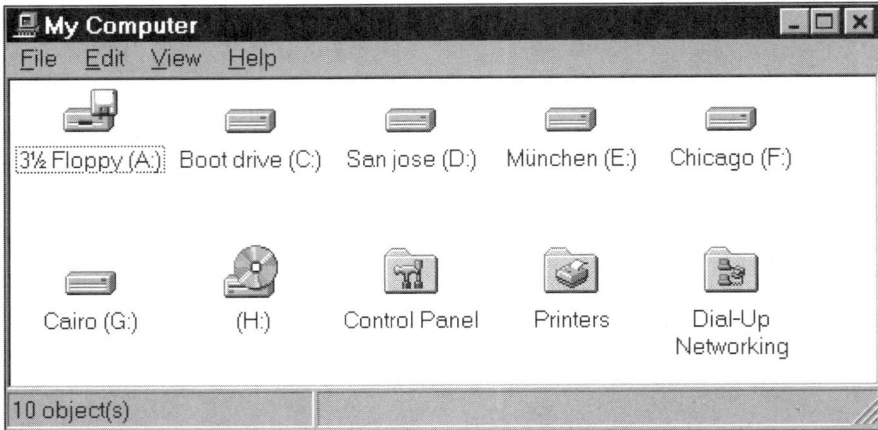

Figure 5.9: A normal window view includes a number of different icons.

If you double-click any of the disk icons themselves, a new window will open up and show you what's inside that disk. Double-click the icon for your disk C now. You will see another window, like the one in Figure 5.10. Double-clicking on one of the folders in the window will open that folder to show you what's inside, and so on. You can repeat

Figure 5.10: Each disk or folder generally contains more folders.

this procedure indefinitely, delving deeper and deeper into folders like a series of Russian dolls, one inside the other. As you know, when you eventually run out of folders to open and double-click a file or application icon, the application will be launched.

Reducing Desktop Clutter This method of opening up window after window can clutter your desktop pretty successfully if you open a lot of folders. Besides, if you're only interested in what's inside the final folder, why leave all the others standing open like that? Well, you can change that situation if you like. Windows NT gives you two ways of handling a cluttered succession of windows, and it's very simple to choose which method you like better.

Click on the View command on the menu bar, and then select Options at the bottom. You will see three tabs, shown in Figure 5.11. As you can see, the first tab, called Folder, offers you one of two choices. You can either browse through folders one after another the

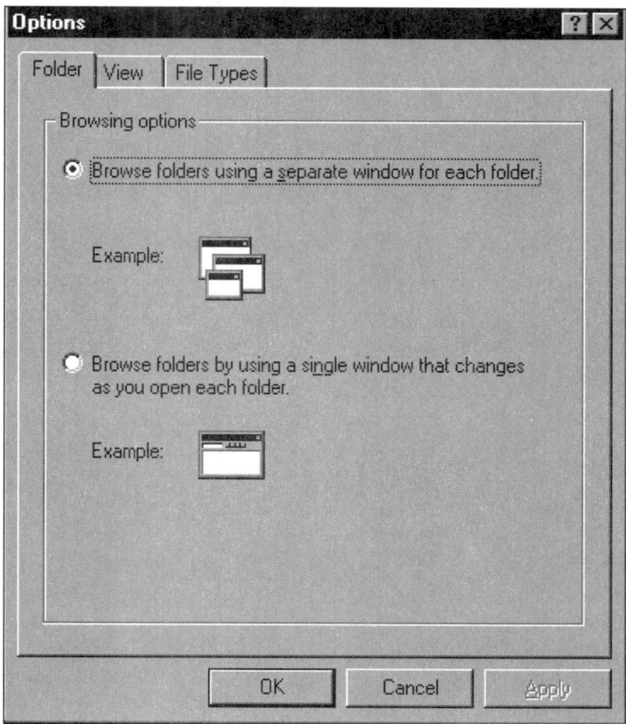

Figure 5.11: You can choose to have only one window open at a time by selecting this option.

way you have been, or you can reuse the same window time after time.

To see what a difference this makes, click on the second radio button to choose that option, and then click on the big OK button at the bottom. Close all the windows on your screen until your desktop is neat and tidy and uncluttered. Now start over by double-clicking on My Computer. So far, nothing out of the ordinary. Now double-click on disk C again, just like before. Continue to double-click on more folders, opening as many as you want. No matter where you click, or how many levels of folders you open, only one window stays open on your screen.

If you prefer to browse through your system this way, then leave everything as it is, and Windows NT will display folders this way from now on. Even after you start up your computer again tomorrow, Windows NT will remember that this is the way you prefer things. If, on the other hand, you prefer the other method with multiple windows, you can change it back by repeating the steps above.

Although many people prefer the "one-window" method because it reduces clutter on their screen, they do often complain about one thing. It's hard to open the folder that comes before the folder you are looking at. In other words, it's more difficult to go backwards through the folders, or move back "up" the directory tree. There are two easy solutions to this problem.

First, you can simply press the <BACKSPACE> key at any time and the window you're looking at will automatically jump "back" one folder, to the folder or disk that contains this folder. You can press <BACKSPACE> as many times as you want, over and over, and each time Windows NT backs up one level. You can back up all the way to the first My Computer window.

The other way is to use the Toolbar. The Toolbar is usually not displayed on windows, but you might prefer to have it visible. Click the View menu and select Toolbar. Now your window should look more like the one in Figure 5.12. The Toolbar adds a lot of one-click buttons to your window to help you do what you want.

The drop-down list at the left end of the Toolbar displays the current disk or folder you are viewing. Clicking on this drop-down list is a quick way to "jump" to another disk or folder. After the drop-down list is a row of buttons.

Clicking the first button is like pressing <BACKSPACE>. It takes you back one level to the folder "above" the current folder, like retracing your steps. The next two buttons are used for attaching and

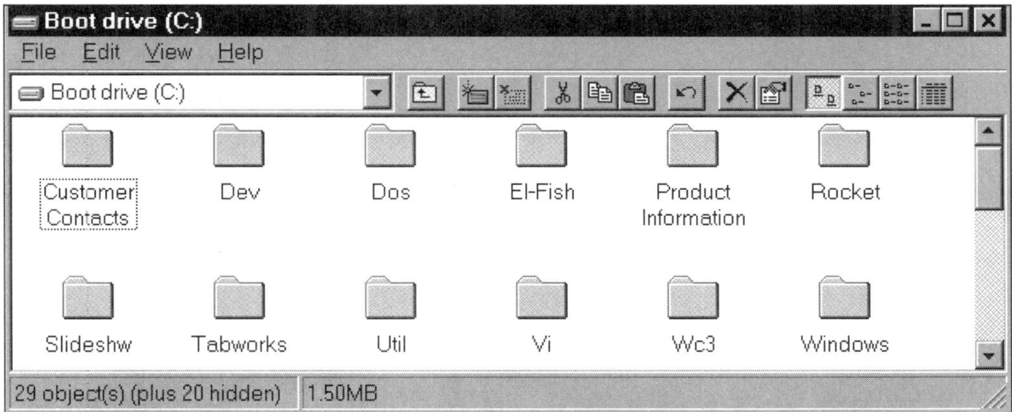

Figure 5.12: Adding a toolbar to your windows gives you one-click access to most common functions.

detaching other people's disks across a network. Buttons are also available for cut, copy, and paste operations. An Undo button will reverse your last action, like restoring a file accidentally thrown in the Recycle Bin. You can also access a file property sheet and change views with the Toolbar.

Changing the Way Files Are Displayed If you're not satisfied with the windows full of icons that Windows NT normally displays, you can change the look of your files windows, by a little or a lot. It's as simple as clicking on the View menu and selecting which of the four views you prefer. Before trying this out, let's choose an interesting window to browse through.

Find the Windows NT home directory on your disk. To start, double-click on the My Computer icon in the upper left corner of your screen. If you know what disk Windows NT calls home, double-click on it. If you don't know, pick the first disk (probably called disk C) that looks like this:

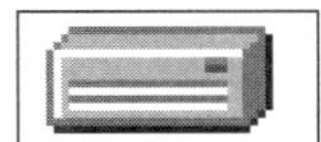

Now look for the folder called Win, WinNT, Windows, or something similar, and double-click on it. You should be greeted with a very full window like the one in Figure 5.13. This is the normal icons-in-a-window view that Windows NT normally uses. To change to

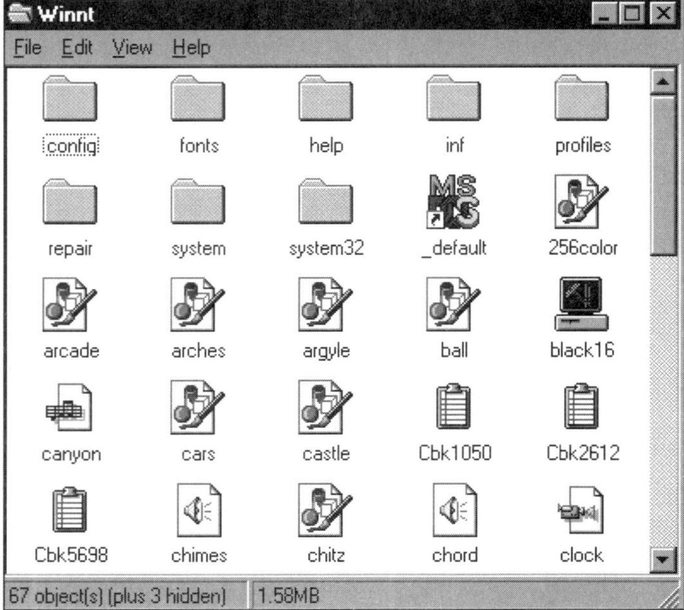

Figure 5.13: The Large Icons view shows a few icons up close.

another kind of view, click once on the View menu, then click once on Small Icons.

Now you window should look more like the one in Figure 5.14. The window still shows all the same files as before, but because the icons are drawn much smaller, a lot more of them fit within the window. You might prefer this view if you have a folder that (like this one) has lots of files in it.

Now it's time to try a second alternative. Again, click the View menu, but this time select List. Your window should now look like Figure 5.15 does.

At first glance, the List view may not look much different from the Small Icons view. If you haven't figured it out already, the difference is that Small Icons view alphabetizes files from left to right, and List view sorts them from top to bottom. That's the only difference.

Now, for something completely different, click on View once more and select Details. This will make your window look something like the one in Figure 5.16. This is very different than the previous views. All your files are arranged in a single regimental column, with details

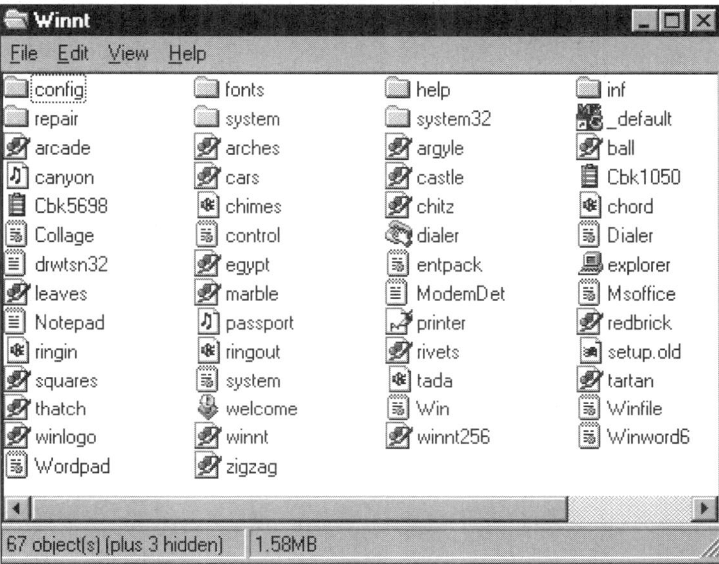

Figure 5.14: The Small Icons view shows more of a window's contents at once.

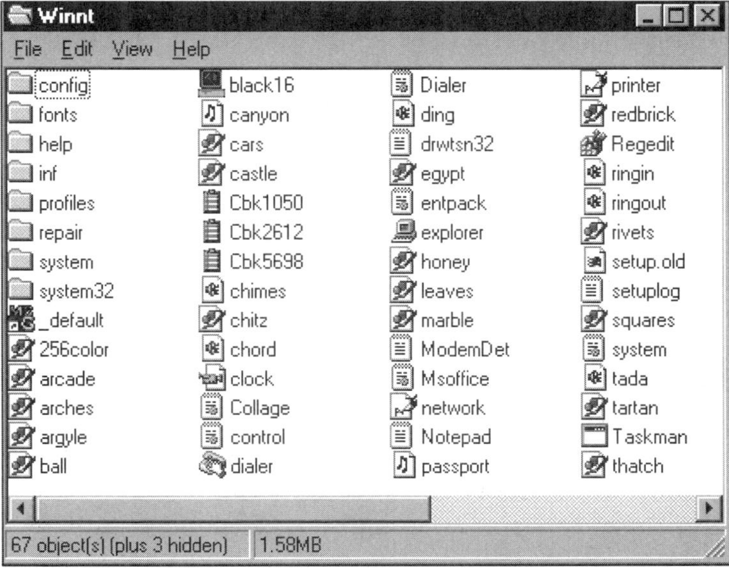

Figure 5.15: The List view is similar to Small Icons but alphabetizes icons vertically instead of horizontally.

Figure 5.16: The Details view shows the maximum amount of information for each file or folder.

about each one, such as its size, its file type, and the date and time it was last modified, all listed in alphabetical order. If you're a DOS aficionado, you may prefer this view because it most closely resembles the DIR command.

Having already found how to select the Details view, there's one more thing to learn about this view that the others don't have. At the top of each column, there's a heading. They read Name, Size, Type, and Modified. Did you know that you can change the width of these columns just by dragging them with your mouse? Try it—place your mouse pointer over the "groove" between the Name and Size headings and drag it a bit to the right. The Name column should get wider, and everything else moves to the right. You can change the width of all four columns this way, including making them narrower, too.

The other neat trick you can use in Details view is sorting the files by clicking on the column headings. If you click once on the heading Names, the files will be sorted alphabetically. But if you click a second time, they'll be sorted backwards, from Z to A. (Folders always get sorted before the A's, because they're special.) You can click on any of the four column headings—Name, Size, Type, or Modified—and your list of files will be sorted by that item. This can be really handy for finding the biggest or the smallest file in a folder. Sorting by date modified is also a great way to decide which file is the most up-to-date from a series of files. Sorting by type puts all similar files together. You'll find lots of uses for this handy little feature.

Hiding Files from View Although you might not know it, the file windows you use to browse through your computer might not really be showing you all the files on your computer. In fact, they might be hiding more files than you think—maybe even the file you've been searching for. In an effort to reduce desktop and window clutter, Windows NT normally hides many types of files from you. And nothing—not even the Explorer or the Find command—can find a file that Windows NT has hidden. That's why you should know how to make Windows NT hide (and seek).

Take another look at Figure 5.16 and notice the message near the lower left corner of that window. It says that there are 67 objects (mostly folders) in the window, but that 3 more objects are hidden. How do you see the hidden items?

If you click in the View menu of any window, you can select the Options command. Then you should see three property tabs. Select the second tab, which is labeled View. It looks like the one if Figure 5.17. The first two radio buttons allow you to turn Windows NT's file-hiding tendencies on and off. If you click Show All Files, then that is what Windows NT will do. Otherwise, Windows NT hides various kinds of files from view. The list of "hideable" files is given right in the middle of the tab.

Notice that Windows NT hides about half a dozen different kinds of files from view. All files with these three-letter extensions will be invisible in any window. Even the Find command won't find them. You cannot change the list of file types that will be hidden; only Windows NT can do that. If you are searching for a special system file or device driver, be sure to turn off file hiding before your search or you might conclude that the file you want has disappeared.

The next two check boxes in the Options window are just for show. You can experiment with them to see if you prefer the results. The first one changes the title in your windows to show the full MS-DOS path name of the window you're looking at. Otherwise, Windows NT displays just the name of the folder itself without a full path.

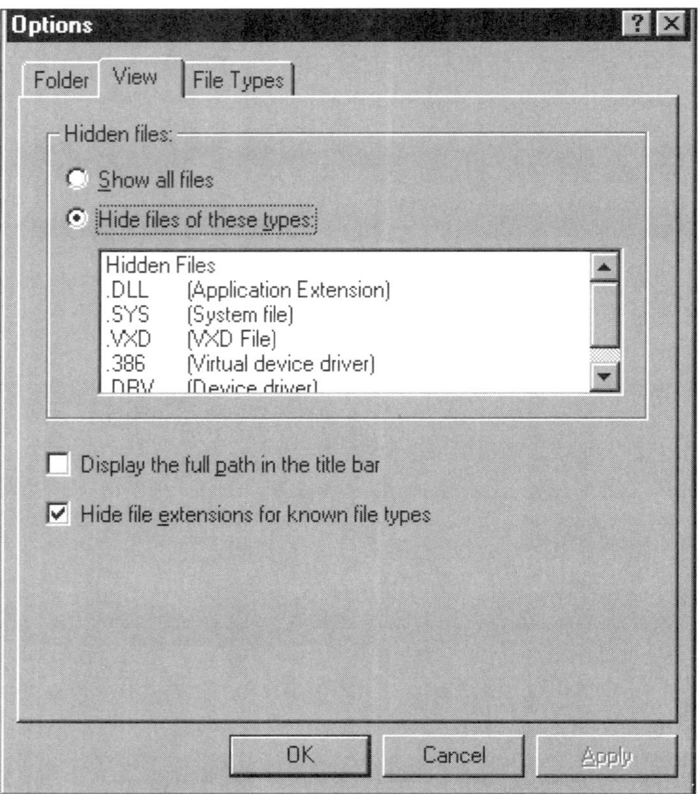

Figure 5.17: Windows NT normally hides several types of files from view, but you can change this option.

The second check box allows you to either show or hide the three-letter file name extension that all files have. Windows NT classifies files based on this extension, and assigns them icons accordingly. This classification is controlled by a list called the Registry (which is covered in more detail later).

Changing Sizes, Shapes, and Colors

In this section, you'll read and learn about all the ways you can change Windows NT's visual appearance: the colors of windows and background designs, the size of the scroll bars, how to space icons closer together or farther apart, and how to select different fonts, to name just a few.

All of the interesting controls for customizing the look of your computer are part of the Display Properties sheet. There are two ways to reach the Display Properties sheet. First, you can find a blank area of desktop on your screen and right-click on it. From the shortcut menu that pops up, select Properties, and you'll see a large property sheet. Click on the third tab, which is labeled Appearance. It should look like the one in Figure 5.18.

The other way to reach the property sheet is to open the Control Panel. This is located on your Start menu under Settings.

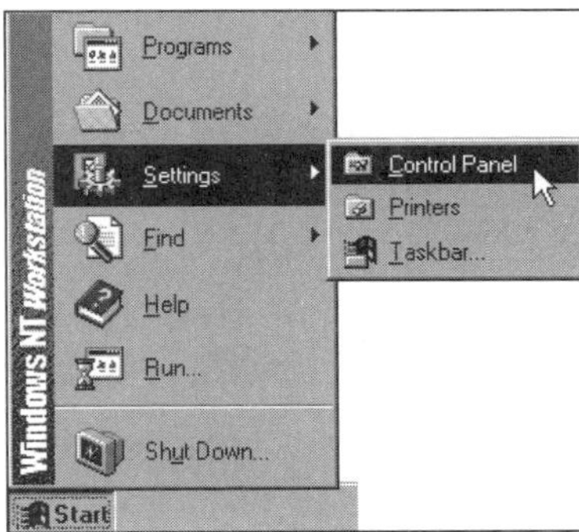

When the Control Panel window opens, double-click the Display icon.

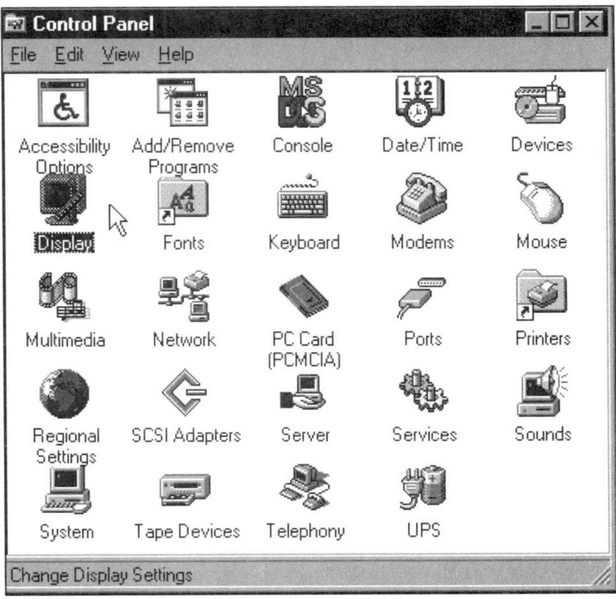

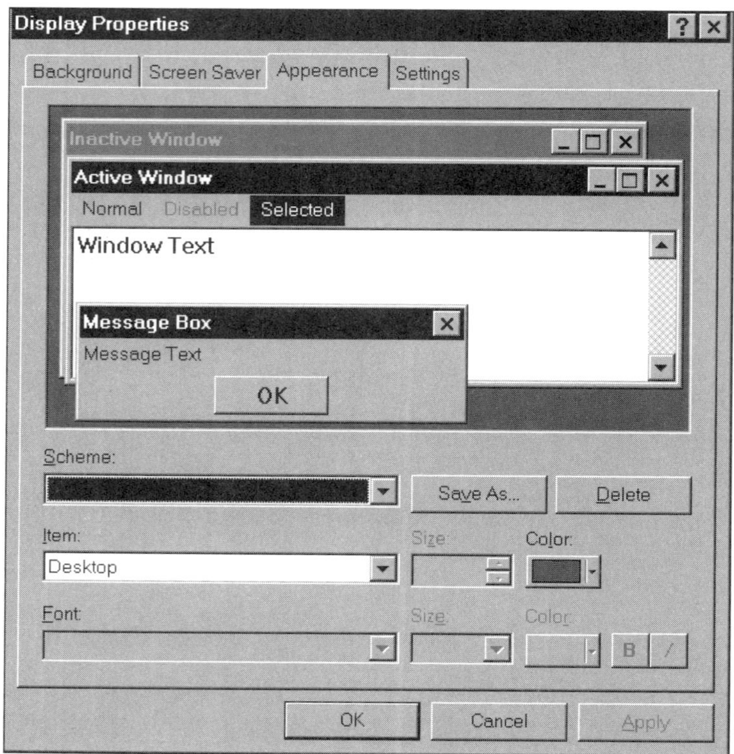

Figure 5.18: Using the Display Properties sheet you can change the color and size of practically everything on your screen.

The Display Properties sheet has four tabs, called Background, Screen Saver, Appearance, and Settings. We'll examine each of these in turn.

Changing Your Desktop Background You can change the background color on your screen in many different ways. Instead of looking at a boring old solid-color desktop all the time, you can jazz it up with different colors, a nice wood- or stone-like pattern, your favorite photograph, or even a picture that you draw yourself! There are literally thousands of different options available to you, even if you have no artistic ability. Windows NT comes with dozens of different color schemes and patterns that you can use right out of the box.

The desktop in Figure 5.19 has no special pattern or design on it at all. It's a basic, not to say boring, kind of screen. In this section, you'll see how you can decorate your desktop in a number of different ways.

Figure 5.19: A desktop with no wallpaper is a boring desktop.

There are too many possibilities to explore them all here, but you'll get a good start. Then you can experiment on your own.

Starting with Patterns Start by opening the Display Properties sheet, as described above. You'll use the Background tab, shown in Figure 5.20, and maybe the Appearance tab, to change your desktop's background.

The Background tab has two scrolling lists. You can use either one of them, or both, to change the way your desktop looks. The list on the left holds simple patterns while the list on the right has fancier patterns called wallpaper.

To see how this works, start by clicking the first pattern listed in the left-hand list. This is called Bricks. The miniature screen at the top of the tab changes to show you what this pattern will look like when it's

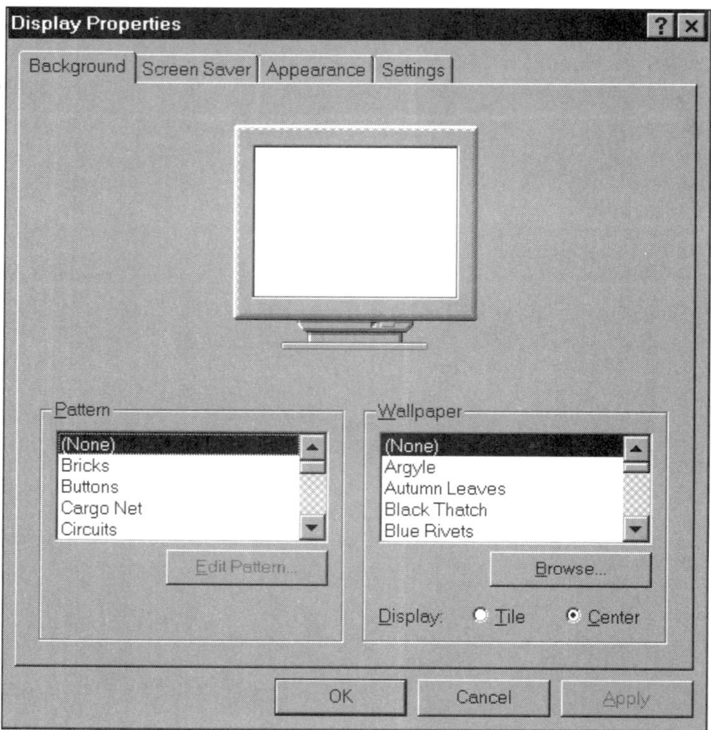

Figure 5.20: Click on the Background tab to explore the options for decorating your desktop.

spread all over your screen. If you like it, you can click on the big OK button at the bottom of the window, and you're all done.

If you'd rather just sample the new pattern for now, click on the big Apply button instead of the OK button. This will apply the pattern to your desktop but leave the Display Properties window open. If you decide you don't like the Bricks pattern after all, you can simply click on a different pattern from the list. There are over a dozen different patterns here for you to try.

All of the patterns are pretty simple, and they only have two colors, usually black and white. For a fancier pattern, read the next section on wallpaper. To learn how to make the patterns more colorful and how you can create your own, turn to *More about Patterns.*

Trying Out Wallpaper Patterns are nice, but they're very simple and they don't have much color in them. To really dress up your computer screen, you need to hang some Windows NT wallpaper. The list on the right side of the Background tab lists all the wallpapers you have on your computer. Later, you'll learn how to change these wallpapers and even add more of your own.

Windows NT comes with many different wallpapers already on the list. To select a wallpaper, click on it once. The wallpaper you pick is displayed on the miniature screen at the top of the window.

You may notice that the wallpaper overlaps the pattern you picked from the other list. That's exactly right—you can pick both a wallpaper and a pattern at the same time and the wallpaper will overlay the pattern like a picture in a picture frame. You may also notice that the wallpaper sample is very tiny. It might be no more than a dot on the miniature screen. That's because the wallpaper has not been tiled.

Wallpaper can be either tiled or centered on your screen. You can control this with the two radio buttons located underneath the wallpaper list. If you choose Center, only one small swatch of wallpaper will be pasted onto the exact center of your screen. Normally, this is no good. Many wallpaper patterns are very small and centering one is like wallpapering your living room with a postage stamp. Click the Tile option to see the difference tiling makes.

When wallpaper is tiled, Windows NT duplicates the pattern over and over until it covers your entire screen. For many wallpapers, this is the only way to get a good-looking design. By the way, if you tile your wallpaper, there's no point in choosing a pattern too, because the wallpaper will completely cover the pattern. Mixing patterns with wallpaper only makes sense when the wallpaper is centered and you can see the pattern around the edges.

If you're not satisfied with the wallpapers that come with Windows NT, you can use other pictures for your wallpaper. Wallpaper files are just normal Bitmap Image (.BMP) files like the kind you create with Paint. In fact, if you look in the Windows NT folder, you'll see all the wallpaper designs stored there as Bitmap Image documents.

That means that you can pick just about any picture file to be your wallpaper. Directly below the list of wallpaper designs a big Browse button. Clicking this button allows you to locate and select a different picture file on your computer and use it as wallpaper. The file must be stored in either the .BMP or the .DIB format. Paint is just one application that creates .BMP files. If you create a picture with Paint and save it, you can use that picture as your wallpaper.

If you have access to a scanning device, you can even scan photographs and create bitmap pictures from them and use those as wallpaper. The possibilities are truly endless.

More about Patterns In addition to the dozen or so patterns you get with Windows NT, you can create your own or alter the existing ones. To change a pattern, highlight its name in the list of patterns and click the Edit button just below the list. The Pattern Editor window will open, like the one in Figure 5.21, and you can edit the pattern.

Shortcut Hint: You can edit a pattern by double-clicking its name.

All patterns are created on an 8 x 8 grid of squares, like a quilt. The window shows a close-up of the pattern on the left, and what it normally looks like on the right. The name of the pattern is written above it near the top of the window.

You modify patterns by clicking on them with your mouse. All patterns use just two colors, so clicking any square flips it to the opposite color. Clicking a black square turns it white and clicking a white square turns it black. Every time you click a square you change a pattern, and the pattern display on the right side of the window will change to show you what your new pattern will look like. Creating pleasant patterns is harder than it looks.

You must decide whether you're going to change one of the supplied patterns permanently or create a new pattern of your own. If you want to make a new pattern, you must type a name for it in the space

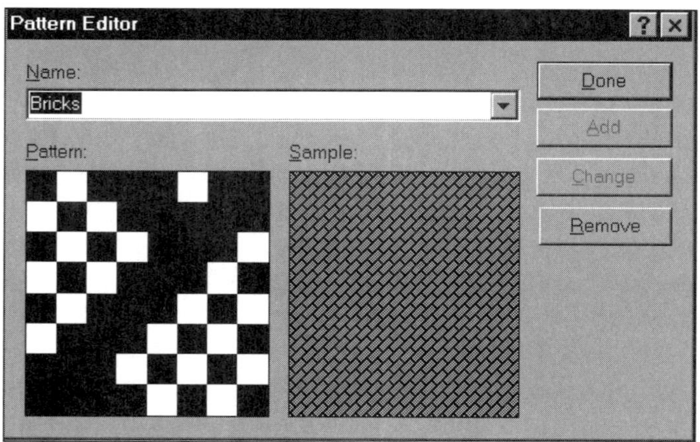

Figure 5.21: If you don't like the desktop patterns supplied, you can create one of your own.

provided at the top of the window. Otherwise, if you leave the pattern name as it is, you will replace the original pattern when you save your changes.

To save your new pattern, click the Add button. The pattern will be saved under the name given at the top of the window. Clicking Add makes this pattern a permanent part of the list of patterns. If you want to permanently remove a pattern from the list, select the pattern and then click Remove. Clicking the Change button saves the pattern under the same name as before, but with changes. You can use this to permanently alter one of the existing patterns.

Patterns are always drawn in just two colors but you get to decide what one of those colors is. Rather than settling for black and white, you can use black and yellow, or black and green, or black and anything.

Changing Colors To change the pattern color, you must skip to the third tab of the Display Properties window. The Appearances tab has many, many options that are covered elsewhere in this chapter. For now, find the drop-down list labeled Item and select the Desktop item. Just to the right of this list is a small drop-down list of colors. Clicking this reveals a palette of 20 colors. The color you pick here will become the "other" color (along with black) that makes your pattern. If you don't like these 20 colors, you can even make your own color by clicking the Other color button. This opens a Color mixing window. If you're not yet familiar with this window, you can read about Paint in Chapter 4.

After you pick (or mix) a color, you must click the big Apply button at the bottom of the window or else your new color will not take effect. After you've done this you can go back to the pattern editor and create your new, multicolored pattern.

No Pattern, No Wallpaper, Just Colors If you prefer a solid-color background with no pattern and no wallpaper, you can choose a solid color for your desktop. This is like painting a room rather than putting up wallpaper, and is less distracting for some people than a busy wallpaper design. To change to a solid-color desktop, use the Background tab to select None for both Pattern and Wallpaper. That will make your desktop a solid color. To choose the color, use the Appearance tab to select one of the 20 desktop colors as described above, or create your own color. Then click the big Apply button to sample your changes or the big OK button to make your changes permanent.

Changing Windows NT Elements You can change more than just the color and pattern that fills the background of your screen—much more. You have control over almost every little thing that Windows NT displays on your screen. The color of the window borders, the size of all the icons, the font (print style) of the writing, the width of the scrollbars—all of these are at your command. You're free to customize Windows NT to look like anything you like. So go ahead, try it out, and make Windows NT your own.

Using Color Schemes To change the "look and feel" of Windows NT, start with the Display Properties window and select the Appearance tab. Then you must decide how much creative control you want. Do you want to pick all the colors and options yourself, or do you want to have Windows NT pick a pleasant combination of colors for you? If you prefer to do everything on your own, skip ahead to *Changing Individual Items*. Otherwise, read on.

Windows NT offers several ready-made color schemes for your approval. Choosing a color scheme is like inviting an interior decorator into your home. You select a scheme from the Scheme drop-down list. These ready-made color schemes offer a range of choices from the traditional to the outlandish. Each one has a name, like Desert or Rainy Day, that suggests what it might look like. To select a scheme, click once on the drop-down list and scroll through the list until you find something appealing. Then click once on the selected scheme.

In the upper half of the property sheet, Windows NT shows a small example of what your new color scheme will look like. Notice that everything is affected: your desktop, the window borders, scrollbars, highlighted text, you name it. If you decide to keep this color scheme, click the big OK button at the bottom of the tab.

If you just want to get a better idea of what the new color scheme will look like, click the big Apply button at the bottom of the window. This will give you a "no obligation" free trial of your new look. If you like it, click on OK. Otherwise, pick a new color scheme from the list.

Changing Individual Items If you're a take-charge kind of person, or if you just like to experiment, you'll like using the second drop-down list on the Appearances tab, labeled Item. The Item list lets you control the appearance of individual items on your screen without affecting any of the other items. For example, you can change the color of an active menu bar while leaving the rest of Windows NT alone.

Clicking on the Items drop-down list reveals well over a dozen different aspects of your screen's appearance you can control. To select an item, click on it once. Just to the right of the drop-down list are the Size and Color selectors. One or the other of these will be active, depending on the item you chose. You can change colors and/or sizes with these two controls. For example, you can change the color of a message box or the spacing between icons. Sizes are always specified in pixels, the little dots of color on your screen.

Shortcut Hint: If you're unsure about what an item is called, click on the preview window and the item will be selected for you.

The big preview scene in the upper half of the window allows you to see what item you will be changing and preview its appearance. Keep tinkering until you get the look you want. In addition to just changing colors, you can change the width of the scrollbars and the size of the print on the windows. This can be helpful if you're having a hard time clicking on small items or reading small print.

Changing Fonts The third drop-down list on the Appearances tab lets you change the fonts (print styles) that Windows NT uses. Windows NT displays writing in a lot of different places and you don't have to use the same font everywhere. There are more than half a dozen items that allow you to change their fonts including icon titles, message boxes, menus, and window borders.

Changing fonts is a two-step process. First, you must select a text item from the Item drop-down list. Then, you select a new font for that item from the Font drop-down list. Clicking this list displays the fonts (printing styles) that you have loaded on your computer. Just to the right of the font list is a fill-in box that lists the point size (height) of the letters. You can change either one of these items, or both. The preview screen in the top half of the window shows you how the changes will appear.

Some items also let you change the size of the print and its color using the two additional controls just to the right of the Font list. If the writing under the icons on your screen is too small to read comfortably, try choosing a larger point size (height) by clicking on the drop-down list for point sizes. Click the big Apply button near the bottom of the window to try out the new font without making your changes permanent.

You can also display boldface or italics print by clicking on the small B and I buttons just to the right of the size and color options. When you're satisfied with all your changes, click the big Okay button at the bottom of the window to make your changes permanent.

Changing the Size and Space Between Icons Among other things, you can change the distance between icons on your desktop or inside windows. Look for the items called Icon Spacing (Horizontal) and Icon Spacing (Vertical) and click one of them. Just to the right of the drop-down list is a small fill-in box with the number 62. This is how far apart your icons are now, measured in pixels. (Pixels are the tiny dots of light on your screen; 62 pixels is about one inch.)

To move your icons closer together, type a smaller number in place of 62. To move your icons farther apart, fill in a bigger number. To try it out, click on the big Apply button at the bottom of the window.

Shortcut Hint: You can click the tiny up and down arrows in the Size box to increase or decrease the spacing between icons.

You can change the size of the icons themselves, too. Normally, all icons are 32 pixels high. You can change them to be as big or as small as you want to by selecting the Icon item from the drop-down list and changing the number in the Size area just to the right. Feel free to tweak the icon size and spacing until you're happy with them. Click the Apply button to sample your changes.

Saving Your Own Windows Scheme When you hit on just the right combination of colors and sizes, you'll want to save your color scheme for posterity. Clicking on the OK button at the bottom of the window will make your changes permanent, and they will be remembered even after your computer is turned off and restarted again. However, if you want to, you can also give your color scheme a name and save it permanently on disk. To do this, simply click the Save As button near the center of the window. Then type in a name for your color scheme and click OK.

Conversely, if there's a color scheme you absolutely hate and never want to see again, choose it from the Scheme list and then click the Delete button.

Screen Savers

Windows NT comes with a number of screen savers you can use. What is a screen saver? It's a simple application that Windows NT runs for you automatically when you haven't been at your computer for awhile. It blanks the screen and displays a random moving picture in its place. No work is lost and nothing is harmed—the screen saver just kills time by making pretty pictures.

The purpose of a screen saver is twofold. First, it prevents possible damage or "burn in" to your computer screen if you leave the computer running too long without actually using it. If you remember the old Pong games, their screens would eventually show a permanent image even after the game was turned off. That's because a computer screen is a bit like a carpet: if you walk on the same places all the time, eventually it gets a permanent rut in it. With computer screens, displaying the same picture hour after hour will eventually wear a "rut" into the screen until the picture becomes permanent.

The second reason to use a screen saver is to prevent prying eyes from looking at your computer while you're not at your desk. You might want to do this to protect yourself, or to protect passersby. If you're evaluating sensitive financial data or personnel records and get up briefly to stretch your legs, you might not want that information displayed on your screen for everyone to see. If you're interested in security, you can take this one step further and create a password that you must enter before you can see what's on your screen.

All screen savers are controlled through the Screen Saver tab, which is part of the Display Properties sheet. The Screen Saver tab, shown in Figure 5.22, has really only one big option and that is the drop-down list that lets you choose your screen saver.

Normally, the screen saver is set to None, which means no screen saver at all. Click the drop-down list and select a different one. After you click once on the name of a new screen saver, you can watch a preview of it in the little screen near the top of the window. All screen savers move—that's the whole point of a screen saver. If it stayed still, the image of the screen saver might burn into your screen.

Most of the screen savers have aesthetic options you can set, like the colors they use, or the number of wiggly lines they draw. Click the Settings button and explore with the options it gives you.

If you want to try out a screen saver, click the Preview button once and then hold your mouse still. This gives you a full-size preview of what the screen saver will look like on your monitor. Any mouse movement or tapping the keyboard will cancel the preview and return you to the Screen Saver tab.

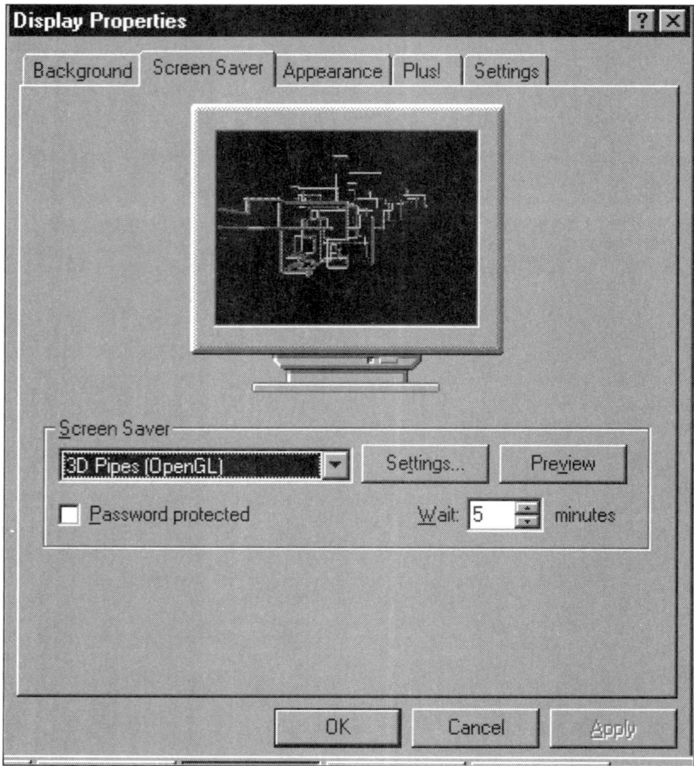

Figure 5.22: Click on the Screen Saver tab to pick your favorite screen saver.

A screen saver works by automatically "kicking in" after a certain amount of time. If you are working with your computer—typing on the keyboard and moving and clicking with your mouse—the screen saver will never start. But if you leave your computer alone long enough, the screen saver will start. You can set your screen saver's "attention span" using the Wait control.

Choosing a very short time, say one minute, will start the screen saver after one minute of inactivity. Pick a time you're comfortable with. If you set it too short, the screen saver might start up just as you're studying a column of numbers. (If that happens, don't worry. Just wiggle your mouse or tap a key and the screen saver will go away.) Setting it too long might mean the screen saver never starts at all. The maximum span you can set is 60 minutes. There is no way to make your screen saver activate early if, for example, you get up from your desk and want to start the screen saver immediately.

Using a Password with Your Screen Saver By checking the Password Protected box you can create a password. Check the box and then click the Change button next to it. Windows NT prompts you to type your new password two times to insure that you're typing it correctly. As you type your password, Windows NT displays just stars so that someone looking over your shoulder can't read your password.

After the screen saver engages, you will need to type the password to dismiss it. If you don't type the correct password, the screen saver will keep running. This can make it very difficult for unauthorized people to see what's on your screen or to use your computer at all.

To stop using passwords, simply uncheck the Password Protected box. Also be sure to click the big Apply or OK button afterwards to put your changes into effect.

Shutting Off Your Screen Automatically Many new computer screens have the ability to shut themselves off. If your screen can do this, you can set up the screen saver to shut your screen off after a certain amount of time. This goes the basic screen saver one better because it saves energy, too.

If the options for Low Power Standby and Shut Off Monitor don't appear anywhere on your Screen Saver tab, it means either your screen or your computer does not have this ability.

Changing Your Screen, Video Card, and Font Size

The last tab on the Display Properties sheet, labeled Settings, is not used very often. The options on this tab are used mainly when you first get your computer and then left alone. From this tab you can change the kind of screen (monitor) attached to your computer, the video display card inside your computer that makes it go, the number of colors your screen can display, the size of the display, and the size of the text on your screen. The latter two are sometimes helpful in day-to-day use.

The Settings tab looks like Figure 5.23. The Color Palette drop-down list gives you a few choices based on the capabilities of your screen and the video-display card inside your computer. You should generally set this to the highest number of colors you can.

Clicking the big Change Display Type button takes you to another window that allows you to pick your screen and your video-display card by brand name. There is no reason to do this unless you think they were not configured correctly when Windows NT was first loaded on your computer.

The slider control labeled Desktop Area can be fun to play with. It allows you to grow or shrink the entire Windows NT desktop so that you can see more or less on your screen. Moving the slider toward More fits more on your screen by making everything smaller. Moving the slider toward Less makes everything bigger, so less fits on your screen. Windows NT may force you to restart your computer after changing this slider.

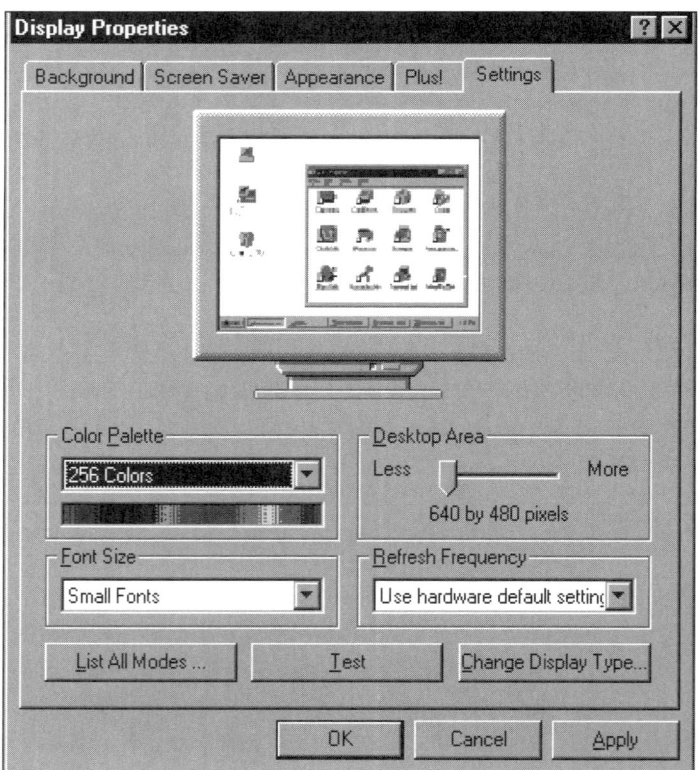

Figure 5.23: You can change the detail level on your desktop and the number of colors displayed from here.

The Font Size drop-down list lets you choose between a few different font (print) sizes. If the writing under all the icons is too small, choose a larger font.

When you change the size, resolution, font, or type of display, you should then click the large Test button to make sure you are happy with the changes before making them permanent. Windows NT will then test the new settings, displaying a color test pattern on your screen for five seconds. A brief message, shown in Figure 5.24, informs you of the test. If you're not happy with anything about the new settings, simply click the No button after the test is done, and nothing will be changed.

Changing Icons

Icons are the most obvious visual element of Windows NT. You can change these icons, and you can change what clicking and double-clicking on an icon will do. You have a lot more control over those little picture on your screen and how they behave than you might think.

How to Change an Icon You can change the icons for some files, but not all of them. The files on your computer come in three basic kinds: those that have their own icons, those that get an icon because of their type (described later, under the Registry), and those that you can change. Unfortunately, the last kind is the smallest group.

Many Windows NT programs come with their own icons buried inside them. Most applications (programs) are of this kind. You cannot, for example, change the icon for Notepad or Paint because those icons are part of Notepad and Paint, respectively. You can, however, "steal" their icons for another file if you want to (see later in this chapter for instructions how).

Many other files (in fact, most of them) do not come with their own icons. Most work files, or documents, are like this. Windows NT assigns them icons from its secret stash of icons based on what type of work files they are. For instance, all the documents you create with

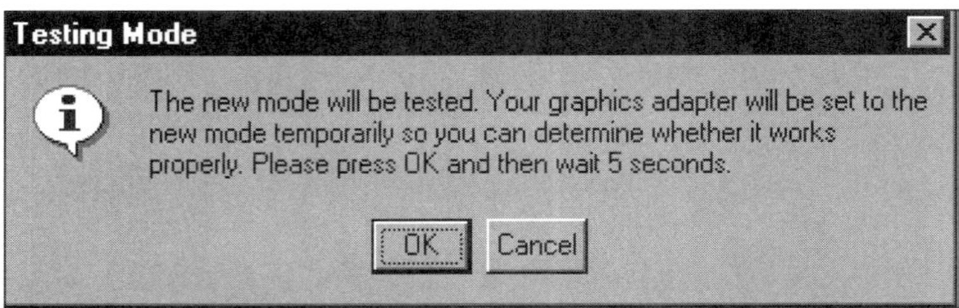

Figure 5.24: Changing your screen's detail level sometimes involves a brief test.

Notepad or Paint get special Notepad-document or Paint-document icons so you can tell what they are.

You cannot change the icon for one individual Paint document or Notepad document. The only thing you can do is assign a different icon to all Paint or Notepad documents. The next section on the Registry, describes how to do this.

The last category of files are those that do allow you to change their icons. Unfortunately, there aren't very many of these—only shortcuts. You can change a shortcut to any kind of file, no matter what kind of file it is. That means that although you can't change the icon for one particular Paint picture, you can create a shortcut to it and change the icon for the shortcut.

To change a shortcut's icon, right-click on the shortcut and select Properties from the pop-up menu. Click on the second tab, Shortcut, and then on the Change Icon button near the bottom of the window. Windows NT will display the Change Icon window, shown in Figure 5.25. This window allows you to go fishing for icons.

Icons are stored in files. Some files contain lots of icons and some have none at all. You can pick the file from which you want to get an icon, and if the file has more than one, you can pick the icon to use. You can enter the name of any file you want to in the fill-in area near the top of the window, but it's usually easier to click the Browse button and locate an icon-laden file that way. When you choose a file, all the

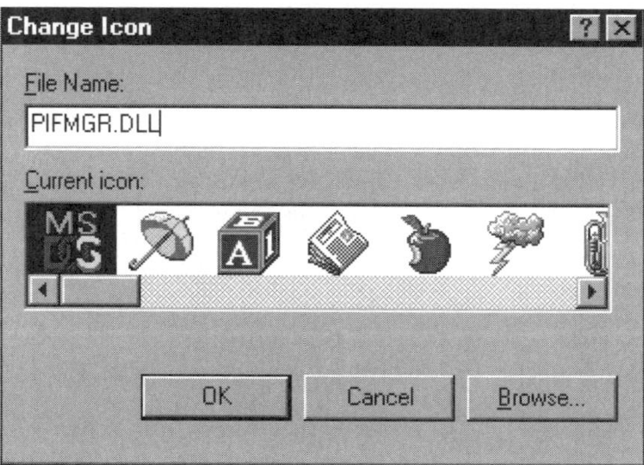

Figure 5.25: You can change the icons of most kinds of files.

icons it contains are displayed in the lower portion of the Change Icon window.

There's no way to know ahead of time which files will have interesting icons in them and which files won't. You may have to do a bit of fishing. If you know that you want to "steal" the icon from FreeCell, for example, use the Browse button to locate FreeCell on your computer and then select its icon from the Change Icon window. Windows NT comes with a few files that contain several icons. One of the richest troves is in a file called SHELL32.DLL , which is found in the System folder inside the Windows NT home folder. It has about 75 different icons from which you can choose.

Here's an icon-hunting hint: Some of the richest icon-bearing files are invisible. To find them, you must first turn on the Show All Files option. To do this, click the View menu from any open window, select Options, click the View tab, and select the Show All Files option. Otherwise, many of the most interesting .EXE and .DLL files will not be visible.

There are files available from other companies and from on-line services like America On-line, CompuServe, and Prodigy, that have nothing but icons in them. These "icon libraries" are packed with hundreds of different icons for all occasions and file types. Many are free or can be bought for a minimal charge. Unfortunately, Paint is not able to create icons. If you want to create your own icons or an icon library, you will have to use a special application. These are also available for sale or from many on-line services.

File Types, Icons, and Shortcut Menus (The Registry)

Windows NT keeps a list of all the different types of files you have on your computer. This list is called the Registry. Like guests in a hotel, new types of files "sign the registry" when they are loaded or created on your computer. This happens behind the scenes and you will not be aware of it. When an entirely new type of file is entered into the Registry, Windows NT assigns an icon to that type of file and chooses the application that will open them.

Windows NT tracks each type of file by its three-letter file name extension. (File name extensions are a carryover from MS-DOS days when all files had an eight-letter name and a three-letter extension.) Like a person's surname, a three-letter extension identifies the "family," or type of file, this file belongs to. If you look at the Property sheet for any file you will see its MS-DOS name, including the three-letter extension. As examples, word-processing documents usually have the extension .DOC, bitmap files (pictures) have .BMP extensions, e-mail messages have the extension .MSG, and so on. You can change the name of a file as much as you want, but its extension never changes.

As mentioned earlier, Windows NT assigns an icon to each type of file based on its extension. Windows NT also associates each type of file with one application so that if you double-click a document icon, Windows NT will always know what application to open for that document. Windows NT also stores a description for each type of file so that when you display a list of files in My Computer or Explorer, you have a meaningful description to read. For example, .BMP files are described as Bitmap Images, .TXT files as Text Documents, and so on. All this information is kept in the Registry. The Registry grows over time. When you set up a new application, the type of files the application creates or uses are added to the Registry automatically. File types are never removed from the Registry unless you remove them yourself.

Working with the Registry Modifying the Registry allows you to make changes to your icons, their shortcut menus, and what happens when you double-click an icon. You should be careful when working with the Registry. Although you can't damage your system or your files, you could complicate things sufficiently that you'll wish you'd never started.

From any open My Computer window, click on the View menu and select the Options command, as shown in Figure 5.26. In the Options

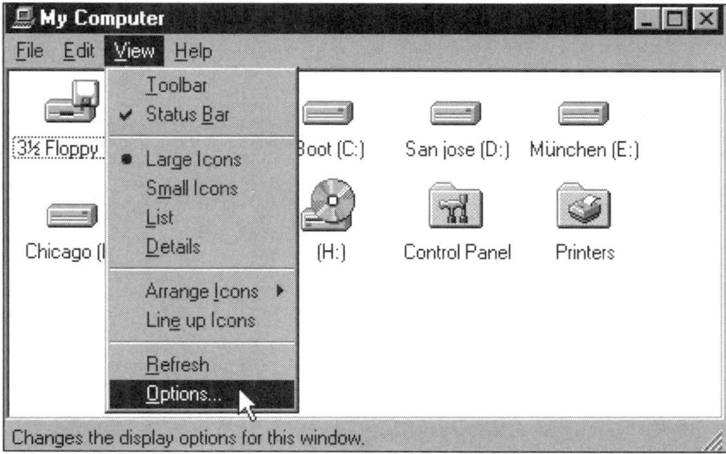

Figure 5.26: To get to the File-type registry, click on View and then Options.

window you'll see three tabs; select the third one, labeled File Types. This displays the most important part of the Registry.

What you will see is a list of all the file types that are registered on your computer. The file types are sorted alphabetically by their descriptions, not by the file name extensions themselves. You can click once on any file type in the list to see its three-letter extension along with an actual-size rendition of the icon that has been assigned to that file type. Below that, Windows NT shows you the name of the program that is used to open that type of file and its icon. You might want to browse this list before going any further and become familiar with the different file types Windows NT has registered. In Figure 5.27, the Paintbrush Picture document type has been highlighted, showing the icon that all .PCX and .MSP files get, and the fact that Paint is used to open all Paintbrush Picture files.

As the three buttons on this tab indicate, you can perform three actions: you can add a new type of file to the Registry, you can remove one of the types already in the Registry, or you can change some of the properties of one of the existing file types. Adding a new file type is an involved process, and removing one is fairly drastic and irreversible, so let's start by editing an existing file type.

Changing the Icon for a File Type Scroll down the list almost to the bottom until you find the file type "Text Document." Click once on this file to highlight it. Notice at the bottom of the window it reports

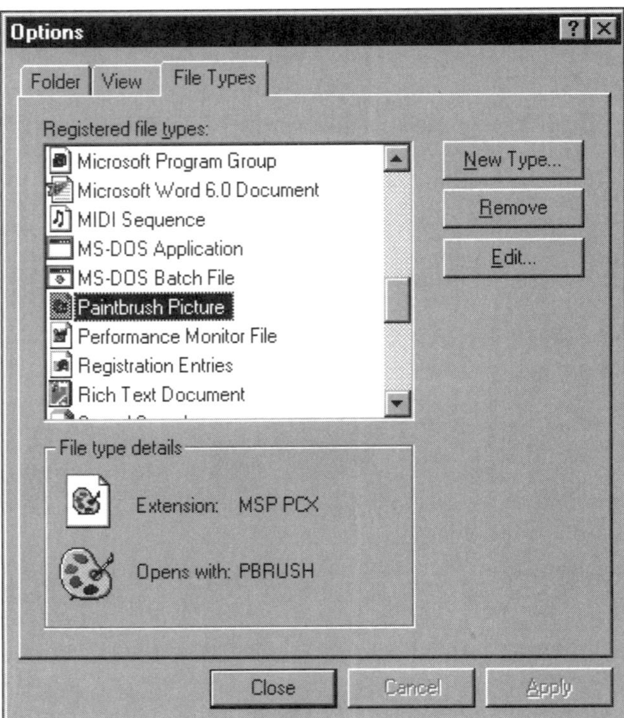

Figure 5.27: The File-type registry allows you to add, remove, and change the applications used for each type of file.

that what Windows NT calls a "Text Document" is really any file with an MS-DOS file name that ends with .TXT. It also shows you what icon Windows NT displays for all .TXT files. At the bottom, Windows NT shows you that these files are opened with Notepad, and what the Notepad icon looks like.

Now click on the Edit button (or double-click on the Text Document in the scrolling window) and you should see the Edit File Type window, like the one in Figure 5.28. This is the nerve center of Windows NT's whole file-association function. This window controls each file's icon, its shortcut menu, and how the file is opened. As you can see, there's a button you can click to change the file's icon, a place to type a description of the file type, and a curious window labeled Actions. Let's look at these in turn.

Click on the Change Icon button and you will see the Change Icon window (see Figure 5.29 for comparison). This one's pretty dull, but they aren't always—it depends on the type of file you're tinkering with. The window shows you where Windows NT is getting the icon

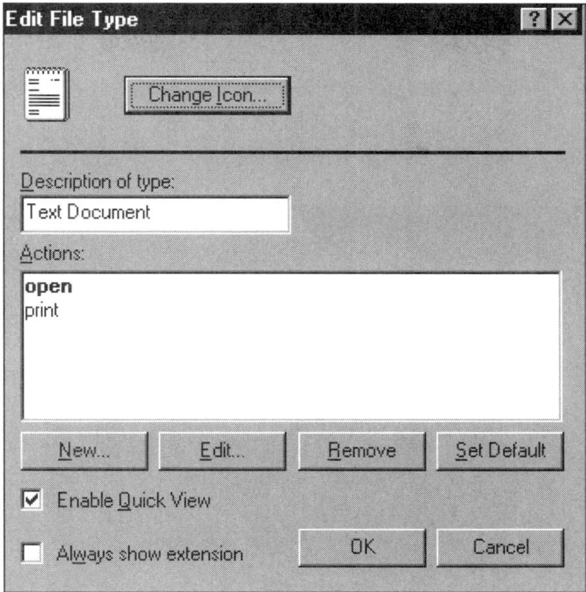

Figure 5.28: From here you can change icons, associations, and double-click behavior.

from, and what icons are available in that file. In the example shown, Windows NT is taking the icon for .TXT files from Notepad, the application used to open .TXT files, and Notepad has only a single icon to choose from.

You can assign any icon to any type of file, and you can get the icon from any of a number of files that contain icons on your computer. In

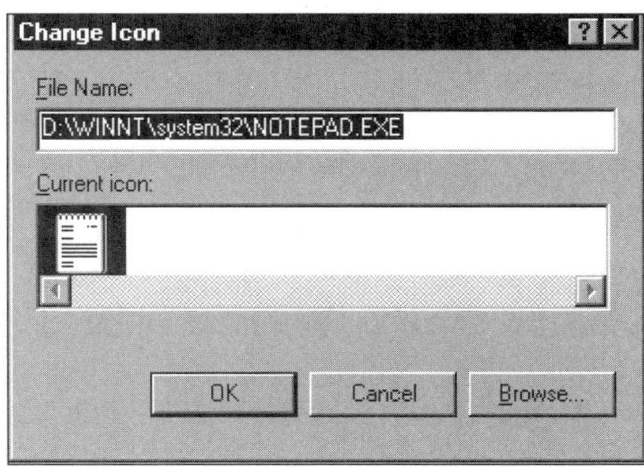

Figure 5.29: You can also assign an icon for each application's documents.

the example, Notepad had just one icon, which looked appropriate for Text Document files. But you could just as easily use different icons from a completely different source if you wanted to. It is not necessary to take icons from the application that opens the file, as is the case with Notepad and Text Document files.

As you might have guessed, you can type in the name of some other file in place of NOTEPAD.EXE and Windows NT will take its icons from that file instead. Rather than type in a long, tedious file name, let's click the Browse button. This will open up yet another window to allow you to peruse your computer looking for a file from which you can pilfer icons. If you click Browse now, Windows NT opens up its own home directory, and that's just fine. Look for the file called Explorer and double-click on it. You should now return to the Change Icon window like in Figure 5.30, but with a more interesting selection of icons. These are the icons contained in Explorer itself. Pick one that you like and double-click on it.

Now you're back at the Edit File Type window, but your Text Documents have a much different icon! Now you know how to change the icon for any type of file in the Registry. Remember that changing the icon will change it for all files of that type everywhere on your computer. In this example, all Text Documents will get the new icon you just picked.

Changing the Description of a File Type If you aren't happy with the description "Text Document," you can change it to suit you.

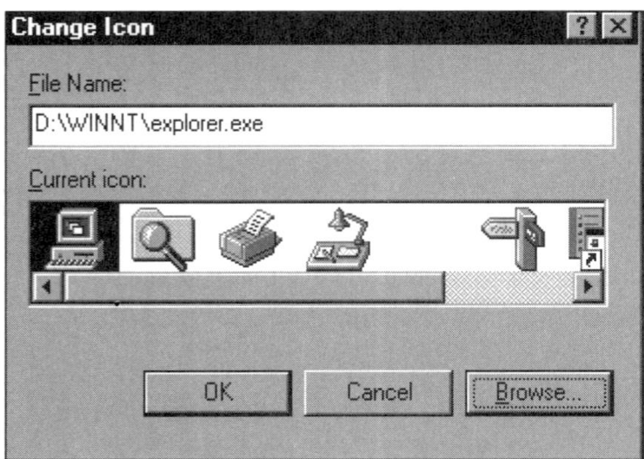

Figure 5.30: You can borrow icons from any file or application, even unrelated ones.

Simply highlight the description and type in a better one in the space provided. You can type in anything, it doesn't even have to be accurate. The description you type here will appear in four places: in the Registry list where this all started; in windows that display file descriptions (such as My Computer when you have chosen the Details view), in the Explorer window; and on the Find command's Advanced tab, where you are allowed to search for files of a particular type.

Changing the Application Associated with a File Type Now for the more advanced features. In the Edit File Type window, the Action area lists the actions that can happen automatically when you click or double-click this type of file. These actions also appear on the shortcut menu when you right-click this type of file. You can change these features by changing the Actions list. Here's how it works.

In the Action window, you can create as many different actions as you like, each one on a different line. The actions will appear on the shortcut menu in the order that you type them here. The first one will become the standard (also called the default) action, which is carried out if you double-click the icon. Therefore, the actions you type here are very important, and can have a big effect on how you interact with your files and your icons. The Open command is almost always the first (default) action.

In our example with Text Documents, two actions have already been defined: open and print. These are very reasonable choices. Since open is listed first, it appears first on the shortcut menu when you right-click a Text Document, and when you double-click a Text Document file it will open, too. The actions in the Action window are just words. You can create any words you like; they don't have to mean anything and they don't have to be technically accurate or match any commands in any application. The only place these words will ever appear is in the shortcut menu when you right-click this type of file. Assigning actual Windows NT commands to these words requires an additional step.

Highlight the first action and open by clicking on it once. Now click on the Edit button. You will see the Editing Action window like the one in Figure 5.31. The top half reminds you that the action word is open. The lower half displays the actual command Windows NT carries out when you select that action. This is where you enter the name of an application that you want Windows NT to run. If the application wants or needs extra parameters, arguments, or switches to make it

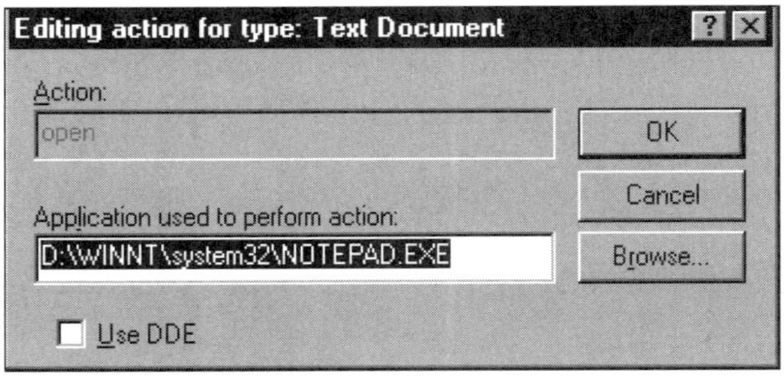

Figure 5.31: Action words can be associated with actual commands.

work, this is also the place to put them. In this example, selecting the open command for a Text Document launches Notepad with no special parameters.

If the application you're launching uses DDE (Microsoft's dynamic data exchange protocol), check the appropriate box. Using DDE is involved and technical. If you don't understand it or aren't sure, leave this option unchecked.

For now, you can click the Cancel button to leave everything unchanged. After returning to the Edit File Type window, highlight the "print" action and click the edit button again. Notice that Windows NT still launches Notepad, but this time with the "/p" option to initiate printing. Even though in this case Notepad is used for both the open action and the print action, you don't have to use the same application for each action. You might use one application to view a file, another to print the file, and still another to edit the file. There are no restrictions. Click Cancel to leave everything unchanged.

At the bottom of the Edit File Type windows are two check boxes. The first adds the Quick View command to the shortcut menu for this file type. Quick View is a small application that comes free with Windows NT. It allows you to see the contents of many different kinds of files even if you don't own the application that created the file. For example, if someone gives you a floppy disk with an Excel spreadsheet on it, but you don't own a copy of Excel, you can display it anyway by using Quick View. Since Quick View is so handy, you'll probably want to add it to the shortcut menu for most types of files. That's why there's a special check box just for Quick View. Quick View is not perfect—it can't display absolutely every type of file. If you know Quick View can't display a certain type of file, there's no point in checking the Quick View box. If you're uncertain, experiment with using Quick View on a new file type.

The final check box overrides the option on the View tab that hides three-letter extensions for registered file types. If you check the Always Show Extension box, Windows NT will always display the extension (in this case, TXT) even though it shouldn't (because .TXT files are registered). This is an odd, but potentially useful option if you think it's important to always show the extension for this particular type of file. One possible use is to distinguish this type of file from another type of file that uses the same icon.

How to Create a New File Type Windows NT normally learns about new types of files when an application creates those files for the first time and registers them. This happens automatically and you aren't aware of it. However, you can "manually" create a new type of file and register it yourself.

To register a new type of file, assign it an icon, select an application to manage it, and define the actions you can perform with it, click the New Type button from the Options window. The Add New File Type window, shown in Figure 5.32, looks very much like the Edit File Type window. There are fill-in blanks on this window for

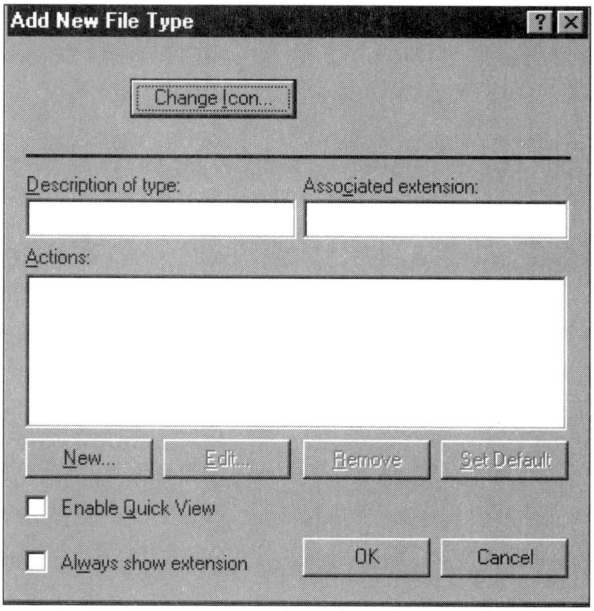

Figure 5.32: Registering new file types allows you to associate any application with any type of file.

the file extension, a wordy description, and the commands you want on the shortcut menu. There's also a button to let you select an icon for your file type.

The first fill-in area lets you type in an English description of what type of file you're defining. This can be anything you like, accurate or not, and it will be displayed in any window that displays file types, and added to the Find command's list of file types. In this example, let's type in "My First Example File Type" but don't press the <ENTER> key yet.

Instead, press the <TAB> key once or use your mouse to move to the next fill-in area. Here you need to fill in the three-letter file name extension for the new file type. You must be accurate here. Windows NT depends on this three-letter extension to recognize all the files of this type. If you get it wrong, Windows NT will not correctly identify this type of file. You must also be careful to use an extension that is not already used. File extensions like EXE, COM, BAT, and DLL are already used to identify other types of files. For our example, type in "XYZ" but don't press <ENTER> or <TAB>.

To start defining the actions for XYZ files, click the New button. Under Action, type "Open Sesame" and press <TAB> or click your mouse to move to the next fill-in area. Now type "NOTEPAD.EXE" and click on OK. Your window should look like Figure 5.33.

Now that you're back at the Add New File Type window, you should see your (admittedly silly) command listed in the Actions window. At this point, Open Sesame will be the only command on the shortcut menu for XYZ files (apart from the few standard commands that appear on all shortcut menus). Just for fun, click the check box to enable Quick View, even though we can be pretty certain Quick View would never be able to open our mythical XYZ files.

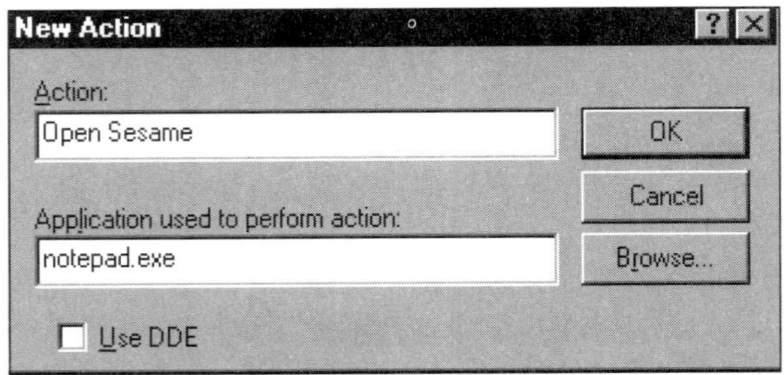

Figure 5.33: Be sure to define one or more action words and to associate them with actual commands.

Now the only thing left to do is to give our file type an icon. At the top of the window, click the Change Icon button and you'll see Windows NT's secret horde of icons. This is where Windows NT gets many of its icons for the files on your computer. They're stored in a file called SHELL32.DLL, as you can see from the window. There are about 75 different icons here; scroll through the list until you find one you like. You should ask yourself, what does an XYZ file look like?

Highlight your chosen icon and click on OK to return to the Add New File Type window. That's it! You're ready to try out your new file. But before you leave this window, let's try one tiny little advanced feature. This step is optional.

Creating Hot Keys on the Shortcut Menu From the Add New File Type window, click the New button one more time. We're going to create a second action for the XYZ shortcut menu, but this time with a difference. In the Action window, type in "Foo&Bar" just as you see it, with the ampersand in the middle of the word. Now fill in the other box with any application you want (you can enter NOTEPAD.EXE again or you can think of another program to name here). When you're finished, click on OK.

What you've done is create a second command, but this one has a shortcut key (also called a hot key) assigned to it. Placing the ampersand in the action word makes the next letter after the ampersand the hot key. In this case, the hot key is the letter B. You can give each of the actions a hot key, as long as they all use a different key. To use a hot key, select the file, press <SHIFT>+<F10> to display the shortcut menu, and then press the key.

Now that your new file type has been defined, it's time to click Close on the Add New File Type window. Look at how your new file is added to the list of registered files. Highlighting it will show its icon, list its extension (XYZ), and identify the application used to open it (Notepad). Click on Close one last time to close the Options window.

Testing Your New File Type To test your new file associations, you need an XYZ file, except there are probably no XYZ files on your computer. No problem—we'll create one by changing the three-letter extension of a Text Document (TXT) file to XYZ.

Right-click a blank area of your desktop to get a shortcut menu. Hover over the New command and select Text Document. This creates a file on your desktop called New Text Document.

Changing a file's name won't change its extension; Windows NT deliberately makes it hard to change a file's extension. The first step is to make file extensions visible. From any open window click the View menu and select Options. Select the second tab (View) and make sure the last box is not checked. This option hides file name extensions, and we want to see the file extensions. Click OK. Now right-click on your file and select Rename. Type the new name "HELLO.XYZ" and press <ENTER>. Windows NT should then warn you about the hazards of changing a file's extension.

Did your file change its icon? Right-click your file again and look at the shortcut menu. You should see the commands you added along with Quick View and the usual items. Select Properties and see what Windows NT says about your file type. The properties sheet should look like Figure 5.34.

You can create more and more new types of files if, for instance, you save your work files with "funny" extensions that Windows NT

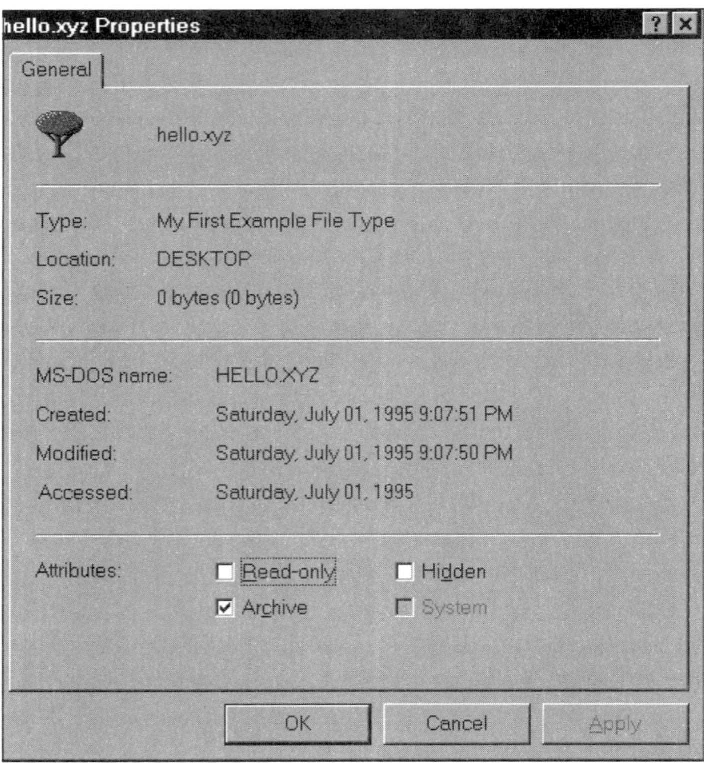

Figure 5.34: The property sheet tells you everything there is to know about a file.

doesn't recognize. For example, if you write a lot of short letters with WordPad, it will normally save each letter with the extension DOC. If you want to personalize your letters a bit more, you could save them all with a different three-letter extension—perhaps your initials. Windows NT would not recognize those files as WordPad files and would give them all a generic "I-don't-know-what-that-is" icon. By following the steps above, you can define all files with your initials in the extension as your personal correspondence, give them all a distinctive icon, and even have WordPad added to the shortcut menu for each one. You can probably think up other uses as well. Enjoy!

Removing a File Type Over time, more and more types of files will be added to the Registry on your computer. This usually happens when you install a new application. But if you stop using a particular application and remove it from your computer (sometimes called uninstalling it), Windows NT might still think you have the ability to manage those files. If you find yourself in this situation, you can make Windows NT "unlearn" what it knows about different types of files. In other words, you can remove file types from the Registry.

To remove a type of file from the Windows NT Registry, just click on the View menu on any open window (like My Computer) and select Options. Then click the third tab, File Types. You'll see a list of all the types of files that are registered. The list is sorted by the descriptions accompanying each file type. Scroll down the list if need be to locate the type of file you want to remove.

When you've located the file type you want, click on it once and look at the information displayed near the bottom of the window. Double-check that both the three-letter extension and the icon match are what you expect. If there is no application listed next to "Opens with," it's a good indication that this type of file is managed by an application that you no longer have. After you've satisfied yourself that you really do want this file type to "check out," click the Remove button and it will be erased from the Registry.

When you unregister a file type, the files themselves are not erased from your computer. If any such files are still on your system, Windows NT will give them a generic file icon like the one below to show that it doesn't know what kind of file this is or what to do with it.

When a File Is Unregistered What happens when you try to open a file whose type is not registered? Without a listing in the Registry, Windows NT doesn't know anything about the file, what it contains, what applications can open it, how to print it, or even what kind of icon to give it. As you saw before, Windows NT assigns a generic-looking icon for lack of anything better, but Windows NT cannot safely guess at what application to use to open or print the file. So what happens? Try it and see.

First you need to locate an unregistered file on your computer. You can use the Find command to do this. Open the Find window and type the letters BAK in the Named fill-in area. Then click the Find Now button or press <ENTER>. After a few moments, Windows NT should locate a few BAK files. Highlight one of them at random, then click on the File menu and select the command Open Containing Folder. This allows you to see the icon. If you right-click on the icon, you'll notice that the shortcut menu does not have the usual open and print commands. Instead, the first command is Open With...

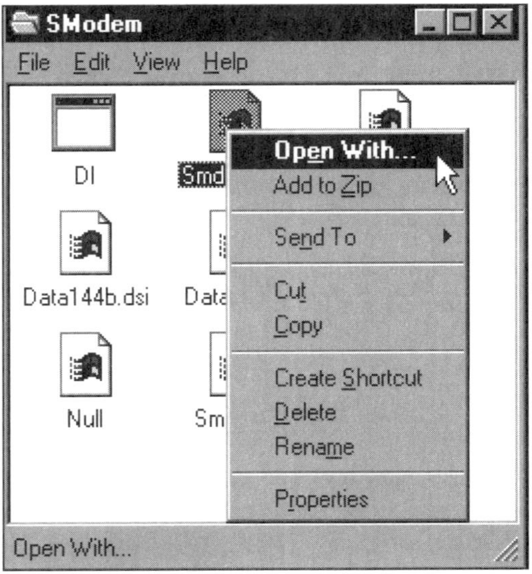

That means that Windows NT has no idea what application to use to open this file. Is it a word processing file? Or is it a spreadsheet, or a picture, or a sound file? If you select the Open With command from the shortcut menu, or if you simply double-click the unregistered icon,

Windows NT will ask you to pick an application to use with this file. The Open With window, shown in Figure 5.35, lets you pick the application you want to use.

All the applications you have used up until now will be listed in this window (if you have loaded other applications but have not used them yet, they may not be included on this list). You can choose which application to associate with BAK files here, or you can click the Other button near the bottom of the window to choose another application that is not listed. At the top of the window you can type in a useful English description of what these files really are so that Windows NT does not have to call them BAK files anymore. Finally, at the bottom of the window is a check box. Leaving this box checked will make your file association permanent. That is, once you decide that this BAK file should be opened with, say, Notepad, then all BAK files from here on will also be opened with Notepad. On the other hand, if the box is not checked, Notepad will only be used this time. The next time you try to open a BAK file, Windows NT will ask you again what application to use.

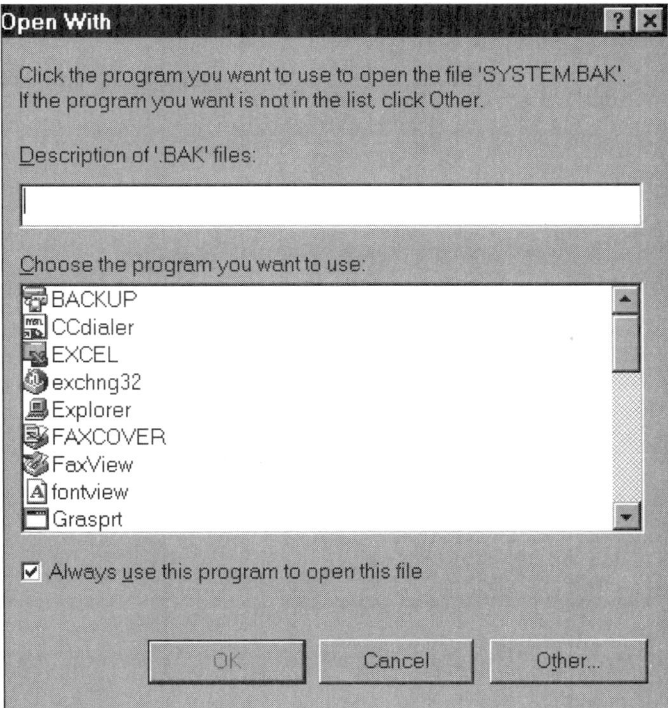

Figure 5.35: Unregistered files have no application associated with them, so you must pick one.

Control Panels

Windows NT comes with a number of small maintenance programs called control panels. Like the control panels in a mad scientist's laboratory, the Windows NT control panels allow you to dial in various settings just the way you want them.

All the control panels are grouped together in one window for easy access. The quickest way to get to them is to click the Start button, select Settings, and click on Control Panel. The Control Panel window, shown in Figure 5.36, has icons for each of the Windows NT control panels.

Changing Date, Time, and Time Zone

Double-clicking the Date/Time control panel allows you to change your computer's idea of what day it is as well as the current time and what time zone you are in. Setting the correct date and time on your computer is important because every time you open, close, and modify a file, Windows NT records the exact date and time you did so. That later allows you to sort files by their age, or to compare two similar files to see which is newer. Besides, it also makes the clock in the corner of your screen more accurate.

The Date/Time Properties window has two tabs, as Figure 5.37 shows. The first tab sets the date and time, and the second sets your time zone. You should always set the time zone first, so click on the Time Zone tab now. This displays a miniature map of the world with your current time zone marked, and its description in the top line (along with hours difference from Greenwich Mean Time, GMT). You can either click on the drop-down list and select your time zone, or simply click on the world map and let Windows NT set your time zone accordingly.

After selecting the proper time zone, return to the Date & Time tab. Now set the date by clicking on the calendar (be sure to check the year) and set the time by clicking on the numbers under the clock. When you change the time, the hands on the clock will move.

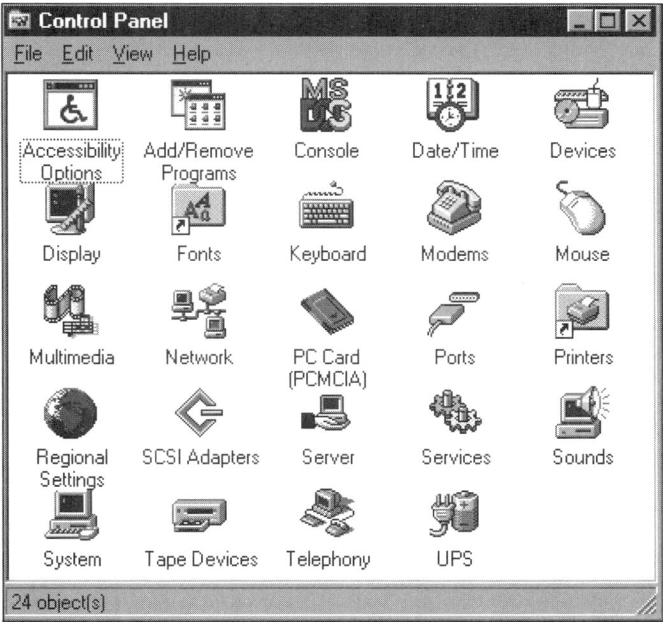

Figure 5.36: There are several control panels, for controlling all aspects of your system.

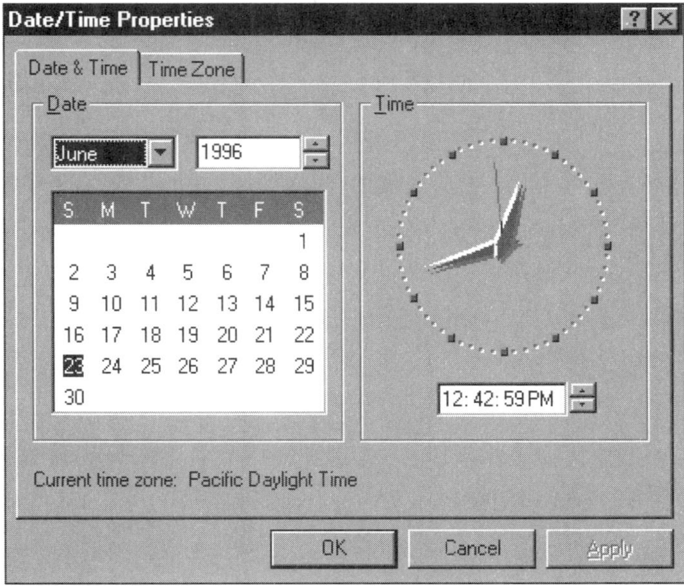

Figure 5.37: To set your computer's clock, calendar, or time zone, use the Date/Time control panel.

If you travel with your computer, you might want to create a shortcut to the Date/Time control panel and keep it on your desktop or another convenient location.

Shortcut Hint: You can adjust the date, time, and time zone by right-clicking on the clock at the right end of your Windows NT Taskbar and selecting Adjust Date/Time from the pop-up menu.

Changing Keyboard Options

The keyboard control panel contains several option that you won't need to change very often. Some are personal preferences and some are language-related. Double-clicking the Keyboard icon displays the Keyboard Properties sheet, which has three tabs. Starting from the last one, the General tab sets up the actual keyboard you are using. You only need to use this tab if you buy a different keyboard and attach it to your computer.

The Language tab, obviously enough, selects the language or languages you work in. The vast majority of people never need to use this tab. But if you are multilingual and wish to be able to type in different languages (with different keyboard layouts), this is a necessary feature. Even though most Western languages use the same alphabet, the letters are often arranged differently on a standard keyboard. American and German keyboards, for example, swap the Y and Z keys.

To add a second language to your computer, click the Add button and then select another language from the extensive drop-down list. You can repeat this process to add additional languages as well. After selecting additional languages, you have some additional choices to make. First, you must pick one language as your normal (default) language by highlighting it and clicking the Set as Default button. You can also select one of two shortcut keys that will switch between languages. Third, you can choose to have a language indicator appear on your Taskbar to remind you what language you are currently using. If you use this option, you can easily switch between languages by clicking the Taskbar indicator and selecting a language from the pop-up list.

Bear in mind that switching languages will not change the menus or anything else that appears on your screen. It only changes the layout of the keys on your keyboard, and since the keys themselves obviously do not change, you will have to remember which keys are where when using an alternate language.

The Speed tab allows you to change three things to suit your personal taste: the rate at which your cursor (mouse pointer) blinks, how fast the keyboard keys repeat, and how long you must hold a key down before it repeats. Each of these options is controlled by a slider that you can drag with your mouse.

Changing Your Region of the World

In addition to language, other things change from region to region, such as the way dates are displayed, or how decimal points are used. The regional control panel understands many of the conventions used around the world and can change them for you all at once.

The easiest and quickest to change regional settings is to select your country or region from the drop-down list that appears on the Regional Settings tab. This will set most of the other options automatically.

The Number tab gives you many options for displaying numbers, including decimal points, decimal places, and English or metric measure system. Likewise, the Currency tab controls monetary options, like currency symbol and number grouping. The Time and the Date tabs have controls for displaying dates and times.

Changing Mouse Options

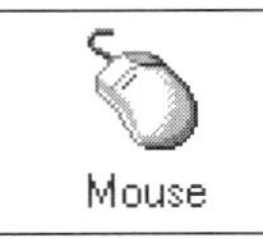

Like the keyboard control panel, the mouse control panel has multiple tabs. The first tab, Buttons, lets you choose between right-handed and left-handed operations. The mouse itself does not change; this option allows you to use any mouse with either your right or your left hand. In actuality, all this option does is swap the meaning of the left and right mouse buttons. If you choose the left-handed option, the right button becomes your primary button for clicking menus, dragging icons, and so forth. Naturally, you can use your mouse with either hand, but left-handers often find it more comfortable to swap the buttons by choosing this option.

In the lower half of this tab you can control how quickly you need to click your mouse button for it to count as a double-click. If you have trouble clicking your mouse button quickly enough to make a double-click, drag the slider control to the left. You can practice double-clicking on the purple jack-in-the-box near the lower right corner of this window. If you can make the jack-in-the-box pop up, you are double-clicking successfully.

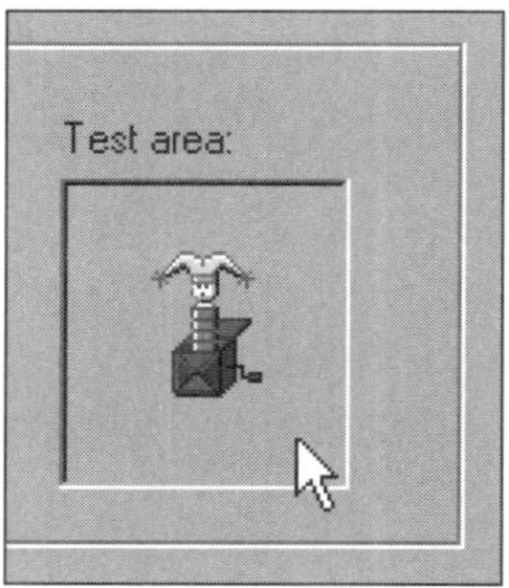

The Pointers tab lets you control what your mouse pointer (cursor) looks like. Although you may not have noticed it, your mouse pointer changes shape frequently as you use it. It sometimes turns into a hourglass, or a double-headed arrow, or even a question mark. These shapes are not fixed, however, and you can change them if you like.

You can change an individual cursor style if you like, or you can select an entirely new set of styles. The drop-down list near the top of the window lists the available sets, known as schemes. Selecting a scheme from this list changes all the cursor styles at once. Or, if you prefer, you can double-click one particular cursor style and choose an alternative. Double-clicking takes you to the Cursors folder, where

Windows NT stores all of its different cursor designs. Pick the one you like and click the big Open button. Some cursors are animated, meaning they actually are tiny little cartoons that move. The animated hourglass is a good example of this.

The Motion tab allows you to turn "mouse tails" on and off and also to control the speed of your mouse. Mouse tails (or pointer trails) can help you find your mouse pointer on a crowded screen, especially if the light is poor or if you are using a black-and-white screen (as with a notebook computer). By adjusting the slider for pointer speed you can make your mouse more or less sensitive. A fast mouse requires little write movement but can be hard to hold still. A slow mouse sometimes requires heavy "rowing" motion to get to the other side of the screen. Choose a setting that suits you.

The General tab determines the brand and model of mouse you have. You should only change this if you buy a new mouse or if your current mouse isn't working.

Viewing Different Fonts

The Fonts control panel, as you can see, is actually a shortcut to the Fonts folder where Windows NT stores all of the fonts (print styles) on your computer. Double-clicking this control panel opens the Fonts folder window. Here you can list your fonts by icon or by name. The Fonts file is unique in that it can also group your font files by their appearance. Click the View menu and select the List Fonts By Similarity command, as shown in Figure 5.38.

This option groups your fonts by how similar they look to another font, which you can specify in the drop-down list near the top of the window. After picking a font, like Arial, the remaining fonts are listed in order of similarity, from very similar to not similar.

Regardless of what view you select, you can always double-click on a font file to see a sample of it. The Font Viewer application will open and display a large window filled with samples of the chosen font at various sizes, just like in Figure 5.39. From this window, you can print a font sample if you like.

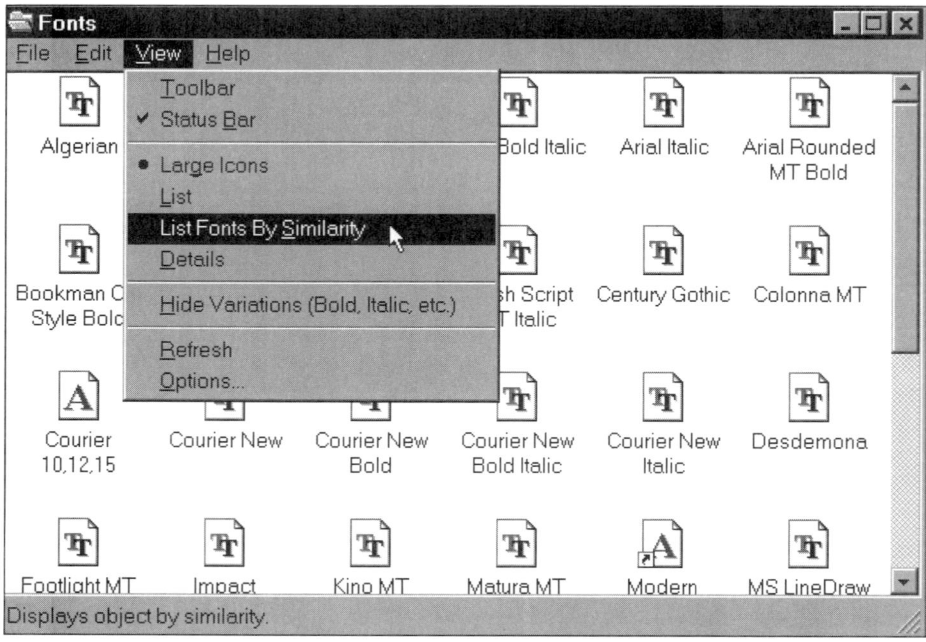

Figure 5.38: The Fonts folder lists all the type styles available on your PC.

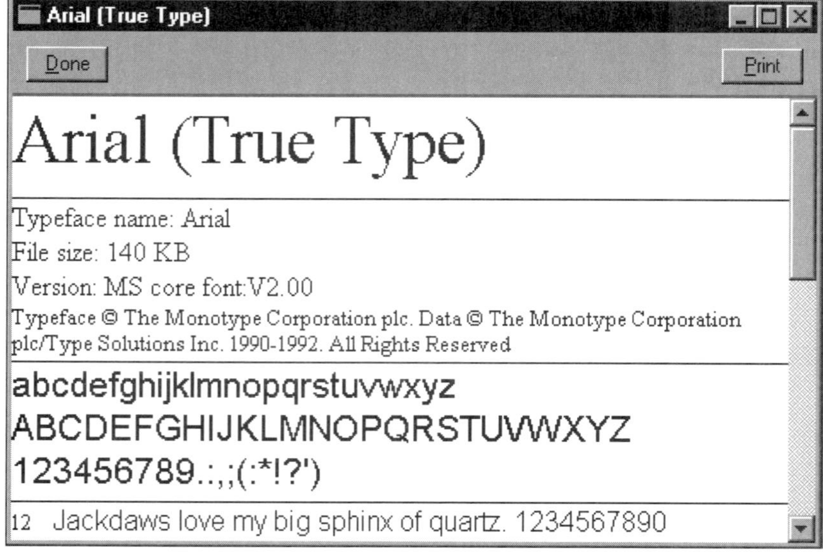

Figure 5.39: Double-clicking a font file displays a sample of that type style.

The Options tab for the Font folder is also slightly different than normal. If you click on the View menu and select Options, you will see the standard Options sheet but with a fourth tab, called TrueType. This tab has only one option. It allows you to hide all fonts that are not stored in the TrueType format so that you will not be inclined to use them. This is primarily of interest to writers and publishers who wish to maintain font compatibility with others who use only TrueType fonts.

Controlling Startup Options & Hardware Profiles

You can use the System control panel to control how your computer starts up, or boots. If you have more than one operating system installed on your computer (such as Windows 97 and Windows NT), it lets you control which one normally gets loaded and run. For Windows NT, the System control panel also selects which hardware profile you want to use.

A hardware profile is a certain arrangement of system-configuration options. For example, if you have a portable notebook computer, you might want Windows NT to run differently depending on whether your notebook computer is plugged into its dock, or whether you're carrying it on the road. You might want all of NT's networking software loaded and running when your computer is docked but not when you're traveling with it. You can define any number of such configurations, or profiles.

To create a new hardware profile, open the System control panel and click in the Hardware Profiles button. To create a new profile, select one of the existing ones (there's generally only one, called Original Configuration) and click on the Copy button. The new profile is now identical to the previous one. You'll use the Services and Devices control panels (described later) to change the profiles.

Given that you now have more than one hardware profile, how does Windows NT decide which one to use? You can tell Windows NT to ask you every time your computer starts up, boots, or is turned on, or you can select a default (normal) choice. The two radio buttons at the bottom of the Hardware Profiles windows help you choose.

Changing System Services

The Services control panel controls the services, or background processes, that Windows NT runs. When you open the Services control panel, you'll see a list of Windows NT services in alphabetical order. Listed after each service is its current status: Manual, Automatic, or Disabled and whether or not it's running. The choice between manual, automatic, and disabled status is determined by the current hardware profile. Some services will be started for a given profile and some won't. You can change the status of a service by double-clicking it or by highlighting it and selecting one of the buttons to the right.

To change a hardware profile, first select one of the services from the list and then click the H/W Profiles button. All your existing hardware profiles will be listed, including whether or not this particular service has been enabled or disabled for those profiles. You can click the Enable and Disable buttons to change the status of the service for each of the profiles.

Changing Hardware Device Drivers

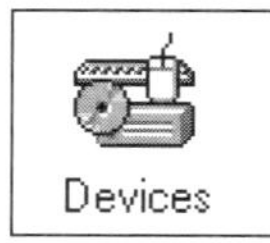

The Devices control panel works much like the Services control panel, but controls which hardware device drivers are loaded and run. You can use the Devices control panel to enable and disable certain hardware devices, based on hardware profiles. That is, you can choose to load your CD-ROM device driver (for instance) when your notebook computer is docked but not when it's portable.

For each device driver, you also have the option of controlling when and how it is loaded. To change its status, highlight one of the device drivers and click the Startup button. You have four choices, plus the option to disable the driver.

Configuring an Uninterruptible Power Supply

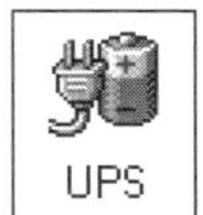

An uninterruptible power supply (UPS) is a special rechargeable battery that keeps your computer running during a power failure or "brown out." A UPS is a useful and important thing to have when a number of people (or just you!) depend on the computer at all times. The UPS provides a steady flow of power even when your main power fails. Usually, the UPS can keep your computer running for a few additional minutes—enough time to finish important work and shut Windows NT down properly.

The UPS needs to communicate with your computer so that it (the computer) knows when the power has failed and the battery has been engaged. That way, Windows NT can initiate an orderly shutdown within a few minutes of the power failure, before the battery runs out. You should use the UPS control panel to configure Windows NT to work with your UPS. Most of the options on the UPS control panel are fairly technical, but the manual that came with your UPS should be able to provide all the answers for you.

Changing the Send To Menu

Every time you right-click an icon, a shortcut menu pops up. Each shortcut menu is a little different, but there is a handful of commands that appear on almost all of them. Commands like Rename, Delete, Copy, and Cut appear on the shortcut menu for almost all icons. Another common command is Send To, as Figure 5.40 shows. The Send To command is an easy way to send a file to another disk, an e-mail recipient, your Briefcase, or to a printer. You can customize the Send To menu, and it's very easy to do.

If you experiment a little bit, you'll find that all folders and files have the same options on their Send To menus. That's because Windows NT keeps a central repository of available Send To destinations. They're in a folder called SendTo, which is inside the Windows NT home folder. If you place a shortcut to a disk, folder, network computer, printer, or other item in the SendTo folder, it will appear in all the Send To menus from then on. Likewise, removing a shortcut from the SendTo folder will remove it from all the Send To menus.

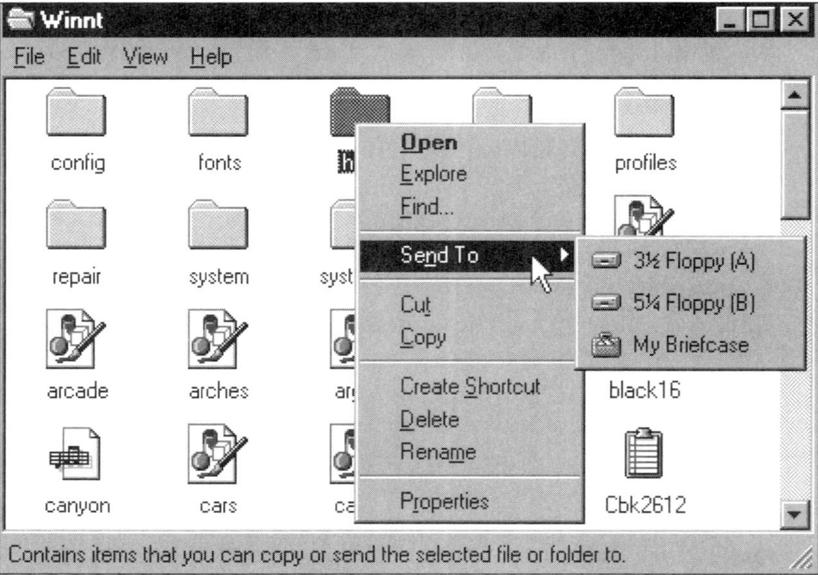

Figure 5.40: The Send To command provides a handy shortcut for copying files to other places.

Chapter 6

COOL STUFF AND HOT TIPS

Now that you've mastered the basics of Windows NT—and even some not-so-basic techniques for getting your work done—it's time to take a look at some of the hidden, unusual, and little-known features of Windows NT. It's also a good time to play around with some of the not-very-business-like features that are just plain cool. The sections in this chapter will show you how to breeze through some common tasks and how to have a little fun along the way.

Event Sounds

If your computer has a sound card (also called a multimedia card) then you've probably already discovered that it can make some interesting sounds and noises. Once upon a time, all PCs had was a simple speaker that could make tinny little noises like beeps and bloops. That was fine for the occasional warning beep, but it was no good at all—and therefore, no fun—for playing music or creating sound effects. Nowadays, most new computers have some kind of advanced sound card in them. Names like Sound Blaster, AWE32, Sound Canvas, AdLib, and others are just some examples of these wonderful things.

Windows NT can play special sounds and noises if you have a sound card. You can "attach" different sounds to particular events, like a doorbell tone when you receive e-mail, or screeching tires if

Windows NT encounters an error. All in all, there are over a dozen different Windows NT "events" that can make noise. Applications can have noisy events, too, with different sounds. Best of all, you get to decide what events will make noise, and what noise it will be.

To assign sounds to events, you must open the Sound control panel. To get there, click the Start button, highlight Settings, and select Control Panel. Then, from the Control Panel window, double-click on the Sounds icon.

The Sounds Properties window, which is shown in Figure 6.1, has several areas you can manage. The upper portion of the window is a list of all the events that you could possibly assign sounds to. In the example, the events Asterisk, Close program, Critical Stop, Default sound, and more are listed. Furthermore, these sounds are all indented under the Windows name. That means that these are all events associated with normal Windows NT functions. If you scroll down the list you may see other applications listed here too, each with its own events.

Next to some of the sounds in the list is a speaker. The speaker means that this event makes a noise. No speaker (like Close program in the example) means that this event currently does not make any noise, but it could. If none of the events have speakers, then none of them are currently set up to make noise.

Making Windows NT Noisy To assign a sound to an event, highlight the event by clicking it once. Then, from the drop-down list labeled Name, select the sound you want to play when that event happens. Windows NT comes with an assortment of basic sounds, called Ding, Chord, Chimes, and so forth. You can also add many, many more sounds of your own (more on that later). Pick a sound by clicking on it.

To hear a sample of your sound, click the little play button next to the Preview area. The play button has a triangle on it, and looks a bit like the controls on a VCR or tape recorder. If you've picked a really

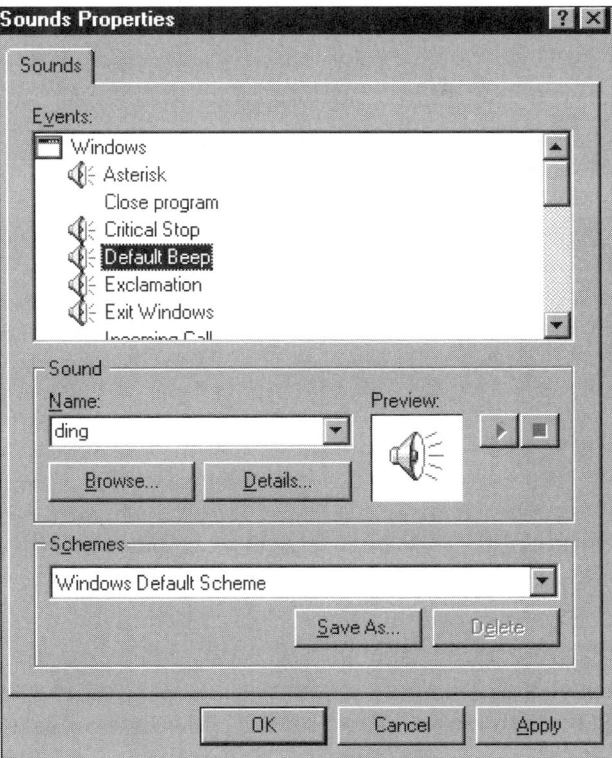

Figure 6.1: A scheme is an entire collection of related sounds. You can switch schemes or just change one sound at a time.

long sound and you want to stop it, click on the square stop button. The big picture of the speaker in the Preview area doesn't do anything; it's just for show (different sounds sometimes have different pictures).

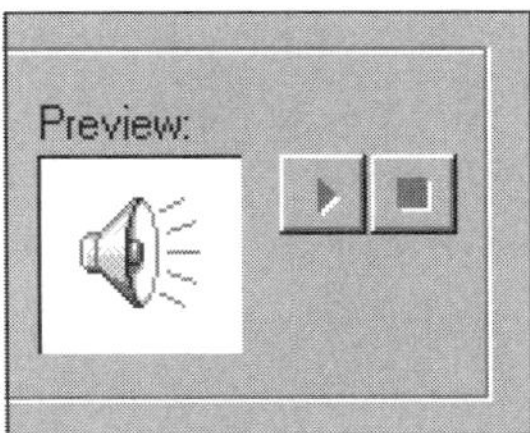

You can repeat the previous steps (highlighting an event, then picking a sound) until you've assigned sounds to all the events. If you don't want a certain event to make a sound, just pick the "sound"

called (None) from the very top of the drop-down list. When you're happy with all of your sounds, click the big OK button near the bottom of the window.

Total Sound Schemes Given that there are more than a dozen events, it might be tedious to assign different sounds to all of them, particularly if you share your computer with somebody else who doesn't share your ear for attractive aural cues. Changing all the event sounds can be a chore, so Windows NT has a shortcut. Near the bottom of the Sounds Properties window is a drop-down list labeled Schemes. A sound scheme is a prepackaged bundle of sounds ready-mixed for all occasions. Like a color scheme for visual Windows NT elements, sounds schemes are (hopefully) pleasant combinations of sounds for Windows NT events.

To select a sound scheme, simply click on the Schemes drop-down list. The number of schemes listed here depends on how many of Windows NT's optional elements were loaded on your computer when Windows NT was installed. Later, you'll be able to create your own schemes. When you click on a sound scheme, all of the event sounds will be changed, en masse. A sound scheme is a package deal but if you don't like all aspects of the sound scheme, you can change individual event sounds using the normal technique, described above.

Creating Your Own Sound Scheme If you've developed a personal sound scheme that you're happy with, you can save it for posterity by saving it as your own sound scheme. Saving a sound scheme on disk makes it easy to restore that collection of sounds later. To save a personal scheme, assign all the event sounds the way you want them, and then click the Save As button just below the Schemes drop-down list. Windows NT will prompt you to give your scheme a name, and then it will be saved. Your personal sound scheme will now be listed with all the others in the Schemes list.

Searching for Sounds When you assign sounds to events, you use the drop-down list in the Sounds Properties window. But what if you're not satisfied with the sounds on that list? What if you want to use different sounds? No problem.

The drop-down list of sounds is no more than the listing of the sound files stored in the Windows NT home folder. This folder contains many files of the type Wave Sound (.WAV). If you add new sound files to this folder, they will appear on the drop-down list. Likewise, moving (or deleting) a sound file from this folder will remove its name from the list.

You can get new Wave Sound files from many sources. Most on-line services and many Internet sites have hundreds of compatible sounds you can download for free, and there are also companies that sell sound collections. Later in this chapter, you'll even see how to record your own sounds.

If you want to use a new sound but the sound file is not stored in the Windows NT home folder, use the Browse button to locate the sound file you want. After you've selected any sound file, clicking the Details button will display a property sheet for the selected sound, including its length (play time), how it was recorded, and any copyright information that may be associated with the sound.

Recording Sounds

If you have the right equipment in your computer, you can record your own sounds and add them to your "sound library." You can then assign these sounds to Windows NT events, if you like, using the procedure described in the previous section.

To record sounds, you'll need the right kind of sound card (multimedia hardware) and either a microphone or an audio CD hookup. These will allow you to record your own voice and other sounds, or audio music tracks. The recording process itself is pretty simple. Open the Sound Recorder window and click the Record button.

Recording a Sound Sound Recorder is located on the Start menu. To find it, click the Start button, highlight Programs, then Accessories, then Multimedia, and finally, click on Sound Recorder. The Sound Recorder window, shown in Figure 6.2, is pretty small, with just a few simple controls. To start right in, click the round, red Record button on the right end of the window and speak into the microphone. To stop recording, click the square Stop button.

As Sound Recorder records, it displays a waveform of the recorded sound. This is primarily of interest to audiophiles, but you might want to watch to be sure the green wave wiggles a bit but never hits the top of its little window. If it does, it means the sound you are recording is too loud, and the quality of the recording will be very poor and distorted.

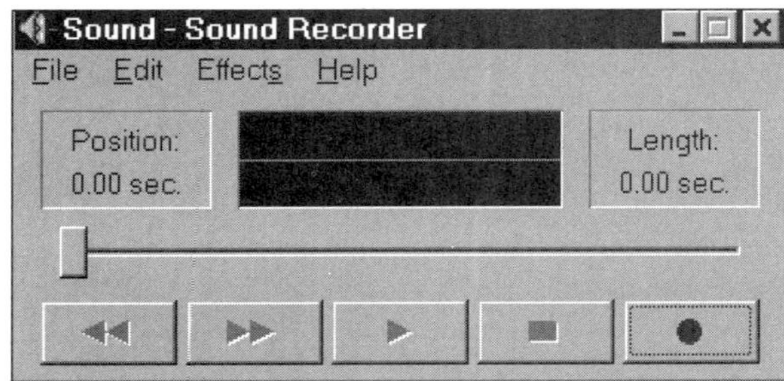

Figure 6.2: The Sound Recorder lets you digitize sounds and store them on disk.

Saving a Sound After you've made your recording, you can save it on disk as a Wave Sound (.WAV) file. Click the File menu and select the Save command. Give your sound file a name and choose where you want to save it. If you are planning to assign this sound to a Windows NT event, you may want to save it in the Windows NT home folder.

Playing a Sound Despite its name, Sound Recorder can also play sounds. From the File menu, select the Open command and choose a Wave Sound file. Then click on the triangular Play button in the middle of Sound Recorder's row of buttons.

Controlling Sound Quality When you save a recording with Sound Recorder, Windows NT stores the sound in a digitized form on your disk. The method is somewhat similar to the way audio CDs are recorded by converting audible sounds into electrical impulses. Recorded sounds are notorious for consuming large amounts of disk space, so over the years, several different formats have been developed for storing sounds. Some formats use less disk space than others, but sacrifice sound quality. Others preserve sound quality but result in large Wave Sound files on your disk. Sound Recorder has the ability to compress, digitize, and record your sounds using a number of these different formats.

To choose a recording format, use the Save As command rather than the Save when saving your recording. At the bottom of the Save As window is a button labeled Convert To. Clicking this button before you save your sound opens the Sound Selection window, pictured in Figure 6.3. The Sound Selection window gives you a number of options for trading off sound quality and disk space.

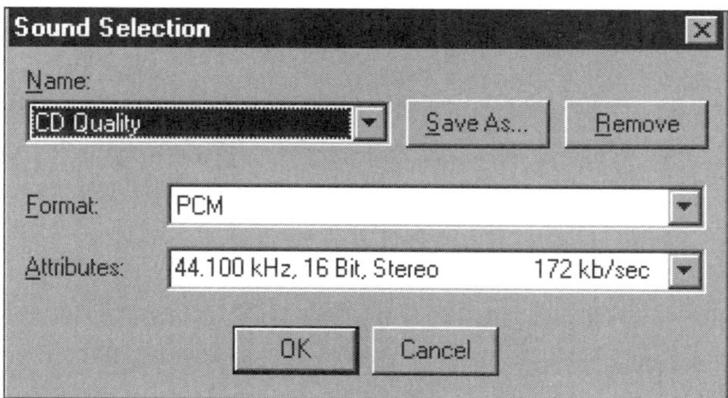

Figure 6.3: When you record a new sound, you can control its storage format and sound quality.

The easiest way to select a recording format is to choose one from the drop-down list near the upper left corner of the Sound Selection window. This list usually gives you three broad definitions of quality, from telephone quality (worst sound, best space savings) through CD quality (best quality, most disk usage). Selecting one of these options sets the others automatically.

If you prefer to tinker with the formatting settings yourself, use the other two drop-down lists to select a codec (a mathematical compression algorithm) and a sample rate (the graininess of the recording). Manually changing either of these items will blank out the quality description in the drop-down list so that you can create your own name for it. After adjusting the settings, click the big Save As button and give your quality settings a name. This name will appear in the drop-down list from now on so that you can use the same settings for subsequent recordings.

Converting Recordings In addition to selecting a recording-quality format when you save a new recording, you can load an existing sound file and convert it to a different format. Click the File menu and select Open to load a sound file. Then, using the Save As command, save the recording with different settings as described previously.

Sound Recorder can display the recording format of a sound file. Click the File menu and select Properties. The property sheet displays the sound's length and recording format. Clicking the Convert Now button gives you an opportunity to save a copy of the sound with different recording-quality settings.

You can also access the recording format by clicking the Edit menu and selecting Audio Properties. This technique has the advantage of allowing you to control your recording and playback volume at the same time.

Controlling the Recording Source and Volume

If your computer is equipped with sound-recording and playback hardware, you probably have a little speaker icon displayed in the corner of your Taskbar.

Clicking this speaker once displays a pop-up master volume control. By dragging the slider control up and down with your mouse, you can control the volume of all the sounds your computer makes. To turn sounds off entirely, click the small Mute box.

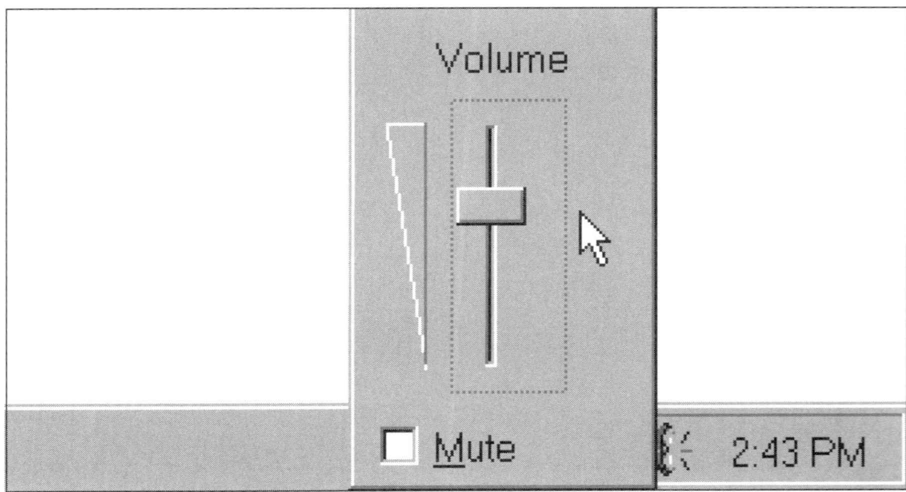

A more advanced volume control is available by double-clicking the speaker icon. This opens the Volume Control window, which has a collection of volume sliders. Your Volume Control window may differ from the one in Figure 6.4; different computers and multimedia boards have different capabilities. The purpose of the Volume Control window is to let you dial in both the recording and playback volume of different sound sources. Depending on your computer, you may be able to control the microphone input, MIDI instruments, Wave Sounds, audio CD player, and other sources independently. The volume control slider on the left is the same as the master volume control you saw by clicking the speaker icon.

The Volume Control window has three distinct uses which are controlled by the Options menu. Clicking Options and selecting Properties displays the volume controller's Properties sheet, as shown in Figure 6.5. You choose between the volume controller's three basic functions with the three radio buttons near the top: Playback, Recording, and Other.

Controlling Playback Volume The usual mode is Playback mode. In playback mode, the Volume Control displays sliders for all the playback sources you could possibly listen to. This allows you to control the volume of each sound source individually. For example, you might want to listen to an audio CD but not have it drown out the Windows

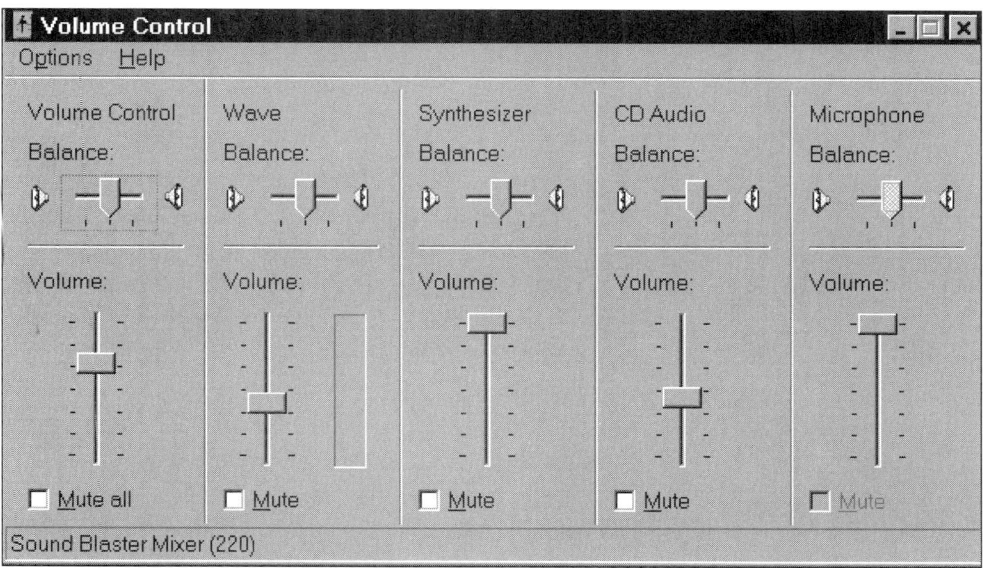

Figure 6.4: With a good sound card in your computer, you will have quite a bit of control over sound volume and mixing.

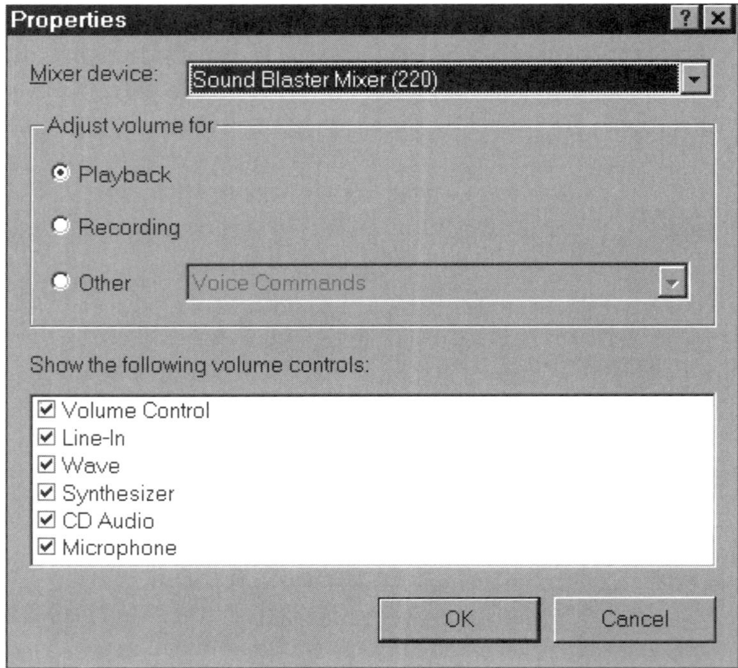

Figure 6.5: Be sure to select the appropriate option—playback, recording, or other—before adjusting any settings.

NT event sounds you assigned earlier. You can turn certain sliders on and off so that you don't see them by clicking the check boxes at the bottom of the Properties window.

Selecting the Recording Source The second mode is for controlling the recording volume (also called the gain). Clicking the Recording option displays your computer's recording input sources. Sliding the sliders allows you to control the gain of each source independently, such as a CD player and a microphone. If you don't want to see the sliders for all of these sources, you can click their check boxes at the bottom of the Properties window.

The recording mode is vital because it's the only way to select the input source for a new recording. If you want to record from a microphone, CD, or other source, you must first select the source by clicking the Select box at the bottom of that source's slider. A virtual VU meter appears next to each slider so you can control the gain of each source.

The third and final mode is for everything else, labeled Other. Clicking the Other button enables a drop-down list of possible other recording and playback sources.

Fun with Compact Discs

Windows NT includes a lot of good support for compact discs, both in the form of CD-ROMs (which hold computer data) and audio CDs (which hold recorded music). If your computer is properly equipped, you can play both kinds of CDs right in your computer.

Playing a CD You can play normal audio CDs through your computer's CD-ROM drive, as long as you have the correct kind of multimedia, sound, or CD-ROM controller hardware (most computers with a CD-ROM can do this). Windows NT has a special application just for playing CDs called, obviously enough, CD Player. It looks like Figure 6.6.

When CD Player opens, it looks for a CD in your CD-ROM drive. If it finds one, CD Player will try to display the artist and title of the CD, along with the title of each one of the tracks. Failing that, CD Player will simply display New Artist and no track titles. As you can see from the figure, CD Player has the usual assortment of controls, like any CD player would. Pressing the Play, Stop, Pause, Fast Forward, and Rewind controls have the expected effects.

Figure 6.6: The CD Player accessory will recognize a music CD the second time you put it in and display all the relevant information.

Storing CD Titles Although CD Player can't often read the artist, title, and tracks directly off the CD itself, you can teach it all these things, and CD Player will remember them the next time you insert the same CD. Each CD has a serial number on it that your computer can read. You only need to "teach" CD Player once what the artist, title, and tracks are called, and it will associate those names with that serial number from then on.

Click the Disc menu and select Edit Play List. In the spaces provided, enter the name of the artist, band, or composer, and the title of the CD. Near the bottom of the window you can enter the names of each of the tracks on the CD, one by one. Start with the title for track one, and after each track, click the Set Name button. When you're all done, click OK.

Rearranging the Play List You can play CD tracks in their normal recorded order, random order, or you can create your own order. To play tracks in random order, click CD Player's Options menu and select Random Order. To create your own order, click the Disc menu and select Edit Play List. As in the previous example, this window displays the artist, title, and tracks for the entire CD. The center portion of the windows contains two lists. One lists the tracks that are on the CD, and the other lists the tracks that will be played. Normally, these lists are identical.

To rearrange the play list, click the name of one of the tracks in the left-hand window, then drag the track up or down the list. To remove a track from the list and not play it at all, drag it from the left-hand list to the right-hand list.

You can also use the four buttons that are placed in between the lists. The Add button moves a track onto the play list; Remove takes a track off the play list; Clear All takes all the tracks off the play list so you can start from a clean slate; and Reset restores the play list to its normal recorded order. The order of your play list is stored along with the artist, title, and tracks for this CD, so you can play the tracks in your chosen order the next time you insert this CD.

Recording from a CD If your computer has a CD player, and if it's connected to your multimedia sound board (which it almost certainly is), you can record tracks off your CD and store them on your computer. Why would you want to do this? So you can use them as event sounds, or be able to play a track without actually having the CD in your computer's CD-ROM drive. Here's how to do it.

First, start Sound Recorder. Click the File menu and select New, then click the Edit menu and select Audio Properties. Choose the recording quality you want to use from the drop-down list near the bottom of the window. When you've made your settings, click OK. Next, start CD Player. Put a CD in your computer's CD-ROM drive and select the track (or part of a track) you want to record.

Third, start Volume Control (you can do this by double-clicking the speaker icon on your Taskbar). Click the Options menu and select Properties. Choose Recording mode. Make sure your CD audio source (usually called CD Audio or Line-In) is checked. Click OK. From the Recording Volume window, make sure the Select box for the correct source is checked. That's it for the preparations.

Ready, set, go! Click the Play button on CD Player and then click the Record button on Sound Recorder. You should see the green line bounce up and down along with the music. If you need to adjust the recording volume (gain), move the slider up and down on Recording Control window. To stop recording, click the Stop button on Sound Recorder, then click the Stop button on CD Player. Now you've recorded your CD!

Having Fun with Your Recordings

If you want to have some fun with Sound Recorder, record a track off your CD and play it back along with the original CD. Use CD Player to play the original CD and Sound Recorder to play your recording of it. You can stagger the recordings by a second or so if you want to and make a "round" out of it.

You can also use Sound Recorder's special effects to modify your recording. Under the Effects menu, you can change the speed and volume of a recording after it's been recorded. You can also add echo (reverberation) or reverse the recording to play it backwards. All of these effects are cumulative. For example, speeding up the recording twice will play it four times faster than normal.

Sound Recorder can edit sound files, too, allowing you to cut, paste, and mix sound files together. To trim part of a sound file, play it to the point you want to cut, then click the Edit menu. You can either delete from the beginning to that point, or from that point to the end. If you want to extract the middle of a sound file, you will have to do it in two steps, saving the intermediate file in between. There is an Undo command on Sound Recorder's Edit menu, but it's called Revert.

To splice two sounds together, load the first sound into Sound Recorder. Play the sound up to the point where you want to splice in a new sound. To record a new sound, click Sound Recorder's Record button. To splice in an existing sound, click the Edit menu and select Insert File. In either case, the rest of the original sound is erased and replaced with the new sound. There is no way to insert a sound into the middle of an existing sound like a word processor. In addition to splicing a new sound over the old sound, you can mix two sounds together. Use the procedure described above, but select the Mix with File command from the Edit menu. Sound Recorder will combine the new sound with the old sound.

You can copy and paste a sound back into itself to duplicate it. You can also mix the same sound file together with itself to create echo effects. Try mixing a sound with a reversed copy of itself. Have fun.

You can cut sounds from Sound Recorder and paste them into most kinds of files, including word processing documents. Not all word processors support this feature. Notepad, for example, does not but WordPad does. From Sound Recorder, click the Edit menu and select Cut. Then from WordPad, click the Edit menu and select Paste. An icon of a speaker will be pasted into the document. If you or somebody you give the document to double-clicks the speaker, the sound will play. Quite a nice way to annotate or personalize your documents, no?

Media Player

Media Player is Windows NT's all-purpose multimedia player. With Media Player you can play Wave Sounds, MIDI sequences, CD audio tracks, or Video for Windows movies. Media Player is a one-stop shop for just about any kind of audio or video file format you're likely to find.

You can find Media Player by clicking your Start button, highlighting Programs, then Accessories, then Multimedia, and then selecting Media Player. The Media Player itself is very small, and looks like Figure 6.7. It has an elapsed-time slider and a row of generic VCR-type buttons to control it. Double-clicking Media Player's title bar makes all the controls disappear.

Media Player works with four types of files, or media. These are video clips (.AVI files), sounds (.WAV files), MIDI sequences (.MID or

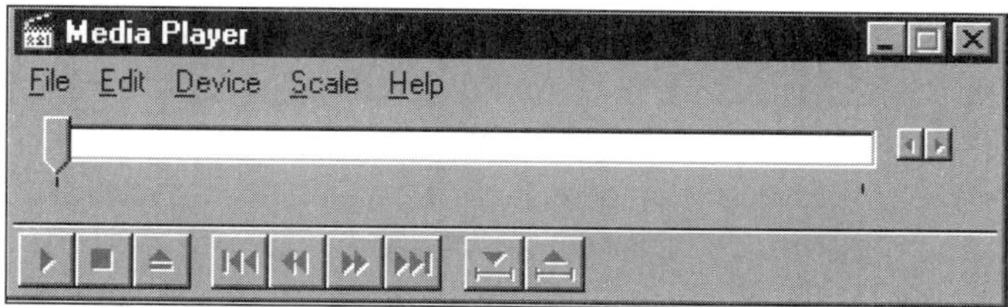

Figure 6.7: The Media Player is good for audio, video, and multimedia files.

.RMI files), and CD audio tracks (no file names, because music CDs are not stored as Windows NT data files). Although sound files can be played with Sound Recorder, and CDs can be played with CD Player, Media Player is the only application that can play video clips and MIDI sequences. In addition, Media Player has a few features that Sound Recorder and CD Player don't have.

Playing Video Clips Video clips (.AVI files) are like small movies or music videos. They're usually just a few seconds long and play in small windows about the size of the palm of your hand. Compressing and restoring moving color pictures on a computer requires a high-performance computer and/or some additional hardware. The better-equipped your computer is, the smoother the pictures will be, and the less they will monopolize the rest of your computer when they're playing. To play a video clip, simply double-click a Video for Windows file. Media Player will start automatically, playing the video in a window. The Media Player window will normally not be visible in this situation. To see it, double-click the title bar of the video window.

Either before or during the time the video clip is playing, you can change the size of the window it plays in by clicking the Device menu and selecting the Properties command. Note that playing a video clip in a larger window than it was intended for tends to make the picture grainy and requires more of your computer's time to keep the video running.

Playing MIDI Sequences MIDI sound files, or sequences, are like recorded music files, but with a difference. MIDI (which stands for musical instrument digital interface) is a standard used by musicians and instrument makers worldwide that allows composers and performers to connect musical instruments to computers, recording devices, and each other. The advantages are many, but in the end, a

MIDI file is essentially a musical score without the instruments. That is, a MIDI file records the notes, but your computer must play them.

In MIDI files, each instrument is numbered, not actually recorded. Your computer must fill in for each of the instruments, and very few hints are given about what instruments should be playing which numbered parts. Thus, MIDI files often sound different on different computers. If your computer is able to play MIDI files, simply double-click one and Media Player will take it from there.

Playing Wave Sounds Double-clicking a Wave Sound (.WAV format) file usually starts Sound Recorder, not Media Player. You can play sounds with Media Player, though, you just have to open Media Player first and then load the sound file. Click on the Device menu, select Sound, and then select the file you want to load. Media Player has a slight advantage over Sound Recorder for editing, because it allows you to mark the beginning and end of a passage before you copy it.

Playing Audio CDs Media Player can also be used instead of CD Player to play audio CDs, although it has none of the titling or play list features of CD Player. To play an audio CD with Media Player, click on the Device menu and select CD Audio. Clicking the Play button will start the CD playing. You can skip ahead or back through tracks using the Fast Forward and Rewind buttons.

Editing with Media Player Media Player lets you cut snippets of a video clip or sound file out and paste them in elsewhere. As a file plays, Media Player's slider moves from left to right. You can mark the beginning and the end of the section you want to copy by clicking the Start Selection and Stop Selection buttons. Media Player fills in the area between the marks to give you a visual indication of the area you've marked. After marking, click the Edit menu and select the Copy Object command.

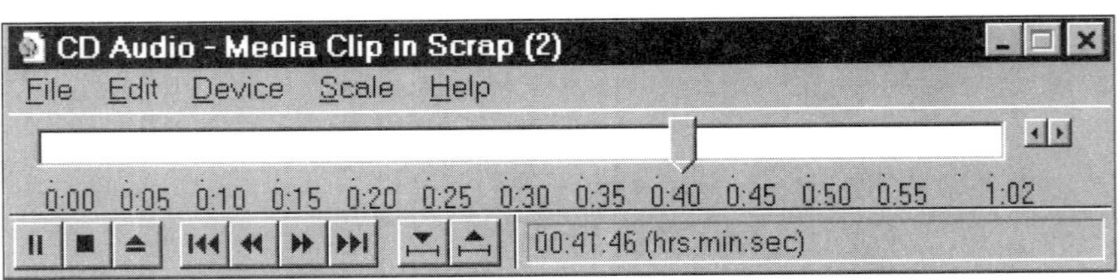

To do precision editing, you can type in the exact time of the start and end marks, or the exact amount of time you want to copy. From the Edit menu, choose Selection. These audio or video snippets can then be pasted into any Windows NT application that accepts OLE (object linking and embedding) pasting. WordPad is a good example of just such an application.

Hot Tips

Herewith is a diverse collection of tips, tricks, and pointers for your enjoyment. Feel free to experiment with the ones that sound interesting and incorporate them into your daily routine.

- There's a secret way to add the Control Panel and the other "special" folders Printers and Dial-Up Networks to your Start button. Right-click on the Start button and select Open. From the Start Menu window, right-click a blank area and select New, then Folder. Rename the folder with the following name: Control.Panel.{21EC2020-3AEA-1069-A2DD-08002B30309D}. The funny name is necessary to get all the control panels to appear on your Start menu. To add the contents of the Printers or Dial-Up Network folders, follow the same procedure but use the names Printers.{2227A280-3AEA-1069-A2DE-08002B30309D} or Dial.Up.Net.{992CFFA0-F557-101A-88EC-00DD010CCC48}.
- If you're trying to right-click on the Taskbar to reach its property sheet but the Taskbar is completely filled with buttons, you can still find an "empty" area by right-clicking the very left edge of the Taskbar, beside the Start button.
- You can have a movie play every time you start your computer, or have it play a tune, or hear your spouse's voice greet you. Simply place the appropriate video or sound file into your StartUp folder. The StartUp folder is located inside the Windows NT home folder. Any application or document file inside this folder is automatically opened every time you start Windows NT.
- Dragging an icon from one folder to another moves the file if the two folders are on the same disk. Holding down the <CTRL> key when you drag makes a copy instead of moving.
- Dragging an icon from one folder to another makes a copy of the file if the two folders are on different disks. Holding down

the <SHIFT> key when you drag moves the file instead of making a copy.

- You can pull sections of a document out and save them as "scrap" files. For example, using WordPad, highlight an area of text (word, sentence, paragraph, or whatever) and drag the highlighted text out of WordPad to another folder or onto your desktop. Windows NT creates a scrap file there. Double-clicking this scrap file will re-open the application (in this case, WordPad) with the highlighted text in it. You can also paste this scrap into other documents simply by dragging its icon into a word processing window. This technique also works with pictures and other types of work files.
- Dragging icons with your right mouse buttons gives you more options than left-dragging does. When you drag and drop with your right mouse button, you will get a short pop-up menu that allows you to choose between copy, move, and make shortcut.
- If you want to drag a scrap file (or or anything else) to a window that is open but obscured under other windows, drag the item to the window's button on the Taskbar instead. Hovering over the Taskbar button for a second will open the appropriate window so that you can drop your cargo where you wanted.
- You can create a new folder while you save a file. Inside the Save and Save As windows, right-click an empty portion of the window. From the shortcut menu select New, the Folder. Name your folder and continue.
- To incinerate a file immediately (that is, delete it without putting it in the Recycle Bin first), hold down the <SHIFT> key and press <DEL>. Or, right-click the file, hold down the <SHIFT> key, and select Delete from the shortcut menu. The file will be lost forever.
- You can highlight multiple icons at once by holding down the <CTRL> key as you click each one. If you click one by accident, simply click it again. You can select any number of icons this way. If you want to highlight a series of consecutive file icons (for instance, all files that begin with the letter C), click the first one, hold down the <SHIFT> key, and click the last one. All files in between will be highlighted, too.

- You can rename a file or folder by highlighting it and pressing the <F2> key. This is an alternative to clicking the file twice (without double-clicking it) or right-clicking it and selecting Rename from the pop-up shortcut menu.
- For a shortcut to a file's property sheet, highlight the file and press ALT+ENTER. Or, hold down the <ALT> key and double-click the icon.
- You can close a series of folders at once by holding down the <SHIFT> key as you click the close box (the little X in the upper right corner of all windows). This will close not only that window, but all of its predecessors as well.
- To pop up an item's shortcut menu without right-clicking it, highlight it and press SHIFT+F10.
- If you're converting from Windows 3.x and want all your old Program Manager groups back, find the .GRP files (they're probably in your original Windows 3.x folder) and double-click each one. This will run an application that places the group on your Start menu.
- To open a file with something other than its normal application, highlight the file, hold down the <SHIFT> key and right-click it. Then select Open With from the shortcut menu.
- Copying a floppy disk is simple with Windows NT, but a special shortcut can be convenient, too. (Normally, to duplicate a floppy, you'd right-click it and select Copy from the shortcut menu.) To create a shortcut on your desktop, right-click any open area, highlight New from the pop-up menu, and select Shortcut. When the Create Shortcut window pops up, type COMMAND and click the button marked Next. In the following window, type any name you like for your shortcut and click the button marked Finish. Now right-click your new shortcut and select Properties from the pop-up menu. Select the Program tab and in the line labeled Batch File type DISKCOPY A: A: and click the big OK button at the bottom. Now any time you want to duplicate a floppy disk, just double-click your shortcut icon. You can change its icon, too, if you like.
- If your mouse suddenly stops working, you can press CTRL+ESC to open the Start menu. From here you can use your arrow keys and/or press the underlined letters on the menus to get where you want to be.

- You can double-click the title bar of any window to maximize it (make it fill the whole screen). Double-clicking the title bar again sets the window back to its previous size.
- If you share your computer with other people and you don't want them to learn what you've been working on, be sure to empty the Recycle Bin (right-click the Recycle Bin and select Empty Recycle Bin) and clear your Documents menu (right-click the Taskbar, select Properties, choose the Start Menu Programs tab, and click the Clear button).
- When you're running an MS-DOS program or the NT Command Prompt in full-screen mode, you can switch back to Windows NT by pressing ALT+ENTER.
- You can print any file without opening it. Right-click the file's icon and select Print from the pop-up shortcut menu. Or, if you have already placed a shortcut to your printer on your desktop, you can drag the file's icon onto your printer shortcut and drop it.
- You can change the name of an application the same way you change the name of any other icon. If you keep applications on your desktop for easy access but are bothered by the clutter of long names, simply give the icon a shorter name. When the application opens, its full name will still appear in the title bar as before.
- Don't be tempted to change all of your folders and files to give them long file names. If you're still using DOS programs or applications that were created for Windows 3, these programs won't understand the long file names and will probably malfunction. Common symptoms are applications that do not open when you double-click them, or that cannot find accessory files, or that are unable to load work files.
- If a file is important and you don't want to delete it accidentally, you can make it unerasable. Right-click the file's name or icon and select Properties from the pop-up shortcut menu. Then check the box labeled Read-Only and click OK. Marking a file read-only prevents you from deleting it but also prohibits you from changing the file, so you won't be able to update it, either.
- You can't change the icon for most applications or documents, but you can change the icon for a shortcut to those files. If you want to give a certain application or document a special icon,

first create a shortcut to it then right-click the shortcut, select Properties from the pop-up menu, and click the Change Icon button.

- If you grow tired of the Welcome Tip-of-the-Day every time you start Windows NT, you can turn it off by clicking the little check box in its lower left corner. To bring it back after you've turned if off, click the Start button, select Help, select the Index tab, and type WELCOME on the entry line. When the Help window appears, click on the shortcut button to jump directly to the Tip-of-the-Day. Now you can click the check box again to turn this feature back on.

Chapter 7

E-MAIL, FAXES, AND EXCHANGE

Electronic mail, instant fax delivery, commercial on-line services, the Internet, the World Wide Web, new telecommunications legislation, and constant advances in technology all make using a computer more interesting—and more complicated—as time goes on. Once, you could draft a letter on your computer but you still had to fold it and put it in an envelope to mail it. Now the letter need never be committed to paper. As you will see in the next few pages, you can compose, edit, and transmit a complex spreadsheet, drawing, or document without ever lifting your hand from your mouse. And, your work will arrive sooner and in better condition than if it had been mailed. To learn how to harness all these capabilities and make them work for you, keep reading.

Exchange

Exchange is an agglomeration of existing applications all rolled into one. If you've used a computer for a few years, you're probably acquainted with electronic mail (e-mail) and fax applications or with on-line services like America Online or CompuServe. Exchange combines many of these features and more to give you a one-stop shop for all your communications and messaging needs. Exchange stands in for your older e-mail program, your fax program, and possibly even your commercial on-line service. It allows you to treat e-mail messages and faxes as just two different kinds of electronic messages. With

Exchange, you can send messages to others on your office network, people outside your organization, and people and organizations on the Internet, all from the same place. Exchange will also collect all your incoming e-mail and fax messages, regardless of where they came from, and present them all to you in one convenient in-box. To start Exchange, double-click the Inbox icon on your desktop.

The Exchange window looks a whole lot like an Explorer window, as you can see from Figure 7.1. On the left are your four personal folders and on the right is the contents of one of those folders. As you can see from the figure, your four personal folders are all part of Microsoft Exchange. If you share this computer with others, they will each have their own personal folders so that you aren't all sharing one Inbox, Outbox, and so on.

Normally you will have four personal folders for your messages: Inbox, Outbox, Sent Items, and Deleted Items. You may create more later on if you want to. The Inbox holds messages that others have sent to you. These can be e-mail messages from people on your

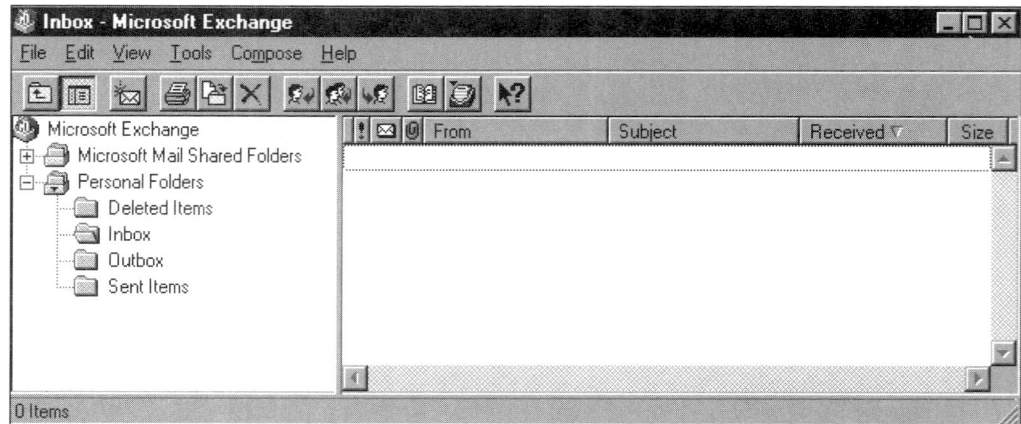

Figure 7.1: The Exchange window is your central repository for e-mail and faxes.

office network, faxes, or messages from outside your office via the Internet. The Inbox is the central repository for all your incoming communiques.

The Outbox, obviously enough, is where all of the messages you send to others go just before your computer actually sends them. Just like in real life, looking in your Outbox shows you what you have asked to be sent but that has not yet been delivered. When your computer transmits an e-mail message or fax from your Outbox, the message will be moved to the Sent Items folder to confirm that it was delivered.

The fourth folder, Deleted Items, acts like a Recycle Bin for your incoming and outgoing items. Messages you delete wind up here, where they will stay until you empty the Deleted Items folder. You can let this folder accumulate discarded messages until you deliberately empty it, or make it empty itself automatically every time you close Exchange.

Reading Your Messages Highlighting any one of the four folders on the left side of the Exchange window displays the contents of that folder on the right side of the window. When you first start Exchange, your Inbox is generally highlighted so you can see if you have any new unread messages. If you have received a new message, it is listed in boldface type to make it stand out. Likewise, the Inbox folder itself will be displayed in boldface type to alert you to the fact that it contains at least one unread message. To read a message, simply double-click it.

When you read a message, a new window will appear, like the one in Figure 7.2. It's similar to a Notepad or WordPad window, with a collection of menus and buttons. After you read the message, you have several options. You can delete it, send a reply to the sender, forward the message to someone else, or save it for later.

Saving a Message Your e-mail messages and faxes are not deleted after you read them. You can leave messages in your Inbox indefinitely. Or, if you prefer, you can drag those messages from the Inbox to another folder. You can place already-read messages in another folder in your Personal Information Store simply by dragging it to one of the folders that appear in the left portion of the Exchange window, or you can drag a message completely out of the Exchange window and deposit it anywhere on your computer. Such a message will

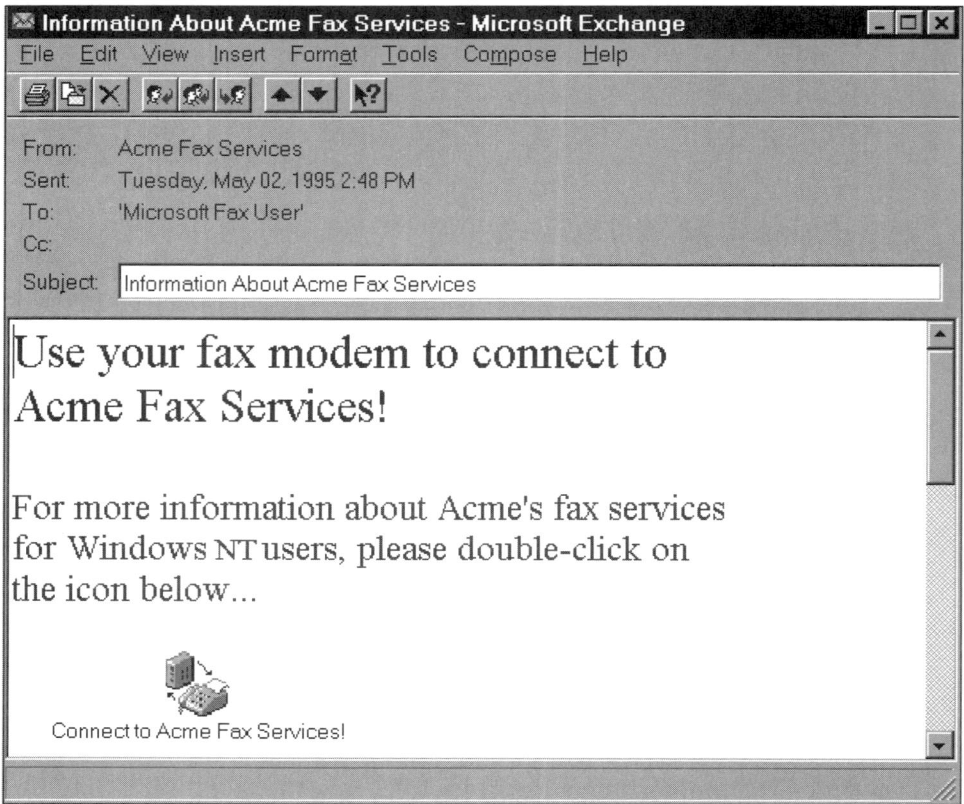

Figure 7.2: Incoming e-mail messages might have pictures or files embedded in them.

appear as a yellow envelope icon and will get the .MSG file name extension. Double-clicking a saved message will open it again.

Writing a New Message From the main Exchange window, click the Compose menu and select New Message if you want to write a new e-mail message, or select New Fax if you want to create a new fax (covered later). If you have the Exchange toolbar displayed, you can also click the New Message button.

The New Message window, shown in Figure 7.3, looks much like the one you see when you're reading messages; it also looks a bit like WordPad. The New Message window is its own word processor, so you can create reasonably fancy e-mail messages from here. You can also cut, paste, drag, and drop text and embedded or linked items into this window from other applications. Although this window has

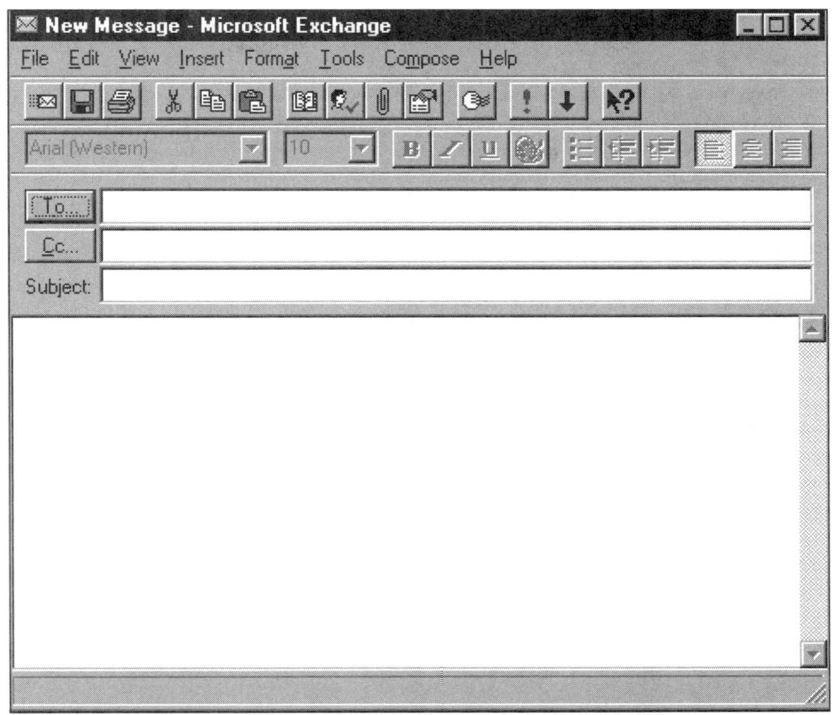

Figure 7.3: To compose a new e-mail message, you must address it and give it a subject.

many buttons, menus, and fill-in areas, you should feel free to start anywhere you want to. You can address your message first, or start typing the message, or fiddle with the formatting—whatever suits you.

The only item you must eventually fill in is the name of the addressee in the To area. If nothing else, you must at least tell Exchange who you want to send this message to. You can either type the person's name in the space provided or you can click the To button and select the person's name from your personal address book (described later). You don't need to do both. If you want to send this message to two or more people at once (something you could never do with real mail), simply enter multiple names with semicolons between each name. If the fill-in area gets full, press <ENTER> and keep adding more names.

If you like, you can also send "carbon copies" to other people, including blind carbon copies. In the CC list, add the names of any more people who should receive this message. These people will receive the same message at the same time as the normal addressees; technically, there is no difference between an e-mail message and a copy. In your workplace, you might attach some significance to receiving a copy, though. Likewise, you can send blind copies by clicking the View menu, selecting BCC Box, and adding more names to the BCC list. These people will also get the same message at the same time as everyone else, but with one important difference: their names will not appear anywhere on the message and nobody will know these people have received it.

When you've completed your message, including any fancy formatting you want to apply to it, you can send it by clicking the File menu and selecting Send, or by clicking the Send button on the toolbar. Exchange will check all the recipients' e-mail addresses against your personal address book to see if they match. If not, Exchange will ask if you'd like to add that person's name to your address book, or if you really meant to enter another, similar name.

Attaching Files You can embed, or attach, files to an e-mail message the same way you might use a paper clip to attach something to a memorandum. To attach a file to your message, click the Insert menu and select File, or click the Attach File button on the New Message toolbar. You will see a standard Windows NT file-browser window. Select the file you want to attach and double-click it. Before you choose the file, you may want to review the options at the bottom of the window.

You can attach either the text of a file or the file itself. In other words, if you are attaching a normal, readable document like a word processing file, you can choose to insert the contents of that document into your message as though you had typed it or you can attach the entire file as a separate document. Using the latter option is like mailing a copy of the file to the recipient and it allows that person to keep and edit a separate copy of the document on his or her computer. If you attach a document, you can also choose to either mail it along with your message, or just send a link to it. If you send just a link, your message will be transmitted faster because the attached file will never be sent. Instead, your recipient will receive a link to the attached file that allows them to access your file on your computer at a later time.

Sending Messages to People without Windows NT Windows NT affords you many opportunities to dress up your e-mail messages with special fonts, colors, underlining, and embedded pictures, files, or other objects. This is considerably more exotic than most e-mail programs, which limit you to basic typewriter-like simplicity. In fact, most e-mail delivery systems, like the Internet, are not equipped to transmit or receive such complex messages. So what happens?

When you send messages from your Windows NT computer to another Windows NT user, the recipient will receive the message just the way you created it, with all the formatting and special features intact. This works regardless of what medium (telephone, LAN, Internet connection, etc.) was used to transmit the message. Exchange compresses and converts the message as necessary. If your message is received by persons who are not using Windows NT or who does not have Exchange, they will still receive your basic message, although it will appear very basic. Any attached files (pictures, enclosures, etc.) will appear as binary attachments to their e-mail software. These people may have to open such attachments separately.

Changing Message Priority and Sensitivity Before you actually send an e-mail message, you can assign it a priority and/or a sensitivity. Priority can be low, normal, or high. Changing a message's priority doesn't do much other than display a red exclamation mark in the receivers' Exchange window when they read their e-mail. If you are sending messages to people outside your office via the Internet, a high-priority message may get delivered sooner, but that depends on your networking equipment.

Sensitivity has four settings: normal, personal, private, and confidential. None of these has any effect on your message except for the private setting. Marking a message private prohibits anyone from modifying your message when they reply to it or if they forward the message to someone else.

Requesting a Receipt Before you send a message, you can request Exchange send a receipt to you when the message is delivered, or when it is actually read, or both. From the File menu, select Properties. Two check boxes near the bottom of the property sheet allow you to choose the type of receipt you want. You can also choose not to have a copy of this message deposited in your Sent Items folder after it is delivered. Clicking the Read Receipt button on the New Message toolbar will also check the option for a Read Receipt.

Using the Address Book Remembering peoples' e-mail addresses can be taxing, like memorizing their telephone numbers. That's why

Exchange provides you with an address book for all your e-mail and fax recipients. The address book allows you to remember people's real names and let Exchange fill in the delivery details. You can store a person's name, company affiliation, several telephone numbers, assistant's name, and random notes to yourself for each person in your address book.

To add a name to your address book just click the Tools menu and select Address Book. You can also click the Address Book button on the Exchange toolbar. The big address book window will appear. To add a new name, click the File menu and select New Entry or click the New Entry button on the toolbar. The New Entry window, shown in Figure 7.4, allows you to categorize the new name before you enter it. In the figure, your choices are to classify this person as a Microsoft Mail user (like yourself), a person you contact via the Internet, or through some other means. You can also create distribution lists, grouping names of people you communicate with often. It doesn't matter a great deal which category you place someone's name in—you can always retrieve any name from any category. Double-click one of the choices to begin entering a person's information.

The new address book window has four tabs. The first three are identical for all categories. These give you a place to enter a person's name, business, mailing address, and so forth. The second tab collects every possible phone number for this person including two for work

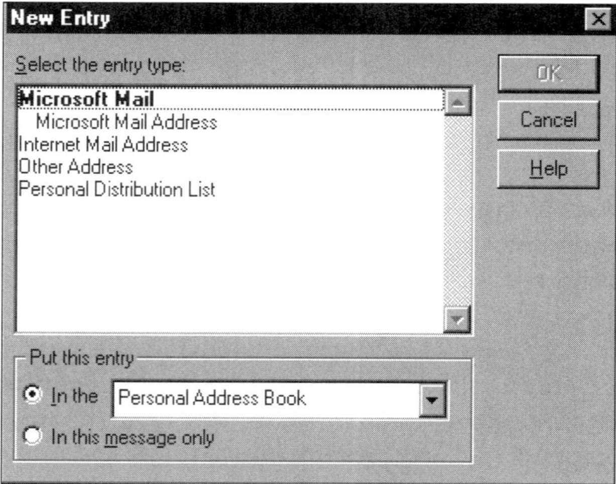

Figure 7.4: When creating your personal address book, you can assign people to various classes of recipients.

and two for home. The third tab is simply for adding notes to yourself about this person. The fourth tab, which changes depending on which category you chose to put this person in, holds specific information about fax numbers, e-mail addresses, or other information.

After you enter a person's name and other salient details into your address book, you'll be able to simply type that person's real name when addressing e-mail messages or faxes, or highlight the name from your address book.

Changing Your Exchange Window You can change the way your incoming and outgoing messages are displayed by sorting them or altering the appearance of the Exchange window. The standard window has seven columns showing who the message was from, the subject, and the date a message was received, among other things. Just like windows in Explorer, you can click these column heading buttons to sort your messages based on that column. Clicking the Received column heading, for example, sorts your messages by the date they were received, from oldest to newest. Unlike Explorer, though, clicking on the heading a second time does not sort them in reverse order. To do that, you must click the View menu and select Sort. Like Explorer, you can change the width of these columns by dragging the headings to the left or right with your mouse.

One feature that Exchange has that Explorer doesn't have is the ability to add or remove headings from the window. If, for example, you don't care about the date a message was received, you can remove that heading from the window to save space and reduce clutter. You could then add one or more new headings in its place. Here's how:

Click the View menu and select Columns. The Columns window appears, listing all the categories you could possibly want to display, and on the right, all the categories you are already displaying. Browse the list on the left; to add one, highlight it and click the Add button. To remove a heading from the Exchange window, highlight it from the list on the right and click the Remove button. You can also change column width from here by changing the number in the Pixels area. Finally, you can change the order in which the columns are displayed, from left to right, by using the Move Up and Move Down buttons.

Sending and Receiving Faxes Sending and receiving faxes is not much different than with e-mail messages, which is only natural since they are both essentially the same thing—documents transmitted electronically between two machines. In this case, you can send a fax from your computer to a fax machine anywhere in the world, or you can "fax" a document to another computer, just like e-mail.

There are more ways to send a fax than there are for composing e-mail messages. You can compose a new fax from the Exchange window, by using the Compose New Fax accessory, by attaching a file to an e-mail message, by faxing directly from an application, or even by "printing" from your application to a fax machine. The results are always the same, but the method for getting there differs.

If you already have an Exchange window open, you can easily create a new fax by clicking the Compose menu and selecting New Fax. This starts the Compose New Fax Wizard, which steps you through the procedure. After answering a few questions about where you're calling from, who you're calling, and what kind of cover page you want, you can finally type out a few lines to send as a fax, or you can attach a file to be faxed.

If you do not have an Exchange window open and just want to compose a quick fax, you can achieve the exact same result by clicking on your Start button, highlighting Programs, then Accessories, then Fax, and then clicking on Compose New Fax. This also starts the Compose New Fax Wizard, the same as before.

Files can be faxed by attaching them to e-mail messages and addressing the e-mail to a person's fax number. If a fax machine answers the call, the attached documents will be printed on the fax machine. If a computer answers, and that computer is also using Exchange (or Microsoft Fax), then the document will be sent as an attached file which the recipient can then open and edit like any other file.

Many newer Windows NT applications have the ability to transmit files directly as a fax. For example, if you are using a high-end word processing application (not Notepad or WordPad) to create a document for the purpose of faxing to another person, you can save yourself a lot of extra steps by faxing it directly from the word processor. The exact command depends on the application, but typically you will find it under the File menu as the Send command. Word processors are not the only applications to have this feature.

Finally, you can often "print" a document to a fax, whether the application supports direct fax transmission or not. In this case, you would select Microsoft Fax as your "printer" and print the document normally. Rather than appearing on your normal printer, Windows NT will intercept the document and forward it to a fax number that you specify. If your intention is to fax the document anyway, this method saves you the work of saving the file, creating a new fax or e-mail message to attach it to, and sending it.

Calling a Fax-Back or Fax Information Service Many companies now provide a "fax-on-demand" service to allow their customers to receive printed information instantly. By simply dialing a telephone number and pressing a few buttons, a catalog, price list, or promotional literature can be returned to you (or more specifically, to your fax machine) in a few moments. Exchange provides the ability to call these services without lifting your telephone.

If you have an Exchange window open, you can click the Tools menu, highlight Microsoft Fax Tools, and click Request a Fax to start this procedure. Exchange will ask you for a fax number to call and off it goes.

Chapter 8

DOS COMPATIBILITY

With Windows NT you can still run many programs that were intended for MS-DOS. If you've had your computer for many years, you probably have a lot of old DOS programs that you still like to use. Sometimes, these old DOS programs have been updated with Windows NT versions, but other times there either is no Windows NT version or you just like the DOS version better. Never fear, Windows NT may let you run most DOS programs anyway.

First, a bit of history. MS-DOS (for Microsoft Disk Operating System) has been around almost since there were PCs. The first PCs didn't run MS-DOS, they used either something called CP/M, or ProDOS, or one of a handful of other operating systems. But when IBM started selling personal computers, it practically gave MS-DOS away with every PC, so MS-DOS became very popular. DOS was still running on more than 80% of the world's IBM-compatible PCs in 1996. In 1984 Microsoft created Windows version 1.0 but it wasn't very popular. In 1987 the company released version 2.0, but it wasn't very popular, either. Then, in 1990, Microsoft announced Windows version 3.0 and it was a huge success. Lots of new applications were created just for this new version of Windows (you may have some of them yourself).

Around that same time, Microsoft began developing an entirely new version of Windows for a new generation of microprocessors to address many of the limitations of Windows and the DOS operating system on which it was based. The project was code-named NT, after the new Intel microprocessor (the i860) it was designed for. The microprocessor never caught on, and Microsoft ported its new OS to the traditional Intel x86 chips as well as new, emerging RISC processors. Windows NT was first released in June of 1993, with the NT moniker officially changed to "new technology."

Although Windows 3.0 and Windows NT were big successes, there were literally millions of PCs around the world that used nothing but MS-DOS and each one had lots of DOS-style programs on it (you may have some of these, too). So it was important that Windows NT be able to run as many of the older DOS programs as possible in addition to the newer Windows NT programs. Windows 3 accomplished this feat reasonably well, and Windows 95 did even better, but it took a lot of tinkering by the computer owner to get some DOS programs to work.

In this chapter, you'll see how easy it is to get 90% of your old DOS programs working in no time. And, if you're sentimental about DOS, you'll see how you can get back to your old C:> prompt any time you want.

Running a DOS Application with Windows NT

The quickest and easiest way to find out if your favorite DOS application will run with Windows NT is to try it. You'll find this method also happens to work most of the time. The first step is to find the DOS program itself. There are at least three ways you can do this:

- Double-click on My Computer in the upper left corner of your desktop, and browse through your disks and folders until you find your DOS application.
- Open the Windows NT Explorer (click the Start button, highlight Programs, and select Windows NT Explorer) and browse through your disks and folders until you find your DOS application.
- Use the Find command (on the Start menu) to search for your application by name.

Once you find your DOS program, just double-click on it. You can recognize the right program file because the icon for all DOS applications looks like this (although it won't have the name Command under it):

Just to make sure this is a DOS application, you can right-click on the icon. When the shortcut menu pops up, select the Properties command. You will see a properties sheet like the one in Figure 8.1. The first tab of the property sheet has the icon of a "generic" DOS application at the top and the Type is listed as either Application or MS-DOS Application. Click the big OK button to close the property sheet and then double-click your icon to let 'er rip!

Try out your program. Experiment with it and make sure everything works the way it should. If there's going to be a problem, it normally shows up in the first 10 minutes. If everything checks out okay, exit your program and you're done.

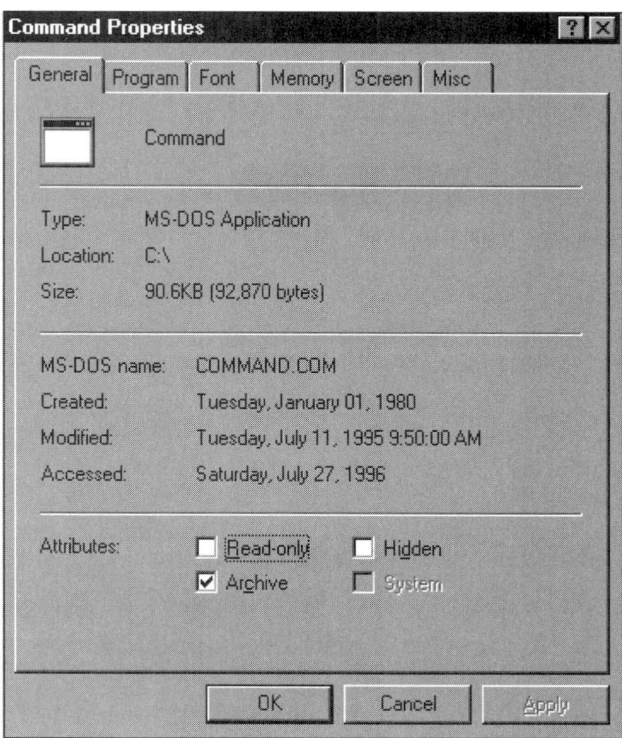

Figure 8.1: The property sheet for a typical MS-DOS application has six tabs.

If Your DOS Program Doesn't Run with Windows NT

If your DOS program doesn't run "right out of the box" by double-clicking it, you'll have to fine-tune its settings a little bit. This is not difficult, but it does require a little trial-and-error experimentation on your part.

You see, Windows NT knows what to do with Windows applications because those applications come with the information Windows NT needs to make them run well. DOS programs, on the other hand, were often created before there was a Windows NT, so they couldn't possibly supply the information Windows NT needs. It's a bit of a chicken-and-egg problem, and you get to sort it out.

No matter what the problem, you always start the same way: by right-clicking on the DOS application and selecting Properties from the shortcut menu.

As you saw in Figure 8.1, there are six tabs on the DOS property sheet. That's six categories of questions you get to answer, and they're mostly technical. The good news is, you don't have to answer them all at once, and you're allowed to guess. The worst that can happen is your DOS program still won't run. If you get stuck, you can click the question-mark button near the upper right corner of the property sheet and then click on one of the properties for a brief explanation. If you give it some thought, study up, and aren't afraid to experiment, you'll probably get your DOS program running in no time. Here goes...

General Properties You should always work through the property tabs in order. Start with the General tab and move ahead from there. Fortunately, the General tab is an easy one. As you can see in Figure 8.2, it's really telling you more than it's asking you. It gives you the name of your program, how much space on your disk it takes up (in both computer-speak and real numbers), its MS-DOS name, and even the last time you accessed (i.e., tried to run) it.

The only things you can change on this tab are a few file attributes at the bottom. If you check "Read-only" then the file will be harder to erase. If you check "Hidden" it won't show up in Explorer or My Computer windows any more (good for hiding things from prying eyes), and the Find command won't find it. The "Archive" attribute is fairly useless, and only says that this program has been copied at some point in its life. Practically all files have the Archive box checked.

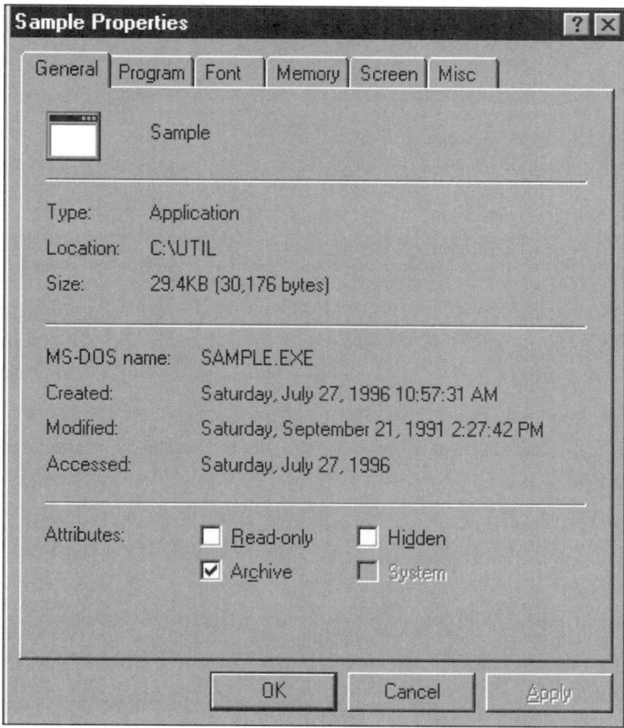

Figure 8.2: The General properties tab is a simple one.

Changing any of these attributes is not going to help your program run, so skip ahead to the next property tab. You can either click on the next tab or you can use your keyboard and press CTRL+TAB to move to the next tab.

Program Properties The Program tab (see Figure 8.3) has several options you can change; some important, some frivolous. The top line is completely unimportant. Whatever you type in here will become the title displayed underneath the icon. You can change this to say anything you like; it doesn't neccessarily have to be the actual name of the application.

The Cmd Line fill-in box is important, but it should already be filled in. It holds the exact name and the folder (technical description: the path) where this application is stored on disk. For more advanced users, you can add parameters or arguments after the end of the file's name. If the program accepts options after its name, you can add them

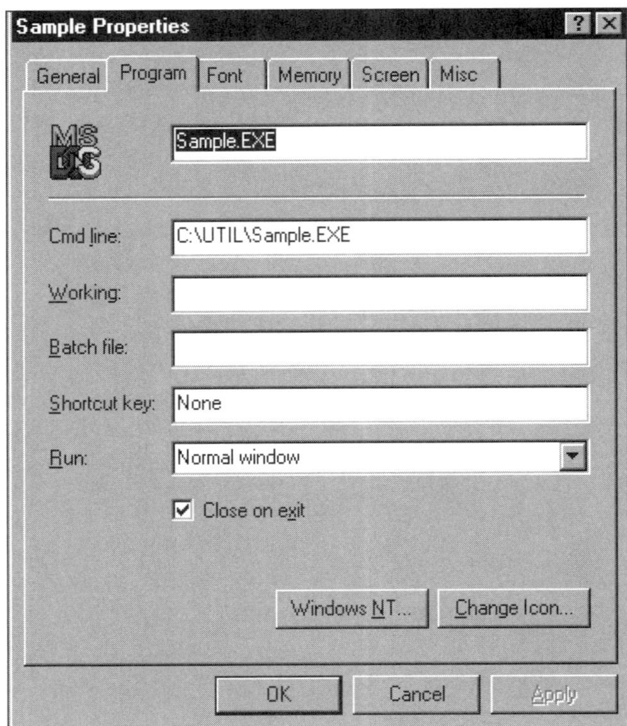

Figure 8.3: The Program properties tab determines an application's working directory and shortcut key, among other things.

here. All your DOS environment variables are available here, too. If you want Windows NT to stop and query you each time you launch this program, you can add a question mark after the end of the file name.

If you're familiar with previous versions of Windows NT, you may have noticed the similarity between the Program tab on the property sheet and the Properties window from Windows, shown below.

Program Item Properties

Description: Generic DOS Application

Command Line: C:\SAMPLE\SAMPLE.EXE

Working Directory: C:\SAMPLE

Shortcut Key: None

Run Minimized

OK

Cancel

Browse...

Change Icon...

Help

The third line down is the program's working directory (folder). Some applications care about this, others don't—there's no way to tell in advance. Entering a directory (folder) name here makes the program think it's running from that directory. That might be important if it's looking for accessory files like overlays, data files, templates, or saved work files. When in doubt, type in the same path as the program itself from the line above but without the program name at the end. In the example, a good working path would be C:\UTIL\SAMPLE.

The line for a batch file is new to this version of Windows NT. If you type the name of a batch file here, Windows NT will execute the commands in the batch file just before it launches the program itself. Why would you want to do this? Because with Windows NT, each MS-DOS window (including the one that this program is about to run in) gets its own private environment, including a set of environment variables, drivers, memory manager, and so forth. If you want to set (or clear) a few environment variables before this program runs, this is the way to do it. By the way, you don't necessarily have to enter the name of a batch file here—any valid one-line MS-DOS command will do.

The Shortcut key option is a really wonderful toy for "power users." With it, you can assign a single, special key that will instantly start this application running or switch to its window if it is already running. You don't have to click on the Start button, find it with a browser, or click on the Taskbar—nothing. Just press a key and there it is.

Well, two keys, actually. It would be foolish to pick the letter "A" as the special shortcut key or you could never type a legible sentence again. Your special shortcut key must be a combination of ALT or CTRL and another letter. It can also be ALT *and* CTRL and a letter.

There is one catch. Your shortcut key must be unique—it can't already be in use by another application on this computer. And, although it's not a rule, you should never pick a shortcut key that's the same as a keyboard command used in an application. For example, if you picked CTRL+S you'd have a tough time saving any documents because most Windows NT applications also use CTRL+S as a shortcut to the Save command.

The last fill-in line asks how big a window you want to give this application. Your choices are normal, minimized, and maximized. Maximized means the whole screen (which many DOS programs do anyway). Minimized means no window at all; the program starts out minimized, as just a button on the Taskbar. Normal means a normal Windows-type window. This is usually a good choice.

The final item on this tab is a check box that says Close on exit. If you check this, the application's window will close as soon as the application itself is finished running. Leaving this unchecked will leave the window open, even though the application isn't running anymore. This is handy if your application believes in lengthy good-byes. If it often displays passing status (or error) messages that you would miss if the window closed too early, don't check this box. If you're having trouble with an MS-DOS application, leave this box unchecked and carefully read anything the application might display after it exits.

Near the bottom of the property sheet are two buttons that you won't find on the other property tabs. They're labeled Windows NT and Change Icon. If you're feeling bold and you click on the Windows NT button, you'll see a special window like the one in Figure 8.4.

Advanced Properties The items on this property page are fairly esoteric, advanced technical options that you normally will never need to modify. They allow you to give this particular DOS application its own MS-DOS environment. That is, you can change your computer's CONFIG.SYS and AUTOEXEC.BAT startup files every time this application runs. When you double-click the application, Windows NT will reboot your computer using the two startup files you've specified.

Normally, Windows NT keeps standard, general-purpose copies of CONFIG.SYS and AUTOEXEC.BAT handy in its home directory, called CONFIG.NT and AUTOEXEC.NT, respectively. Using these two fill-in boxes, you can specify alternates.

The check-box option, Compatible Timer Hardware Emulation, is a technical detail regarding Windows NT's manner of handling time slicing. There's no good rule of thumb here; just guess.

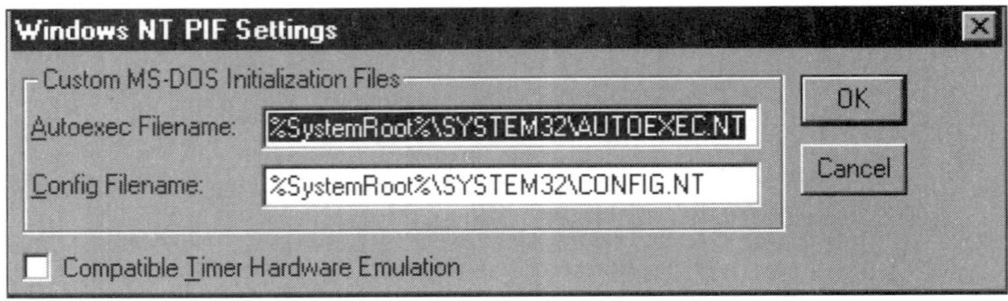

Figure 8.4: On the Program properties tab, clicking the Windows NT button displays this window.

Changing the Icon The last button on this property tab is labeled Change Icon, and it does just what it says. Since MS-DOS programs don't come with their own icons (icons are a Windows thing), you might not like the dreary, generic one that Windows NT assigns to all MS-DOS applications. Clicking this button allows you to choose from a small gallery of icons, as Figure 8.5 shows.

Now, if MS-DOS programs don't have icons, where did all these icons come from? They come from a little library of icons that Windows NT keeps stashed away for just this purpose. If you read the top line of the property window, you'll even see which file this library is in (PIFMGR.DLL). The library contains about two dozen different icons from which you can choose. Simply click on the one you want, and then click on OK.

But wait, there's more! If you still can't find an icon you like, you are allowed to "borrow" icons from other applications. If you type the name of a different file or application in the fill-in box (please be complete, Windows NT needs the entire path name and file name), you will see all of its icons. As an experiment, type in the name of a file that you know contains some interesting icons and see what new choices you get. (Hint: Try SHELL32.DLL.)

There's nothing wrong with using icons from one file or application to decorate another application. The only problem you might possibly encounter is losing your icon if you ever delete the file that it came from. If an application unexpectedly loses its icon some day, that might be the cause.

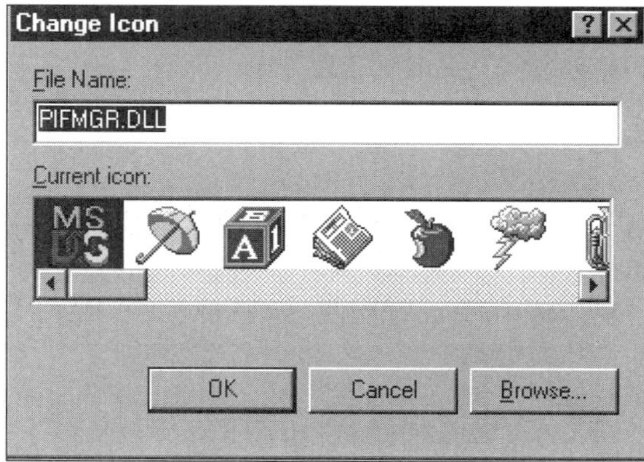

Figure 8.5: Clicking the Change Icon button allows you to pick a file to take an icon from, and which icon to use.

Sadly, choosing a new icon only changes the appearance of the shortcut for your application, not the application itself. That's okay, because it's probably better to launch your application by double-clicking on the shortcut icon anyway. Besides, you can move the shortcut icon onto your desktop or onto the Start menu, where your new icon will be more visible.

Font Properties The Fonts tab is mostly frivolous, so don't worry too much about choosing the right answer here. It only affects how MS-DOS programs will display their messages, and even then, only when they're running in a window. As you can see from Figure 8.6, the tab is divided into four quadrants. The two top ones are for you to fiddle with while the two bottom ones show you the effects of your labor.

Your job here is to pick the font (that is, the typeface or style of print) that you like best. The scrolling list on the upper right shows you all

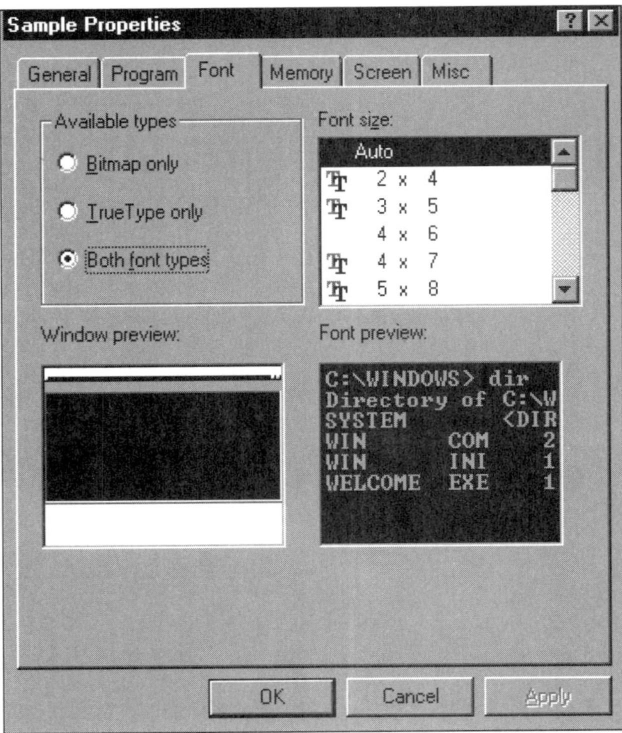

Figure 8.6: The Font properties tab controls text-based DOS applications.

your choices. There's nearly two dozen of them. Go ahead and click on each font size to see what happens. The numbers, like 5×7 or 8×12, are a technical description of how big each letter is. For example, in the 5×7 font, each letter of the alphabet is five dots wide and seven dots high. Exciting, huh?

The purpose of the three options on the left is to let you narrow down your choice of fonts. Among aficionados of typefaces, there's a difference between so-called bitmap fonts and TrueType fonts. You may be hard-pressed to notice (or care). In general, it's best to choose "Auto" from the list of fonts on the right and be on your way.

Memory Properties The Memory tab is a nasty one. Allocating your computer's memory (that's the RAM, not the disk) is a tricky task and one of major reasons Windows NT exists at all. In the bad old days when you could only run one application at a time, each application could use all the memory your computer had. Now they have to share, and they're not always good at it. Your goal here is to discover how much memory your application needs, and fill in all the boxes accordingly.

As Figure 8.7 shows, the Memory tab has five drop-down lists, each one having something to do with memory. Throughout the Byzantine history of PCs, different methods emerged for managing the memory inside your computer, and they are all still with us. The terms conventional, expanded, extended, and protected-mode all refer to the same memory inside your PC, but divided up and managed in different ways. Some applications will want it one way, and some will want it another. There's no single right answer for all of them—that's why each application has its own property sheet.

When in doubt, leave everything set to Auto as they are in the figure. If that doesn't work, read the manuals that came with your application slowly and carefully, looking for any descriptions of how much memory the application needs. After that, guess.

Screen Properties Most of the Screen properties are not vitally important to solving a problem, but they can increase your enjoyment of the application. The first two questions are the big ones. They decide whether your application will run in a window (like any well-behaved Windows NT application) or have the screen all to itself (like practically all MS-DOS programs).

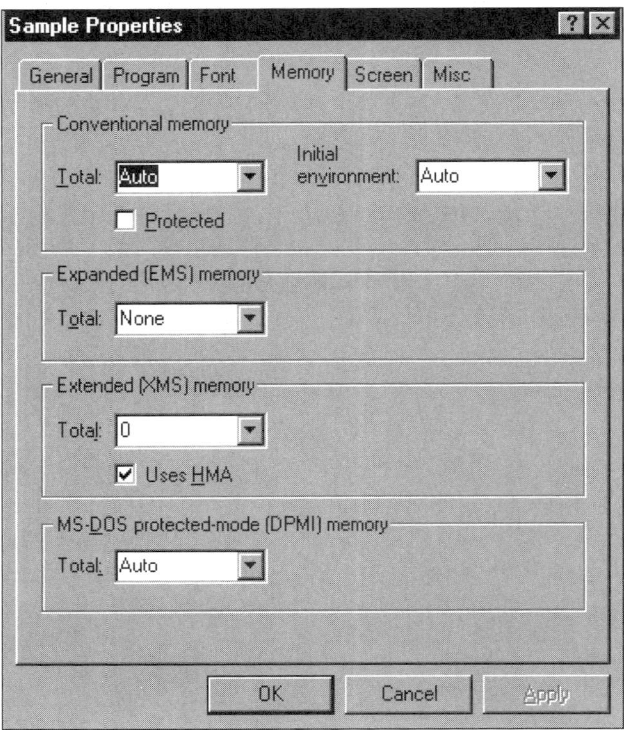

Figure 8.7: The Memory properties tab is a tricky one that sometimes requires some experimentation.

As Figure 8.8 shows, the normal choice is to run the application in a window (this is Windows NT, after all). To the right of these two options is a drop-down list that lets you choose how big that window is going to be. It's a little-known fact, but when you're running MS-DOS, your PC can display more than the usual 25 lines of text on the screen at a time. If you don't mind small print, you can squeeze as many as 50 lines in at once. Use the drop-down list to pick the print density you're happiest with.

The next two check boxes only work if you chose to run the application in a window. If you did, these control the look of the window. Do you want a Windows-style toolbar to appear in the window? If so, check the box. Do you want the window to go back to its previous place on the screen after the application quits? If yes, check the box.

The last two check boxes are fairly technical, and you should leave them checked if you can. If your program does odd things, try turning these off one at a time.

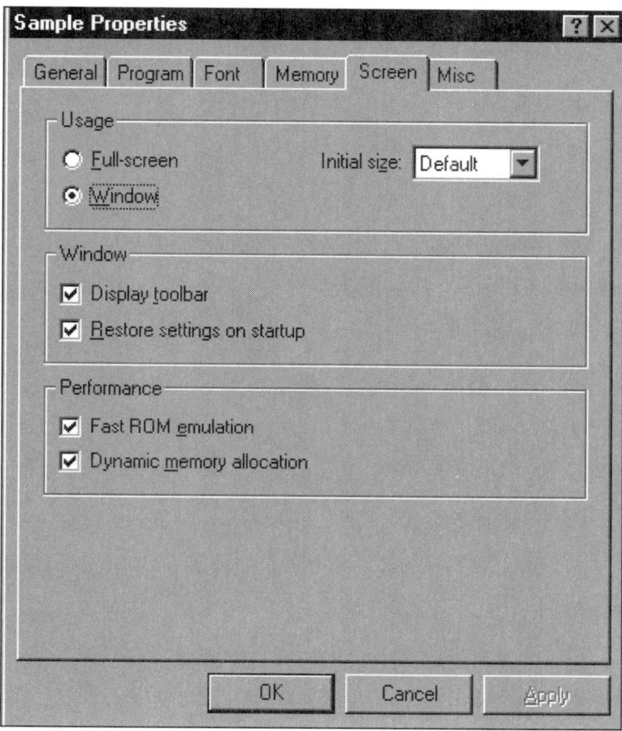

Figure 8.8: The Screen properties tab controls how and how big the DOS application will be displayed.

Misc Properties The Miscellaneous properties holds all the options that didn't fit in the other tabs. Some of these are important, others are downright strange. Take a look at the sample Misc tab in Figure 8.9 and follow along.

Starting from the top, the first check box allows you to turn your Windows NT screen saver off when this program is running. Normally, a screen saver kicks in after about 15 minutes (you get to choose the time) if you leave your computer alone. It's usually harmless, but it's possible that an unwanted screen saver might possibly cause your application to misbehave. Or you just might want to turn the screen saver off because you'd rather look at the DOS screen. Either way, click the box to remove the check mark and the screen saver won't bother this program.

The Always Suspend box is somewhat technical, but here goes. Because your PC can run lots of applications at once, it has to divide its attention among each of those applications. If you minimize an

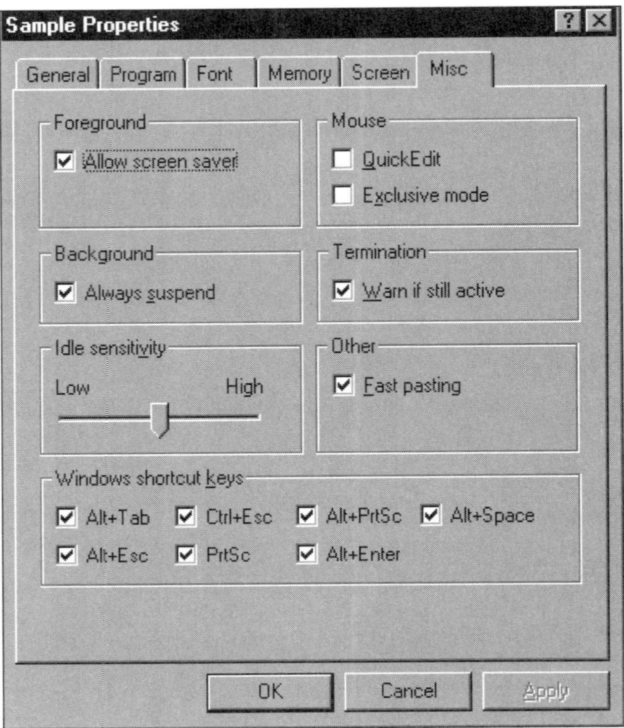

Figure 8.9: The Misc properties tab controls a relatively unimportant collection of features.

application or leave it at the back of your screen behind a lot of other windows for a long time, Windows NT figures you aren't very interested in that application and doesn't waste a lot of time on it. This happens all the time and you normally wouldn't notice it. Like any good kindergarten teacher, Windows NT is very good about giving applications attention when they need it and ignoring them when they don't. If you happen to have an application that (for whatever reason) doesn't need any attention at all, you can check this box and Windows NT will give its portion of time to the other applications.

The slider control labeled Idle Sensitivity is related to the check box just mentioned. This control lets you decide the application's "attention span." If you move it toward Low, Windows NT will keep giving it attention for a long time, even if you've minimized the application or put it in the background behind other windows. Moving the control toward High will allow Windows NT to move its attention elsewhere more quickly.

Moving back to the top of the property sheet, you'll find two mouse-related items. The first one lets you use something called QuickEdit to cut text out of the application's window. This normally works okay, but some DOS applications don't like it. If you don't plan on snipping bits of text out of the DOS window, this option doesn't matter.

The Exclusive Mode check box tells Windows NT that you want to give total and exclusive control of the mouse to this application. That means that Windows NT itself will not be able to follow your mouse. Think twice about checking this option, unless you're good at operating Windows NT without a mouse. The only reason to check this option is if the DOS application simply won't work any other way. Of course, this option is not permanent; when the application ends, Windows NT always gets its mouse back.

The Termination Warning check box keeps you from accidentally closing a DOS application before you mean to. DOS applications aren't used to having windows around them, and if you click on the window's close box, the DOS application might not be ready to quit yet. With this option checked, if you accidentally (or on purpose) click on the close box for a DOS window, Windows NT will warn you and give you a chance to change your mind. If you're adventurous or you never make mistakes, go ahead and clear the check mark.

The Fast Pasting check box allows you to turn off a Windows NT feature that some older DOS programs don't like. Like the QuickEdit feature, you can paste text into a DOS window using the normal cut and paste commands that are available in any window. Sometimes, Windows NT has to do the pasting very slowly or the DOS application gets confused. If this is the case with your DOS application, clear the check box.

At the bottom of the Misc tab are seven check boxes, one for each special shortcut key that Windows NT uses. Here's a puzzle: You're running a DOS application and you press a special key combination, say, ALT+TAB. Is the ALT+TAB meant for the application or for Windows NT? What if the application uses ALT+TAB to do something special? Should the application do its ALT+TAB thing or should Windows NT do its ALT+TAB thing (which, by the way, is to show you a list of the applications you're running)? Here's your opportunity to solve this conundrum. If you leave a box checked, then the shortcut key belongs to Windows NT. If you clear the check mark, then the shortcut belongs to the application.

Finishing the Property Sheet After you've navigated through all six tabs of the property sheet, don't forget to click the big OK button at the bottom of the property sheet! If you forget and click the close box or the Cancel instead, all your changes will be thrown away. On the other hand, if you change your mind and want to undo all the changes you started to make, you can click the close box or the big Cancel button and everything will be left as it was.

Property Sheets and PIF Files All the changes you make to a program's property sheet are stored in a special file called a program information file, or PIF. You can identify PIF files from the MS-DOS prompt because they always have the three-letter file extension .PIF. These shortcuts also look like the following icon.

You can change this icon by right-clicking it and selecting Properties. Then refer to the Program tab, above, for instructions. It doesn't matter whether you launch an application by double-clicking its shortcut or by double-clicking the application itself, although shortcuts can be moved around for convenience and have their icons changed.

DOS and Long File Names

One of the most-requested changes to Windows NT was the ability to use long file names. With MS-DOS and every version of Windows before 1995, file names could only be eight letters long. Now they can be 255 characters long, including spaces and most punctuation marks. While that's all well and good, don't start renaming all your files and folders right away to take advantage of the long names. If you do, most MS-DOS, Windows 3, and earlier Windows NT programs will stop working.

That's because your older DOS and Windows applications won't know how to find files that have long file names. Those applications were created by people who were absolutely, positively, dead certain that all files and folders (directories) would have eight-letter names. They don't even look at anything after the eighth letter. If you change the name of a folder and give it a long, 255-character name, your DOS and older Windows applications won't understand and won't be able to load or save any files in that folder.

Neat Tricks at the DOS Prompt

Although Windows NT is supposed to discourage people from using DOS anymore, there are still die-hard fans of the world's most popular operating system. In fact, Windows NT comes with a new and improved version of DOS that has more features than any version before it. So you're bound to want to play with the new features, right?

The new version of DOS that comes with Windows NT includes a new START command. You can type START and the DOS prompt and follow it with the name of either an application or a document file. The named application will start running in a new Windows window and your MS-DOS window will remain open.

Even more interesting, if you put the name of a document file after the START command, Windows NT will start the application normally associated with those files in a new window, with the document already loaded. For example, you can type START README.TXT and Windows NT will open a new Notepad window with README.TXT in it.

The START command accepts one of four options to control window size, which you must place before the name of the application or document. Typing START /MIN <filename> starts the new window minimized (as a Taskbar button). The /MAX option starts the window maximized (full screen); the /R option (for Restored) opens a normal sized window. Using the /W option (for Wait) prohibits you from returning to the DOS window until the newly opened window is closed again.

START also has a few truly weird uses. Typing START followed by a single period dot opens a new window with the contents of the current folder displayed. In essence typing "START ." is like getting a graphical DIR listing. Likewise, typing "START .." (with two dots) displays the parent folder in a window.

Although it doesn't work with the START command, the new DOS accepts more than just one or two dots to represent parent directories (or, if you prefer, enclosing folders). For example, you can type "DIR ...." (with four dots) to see a directory listing of the "great-grandparent" of the current directory. You can use any number of dots, up to the limit of your actual directory structure. This syntax also works with the CD (change directory) command.

MS-DOS windows run a whole lot faster if they're not windows at all. Pressing ALT+ENTER enlarges your DOS session to fill the entire screen: no Taskbar, no title bar, no nothing. Pressing ALT+ENTER again returns it to its windowed state.

Because you can have an MS-DOS window open beside a traditional Windows window, there is the potential to drag and drop items from one to the other, and this works surprisingly well. Dragging an arbitrary icon into a DOS window and dropping it there places the icon's full path name at the DOS prompt. If you type START first and then drag the icon of a document file into your DOS window, you can open the document by pressing <ENTER>. It's not clear what advantage this technique has over simply double-clicking the icon itself, but there you are.

Chapter 9

WINDOWS NT 4.X FOR WINDOWS NT 3.X USERS

While there's no question that the latest version of Windows NT is based on earlier versions of Windows, Windows NT, and Windows 95, there's also no question that it's very different from those versions. Moving from one to the other can take some time. If you're a Windows NT 3.x user, and you're having trouble getting used to the new look of Windows NT, take heart. In this section, you'll see what's new and different—and also what's the same. From starting up to shutting down, you'll walk through a typical day using your PC to do what you already do—better!

How to Start Windows NT

Starting Windows NT couldn't be simpler. You just turn your computer on and there it is. Your PC may have already started Windows NT automatically before, but on many computers you have to type WIN first at the MS-DOS prompt. No longer. Windows NT always starts automatically after you turn your computer on.

Technical Note: If you don't want Windows NT to start, you can abort the loading process and boot MS-DOS instead. To do this, you must watch for the words Starting Windows... and then press <F5>. Your computer will boot the version of MS-DOS you had before loading Windows.

After your computer makes some routine systems checks, you should see the basic Windows NT desktop with a big Welcome window in the middle of it, like the one in Figure 9.1. The Welcome window pops up every time you start Windows NT and provides a (hopefully) handy tip about something you might not know. If you find this little daily tip annoying (or just think you know it all by now), you can click on the little check box down in the lower left corner. With the check mark gone, the Welcome window won't come back. To dismiss the Welcome window for now, click once on the button in the lower right marked Close. You're all set to go!

Before you got to the Welcome screen, Windows NT will have asked you to enter your name and your password. By entering your name before you get started, Windows NT can customize the computer just for you. This is handy when several people are sharing the same computer. If Windows knows who you are, it can change your screen's "wallpaper," the items on your Start menu, and lots of other things. Windows NT, of course, also enforces a certain amount of system security. When two or more people share the same computer, Windows NT keeps their files private and separate from one another.

Figure 9.1: When you start Windows NT, you should see this welcome screen.

Now you should be looking at the Windows NT desktop. Windows NT 3.x had a desktop, too. It was colored solid, or you might have had a pretty pattern or "wallpaper" design on it. All your windows, like the Program Manager and the File Manager, sat on the desktop. It's essentially the same arrangement here. This is your desktop and you can decorate it with different colors or patterns just like before.

This desktop is a little bit like the Program Manager in Windows NT 3.x because all of your programs, groups, and documents are in here somewhere. It's different from Program Manager because you can never minimize it or close it. Notice that there is no window frame around the desktop, no scroll bars, and no buttons in the upper-left and upper right corners. Your new desktop is more open and unrestricted than the old one was. In a way, it's as if you have the Program Manager window open all the time.

How to Quit Windows NT

First things first. Now that you've successfully started Windows NT the very next thing to know is how to stop it. In Windows NT 3.x, you closed the Program Manager and that closed Windows NT. But as you can see, there is no Program Manager any more, so there must be another way. Ironically, the way to stop Windows NT is with the Start button. Click once on the Start button (with the spiffy Windows logo) in the lower left corner of your screen. A menu should pop straight up from the button, as shown in Figure 9.2.

Without clicking anything yet, move your mouse pointer up just a bit until Shut Down is highlighted. Notice that you didn't have to hold

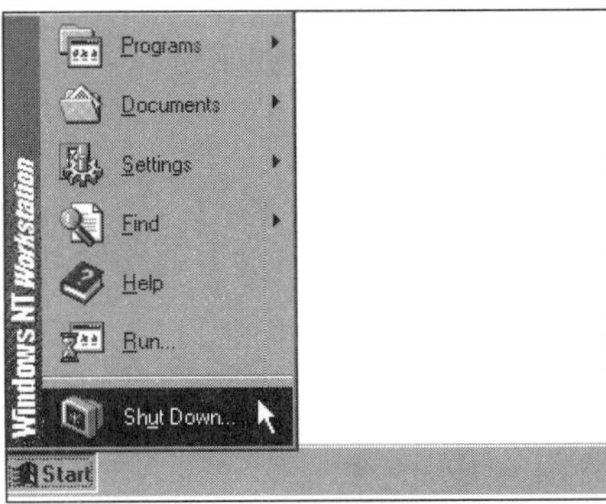

Figure 9.2: Finding a file or application generally starts with a single click on the Start button.

down the mouse button or click anything. With Shut Down highlighted, click once. The screen should go dim and Shutdown gives you a window with three options, shown in Figure 9.3. For now, ignore the three options and just click the big square button at the bottom that says Yes.

Now you wait. It's not okay to turn the power off until Windows NT says it's okay. It usually takes less than ten seconds before your screen goes dark and Windows NT says, in big friendly letters, that it is safe to turn your computer off. You must always, always remember to use the Shut Down command every single time before you turn your computer off.

Why all the fuss about turning off a computer? It's because Windows NT does a lot of work behind your back that you don't know about. Like any team effort, you need to coordinate quitting times. If you turned your PC off without choosing the Shut Down command first, you would probably lose some files on your disk. Part of what makes Windows NT fast also makes it temperamental about shutting down. That's just the way it is. If you've ever used a Macintosh or a computer running UNIX, you've already experienced the ritual of shutting it down. MS-DOS users should count themselves lucky for avoiding it for so long.

Some Basic Differences from Windows NT 3.x

We'll take a complete walk-through of the system in just a moment, but before we start, there are some common points you should be familiar with. Most Windows NT 3.x users have developed certain

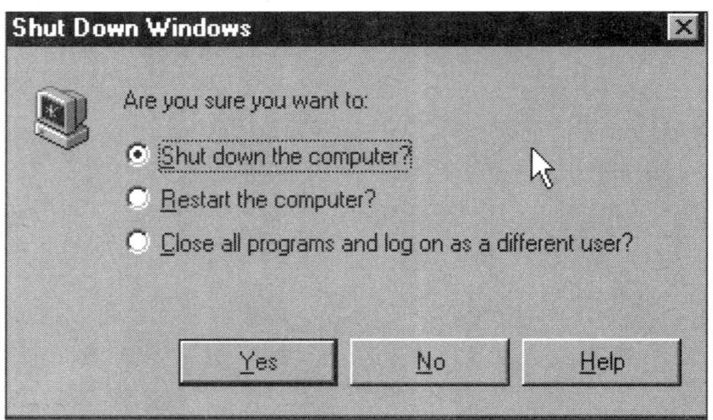

Figure 9.3: There are multiple ways to shut down your computer.

habits, and habits can be hard to break. Although your new Windows NT is a lot like the earlier versions of Windows NT, some of your unconscious habits may have to change. For example:

- You rarely need to double-click.
- A window's "close" box is now in the upper right, not the upper left, corner.
- The right mouse button actually works.
- There is no Program Manager to hold groups of programs.
- File names can be more than 250 letters long, with spaces between words.
- Windows NT does not run on top of DOS (DOS now runs on top of Windows NT).
- You cannot double-click the wallpaper to see a task list.

These little gems should help you adjust to the new look of Windows NT. At first, most people have trouble with the first two items: they tend to double-click a lot, and they inevitably reach for the upper left corner of a window to close it.

Starting an Application

With Windows NT running, click once on the Start button. This pops up the Start menu. The Start menu is the easiest way (although not the only way) to reach your programs. It is somewhat comparable to the Program Manager groups you used to have. Without clicking anything, move your mouse up and down the Start menu. Notice how items are highlighted even though you aren't clicking on them. The uppermost items have arrows on them that point to the right. If you rest your mouse pointer over one of these (called "hovering") for a moment, a submenu will pop up.

These are called cascading menus, and they only appear on the Start menu. To reach an item on a cascaded menu, move your mouse pointer to the right, over the new submenu, as shown in Figure 9.4. These submenus might also have arrows and submenus themselves. Hovering over one of these will open another submenu, and so on. When you finally reach an item you want, you can click once on it.

Remember that you only clicked once to pop up the Start menu and once to finally select the command or application program that you wanted. You should not have been holding your mouse button down or clicking each item along the way. Yes, this is different than it was

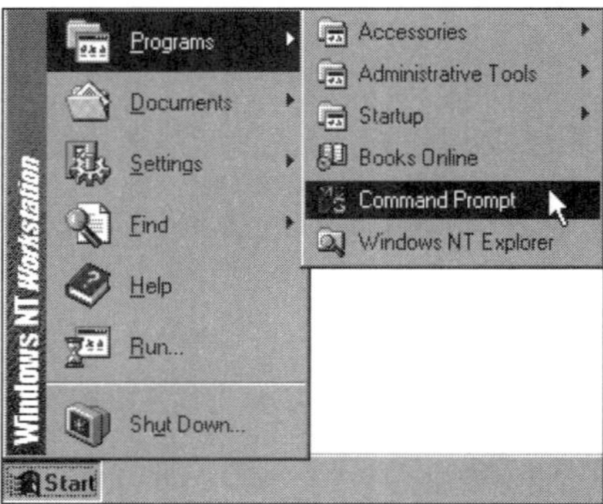

Figure 9.4: Some items on the Start menu will show additional choices if you let your mouse pause over them for a moment.

with Windows NT 3.x, but you'll find that this way is not only easier, but it's also faster and not as hard on your finger.

If you accidentally "fall off" a cascading submenu, it might disappear. You may need a little practice before you can speed through the Start menu, highlighting the items you want from a series of cascading menus, before you click on your goal. For now, click somewhere on the blank desktop, away from any of the menus, and they'll all go away.

Click the Start button. Hover over Programs, then move to Accessories, then move to Notepad, and click once on it. This should start up the Notepad application that comes free with Windows NT. The basic Notepad window should open in the middle of your screen. Notepad is a simple word processor (also called a text editor), so process some words!

Type something. It doesn't matter much what you type, but you should enter a couple of lines before going on. Don't worry about spelling or making it pretty.

Navigating Application Menus

Now it's time to take a look at how to use the menus that all Windows NT applications have. Basically, the Notepad window in Windows NT looks very much like any similar applications did in Windows NT 3.x. The blue title bar across the top, the line of menu commands below it, and the scroll bars along the edges are all nearly the same. There is a subtle difference in how the menus work, though. Brace yourself.

Click once on the word Edit on the menu bar in Notepad. Move your mouse around and see how the commands are highlighted without clicking on them. Now move your mouse to the right, passing over the other menus, like Search and File, and notice how each menu drops down all on its own. Just like the Start menu, you can glide over the menus without selecting anything.

Go back to the File menu and click once on Save. Windows NT now shows you a generic "Save As" dialog box like the one in Figure 9.5. Get used to this. This type of dialog box is not specific to Notepad; it's the same for all new Windows applications. This dialog box is meant to help you, letting you browse through your computer looking for the right disk or folder in which to save your file. Click on the drop-down list near the top of the window. A list drops down showing you all the disks on your computer. Pick the one you want. Notice that two items called Desktop and My Computer are among the choices. After you pick a disk (click on it once) the main window changes to a list of folders. See how this works? The main window is showing you the folders that are inside the disk named at the top in the drop-down list. If you double-click one of these folders to open it, it will get "promoted" to the top, and the main window will show you the folders that are located inside it, and so on. Keep going until you find the folder you want.

If you accidentally navigate too far into a series of folders and want to go back "up" the directory tree, you have three options. You can

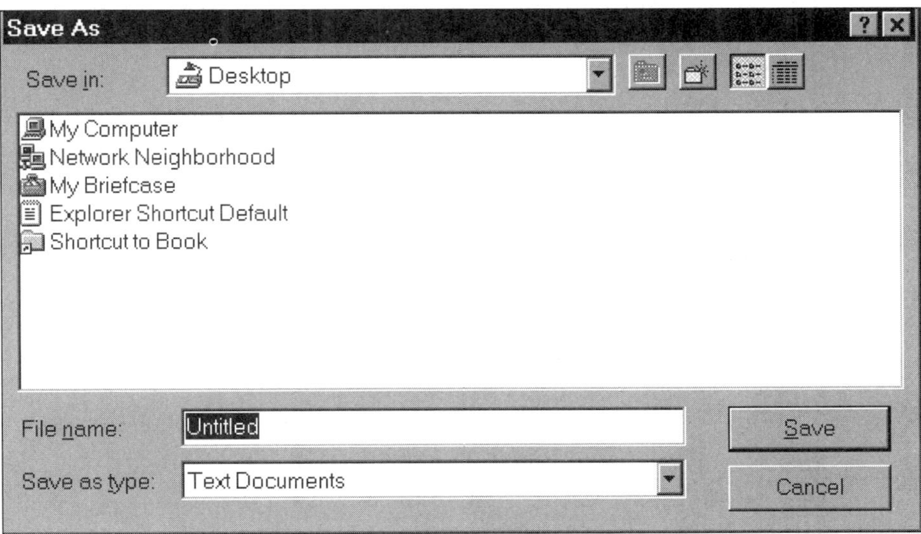

Figure 9.5: Dialog boxes for loading and saving files let you browse through your computer's disks and folders.

either select the drop-down list near the top of the window again, or you can press your <BACKSPACE> key, or you can click once on the up-folder icon on the window's toolbar. That's the icon with the little yellow folder with an arrow in it. Clicking it once takes you to the current folder's parent folder.

If you want to create a new folder for the file you're saving, you don't have to switch to the File Manager (or, in this case, Windows NT Explorer). Instead, click once on the new-folder button in the toolbar. That's the icon with the sparkly new folder, right next to the up-folder icon. You can also use a new trick by right-clicking (that's clicking your right mouse button one time) somewhere in the white area in the window. When the pop-up shortcut menu appears, hover over the New command, then highlight and click the word Folder. A brand-new folder will be created for you.

When you're ready to save your Notepad file, type a name for it by double-clicking on the word Untitled in the fill-in area near the bottom of the window. Notice how large the space is to type your name? That's because Windows NT can now accept file names that are up to 255 characters long. You don't have to try to squeeze names into eight letters any more. Feel free to type a long file name like "This is my first experience with Notepad." When you're satisfied, click on the big Save button.

That's right, "This is my first experience with Notepad" really is the name of your file, not just some title that shows up in a program group. That may take some getting used to, but it's guaranteed to be a happy change.

Managing Windows NT Windows

Now you should be back at your Notepad window. The blue title bar should have the name of your file in it now. Take a look at the three little square buttons in the upper right corner of the window. These fulfill much the same function as the minimize and maximize buttons did in Windows 3. Going from left to right, they are the minimize button, the maximize button, and the close button.

Clicking once on the minimize button will shrink the application, but not close it. Try that now. The entire Notepad window shrinks, but instead of becoming a minimized window on your desktop like with Windows NT 3.x, it becomes a button on the Taskbar. Clicking once on that button restores Notepad to its original size and position.

Click once on the maximize button. Notepad expands to fill the entire screen except for its title bar at the top and the Windows NT Taskbar at the bottom. Clicking the maximize button again (although now it looks different) restores Notepad to its previous size.

Finally, clicking on the close button ends the application. In Windows NT 3.x, you could do this by double-clicking on the application's upper left corner, or by selecting Exit from the program's File menu, or by pressing ALT+F4. Happily, all three of these techniques still work, but now you should get in the habit of reaching for the close box in the upper right corner instead of the upper left corner.

Where's File Manager?

Few people ever really liked the File Manager that came with Windows NT 3.x. It was a necessary evil, and sometimes the only way to accomplish certain jobs. Now Windows NT has replaced the venerable File Manager with not one, but two different ways to browse your system's disk. They are called the Windows NT Explorer and simply My Computer.

Explorer is the more advanced of the two and more technical. Explorer is also more nearly like File Manager. For most people, Explorer is more advanced than they need and so they never use it at all. For them, opening My Computer is sufficient. If you want to become familiar with the Windows NT Explorer, turn to Chapter 2 and follow the guidelines there.

If you want to compare Windows with File Manager, take a look at Figure 9.6, which shows a typical File Manager session. File Manager has one big window with separate windows inside it for each disk. Each of those disk windows is divided into left and right "panes." The left pane shows the disk's directory structure (folders), and the right pane shows the files that are located inside that folder (in this case, "win31"). Clicking a different folder on the left would show a different set of files on the right. Right?

One of the problems with File Manager was that most people who weren't already engineers had a tough time grasping the concept of the

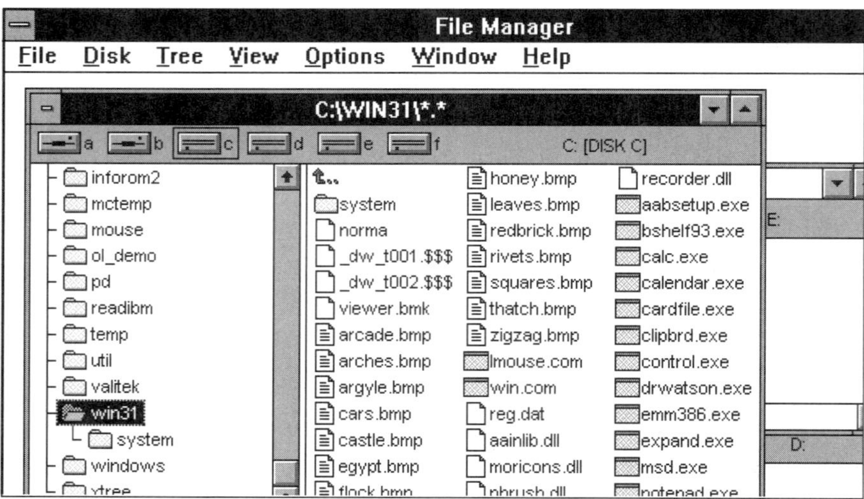

Figure 9.6: Windows NT has dispensed with the old FIle Manager.

two window panes. Do I click on the left side or the right side? Where is my file located? It's not obvious how the files on the right side are related to the diagram on the left side. It was also troublesome to need different disk windows for each disk. Finally, if you wanted to copy or move a file from one folder or disk to another, you had to carefully arrange all the windows so that both folders were visible at once so you could drag the icon to its destination. All in all, not an ideal solution.

Now with Windows NT, "My Computer" is different. To open My Computer, simply double-click the My Computer icon that sits in the upper left corner of your desktop. A window will open showing you the first-level contents of your computer. That is, you'll see icons for each of your computer's disk drives, plus a couple of extra folders filled with useful goodies. Your window should look something like the one in Figure 9.7.

This is your alternative to File Manager. The disk and folder icons should be fairly self-explanatory. Double-clicking either a disk or a folder will open it up and show you its contents in a new window. If you continue opening folders this way you will soon have a screen filled with many different windows. Whereas File Manager had one big window with smaller windows fitting inside, My Computer lets you open a new window for each disk and folder. You can move them around, change their sizes, close ones you don't care about anymore, or anything you want—no restrictions. To close any of the windows, you should, of course, click on its close box.

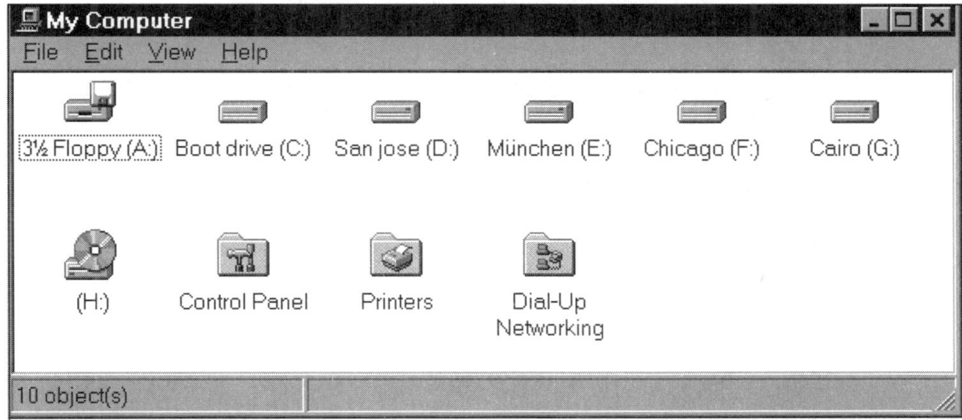

Figure 9.7: This is the normal view that replaces File Manager.

In addition to File Manager, Windows 3 also had Program Manager. Program Manager was another big window that held something called groups, and groups held the icons for the applications you wanted to run. You probably had groups called Main, Applications, Games, and the like. Although the windows in My Computer may remind you of the windows and groups you used to see with Program Manager, they're really not the same at all. Program Manager only showed you icons for a limited selection of applications and documents that were already in groups. With Program Manager, the rest of your files were hidden. Now the Start button fulfills that role. It holds the icons for your most frequently used applications. The folders and files you see by opening My Computer are your entire computer—files, folders, and all—just the way they're stored on your computer.

If you are a Macintosh user, you should be familiar with this style of showing what's stored on a computer. By experimenting with the View menu, you should be able to customize the display windows to suit your taste. You can choose to either show or hide dates and file sizes, for instance, or change the way files are sorted.

Some differences to watch out for: Windows NT normally hides certain kinds of files in the My Computer windows. Normally, this isn't a problem. For example, Windows NT hides about a half dozen classes of system files unless you specifically tell it not to. Windows NT also does not display the three-letter file extension for most files such as applications, help files, and device drivers.

How Do I Switch between Applications?

With Windows NT 3.x, you could switch between running applications a few different ways. If you could see the application's window, you could click on some visible portion of it; you could double-click the background to get a task list and then select from the list; you could press ALT+ESC to activate each of the applications in turn; or you could press ALT+TAB to cycle through the names of all the running applications. Fortunately, with Windows NT, it's easier than all that.

You've already had a taste of the Taskbar from using Notepad. Whenever an application is running, it appears as a button on the Taskbar. The more applications you have running, the more crowded the Taskbar will be. When an application is active (that is, when it's foremost on your screen) its button is pushed in. All the other applications' buttons are pushed out. To switch between applications, you simply push the right button. Since the Taskbar never disappears, and since every running application or open window automatically gets a button on the Taskbar, you can always take a quick glance at the Taskbar to see what's running. A quick click on the appropriate Taskbar button will bring that window right back up. There's no need to hunt for the window you want, just find its button and click.

If you're in the habit, you can still use ALT+ESC on the keyboard to switch from application to application. You can even still use ALT+TAB, though it works a little differently (try it). Naturally, you can also click on any visible portion of a window to select it as well. The only technique you can't use anymore is double-clicking the background screen. That behavior won't get you anywhere.

What about Groups and Programs?

With Windows NT 3.x, you probably had all your program icons arranged into groups. The groups were all inside one big Program Manager window, like the one shown in Figure 9.8. There was probably a group called Main, a Programs group, maybe a Games group, and an Accessories group. Finding and running the program you wanted was just a matter of opening the correct group window and then double-clicking the program icon.

Well now it's even easier. All the your programs are now on the Start menu. The big Program Manager window is gone, and so are all of the

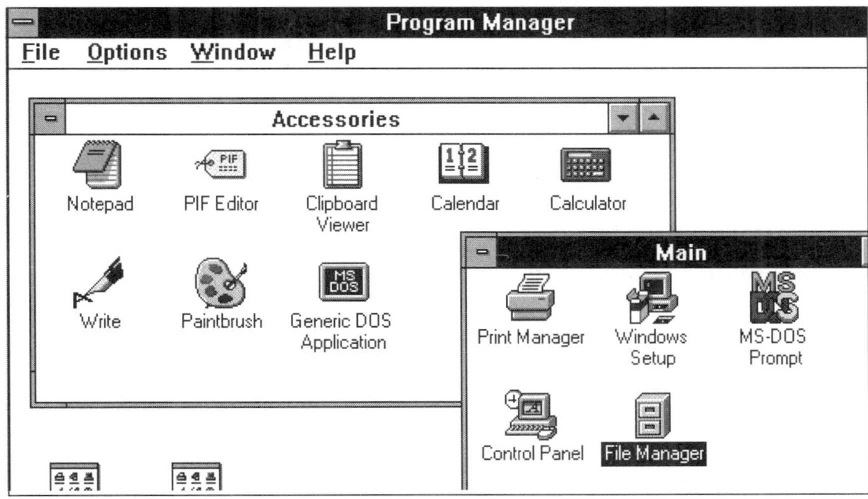

Figure 9.8: The application icons seen in these groups will now be found on the Start menu.

group windows that went inside it. You don't have to cover up most of your screen with Program Manager anymore, either. No matter how cluttered your screen gets, you'll always be able to find the Start button, right in the corner of your screen.

Windows NT comes with a dozen or so applications already listed on the Start menu. Items like WordPad, Calculator, Paint, and the other free applications that come with Windows NT are already there. Your favorite programs from before may or may not be there, too—it depends on how Windows NT was installed. For help on each of these free applications, turn to Chapter 4.

With Windows NT 3.x, you could add a new program to one of your Program Manager groups by dragging the icon into the group window, or you could use the Program Manager's File * New command, and get a dialog box like this one:

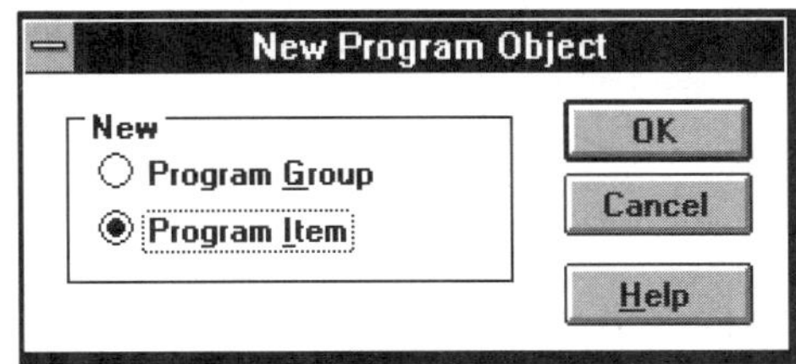

When you're ready to add your own programs to the Start menu, turn to Chapter 5 and it will describe a number of different ways you can do just that. When you install new applications, they'll add themselves to your Start menu automatically, just like they used to get added to the Program Manager automatically under Windows NT 3.x. And, like the old Program Manager, you can cluster your program and document icons into meaningful groups on the Start menu.

If you want your old Program Manager groups back, you can recreate them as new menus that are part of your Start menu. Use either the Windows NT Explorer or My Computer to locate your old Program Manager group files. These will probably be in your \WINDOWS directory and have the .GRP file name extension. If you double-click one of these, Windows NT will create a new Start Menu item that corresponds with your old group.

What about DOS Programs and PIF Files?

Windows NT can still run many of your old MS-DOS programs. In fact, it probably runs DOS programs better than Windows NT 3.x could. And, of course, Windows NT runs earlier Windows NT applications, too. Under Windows NT 3.x, it sometimes took a little bit of tinkering to get DOS applications to run well (or at all). Well, with Windows NT 4.x it still does, but you go about it in a different way.

Previously, you could select a program's icon and press ALT+ENTER or pull down the File menu to set the program's properties (see Figure 9.9). This would allow you to change only simple things like a program's title, or to choose its icon. Now, you can do this by right-clicking on an icon, as shown in Figure 9.10, and glide down to the Properties command at the bottom of the menu.

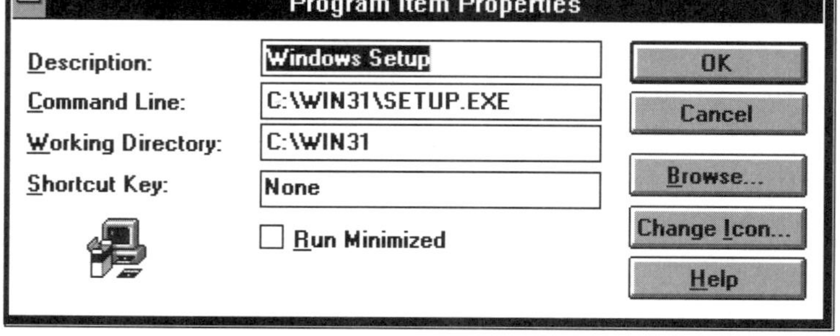

Figure 9.9: The old properties box has been replaced with a new one.

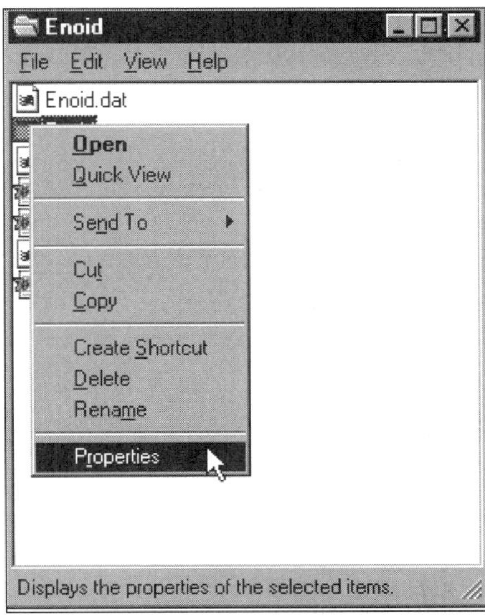

Figure 9.10: The new properties sheet is available by right-clicking on the application.

The properties sheet you'll see is more elaborate than the one you saw with Windows NT 3.x. It also changes depending on what kind of file (program, data file, batch file, etc.) you selected. For more information on filling out these property sheets, turn to Chapter 2 or Chapter 5.

It's still possible to get an MS-DOS prompt from Windows NT. In fact, DOS is right on your Start menu, although it's now called Command Prompt. Running a DOS session with Windows NT allows you to do a couple of things you couldn't do with previous versions of Windows NT. For starters, you can run DOS in a window, change the size and color of the text, and even cut and paste between the DOS windows and a standard Windows NT window. The new Command Prompt window, shown in Figure 9.11, also has its own control panel that you can use to modify all its properties.

Your DOS window also has scroll bars, both vertical and horizontal, and the ability to "remember" things that scroll off the top of the screen. Using the Command Prompt control panel, you can configure how large the off-screen scroll buffer is. There's a shortcut to this control panel hidden in the upper left corner of the Command Prompt window. Click there to reach the shortcut menu.

Windows still uses PIF files (program information files) to run MS-DOS programs, but now they're called *shortcuts*. There's no separate PIF Editor program anymore, like there was with Windows NT 3.x.

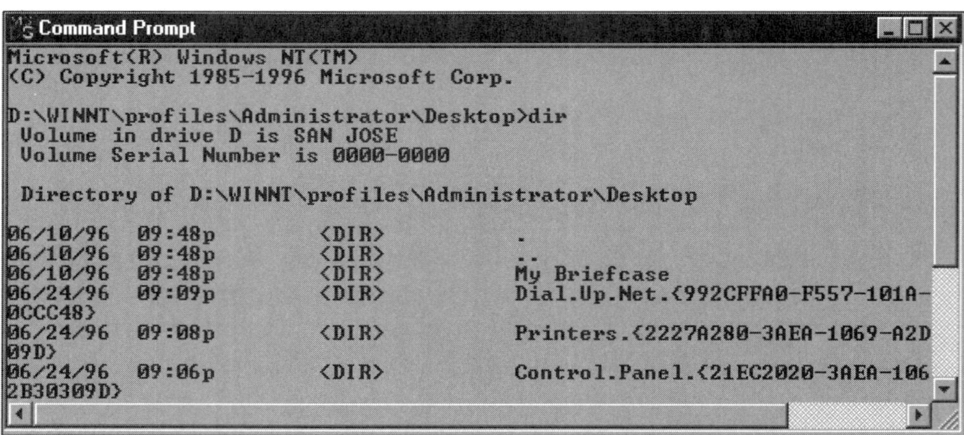

Figure 9.11: To reach the old MS-DOS prompt, open a Command Prompt window.

Instead, you just right-click on the DOS program, and select the Properties command from the pop-up menu. The information you enter into the property sheet will actually go into a PIF file (a shortcut) automatically. The PIF file is generally stored in the same folder (directory) as the MS-DOS application it belongs to. (If the application is on a write-protected medium such as a CD-ROM, Windows NT stores the shortcut in an internal folder.) Like other Windows shortcuts, you can move this file around to put it in a convenient location.

How Do I Install New Software?

Installing new Windows applications has always been pretty easy. New software packages inevitably come with instructions that read something like:

- Insert Disk #1 in your floppy drive
- From the Windows Program manager, select File, then Run
- Type A:\SETUP and press <ENTER>

But wait a minute—there's no File menu anymore and no Program Manager! What do you do?

It's really very simple. The Run command has now moved to the Start menu. As you can see in Figure 9.12, the Run command is still alive and well and it works just like it always did. In time, new Windows NT applications will say:

- Click the Start button and select Run
- Type A:\SETUP and press <ENTER>

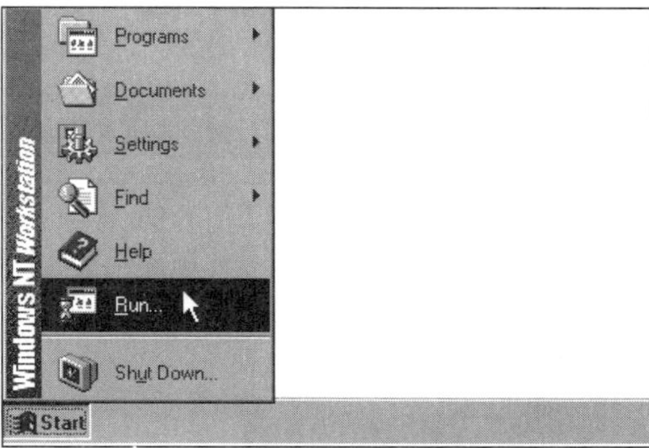

Figure 9.12: To type an arbitrary DOS command, start by choosing the Run command.

But there's an even better way. Windows NT has a new control panel just for installing other new applications. When you're ready to install new software, click the Start button, highlight Settings, and click Control Panel. The Control Panel window will open. Look for the Add/Remove Programs icon and double-click it.

When the big Add/Remove Programs Properties window appears, click the big Install button near the top. That's it. Windows NT will look at the diskette in your floppy drive (if there is one) and the CD-ROM in your CD-ROM drive (if there is one) and automatically select the Setup program from that disk. All you have to do is click another button to say "go" and the rest is automatic.

This same control panel can also be used to remove, or "uninstall," some Windows NT applications. You may see a list of potentially uninstallable applications near the bottom of the control panel already. Not every application that you install will be uninstallable. Only newer, well-behaved Windows 95 and Windows NT applications can be automatically uninstalled.

Chapter 10

THE TECHNICAL MANAGER'S TOOLBOX

There are some tools and applications that come with Windows NT that you may never need to use. These are the technical manager's, system administrator's, MIS directors, or "power user's" tools. You will find them in a special group all their own called Administrative Tools. You can use these Administrative Tools to back up your computer's most valuable files, create, remove, and manage user profiles, control how the Recycle Bin works, optimize and check your disk drives for errors, and even increase their capacity for free. In short, if you're an advanced Windows NT user or in charge of your office's Windows NT computers, you need to know how to open the technical manager's toolbox.

Backup

Backup is a free file-system backup program, and a good one. With Backup, you can make complete or incremental backups of your hard disks to a backup tape or to floppy disks. At a later date you can then restore some or all of the backed-up files. You can also compare backed-up files to the files on your hard disk to see if any have changed, or just to verify the integrity of the backup.

You can start Backup by clicking your Start button, highlighting Programs, then Administrative Tools, and selecting Backup. Backup is also one of the three system tools you can run by right-clicking a disk icon, selecting Properties from the shortcut menu, and clicking the Tools tab.

Making a Backup The Backup window, shown in Figure 10.1, is the first thing you will see on starting Backup. (The very first time you run Backup you will also see some preliminary advisories.) The three tabs correspond to the three major operations: backup, restore, and compare. The Backup window looks somewhat like an Explorer window. Your purpose here is to select which drives, folders, and files you want to back up. In the left-hand pane of the Backup window you will find every disk on your computer. Clicking the empty box next to a disk places a check mark in the box. This action marks every folder and file within that disk for backup. This is the quickest way to back up an entire disk.

To back up just a portion of a disk, you must mark the folders or files you want. This works just like it does with Windows NT Explorer. (If you're not yet familiar with Explorer, turn to Chapter 2.) Briefly,

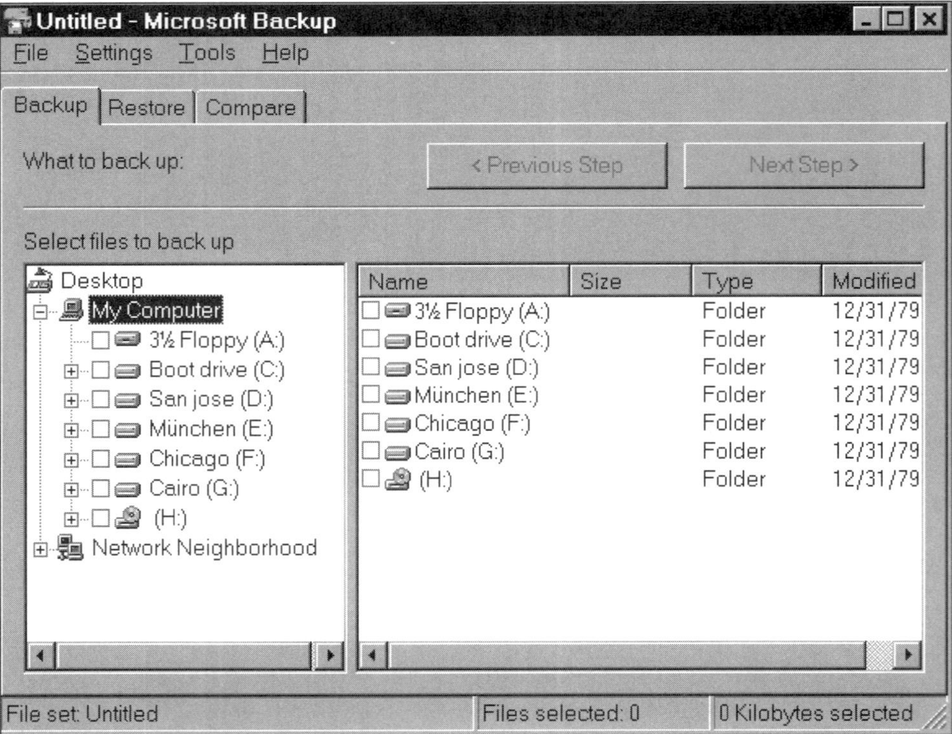

Figure 10.1: The Backup application manages your backup tapes and helps catalog them.

you can double-click a drive to "unroll" it and see the first-level folders inside it. You can check as many of these folder as you like. To open a folder to see more folders, double-click it. Again, checking the check box next to a folder will mark it and everything inside it for backup. You can check (or uncheck) individual files by clicking their check boxes in the right-hand pane of the Backup window.

When an entire disk or folder and everything it contains is marked for backup, its check box is checked. Clicking the check box again unmarks everything and the check box will be unchecked. When a check box is gray it means some folders within a disk are checked and some are not. After one or more items are marked for backup, you can proceed to the next step by clicking the big Next Step button near the top of the Backup window.

In this step, you must identify the device you are backing up to. This is usually a tape drive, but if you don't have a tape drive attached to your computer, you can back up files to floppy disks or to another computer via your office network. Using the display on the left side of the window, click the destination for your backup. To begin, click Start Backup.

Saving Backup Sets If you frequently back up the same set of disks, folders, or files, you can save yourself a lot of time by storing the list of items in a backup set. A backup set is a special file Backup creates for you with your file criteria and backup destination recorded. First, go through the motions of making a backup. Select all the disks, folders, and files you want backed up and the backup destination. Then, before you actually start backing up, click the File menu and select Save As.

To use a backup set you have created, start Backup and select Open File Set from the File menu. You can also double-click the backup set file itself, which is normally located in the Accessories folder inside the Program Files folder on the same disk as Windows NT. Creating a shortcut to this file is an excellent way to automate backups.

You can go this one better by creating a shortcut to Backup itself, possibly on your desktop, and then dragging a file set onto it. The operation is then completely automated, including starting and stopping Backup when the operation is complete. You can fine-tune some of this operation by clicking on the Settings menu and selecting Drag and Drop.

Restoring Files Every time you back up files, Backup creates a special log called the backup set. The backup set is a file that records the conditions and process of the backup. To restore the files that were backed up, you need to locate this backup set so that Backup can reverse the procedure. To restore your files from a backup, open Backup and click the Restore tab. Then, using the left-hand pane of the Backup window, locate the drive on which the backup set was stored (this is usually the same drive that contains Windows NT). Backup will display the available backup sets in the right-hand pane of the window. Select one of these by clicking it and then click the big Next Step button.

You don't necessarily have to restore everything that you backed up. At this point, you can click different disks, folders, and files that have been checked, to uncheck them. Backup will not restore files that have been unchecked, even if they were part of the original backup step. This allows you to restore just a few files that were missing or damaged, rather than the entire set of files you originally backed up.

Comparing Backups Comparing a backup set is a lot like restoring it, but without actually restoring any files. Times when you might want to compare files with a backup set is immediately after a backup, to double-check the integrity of the backup tape or floppy disks or to find out if the contents of a file or folder have changed since a certain backup was made.

To compare the files on your computer with a backed-up copy, start Backup and click the Compare tab. Then, just as if you were restoring files, use the left side of the window to select the disk on which the backup set (the log file Backup creates after a backup operation) is located. After selecting the disk, highlight the correct backup set from the right side of the window. You can limit the comparison operation to selected disks, folders, or files by clicking their check boxes in the left side of the window. When you're ready to proceed, click the big Start Compare button.

Disk Administrator

The Disk Administrator is a grab bag of disk-related utilities. With Disk Administrator you can check your hard disk drives for errors, format and reformat them, and alter disk names and labels. Disk Administrator also gives you a bird's eye view of all your computer's disks with a graphical representation of the used and free space on each one.

To open Disk Administrator, click on the Start button, highlight Programs, then Administrative Tools, then Disk Administrator. The standard Disk Administrator window looks like Figure 10.2.

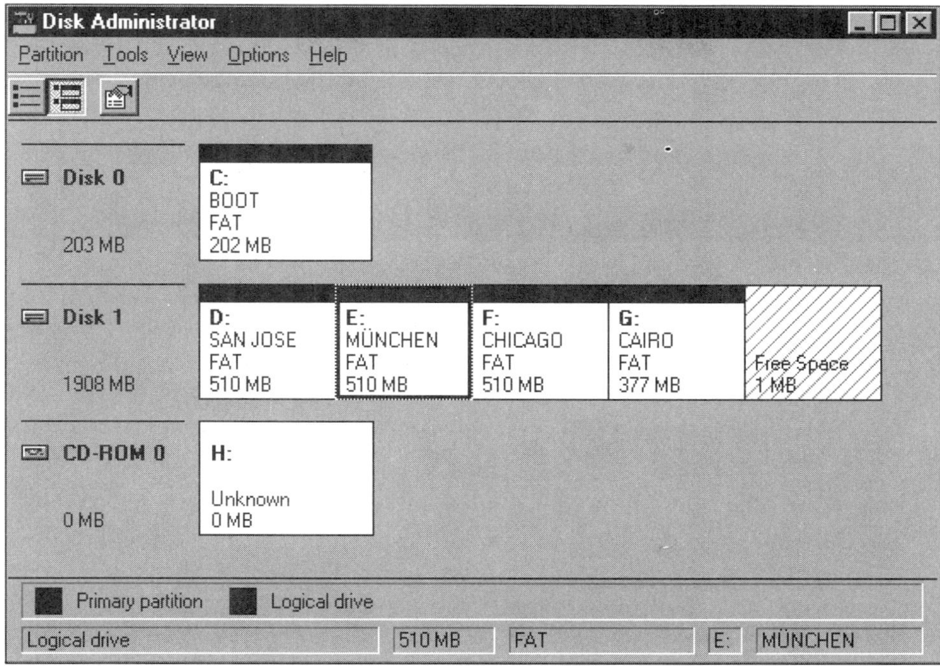

Figure 10.2: Disk Administrator is your entry point into disk-formatting, checking, and labeling functions.

This display separates physical disks from logical disks. If your computer has a large physical disk drive (say, 2GB or more), it may be divided into two or more logical disks just to help make file maintenance easier. In the figure, the second physical disk is divided into four roughly equal logical disks. You can switch from this graphical view to a more list-oriented view by clicking on the View menu and selecting Volumes.

There are four basic "tools" available from the Disk Administrator. All of them are listed under the Tools menu.

Changing Format After Windows NT is installed on your computer, you can change the format of a hard disk using the Change Format command. Windows NT offers two different disk formats: the traditional file-allocation table (FAT) format used by DOS, Windows, Windows 95, OS/2, and all previous versions of Windows NT; or the NT file system (NTFS) format. The latter format is more efficient in terms of storage space and access times, but is incompatible with those other operating systems.

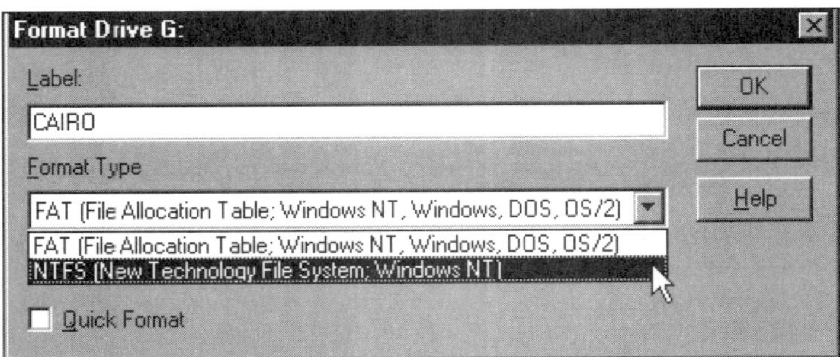

Checking for Errors Under the Tools menu you'll find the command Check for Errors. To check a disk for errors, first highlight one of the disks in the Disk Administrator window, then click on the Check for Errors command. A dialog box will pop up asking you how thorough you want to be with your check.

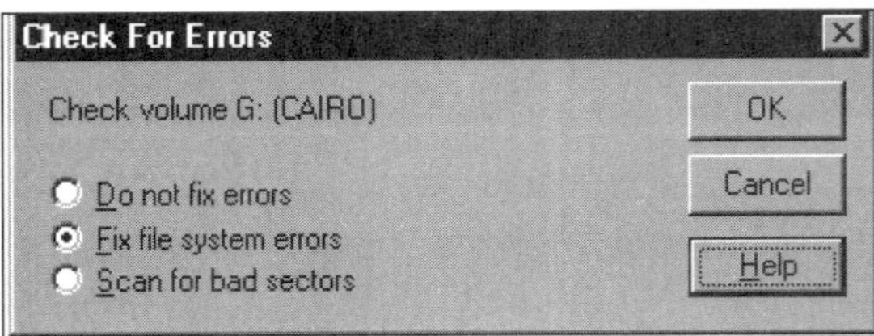

You can also check for disk errors without using the Disk Administrator. With a window open, right-click on a disk icon, select Properties from the shortcut menu, and click on the tab marked Tools. Again, a dialog box will pop up, although this one is not quite the same.

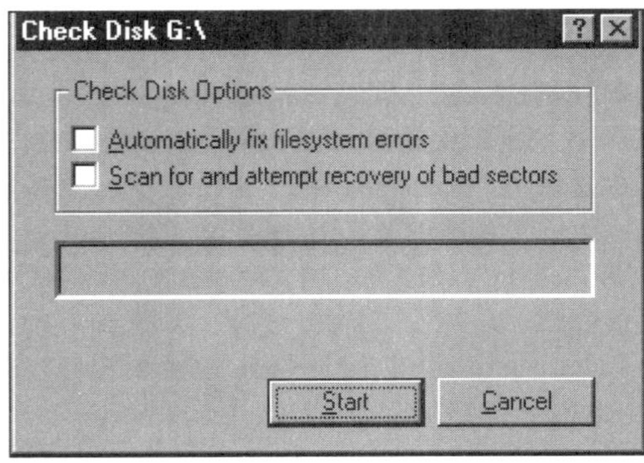

Changing Volume Labels Changing the volume label of a disk is quite straightforward. Simply highlight the disk whose name you want to change, click on the Tools menu, select Set Volume Label, and type a new name for that disk.

Changing Drive Letters To change the assigned drive letter for a disk, use the Drive Letter command under the Tools menu. You can change the drive letter of a drive to any available letter of the alphabet, or you can choose not to assign a letter at all. This option is useful if you have more logical disk than there are available letters in the alphabet. By not assigning a drive letter to a disk, you put that disk into "cold storage," since it can't be used unless it has a drive letter assigned to it.

Event Viewer

The event viewer is your window into the detailed event logs that Windows NT keeps. These event logs record every major and minor occurrence within your system, recording things like when the computer was turned on, what device drivers were loaded, who logged into the computer, and when certain applications were run. Because the event logs can grow to be very large, Event Viewer also lets you archive them for later retrieval.

You'll find Event View in the Administrative Tools group on your Start menu. Launching Event Viewer presents you with a packed window like the one in Figure 10.3. This is the system log, one of three separate logs that Windows NT creates for you. The other two are the security log and the application log.

The system log lists, in reverse chronological order, every significant event that occurred in your computer since it was turned on. Even the normal process of booting up can add several events to the system log. Double-clicking a line in the log opens a window that provides you with more detailed information about the event.

To view the security log, simply click on the Log menu at the top of the Event Viewer window and select Security. The security log normally records all changes to security levels, successful and unsuccessful attempts to log into the computer, and similar events. The actual events recorded depends on the auditing options you have enabled (see the User Manager). Only users who are part of the security group Administrators are allowed to view the security log.

Event Viewer - System Log on \\JIM'S COMPUTER

Log View Options Help

Date	Time	Source	Category	Event	User
6/11/96	7:40:54 PM	Nwlnklpx	None	9005	N/A
6/11/96	7:40:54 PM	Nwlnklpx	None	9006	N/A
6/11/96	7:40:53 PM	Service Control Mar	None	7000	N/A
6/11/96	7:40:53 PM	Elnkii	None	5004	N/A
6/11/96	7:40:53 PM	Elnkii	None	5018	N/A
6/11/96	7:40:53 PM	EventLog	None	6005	N/A
6/10/96	9:47:51 PM	Service Control Mar	None	7023	N/A
6/10/96	9:47:51 PM	Server	None	2503	N/A
6/10/96	9:47:51 PM	Server	None	2504	N/A
6/10/96	9:47:51 PM	Server	None	2504	N/A
6/10/96	9:47:51 PM	Service Control Mar	None	7001	N/A
6/10/96	9:47:51 PM	Service Control Mar	None	7001	N/A
6/10/96	9:47:51 PM	Service Control Mar	None	7024	N/A

Figure 10.3: The Event Viewer log records everything of note that happens on your system.

The application log records events from applications that have caused events to be recorded. Not all applications produce events and not all events get recorded. Thus, the application log is an irregular source of information, but presumably anything important enough to warrant your attention will be recorded in the log.

Because the logs—particularly the system log—can grow quite large, you may want to either purge the logs from time to time or save them. To purge any log, click on the Log menu and select Clear All Events. Windows NT will warn you before carrying out this command and give you an opportunity to save the log first.

To save an event log, choose Save As from the Log menu and select a file format for the log file. The text and comma-delimited formats are handy for transferring logged data to another application or another computer.

Performance Monitor

The Windows NT Performance Monitor is kind of a fun toy for statistics fans. You can use Performance Monitor to track all kinds of technical esoterica and produce colorful graphs in real time. You can select from a number of processor-related events and graph each one in a different color. Even Monitor also lets you select the update rate (in fractions of a second) and the style of the graph. In many cases, Performance Monitor can help you pinpoint problem areas in your computer, operating system, or network. Often, however, it's just interesting to look at.

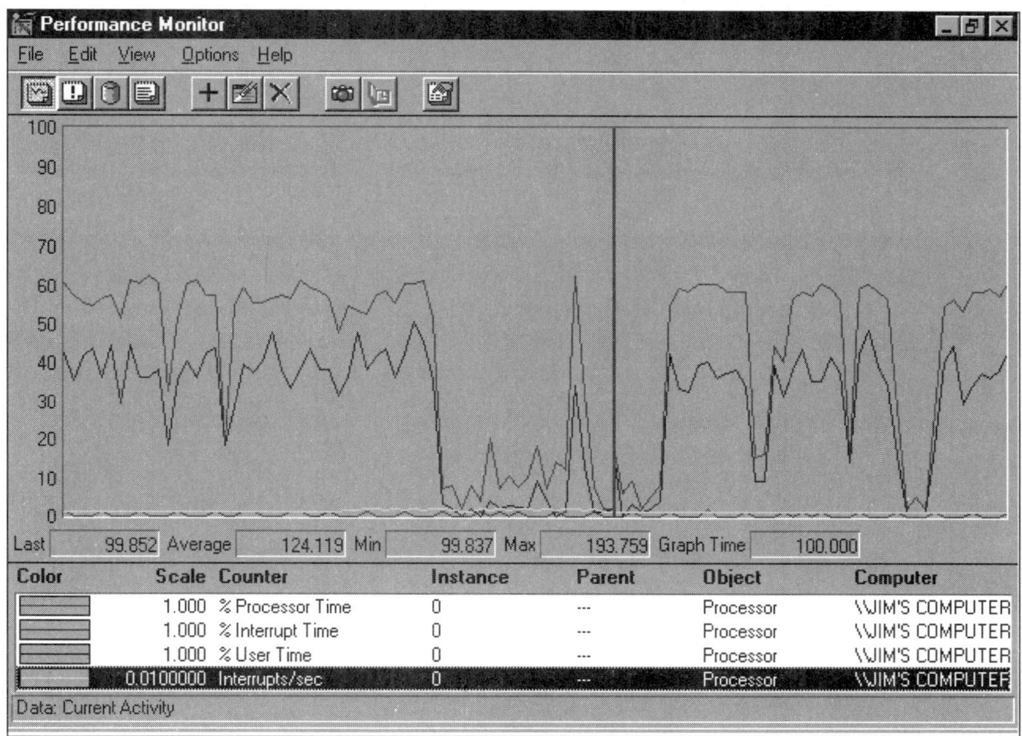

User Manager

The User Manager is probably the most important and most frequently used application in the Administrative Tools toolbox. If you're the Windows NT system administrator, you'll use User Manager to create, delete, and modify user accounts, manage groups of users, and control user- and group-level security.

When you first open the User Manager you'll see a window not unlike the one shown in Figure 10.4. The upper half of the window lists all of the existing user accounts, while the lower half lists the defined groups to which those users can belong.

Every person who expects to use this Windows NT system must have an account. It is permissible to share accounts—that is, to have more than one person use the same account name and password—but

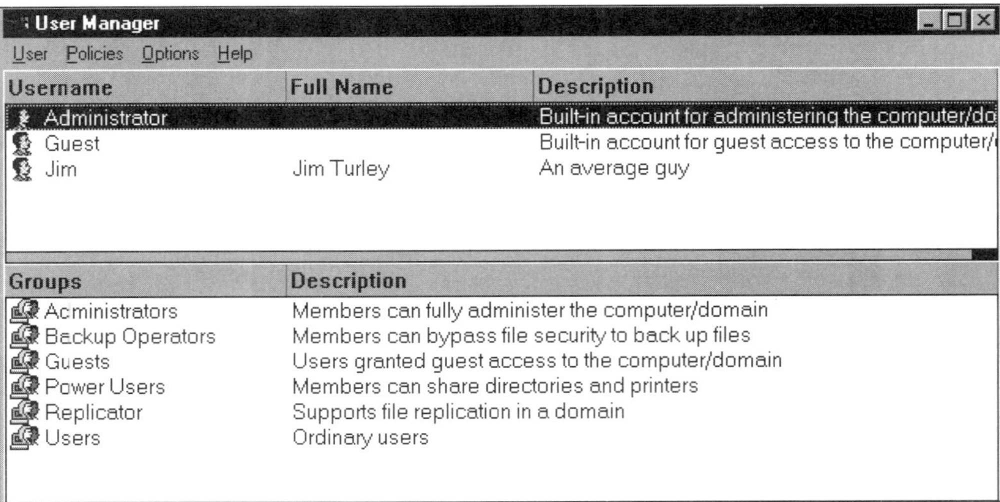

Figure 10.4: User Manager is a vital tool for creating, modifying, and controlling user accounts and privileges.

there is little advantage to doing this. As the system administrator, you should create an account for every person who might potentially use this system.

New Users When Windows NT is first installed, only two accounts exist. They're called Administrator and Guest. You can create any number of additional accounts. In the figure, one additional account has been created. To create a new account, simply click on the User menu and select New User. The New User dialog box appears, shown in Figure 10.5. The dialog box allows (and requires) you to fill in certain information about new users, such as their real names, their usernames (the name they will type in to log into the computer), and any description you care to add. Next, you must give new user a password, which must be typed in twice, on two different lines, to make sure you haven't made a mistake.

The four check boxes near the bottom of this window allow you to control the user's password. For example, you can either require or prohibit this user from changing his or her password. By forcing the user to change the password after the first login, you can globally assign all new users the same password (like "password") and then force them to pick a new one right away. Conversely, you can prevent users from ever changing their passwords.

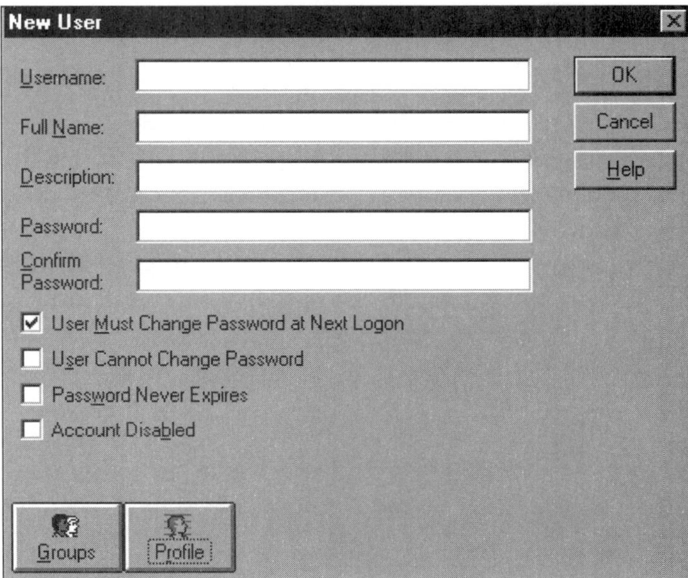

Figure 10.5: When creating a new user account, be sure to enter a password and check the password-control options.

Everybody's passwords normally expire after a fixed amount of time (which you get to determine with the Account Policy command, described later), but you can selectively make some users' passwords "immortal." This is not good policy for most users, but can be handy for the accounts of pseudo-users such as the Guest account or for remote services from across the network.

New User Profile Clicking the Profile button allows you to set up some automated tasks whenever the user logs in successfully. For example, you can assign the user a home directory (whether on the computer itself or on another computer across the network), and designate a batch file (with the .BAT extension) to be run. In all, these options allow you to make new users right at home as soon as they log in.

New User Group Every user account is generally considered to be a member of one or more groups. Group membership is not required, but groups allow you to assign security privileges to several members simultaneously. Assigning group membership is very simple. Just click the large Group button in the New User dialog box and double-click the groups you do or don't want this user to be a member of.

Belonging to multiple groups is okay; so is belonging to none of them. Only groups you've already defined (see below) will be listed here.

Groups Groups, by themselves, aren't worth anything. But they are useful for granting (and revoking) privileges to multiple users at once. Groups also make it easier to crease new users that have the same rights and privileges as other, existing users.

Several groups have already been defined for you by Windows NT. Should you feel the need to create one or more additional groups, you can do so by selecting the New Local Group command from the User menu.

Double-clicking any of the groups listed in the User Manager window will open a window showing you a brief description of that group's characteristic or purpose and a list of the members belonging to the group. Some groups might not have any members; some may have several.

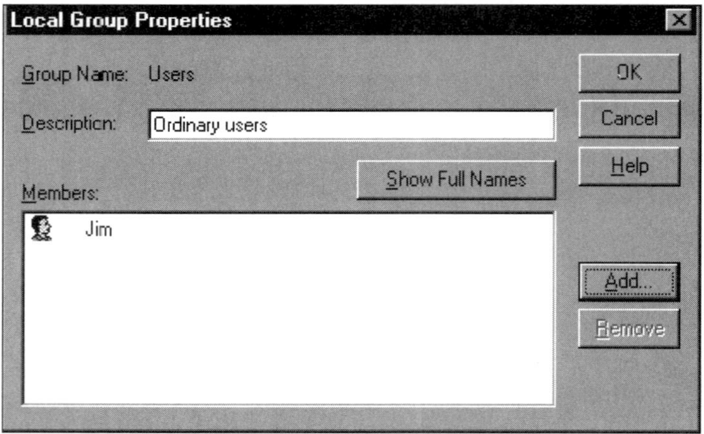

Clicking the Show Full Names button replaces the short usernames with each user's actual full name (assuming it was given at the time the user's account was created). You can add more users to the group by clicking on the Add button; all the existing user accounts will be listed and you can double-click on the ones you want to add.

User Rights Where groups really come in handy is in assigning user rights and privileges. Rights are assigned to groups, not to individual members, so group membership is an important criterion. To review and change access rights, click on the Policies menu and select User Rights. At the top of the window, shown in Figure 10.6, is a drop-down list of available rights and privileges. For each of those privileges, the groups that enjoy that right are listed in the area below. Selecting different privileges from the drop-down list will produce a different list of privileged groups. Selecting the check box called Show Advanced User Rights, makes the drop-down list considerably longer and more detailed.

Password Policy Each user's password is the most crucial key to protecting the security of your Windows NT system. If passwords are compromised, your system might be too. Thus, it's important to maintain strict password security, even among users who don't understand (or don't care) about system security.

You assign each user an initial password when his or her account is created. At that time, you can decide whether the user passwords are in their hand or in yours. That is, you can allow users (and even force them) to change their own passwords, or you can prevent them from changing their own passwords. Assuming they can change their own passwords, you can still exert considerable control over what they choose and how often.

Click on the Policies menu and select Account to see the Account Policy window in Figure 10.7. This window allows you to control system-wide password policy. As you can see from the figure, you can

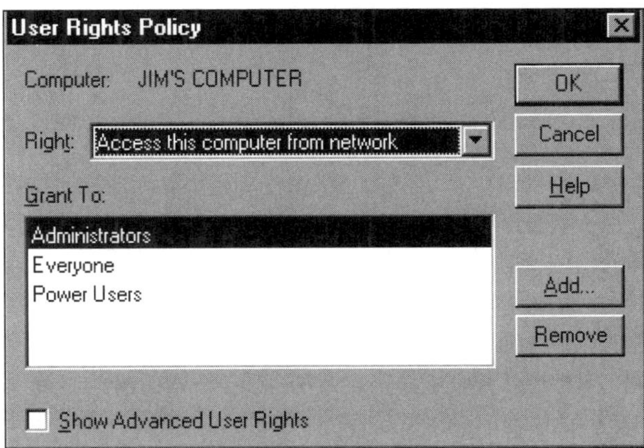

Figure 10.6: The basis of a user group is the privileges it has; use the User Rights Policy window to control these rights.

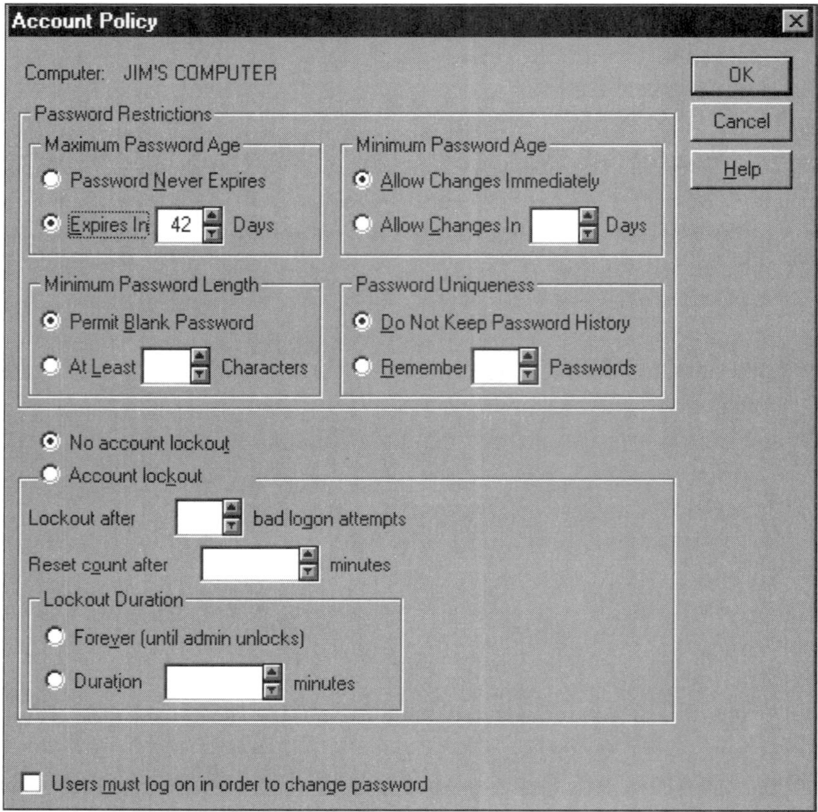

Figure 10.7: Your Accounts Policy determines a number of aspects of password security.

enforce both a minimum and a maximum password length. Enforcing a minimum length prevents lazy users from creating one-character passwords that are easy to break. You can also decide whether blank, or null, passwords are allowed.

Enforcing a maximum password age means that users will be required to change their passwords every so often. This helps reduce break-ins because even a compromised password will only be good for a limited time. Users often grumble when they are forced to change passwords and may try to circumvent your efforts, so use the remaining options carefully. For example, enforcing a minimum password age prevents users from complying with the letter of your edict by changing their password for one day and then changing it back. The requirement for password uniqueness also forces users to think up new passwords, rather than swapping back and forth between their two favorites.

What happens when someone tries to enter the system with a bad password? You can control Windows NT's behavior with the remaining options. If a person makes repeated attempts to log in with a valid username but a bad password, you can lock out the account (disable it). You can choose how many bad attempts in what time period (e.g., three bad tries in a ten-minute span) before the lockout is enforced. If an account is locked out, you can also control how long the account is disabled (in days), or have it disabled forever (or until you reset the policy, whichever comes first).

Auditing Account Activity Windows NT can keep a log of all account activity for the security-conscious administrator. To enable auditing, select Audit from the Policies menu. The Audit Policy window, shown in Figure 10.8, presents you with a checklist of events you may wish to have recorded in the security log. (Recall that you can examine the security with the Event Viewer application.) The options here are pretty straightforward, and any changes you make take effect immediately.

Managing the Recycle Bin

The Recycle Bin, seemingly an inert and featureless function, actually has some interesting properties that you can control. You can control the

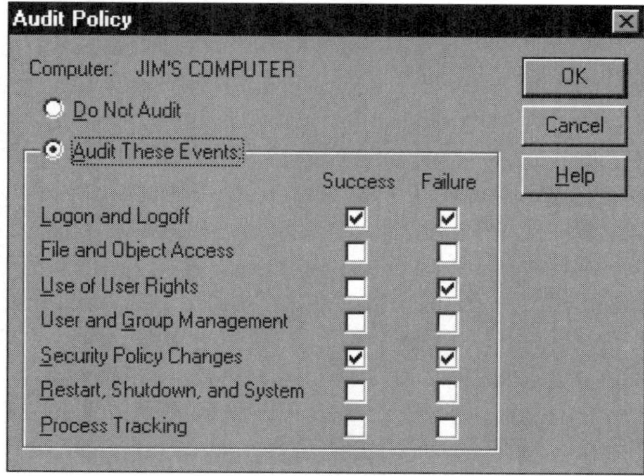

Figure 10.8: You can control which account activities will be recorded or not.

"size" of the Recycle Bin and you can make it a different size for each disk. You can also control how items are emptied from the Recycle Bin.

To view or modify any of these parameters, you must access the Recycle Bin's property sheet. Right-click the Recycle Bin and select Properties from the pop-up shortcut menu. The Recycle Bin Properties window opens, similar to the one in Figure 10.9. As you can see, there is one tab for each hard disk drive plus a Global tab. Clicking the second option (Use One Setting...) on the Global tab renders the remaining tabs useless.

The first check box item is the most important. Checking this box turns the Recycle Bin into an incinerator. That is, all items dragged into the Recycle Bin are permanently deleted right away—the Recycle Bin perpetually empties itself. This somewhat drastic measure keeps the Recycle Bin from filling up.

Assuming this box is not checked, you use the large slider to allocate a portion of each disk (or all disks at once) to be used as a Recycle

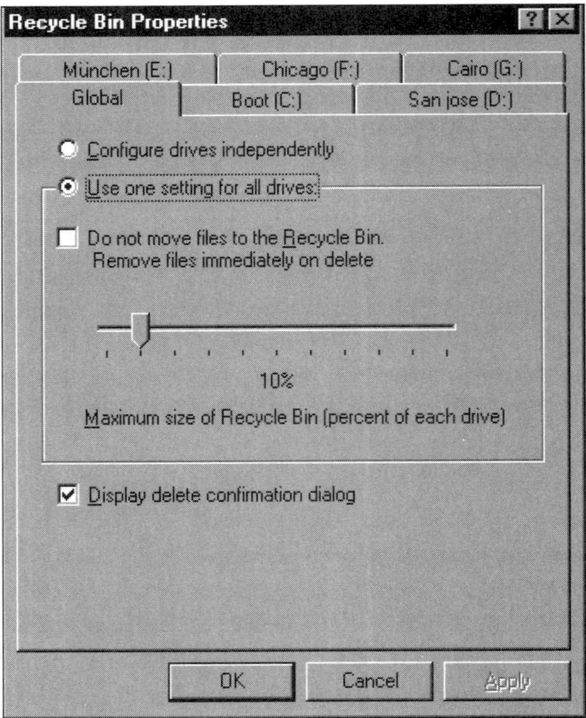

Figure 10.9: The Recycle Bin includes a surprising amount of control options.

Bin. You see, the Recycle Bin is nothing more than a folder like any other folder. Moving a file to the Recycle Bin is technically no different than dragging a file to any other folder. As you have seen, you can even drag items back out of the Recycle Bin, just as you can with any other folder. In fact, the only difference between the Recycle Bin and, say, the Accessories folder is that the contents of the Recycle Bin are deleted on a regular basis. Therefore, throwing files into the Recycle Bin does not actually free up any disk space at all. That is why you can use the slider control to limit the amount of space the Recycle Bin may occupy on your disk. When its size grows beyond the limit, files are deleted to bring it below the threshold again. That is why you can often—but not always—retrieve a file after it has been thrown into the Recycle Bin. Allocating more disk space to the Recycle Bin effectively extends a deleted file's half-life and improves the odds of retrieving it again.

Windows NT actually maintains a separate Recycle Bin for each disk on your computer, although only one appears on your Desktop. This allows you to allocate different amounts of space to each disk's Recycle Bin using the slider control described above. Because of this, files deleted from one disk might easily disappear from the Recycle Bin much sooner (or later) than files deleted from a different disk.

The final check box controls a warning. If you delete a file by highlighting it and pressing the <DEL> key or by right-clicking and selecting the Delete command, Windows NT displays a warning and asks if you really meant to delete the chosen file. This warning is not displayed when you drag a file into the Recycle Bin, on the theory that you're not as likely to do that by accident. If this final check box is not checked, no warning will be displayed, no matter how you delete a file. Note that if you configure the Recycle Bin for "incinerator mode" with the previous check box, this box is always checked and cannot be changed.

You can create shortcuts to your Recycle Bin or to the individual Recycled folders on each disk. And you can change the name and the icon assigned to these shortcuts. It's difficult to imagine a situation where this would be necessary, but not hard at all to imagine the problems it could cause.

WINDOWS NT AND SPECIAL NEEDS

As computers have become more a part of everyday business and home life, they have moved out of the laboratories and spread into every country, every industry, and onto nearly everybody's desk. That growth has demanded that computers become more accommodating of people who are not technically trained, not English-speaking, and not equipped to handle a keyboard, mouse, or computer screen. Windows NT does an admirable job of making a garden-variety PC more useful to a greater number of hearing- and sight-impaired people through the use of several accessibility options.

Turning Accessibility Options On

All six of Windows NT's new accessibility options are available in the Accessibility Options control panel, shown below. To reach it, click your Start button, highlight Settings, and click on Control Panel. When the Control Panel window opens, double-click the Accessibility Options control panel.

Each of the six accessibility options can be turned on or off by using the Accessibility control panel. But what if you can't get to the Control Panel without the help of the accessibility options? To avoid such a frustrating Catch-22 situation, four of the options can also be turned on and off through special keyboard shortcuts. For these four options, you can choose to use either the keyboard shortcut or the Control Panel to enable or disable the accessibility options. A summary of these four shortcuts is provided in Table 11.1.

Turning Accessibility Options Off Automatically

There is an option to turn off almost all the accessibility features automatically if the computer is not used for more than five minutes (ShowSounds is exempted from this feature). This automatic time-out period is meant as a convenience for people who do not need the accessibility options and who might be confused by them if they share a computer with somebody who does need them. You can disable this time-out, thus making the accessibility options more or less permanent, or you can extend the time-out period up to 30 minutes, in five-minute increments. To disable or change the time-out period, open the Accessibility control panel and click the General tab.

Sticky Keys

StickyKeys allows you to type with one finger. This option is useful for people who have trouble pressing two keys at the same time. For example, there are often times when Windows NT requires you to hold down the <SHIFT> key, the <ALT> key, or the <CTRL> key while pressing another key. If this is too difficult, turn on StickyKeys and

Table11.1:

To Turn On	*Press*
StickyKeys	<SHIFT> Five Times
FilterKeys	Right <SHIFT> for Eight Seconds
ToggleKeys	<NUM LOCK> for Five Seconds
MouseKeys	Left <ALT> + Left <SHIFT> + <NUM LOCK>

you'll only have to press one key at a time. These three keys become "sticky" and remain active after you press them.

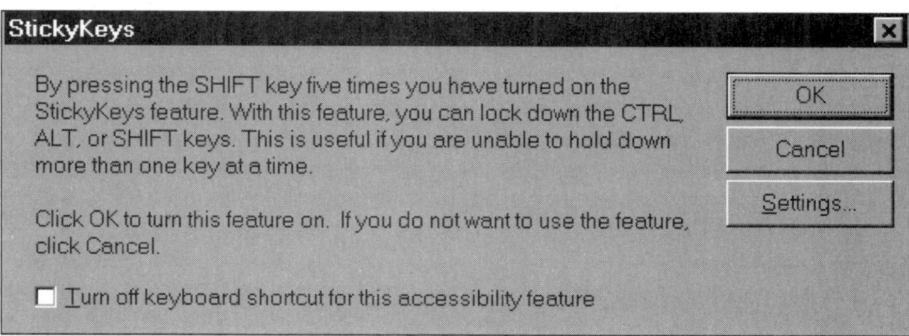

To enable StickyKeys, you can either open the Accessibility control panel or use the keyboard shortcut. The shortcut for StickyKeys is to press one of the <SHIFT> keys five times in a row. When StickyKeys is turned on, you will see a little indicator at the bottom of your screen, at the right end of the Taskbar. The indicator is intended to look like the <SHIFT>, <CTRL>, and <ALT> keys on your keyboard. When one of these keys is being "sticky," it will be colored in to let you know it is active.

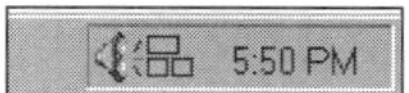

To use StickyKeys, simply press the <ALT>, <SHIFT>, or <CTRL> key once and then press the second key after it. For example, to type a capital S, press the <SHIFT> key once, and then press the S key once. StickyKeys will make this into a SHIFT+S combination. Likewise, to press ALT+F, press the <ALT> key followed by the F key.

Filter Keys

FilterKeys instructs Windows NT to ignore keys that are held down for too long or that get pressed repeatedly. This option is helpful if you accidentally press a key too many times or have trouble releasing a key rapidly enough. For example, if you meant to type "the" but it comes out "thhhhe" then FilterKeys can help.

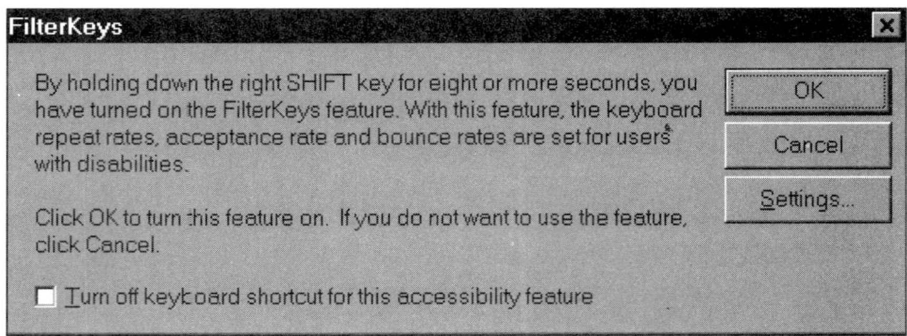

To enable FilterKeys, you can either open the Accessibility control panel or use the keyboard shortcut, which is holding the right <SHIFT> key down for eight seconds. When FilterKeys is activated, a small stopwatch appears at the right end of the Taskbar.

When FilterKeys is active, you must type double characters slowly. For example, you must pause between the two Es in meet so that FilterKeys does not think that you accidentally pressed E twice. Typing two different letters in quick succession is no problem; FilterKeys only filters out accidental double keystrokes.

Toggle Keys

ToggleKeys plays tones when you use any of the "lock" keys: <CAPS LOCK>, <NUM LOCK>, or <SCROLL LOCK>. On most keyboards, these three keys have small lights associated with them, but if the lights are not visible to you, ToggleKeys supplements these with tones. A high-pitched tone means the key is on, while a low-pitched tone means it is off.

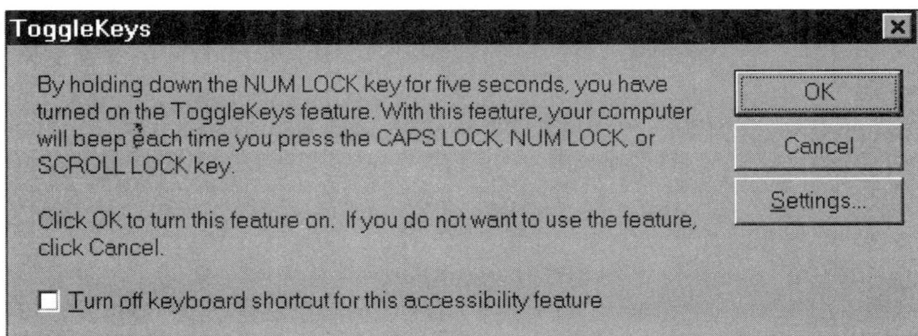

To enable ToggleKeys, you can either open the Accessibility control panel or use the keyboard shortcut. The shortcut for ToggleKeys is to press the <NUM LOCK> key for five seconds. When ToggleKeys is enabled, you will hear a high-pitched tone whenever any of the three "lock" keys is engaged, and a low tone when any of them is disengaged again. There is no way to tell from the tones which of the three keys is engaged or disengaged.

Sound Sentry

SoundSentry converts audible warning tones into visible flashes so that you don't miss important warnings. With SoundSentry enabled, a window, a window's title bar, or the desktop will flash briefly to indicate that a warning tone was just sounded. To enable SoundSentry, you must open the Accessibility control panel and select the Sound tab. There is no keyboard shortcut for SoundSentry.

Show Sounds

The ShowSounds option works like closed captioning for computer applications. Turning ShowSound on tells all Windows NT applications to use caption boxes or printed messages rather than audible indicators. Many applications that use tones or beeps to indicate status can also display descriptive text instead. Unfortunately, many more applications do not offer this option. Thus, ShowSounds will only have a limited effect on many computers.

To enable ShowSounds, you must open the Accessibility control panel and select the Sound tab. There is no keyboard shortcut for ShowSounds.

Mouse Keys

MouseKeys allows you to use your keyboard in place of a mouse. The arrow keys on the keyboard take the place of mouse movement, with the numeric keypad keys standing in for the mouse buttons.

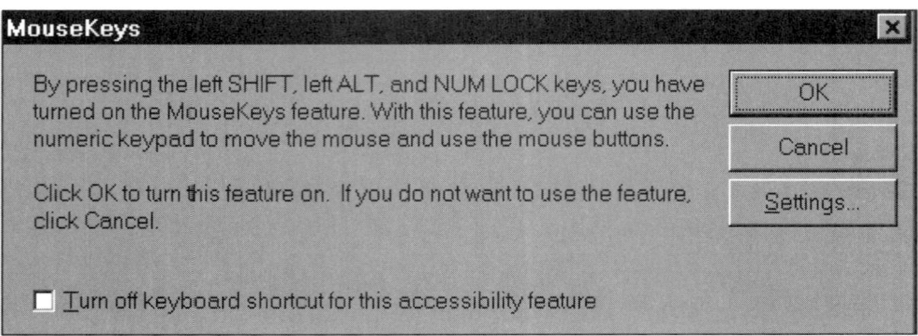

To enable MouseKeys, you can either open the Accessibility control panel or use the keyboard shortcut. The shortcut for MouseKeys is to press the left <SHIFT> key, left <ALT> key, and the <NUM LOCK> key all at once. When MouseKeys is enabled, a small indicator appears on the right end of your Taskbar

To move your mouse pointer with MouseKeys, press the up, down, left, and right arrows (or the 2, 4, 6, and 8 keys on the numeric keypad). You can also move diagonally by pressing the 1, 3, 7, and 9 keys. To move your mouse pointer faster, hold down the <CTRL> key; to move slower, hold down <SHIFT>. When it's time to click, press the 5 key in the middle of the numeric keypad on the right side of your keyboard. To double-click, you can press 5 twice or press the big + key on the numeric keypad once.

To switch between the left and right "mouse" buttons, press the -, *, or / key on the top of the numeric keypad. Pressing - switches to the right mouse button; pressing 5 or + after that is considered a right-click or a right-double-click, respectively. To switch back to the left mouse button, press /. To click both mouse buttons at once (a rare occurrence), press * and then press either 5 or + to click or double-click. Again, pressing / switches back to the left mouse button.

Index

A

B

E

F

M

N

O

P

Q

R

S

V

W